# THE
# COOK'S
# COMPANION

# THE
# COOK'S
# COMPANION

## SUSAN
## CAMPBELL

M

**The Cook's Companion**
was conceived, edited and designed
by Dorling Kindersley Limited,
9 Henrietta Street, London WC2

**Project Director**
Bridget Morley

**Editors**
Jenny Barling, Jeanne Ruzicka
Anne Johnson
Louis Jordaan, Christine Lowe

**Designers**
Dave Whelan, Julia Goodman

**Researchers**
Gill Sanders, Martha Ellen Zenfell

**Editorial Director**
Christopher Davis

**Consultants
and technical advisers:**
DIVERTIMENTI
(Cooking Utensils) of
Marylebone Lane, London W1

ISBN 0 333 28790 8

First published 1980 by
**MACMILLAN LONDON LIMITED**
London and Basingstoke
Associated companies in New York
Dublin Melbourne Johannesburg
and Delhi

Made and printed in England

# CONTENTS

# PREFACE

*Every art or profession requires the skilful and proper use of the appropriate tools; learning about the tools of the trade and their associate techniques is the first and most essential part of any apprentice's training. Thereafter, the possession of the right equipment and the knowledge of how to use it is certainly helpful to anyone who wishes to work comfortably and competently.*

*It was challenging therefore, to be asked to write a book about the tools of cookery, for although recipe books are to be found in almost too much abundance, there are very few books devoted solely to the tools and techniques of this art.*

*This book seems all the more timely today; we live in a world so technologically conscious that even the simplest tasks—once competently dealt with by hand or with the most basic tools—are now executed by sophisticated implements in a fraction of a second. The art of cookery is not immune to this trend, and this book is as much a guide to what is genuinely useful as to what is not. Indeed I couldn't help noticing, during my researches, that professional cooks tend to use fewer and more basic tools than most amateurs.*

*The choice of which tools to include was not always easy, but the governing factors were: efficiency, ease of use, cost in relationship to usefulness and durability, excellence of design and, occasionally, charm. I have also included several tools which are special to particular cuisines, as long as those cuisines are fairly well established outside their countries of origin.*

*Techniques for using the tools are shown whenever the following rules apply: where the way a tool is used is not obvious from its appearance; where, although the tool is familiar, it has unexpected uses—for example, using a rolling pin to shape the curved biscuits known as "tuiles"; and where a tool can be used to demonstrate professional tricks of the trade.*

*I have given no hard and fast rules as to the tools which each kitchen should have. Ultimately the tools chosen by the readers of this book will reflect their way of life. It is not necessary for a single person who rarely entertains to have a saucepan large enough to cook pasta for a family of eight, or a 14 inch ham knife, but he or she may be delighted to learn about the feasibility of baking, frying or stewing food in a portable electric pan. Nor will a person with a small kitchen wish to fill it with cumbrous implements, no matter how great his or her enthusiasm for cake decorating, barbecuing or pasta making. For this reason I have tried to show how versatile some of the most basic tools can be.*

SUSAN CAMPBELL

# HANDS

Somewhat perversely, the first chapter of this book is not devoted to any tools at all but to hands. Hands may be regarded as an integral part of any tool, since a tool is usually held in the hand to make it work. This chapter, however, deals with the many tasks in the kitchen that can be performed by hand, without the help – or in some cases hindrance – of any tools. By reading this chapter first you may save yourself the expense of buying some of the special equipment described further on, as well as the time and bother of washing up things that you can perfectly well manage without.

No really satisfactory domestic tool has yet been invented for fiddly jobs like peeling shrimps or shelling peas, but there are dozens of tools for simple tasks like mixing things. Bare hands are as good if not better than many of these, especially when making cakes, pastry and bread. When mixing sponges, for example, use the whole of your hand with the fingers spread out to fold the flour into a foamy egg and sugar batter. Feel with your fingertips for any pockets of unmixed flour. When mixing pasta and brioche dough, make a little well of flour on a pastry board and gently incorporate eggs into it with your fingers. Do the same for pâte brisée and add the butter by pressing it in with the heel of your hand.

Rub fat into flour with your fingertips when making pastry, and mix in water with them as well, but only if you are blessed with cool hands. But if your hands are warm they will be all the better when kneading bread dough. By doing this with your hands, you will know the right moment to stop for you feel the smooth elasticity of dough that is ready to "prove". Warm hands are also useful for creaming together butter and sugar, as the warmth will help the butter to soften. This also applies when kneading together flour and butter for beurre manié to thicken a sauce. Use your whole hand to knead a slab of butter to soften it before incorporating it into puff pastry or brioche dough – this knocks some of the water out of it as well. (You can also use your fingertips to mark the number of turns you have given your puff pastry.) Smear butter round baking dishes and cake tins with the tips of your fingers; the warmth helps to soften it and you can get right into the corners.

It goes without saying that your hands should be scrupulously clean for all these jobs. It helps if you remove any chunky rings and bracelets which may get in the way and be difficult to clean. Flour your hands for dough and pastry making, so that they are nice and dry. Do the same when using your hands for shaping things like dumplings, quenelles, plaited loaves and knotted rolls, chapattis, pizzas, capelletti, wun tun noodles, Chinese dumplings and marzipan animals.

Wet your hands when mixing and shaping raw minced meat with herbs and eggs for beefburgers or meat balls. This will prevent the mixture from sticking to them. Do the same when mixing tabbouleh, a Middle Eastern salad of burghul – cracked wheat – soaked in water and then mixed with oil, lemon juice and minced onion.

## Kneading bread dough

*Press a ball of dough into a flat shape, stretching and pushing it as you do so (1). Then roll it into a ball again (2). Repeat these actions until the dough begins to feel silky and elastic. It is then ready to prove.*

(1)

(2)

Another Middle Eastern speciality, Syrian kibbeh, depends for its shape on a cook with long, slender fingers. A hollow, torpedo-shaped shell of cracked wheat, raw minced meat and onions is first shaped round the finger. It is then stuffed with another mixture—this time of raw meat, onions and nuts—sealed up and deep fried. Couscous, from North Africa,

is broken up and worked over by hand, both before and after cooking. This is to separate the grains and is one of the occasions when an ability to tolerate heat proves useful.

In fact, many of the tricks of the cook's trade depend on being able to tolerate considerable heat with the hands. If you are unable to do this and you do burn yourself, hold the finger or

### Cracking walnuts

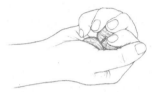

Squeeze two walnuts together in your hand—one of them will crack against the other.

### Skinning almonds

Pour boiling water over unskinned almonds to loosen the skin. When it cools, press each nut between your fingers so that the skin slips off. The almond will slide backwards into your hand.

### Arranging apple slices on a flan

Starting at the edges of the dish, fan out apple slices between your thumb and forefinger. This is much easier to do if you have cut the apples with a mechanical slicer.

### Opening a cooked crab

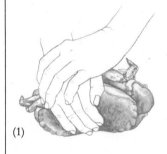
(1)

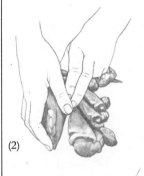
(2)

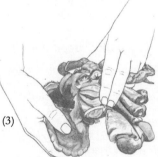
(3)

Stand the crab on its edge. Press down hard where the top shell joins the tail (1): you should hear a slight crack. Prize the top shell away from the rest of the body (2) pressing hardest where the tail joins it (3).

### Shelling prawns

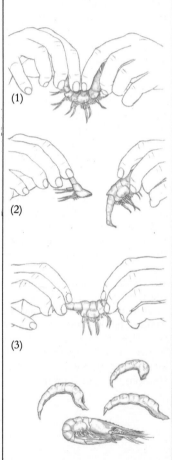
(1)

(2)

(3)

Uncurl the prawn to loosen the shell (1). Pull the shell from the tail end (2), then gently pull the head and legs from the other end (3).

hand under cold running water for several minutes. Some people say that clutching your ear lobes with the afflicted fingers will also relieve the pain. An experienced chef thinks nothing of removing a blanched onion from a pan of boiling water with his fingers or testing a bubbling sauce for flavour by dipping a clean finger into it. You can test rice for tenderness by squeezing a cooked grain between thumb and forefinger. Similarly, you can see if a piece of roasting meat is done by gently pressing it with the fingers – raw meat is soft and mushy, medium done is soft but springy, and over-done meat is hard and unyielding. With this method you can dispense with meat thermometers and timers.

There are many other jobs that you can do by hand and so dispense with pieces of equipment that will merely clutter up your kitchen. You can, for example, do without egg separators, olive stoners and nutcrackers. Separate eggs by cracking the shell in half and, using each half as a cup, tip the yolk from one to the other, letting the white fall into a bowl underneath. A professional chef will tip the raw egg into the palm and, cupping the yolk, let the white run away between the fingers. If he has hairy hands, he may finish by rolling the yolk on the back of his hand, where the hairs will catch any remaining white. Stone an olive by pressing it between thumb and forefinger – the stone squirts out and the olive skin stays behind.

There are dozens of other tasks in the kitchen which you may find are done best by hand. The arrangement and decorative presentation of food can only be done by hand, for example: arrange fruit prettily on open tarts and fan out apple slices like a pack of cards on the base of crème pâtissière. Run the side of your thumb round the edge of a soufflé mixture before putting it in the oven – this makes a little trough which helps to prevent the rising mixture from toppling over (see SOUFFLÉ DISHES). Take the gut from a trout by hooking your finger into its gill and pulling gently. Skin fish fillets by hand, getting a grip on a slippery tail by sprinkling it with salt. Finally, always sprinkle salt into a dish by hand if you want to know exactly how much you are putting in – a pinch of salt means just that.

## Making pâte brisée

1. Soften the butter by pounding it with your fist.
2. Make a well of flour on a marble slab or pastry board and, using your fingers, gradually incorporate egg yolks and the pieces of butter.
3. Knead the mixture with the heel of your hand.
4. Continue until the original crumbly mass is worked into a smooth cohesive paste.
5. Pat the pastry into a ball and refrigerate it to firm it up.

(1)

(2)

(3)

(4)

(5)

# KNIVES

A good, sharp knife is the cook's most useful tool. A blunt knife slows down work and makes cutting a tiresome chore, not the pleasure it should be. Fine artists and craftsmen look after their tools. Serious cooks cherish their knives; for a knife to a cook is the same as a brush to a painter or a bow to a violinist.

Over the centuries kitchen knives have hardly altered in shape or purpose. Where they have changed is in the materials from which they are made.

### Early knives

The earliest knives were made of sharp-edged pieces of stone and bone. Once metal working developed, the strength of bronze and the thinness to which its edge could be shaped made it the material for the finest blades until the beginning of the Iron Age.

Iron was not an immediate success; for at least 1000 years the value of alloying it with carbon to produce steel was not properly understood or even recognized, so some iron blades were mysteriously sharper and stronger than others. Indeed, primitive iron was such an unreliable material that during battle it was routine for warriors to go to the back of the ranks to straighten out their swords. The man who wielded a blade which withstood every shock and continued to cut efficiently was, therefore, regarded almost as a god. No wonder in folklore these swords were invested with magical properties; given names; described as god-given, made by giants or seethed with spells. They must have been made of steel, which had been either imported or was the result of a chance introduction of exactly the right amount of carbon into the iron.

Today knives are still surrounded by a confusion of myths. The modern magic words are molybdenum, carbon, vanadium, Rockwell, high carbon no-stain, surgical (see GLOSSARY).

These various labels make it very difficult to select a good knife, unless you know what they mean and know what you are looking at – and the choice is vast.

### Cost and quality

There are some extremely sharp, cheap, mass-produced knives on the market today, but they are not used by professional cooks. They prefer good quality knives, which have weight, balance and flexibility as well as sharpness and they are prepared to pay highly for them.

It is easier to understand the quality that makes some knives more expensive than others if you know how they are made.

Knives for professional use and some of the more expensive household knives are forged in one piece from bar steel, with blade, bolster and tang individually shaped in a series of processes to produce a well-balanced tool. The handle is added before the edge is ground.

After forging, the blade is machine ground all over to produce a taper from back to edge and from handle to blade tip, making a strong knife with weight and resilience where it is most needed – at the place where the blade joins the handle. These knives, which can be made of either carbon steel or stainless steel, are described as "taper-ground".

Some knife-blades are cut out of wedge-shaped strips of steel. When these blades are also taper-ground they are just as good as forged ones. They are usually cheaper in price because the manufacturing process has been simplified. You can distinguish them from forged knives because they do not usually have a bolster forged in one with the blade. Some continental knives have a separate collar (which looks very like a bolster) into which the handle fits. This method of construction is not so robust as the forged bolster.

*These three ancient weapons show how little the knife shape has changed in 5000 years, from the Egyptian flint knife (top) and the Near Eastern Bronze Age dagger (centre) to the more sophisticated medieval Swiss peasant's knife of steel (bottom).*

## How knives are forged

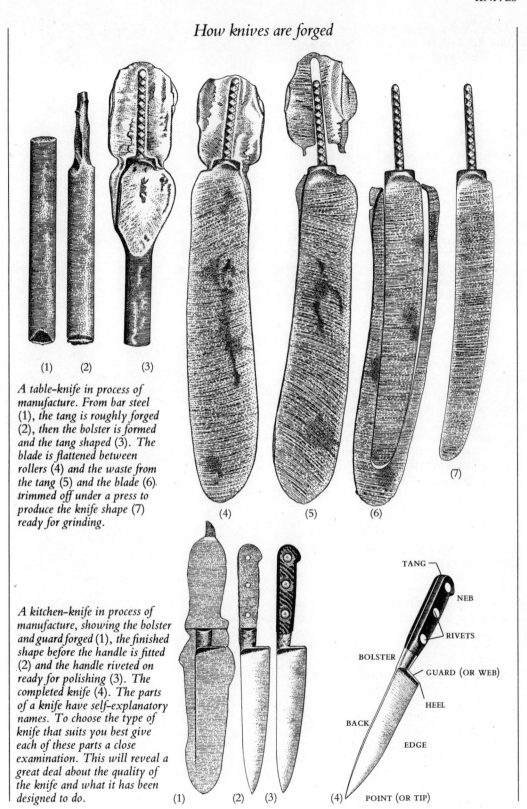

(1)    (2)         (3)

*A table-knife in process of manufacture. From bar steel (1), the tang is roughly forged (2), then the bolster is formed and the tang shaped (3). The blade is flattened between rollers (4) and the waste from the tang (5) and the blade (6) trimmed off under a press to produce the knife shape (7) ready for grinding.*

(4)         (5)         (6)

(7)

*A kitchen-knife in process of manufacture, showing the bolster and guard forged (1), the finished shape before the handle is fitted (2) and the handle riveted on ready for polishing (3). The completed knife (4). The parts of a knife have self-explanatory names. To choose the type of knife that suits you best give each of these parts a close examination. This will reveal a great deal about the quality of the knife and what it has been designed to do.*

(1)    (2)    (3)

TANG

NEB

RIVETS

BOLSTER

GUARD (OR WEB)

HEEL

BACK

EDGE

(4)    POINT (OR TIP)

Most of the cheaper knives are cut from thin strips of stainless steel. The cutting edge (often hollow-ground) is produced by machine in one grinding operation and the blade is polished before the handle is added. This is a less expensive way of manufacturing knives, but there are disadvantages.

## Strength and flexibility

Blades cut from strip steel are not as strong as taper-ground ones because they are thinner and flat-sided, lacking the strengthening thickness at the junction of blade and handle where the greatest stress occurs. They often lack weight where it could be an advantage and the balance which makes a taper-ground blade so pleasant to use. If a flat-sided blade is flexible, it may be so only in one part (and the wrong part) of the blade and it will not have the resilience of a taper-ground blade. These blades, however, often have extremely hard, thin, cutting edges, which make them very sharp – if that is all you really want.

## An edge for every purpose

Knives with fluted edges are used for cutting soft foods such as ham, roast meat or smoked salmon. The flutes are sometimes on one side only. When they are on both sides they are staggered to give extra flexibility and strength. They can be sharpened with a steel in the normal way because the edge itself is straight.

Serrated edges are more finely toothed than saw edges and the points are cut on one side only, not set like saw teeth. They can be sharpened on the flat side of the edge with a steel in the normal way. They are used to cut smooth, soft foods, such as tomatoes, grape-fruit and cucumber. Some bread knives with deeply serrated edges have to be sharpened professionally however.

Scalloped-edged knives cut the same things as fluted ones. The scallops are designed so that the points protect the sharpness of the curves. These blades are usually made of very hard, stainless steel, so frequent sharpening is not necessary. They can be sharpened on a steel using a particular method (see STEELS).

Corrugated edges are found on knives designed for decorative cutting. These edges cannot be sharpened.

Butcher's saws and freezer knives have saw edges, with teeth set alternately to left and right. They make a cut slightly wider than the thickness of the blade and this prevents it getting jammed when sawing.

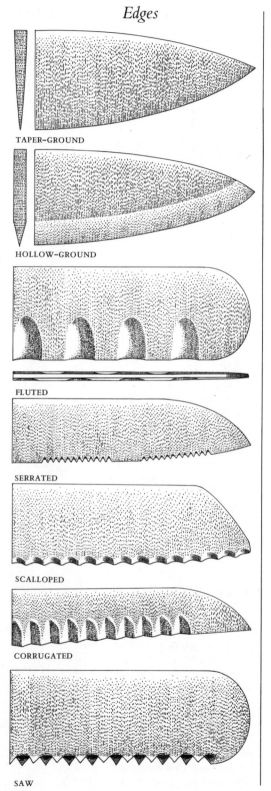

*Edges*

TAPER-GROUND

HOLLOW-GROUND

FLUTED

SERRATED

SCALLOPED

CORRUGATED

SAW

Knife handles are attached by means of the tang. Full tangs are found on heavy-duty knives, cleavers and choppers. They add weight and balance to the knife, which is helpful when cutting or chopping hard substances. Sometimes, in a forged blade, if extra weight is needed, they are thicker than the blade itself.

Half, or canoe, tangs are good enough for lightweight knives which are not likely to be used for heavy work. They are usually found on carving, boning, filleting, vegetable and fruit knives. Pin, rat-tail and whittle tangs add no appreciable weight to a knife.

### Materials used for handles

Traditional handles of wood, bone, horn and leather are still found on knives today, but public health regulations permit only plastic handles, which can be sterilized at temperatures that would ruin natural materials, on tools used where food is prepared for the public. Because of this, if you go to kitchen supply shops to buy the quality of knife used by professional cooks, you will now find that water-resistant, heatproof, plastic handles considerably outnumber wooden ones.

### Caring for knives

When cutting anything make sure that the edge of the blade lands on something relatively soft, such as a wooden block or board, rather than a ceramic, stone, metal or laminated plastic surface (see BOARDS). It is the continual striking of unyielding surfaces that dulls a blade, not the cutting.

Wooden handles tend to swell and work loose and carbon steel blades rust and stain if left wet or in water, or in contact with moist foods. So get into the habit of washing and drying a knife as soon as you have finished with it. Jostling them in the washing-up bowl with other tools harms their edges and putting them in a dishwasher ruins all handles made of natural materials.

Stained or rusty carbon steel blades can be cleaned with a piece of wet cork dipped in scouring powder, or with a mildly abrasive scouring pad; but once used their shine will never be as bright as it was when new.

To check whether a knife is sharp, hold the edge towards the light against a dark surface. Any sparkles of reflected light upon it indicate blunted or burred areas.

The ease with which a knife is sharpened depends upon the thickness of the edge itself and the width of its included angle. The thicker

## Handles and tangs

*Full tangs extend the whole length and breadth of the handle, like the filling in a sandwich. In forged blades the bolster forms part of the handle.*

*This lighter knife has a full tang but no guard or bolster. The shape of the handle itself forms the guard.*

*Half, or canoe, tangs extend one third, half or three-quarters of the way along the handle. They are slotted into the handle, which is made in one piece and secured with rivets.*

*A pin tang goes right through the handle and is secured at the end with a pin or rivet, visible from the outside. It is often used with a decorative collar.*

*A rat-tail, or whittle tang, is long, thin and pointed, extending well into the handle, but invisible from the outside. The handle is hammered on, so in time can work loose.*

the edge, or the wider the angle, the more metal must be removed in sharpening. The hardness of the blade can also make steeling difficult. That is why it rarely exceeds 59 Rockwell (see GLOSSARY). Stainless steel blades are harder than carbon steel ones and keep their sharpness longer for this reason; but they also take more steeling to re-sharpen them once they lose their edge. Carbon steel blades are softer and blunt more quickly, but are swiftly sharpened with a few flicks on a steel.

Blades which have edges worn to more than ·010 in. (0·25 mm) thickness cannot be steeled. Cutlers check this thickness by pressing the cutting edge on the flat of a thumb-nail. The edge should "give" with a ripple, if thin enough for steeling. Otherwise the knife must be sharpened on an oilstone.

(a) **Size.** (Blade) L. 8 in. (204 mm).
**Material.** Carbon steel blade, stag horn handle.

(b) **Size.** (Blade) L. 12 in. (305 mm).
**Material.** Carbon steel blade, wooden handle, brass swivel ring and guard.

(c) **Size.** (Blade) L. 2¾ in. (70 mm).
**Material.** Carbon steel blade, stainless steel handle, leather case.

Sharpening steels are made from a high carbon steel, similar to that used for engineer's files, which is much harder than that used for knife blades. A steel, in fact, acts as a file on the knife's edge. The finer it is the gentler its action.

# Sharpening steels

(c)

(a)

(b)

Most domestic steels, which are often sold with carving sets, are very finely grooved; but for kitchen use it is best to have a coarsely grooved steel with plenty of cut. For efficiency the blade of a steel should be longer than the knife blade to be sharpened.

The domestic steel (a) has the short blade typical of steels sold with carving sets. Some people find these too short. The butcher's steel (b) is of medium size. They range from 10 to 14 in. (255 to 355 mm) in blade length. A 10 to 12 in. (255 to 305 mm) butcher's steel with fairly coarse grooves is a good kitchen tool.

The pocket steel (c) is not a toy, but an efficient sharpener of steak knives. It is a discreet tool for surreptitious use in restaurants.

## Steeling a blade vertically

## Steeling a blade horizontally

## Steeling a scalloped blade

*Knives with scalloped blades cannot be sharpened in the normal way on a steel, because the points of the scallops are long and prevent the "valleys" coming in contact with it. Sharpen each "valley" separately with a firm, scrubbing action on the steel.*

*Hold the steel vertically in confined spaces. Start behind the steel with the heel of the blade by the guard and swoop down to finish with the point at the tip of the steel. Bring the knife in front to sharpen the other side.*

*Keep the blade of the knife at an angle of 30° to the steel and bring the whole length of the edge in contact with it. Keep your elbow still and move just wrist and forearm. Don't overdo it, up to ten gentle strokes are all that is needed. Start with the heel of the knife by the guard and end with the point at the tip of the steel. Sharpen the other side of the blade similarly under the steel.*

## Oilstones

(a)
(b)

(a) **Size.** L. 8 in. (204 mm).
   **Material.** Silicon carbide.
(b) **Size.** L. 4 in. (100 mm).
   **Material.** Silicon carbide.

Oilstones are made of a very hard fine-grained, man-made composition of silicon carbide. The most useful have one side of finer grain for giving a keen finish to the edge. Knives should be honed on oilstones three or four times a year to keep them really sharp.

Oilstone (a) is a convenient size for the kitchen, but has only one grade of surface. The little oilstone (b) has two. It is rather small for large blades, but useful for scissors (see SCISSORS).

*Lubricate the stone with cooking oil or water and put a damp cloth beneath it for stability. Tilt the blade at 20° to the stone and lay it, edge leading, across the top, left-hand corner. Draw the blade gently towards you from left to right, guiding it with your fingertips. Turn the knife over and repeat the action in the opposite direction.*

## Some patent sharpeners

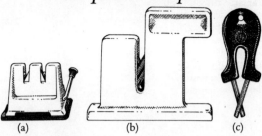

(a)
(b)
(c)

(a) **Size.** H. 2 in. (50 mm).
   **Material.** Sharpening files, plastic body, suction base.
(b) **Size.** H. 4½ in. (115 mm).
   **Material.** Sharpening steels, enamelled cast-iron body.
(c) **Size.** L. 4¼ in. (107 mm).
   **Material.** Sharpening steels, plastic handle.

The double-slotted sharpener (a) works well if you do not exert heavy pressure. Each slot contains a wedge-shaped file and a spring-loaded ball-bearing. The knife is drawn through each slot in turn to sharpen both sides of the edge.

Sharpener (b) is designed to reproduce the action of a steel as closely as possible and is a foolproof tool for those who feel they will never master the art of using a steel. Two crossed steels, cunningly set on springs, rotate and give against the blade as it passes through the slot. This rotation cuts micro-serrations on the edge, unlike hand-held steels.

If a knife is placed plumb between the crossed steels of sharpener (c) it is at the correct angle for sharpening. It is difficult to keep this angle with any but the smallest knives and the sharpener grips the blade rather tensely.

(a)

(b)

(a) **Size.** H. 2¼ in. (57 mm).
   **Material.** Tungsten carbide discs, plastic body.
   Wall-mounted.
(b) **Size.** L. 5 in. (127 mm).
   **Material.** Tungsten carbide discs, plastic handle.

These sharpeners consist of little discs set in two interleaving stacks. The discs rotate as a knife-edge is drawn across them (in one direction only). They sharpen with a fierce, milling action. Don't press too hard, this could damage a blade.

## Electric sharpener

**Size.** H. 5¼ in. (133 mm).
**Material.** Silicon carbide grinding wheel, plastic body.

This machine has slots for knives and scissors. Switch on and draw the blade towards you once through the slot with light pressure. The wheel spins fast and puts an edge on the bluntest knife, but can wear a blade down quickly—so take care.

# Cook's knives

(a) **Size.** (Blade) 4 in. (100 mm).
**Material.** Stainless steel blade, wooden handle.

(b) **Size.** (Blade) 8 in. (204 mm).
**Material.** Carbon steel blade, wooden handle.

(c) **Size.** (Blade) 10 in. (255 mm).
**Material.** Stainless steel blade, plastic handle.

These knives are made in the classic "French pattern" with strong, broad, pointed blades. Their edges are very sharp, dead straight from the heel to about half way along the blade, then gently curving upwards towards the point so that they can be used with a rocking motion when chopping things finely. Knife (a) is used for vegetable paring and has a full tang, making it quite heavy for its size—2 oz. (56 g). More than half the weight is in the handle, giving it good balance for intricate work. It is taper-ground.

A pin-tang and collar instead of a full-tang and bolster, make knife (b) a relatively light cook's

(a)

(b)  (c)

knife for its size—4 oz. (113 g). It has a taper-ground blade, but is less rugged than knife (c), which weighs in at 7½ oz. (212 g). The 8 in. (204 mm) blade makes knife (b) a good size for slicing and cubing, but the greater weight of knife (c) and its larger, taper-ground blade make it a more useful knife and ideal for fine chopping and mincing.

The best cook's knives have firmly riveted full tangs, which withstand the shock of chopping and also give weight to the handle. This makes these knives work better and means that if they fall they will land handle first, thus avoiding damage to the blade.

Professional cooks, who are in the habit of economizing where time and utensils are concerned, use this one versatile tool in preference to a number of more specialized gadgets. Not only the edge and the point (which is sometimes slightly flexible), but also the heel and the flat of the blade of a cook's knife can be used in various ways.

## Balance

A full tang puts weight into the handle of a cook's knife and helps to balance the blade. The point of balance in the knife should be on the blade, just in front of the handle. Test this by balancing the knife on a finger.

## Holding a cook's knife when cutting something resistant

The thumb and first finger should be placed on the blade just in front of the guard when you are cutting something that needs pressure as well as a degree of precision—for instance when cubing carrots or making equal strips of tagliatelli.

## Holding a cook's knife for chopping and mincing

To use a cook's knife with the rocking action needed for chopping there needs to be plenty of room for your thumb and all your fingers to grasp the handle firmly when the heel of the blade meets the board.

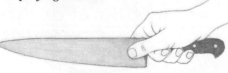

## Slicing vegetables

To slice a firmly textured vegetable (carrot, potato, cabbage), peel and trim it first, squaring off the sides and ends of potatoes. Hold it with your fingers in a grab-like position. The blade should slide up and down against the middle joints of your first two fingers as the edge cuts into the vegetable. Move your hand back with each slice and follow it with the knife keeping close like a dancing partner.

## Julienne strips

After making slices of the required thickness, pile them up together. Cut the slices into even, square-sectioned strips. Use these to garnish soups or salads.

## Cubing vegetables

Having cut slices of vegetables into square-sectioned julienne strips, gather them together and cut them across into neat little cubes.

## Dicing an onion

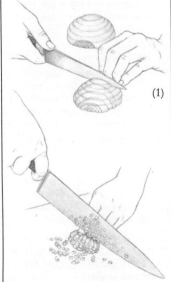

(1)

(2)

Peel an onion and halve it through the root. Lay one half cut side down and make three or four horizontal cuts through the onion, stopping short of the root. Hold the onion with the root to one side and make close vertical cuts still keeping the root intact (1). Finally cut across the previous cuts to make little dice. Discard the root or use it for stock (2).

## Slicing mushrooms into julienne strips

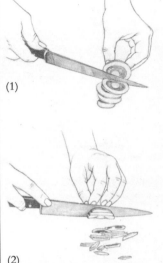

(1)

(2)

Hold the mushroom by its stem and slice it thinly. Discard the stem with the last slice (1). Reassemble the slices into a mushroom cap and make julienne strips by slicing downwards (2).

## Mincing herbs or making a mirepoix

Use the largest, heaviest cook's knife available to make the finest, mushiest mince of herbs or vegetables. With one hand lightly holding the handle and the other counterbalancing it across the back of the blade near the tip, rock the knife rapidly up and down over the vegetables. Gather the bits together from time to time with the flat of the blade until all is chopped finely.

17

(1)

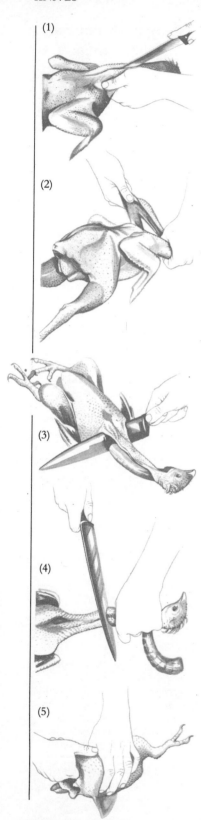

(2)

(3)

(4)

(5)

## Gutting a chicken

*1. With the bird lying on its breast make a slit with a boning knife along the back of the bird's neck.*

*2. Pull the neck free of its skin for its entire length.*

*3. Turn the bird over and with a large cook's knife sever the neck (but not the skin) as close as possible to the shoulders. The head is still joined to the skin and neck.*

*4. Holding the head and neck in one hand, cut the head from the skin, leaving as much skin as possible attached to the bird. Cut the head from the neck. Trim off the wing tips. Keep these and the neck for stock.*

*5. Free the crop and windpipe from the neck skin and work your fingers around inside the bird, detaching the entrails from the back and sides of the spine and ribs.*

*6. Make a vertical cut through the vent and after removing the fat at the tail and thighs, pull out all the entrails, if possible in one handful, without bursting any of the gut. Keep the liver, heart and gizzard and carefully remove the gall bladder from the liver.*

*7. With the point of a boning knife make slits between the bone and tendons on the backs of the legs.*

*8. Insert the point of a steel, or, if the bird is small, the handle of a wooden spoon, between the bone and tendons.*

*9. Twist it until the tendons slip out of the thighs. There should be five in each leg. The claws will contract as you do this.*

*10. Hold the bird steady on its back and chop off both the legs at the same point below the first joint, removing the feet. Trim the claws from the feet and add the feet to the giblets.*

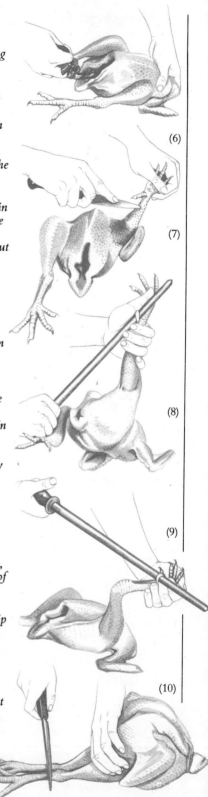

(6)

(7)

(8)

(9)

(10)

## Cutting up a chicken

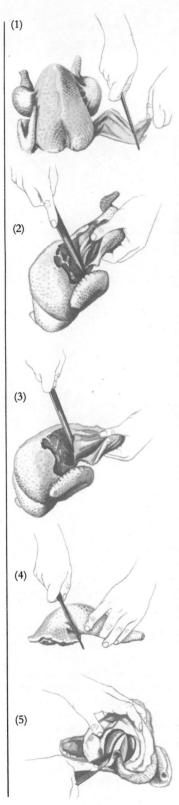

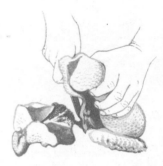

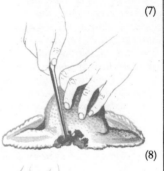

1. If the feet and wing tips have not already been removed, do this using a medium-sized cook's knife.

2. Cut carefully through the ball and socket thigh joint.

3. Remove the legs, including all the meat lying beside the tail; try to include the oysters too.

4. Divide the legs into drumsticks and thighs.

5. Pull back the skin from the shoulders so that you can see and feel the wishbone. Cut it free at the top with the point of a boning knife, then hook it forward with your finger and cut it free from the shoulder joints. Make a mental note of the position of these joints as you will need to find them twice more.

6. With the bird breast uppermost, cut between the breast and the pelvis, using a cook's knife. Slice between the ribs on either side.

7. Continue cutting until you reach the shoulder joints. Sever the carcass at these joints, leaving the breast and wings on one piece and the ribs, backbone and pelvis on the other.

8. With the breast right side up cut just above the thick, fatty line of skin above each wing and aslant of the breast.

9. Carefully cut through the shoulder joints, leaving a diamond-shaped breast.

10. Chop straight across the highest point of the breast, right through the bone. You now have eight pieces of bird, each with an equal share of meat, skin and bone.

## Preparing a pineapple

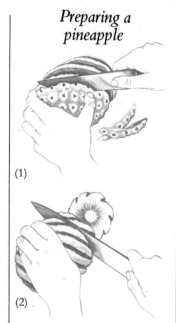

(1)

(2)

Using a medium-sized knife, cut off the top and the stem and trim the peel in wide, thin strips. Following the diagonal lines of little "eyes" now revealed, cut narrow grooves from the flesh to remove them (1). Then cut the pineapple into slices (2), removing the core, if it is tough, from each slice with a round biscuit cutter.

## Crushing garlic

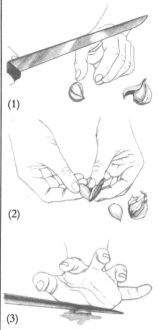

(1)

(2)

(3)

One quick tap with the flat of the blade will split the skin of a garlic clove (1). Peel off the skin (2) and then crush the clove with heavy pressure from the palm of your hand pushed down flat on the blade (3).

## Making chocolate curls

Spread melted chocolate thickly and evenly on a marble slab. When set, draw a knife edge across it towards you. This pulls the chocolate up in large flakes. Use them to cover cream-coated cakes.

## Halving a cooked lobster

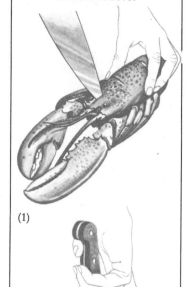

(1)

(2)

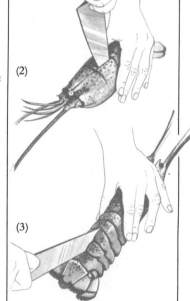

(3)

Make a small cut between the lobster's eyes (1) and shake out any liquid inside. Twist off the claws and legs. Cut into the body where it joins the tail (2) and then along the central line towards the head. Turn and cut down the centre of the tail (3) and remove the food sac and gut.

## Preparing artichoke fonds

1. Break the stem from the artichoke to pull out coarse fibres.
2. Trim the base quite flat.
3. Pare off the leaves to expose the choke.
4. Chop the tops from remaining leaves close to the fond (bottom).
5. Trim the fond with a small knife.
6. Rub it with a cut lemon and put it in a pan with plenty of water. Add one cut lemon to every four fonds. Cook till tender, drain and refresh under cold water.
7. Use a spoon or your thumb to push out the remains of the choke.

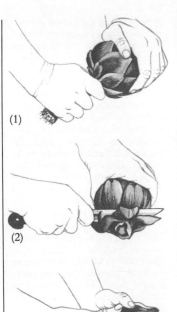

(1)

(2)

(3)

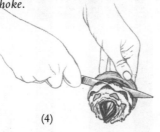

(4)

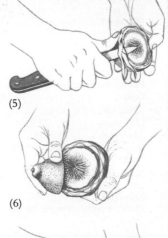

(5)

(6)

(7)

## Milking a corn cob

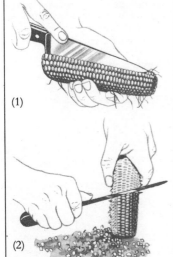

(1)

(2)

To milk an ear of corn, slit each row of kernels with the whole length of the edge (1). Then scrape away the soft flesh from the kernels (2) with the back of the knife blade.

## Making puff pastry cases

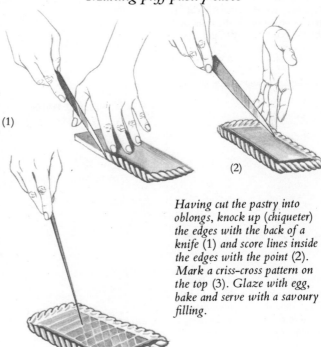

(1)

(2)

(3)

Having cut the pastry into oblongs, knock up (chiqueter) the edges with the back of a knife (1) and score lines inside the edges with the point (2). Mark a criss-cross pattern on the top (3). Glaze with egg, bake and serve with a savoury filling.

(a) **Size.** (Blade) L. 6½ in. (165 mm).
**Material.** Carbon steel blade, wooden handle.

(b) **Size.** (Blade) L. 5½ in. (140 mm).
**Material.** Carbon steel blade, wooden handle, brass collar.

(c) **Size.** (Blade) L. 10 in. (255 mm).
**Material.** Carbon steel blade, wooden handle, brass collar.

(d) **Size.** (Blade) L. 12 in. (305 mm).
**Material.** Carbon steel blade, wooden handle, brass collar.

Japanese cook's knives are made in the same way as Samurai swords. The blades are flat on one side and angled to the edge on the other. They are extremely sharp, but compared with Chinese or Western knives, are made of rather soft carbon steel. Traditionally, the flat side is made of harder steel than the angled side so that the extreme tip of the cutting edge keeps its sharpness longer.

The blades are sharpened on a stone which is not so hard as carborundum. Once again following Samurai tradition the flat side is given one sweep on the stone and the angled side five, to get a perfect edge.

These chisel-edged blades give greater accuracy and control over the thickness and depth of a cut

# Japanese knives

(a)    (b)    (c)    (d)

(when used in the Japanese manner) than do European knives. They are usually attached to the wooden handles with whittle tangs, although some have half, or canoe, tangs with rivets. The handles generally have brass collars and are flat or oval in section with sometimes a flattened area to allow your thumb to rest comfortably – in keeping with the tradition of Samurai sword-making. Because the blades are chisel-shaped, "south-paw" knives are manufactured for left-handed cooks.

Most Japanese households have three different kitchen knives. The nagiri (a) is used for shredding vegetables, such as daikon (long white radish), cucumber or carrot and cutting them into decorative shapes. The deba (b) is for boning, skinning and slicing fish. It can also be used for chopping meat. Although the blade is too soft to go through bone, the heel can be used to sever tendons.

The yanagi (c) is a most useful knife. With it a cook cuts elegant even slices of fish and meat for dishes like sashimi (sliced raw fish) and sukiyaki and cuts and chops vegetables for basic cooking and for decorative garnishes. The whole length of the edge is used in slicing; the tip and heel for cutting and the middle of the cutting edge for chopping.

The square-tipped tako-biki (d) is a professional cook's knife, used in restaurants for making sashimi.

## Shredding roots

(1)

(3)

(2)

*1. Using the nagiri, cut the root into lengths (according to how long you want the shreds to be). Then start shaving the thinnest possible strip from round the outside of the root, controlling the depth of the cut with your thumbs.*

*2. When you have trimmed the root to a finger's thickness, stop cutting.*

*3. Carefully fold up the strip and slice it lengthways (closely for hair-like shreds, less finely for stouter sticks). Put the shreds in a bowl of iced water to crisp up.*

## Decorating cucumber

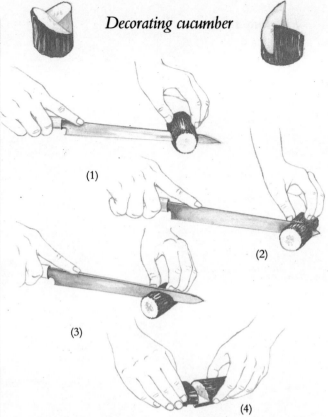

(1)

(2)

(3)

(4)

1. Cut the cucumber into equal lengths, using the yanagi. Then push the point of the knife into the centre of each section, making a slot from side to side. (For a pretty final effect, this central section can be peeled).

2. Slice diagonally through the cucumber without cutting to the ends, and stopping at the depth of the slot.

3. Turn the cucumber over and cut similarly through on the other side.

4. Pull the two pieces apart… …and stand them on end.

## Cutting cucumber fans and "pine needles"

(1)

(2)

Quarter a section of cucumber lengthways with the yanagi. Remove the seeds and make two cuts in each quarter: one going from the left not quite through to the right and the other vice versa (1). Gently pull the closed Z-shape open. Twist the right-hand end under the central bar and over the left-hand end (2) to make "pine needles".

Alternatively, cut the sections into thin strips, leaving them attached at one end (1). Open the strips into a fan. Make decorative leaves similarly to the fan, but cut only five strips. Curl these as shown (2).

## Making garnishes from cucumber peel

Cut a section of cucumber with the yanagi and remove the peel in one piece. Carefully cut the peel in two through the centre in a zigzag. Gently draw the halves apart to produce attractive fronds.

## Making turnip chrysanthemums

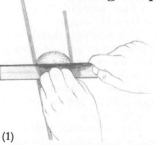

(1)

(2)

Put a peeled turnip between two chopsticks to restrict the depth of the cut (1). Then, using the nagiri, cut down to the chopsticks in a criss-cross pattern. Parboil the turnip, drain and refresh in cold water. Rub salt into the cuts. Soak the turnip in cold water to widen and soften the cuts, giving the turnip a chrysanthemum-like shape (2).

# Filleting a fish
### (USING A DEBA)

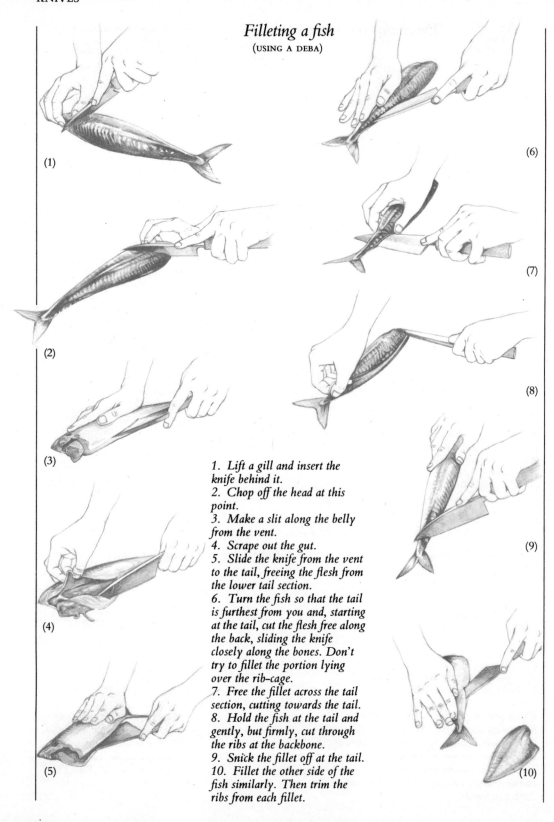

(1)

(2)

(3)

(4)

(5)

(6)

(7)

(8)

(9)

(10)

1. Lift a gill and insert the knife behind it.
2. Chop off the head at this point.
3. Make a slit along the belly from the vent.
4. Scrape out the gut.
5. Slide the knife from the vent to the tail, freeing the flesh from the lower tail section.
6. Turn the fish so that the tail is furthest from you and, starting at the tail, cut the flesh free along the back, sliding the knife closely along the bones. Don't try to fillet the portion lying over the rib-cage.
7. Free the fillet across the tail section, cutting towards the tail.
8. Hold the fish at the tail and gently, but firmly, cut through the ribs at the backbone.
9. Snick the fillet off at the tail.
10. Fillet the other side of the fish similarly. Then trim the ribs from each fillet.

# Chinese cleavers

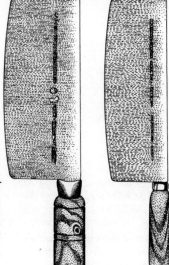

(a) **Size.** (Blade) L. 7¾ in.
   (197 mm).
   **Material.** Carbon steel
   blade, wooden handle.
(b) **Size.** (Blade) L. 7¾ in.
   (197 mm).
   **Material.** Carbon steel
   blade, wooden handle,
   brass collar.
(c) **Size.** (Blade) L. 8 in.
   (204 mm).
   **Material.** Stainless steel.

Cleaver (a) is, for Chinese cooks,
the equivalent of the French
cook's knife and is equally versatile. It is used for every kind of
light chopping, mincing, dicing,
scraping, mashing and shredding
of meat, fish and vegetables. Each
part has a special purpose. The
sharp corner of the blade scores
lines and cuts things into strips;
the back is a pounder and tend-
erizer; the flat of the blade crushes
and scoops and the end of the
·handle acts as a pestle for grinding
spices. It weighs ¾ lb (340 g), but
as it has a pin tang, two-thirds of
its weight is in the blade.

Decorative cutting is best done
with the lightweight cleaver (b)
which weighs only ¼ lb (113 g)
and has a whittle tang.

The heavy cleaver (c) weighs
1½ lbs (680 g) and is used like a
butcher's chopper to quarter
poultry, joint meat and slice
whole fish. It is much the same
size and shape as the medium-
weight cleaver (a), but has extra
weight and strength in its thicker
blade of stainless steel.

(a)    (b)

(c)

## Making green pepper fans

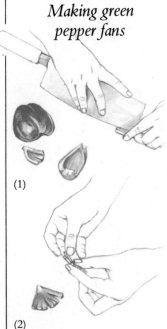

(1)

(2)

1. Using a lightweight cleaver
slice through the pepper lengthwise. Remove the seeds and trim
the inner ribs. Quarter the pepper
lengthwise, then cut each quarter
across into fan-shaped eighths.
With the cleaver tip cut slits
close together along the top of
each fan, leaving it intact at
the base.
2. Gently spread out each fan.

## Cutting squid decoratively

(1)

(2)

1. Clean and skin a squid, then
using a lightweight cleaver slit
and open out the body.
2. Score the surface of the squid
with the tip of the cleaver. Make
a fairly deep criss-cross pattern,
with the blade held slightly on
the slant. Then cut the squid
into 1 in. (25 mm) strips or
2 in. (50 mm) squares. The
pieces will curl a little and open
out as they cook.

## Chopping up chicken

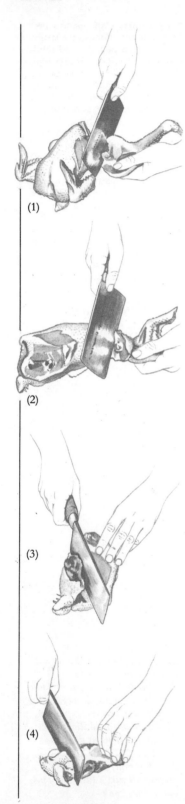

(1)

(2)

(3)

(4)

1. Using a heavy cleaver, cut through the skin at the thigh and lever back the leg, exposing the thigh joint. Cut through this joint. Cut off the other leg similarly.

2. Extend the wings in the same way, severing them by cutting through the shoulder joints.

3. Put the bird on its side and separate the breast from the back, chopping exactly along the middle of the row of ribs that joins the front to the back. Use more than one blow, if necessary.

4. Chop the back, crossways, into two or three pieces.

5. Score down one side of the breast bone with the cleaver, using the tip of the blade.

6. Set the blade in the scored mark and strike the back of the cleaver with the side of a mallet to divide the breast in two.

7. Chop each half into three or four pieces.

8. Chop each leg and wing across into five and three pieces respectively, leaving the joints intact and chopping through the bones.

In some Chinese recipes the chicken is reassembled after cooking so that it looks good on the serving dish. To do this arrange the back pieces down the centre of the dish first; then build up the rest of the fowl, placing the wings and legs in position and laying the pieces of breast on top of the back pieces (as above).

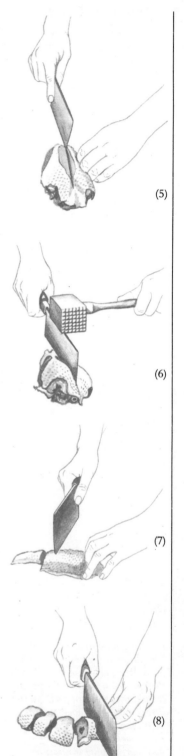

(5)

(6)

(7)

(8)

## Chopping lettuce

(1)

(2)

(3)

(4)

1. (Use a medium weight cleaver for chopping leafy vegetables.) Pile up lettuce leaves with the stems all lying one way and slice the leaves down the midribs to flatten them.

2. Slice the leaves into narrow shreds.

3. Hold the shreds together and slice them across into smaller pieces.

4. Then chop them as finely as you wish. This process can be speeded up by using two cleavers at once.

## Puréeing chicken breast

Place the skinned breast, membrane side down, on the chopping board. Scrape away from your hand along the grain of the flesh with the tip of a wet cleaver. Chop the fine shreds to a purée.

## Chopping walnuts

Use the tip of the blade as a pivot, resting the heel of your hand over it on the back of the blade. Chop backwards and forwards across the nuts, lifting the handle up and down to produce a rocking motion similar to that used with a cook's knife.

## Slicing raw meat thinly

First half-freeze the meat as this makes it easier to cut thinly. Slice it through, sliding the side of the cleaver blade against the knuckles of the hand steadying the meat. Move your fingers backwards with each cut to regulate the thickness.

## Mincing meat

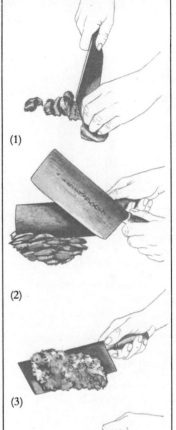

(1)

(2)

(3)

(4)

1. Cut the meat into small pieces.

2. Hold two cleavers and let each blade drop alternately on to the meat in a steady rhythm, moving to and fro across it.

3. Use the flat of one blade to scoop up the mince . . .

4. . . . and flip it over, like a pancake. Continue this chopping and flipping until the desired consistency is reached.

# Salad knives

(a)  (b)  (c)

(a) **Size.** (Blade) L. $4\frac{1}{2}$ in. (115 mm).
**Material.** Stainless steel blade, wooden handle.
(b) **Size.** (Blade) L. $3\frac{3}{4}$ in. (95 mm).
**Material.** Stainless steel blade, wooden handle.
(c) **Size.** (Blade) L. 5 in. (127 mm).
**Material.** Stainless steel blade, plastic handle.

Long, narrow blades with very finely serrated edges are characteristic of knives used for preparing salads. They are ideal for cutting smooth-skinned vegetables with soft centres, such as cucumbers and tomatoes, or for slicing citrus fruit thinly.

The extremely narrow blade of knife (a) makes it light to work with. It is particularly useful for slicing soft, ripe tomatoes because the slender blade does not crush the flesh as much thicker blades do. It is also good for cutting very fine slices of salami. The "sheep's foot" shape of blade (b) is preferred by some people for peeling and the shape is usually found on strong, very rigid, broad blades which suit this work. Knife (c) has a very finely scalloped edge which cuts more smoothly than a serrated one. It has a dishwasher-safe handle, injection moulded to conceal the riveted tang. With its longer blade it is a useful knife for halving grapefruit.

# Paring knives

(a)  (b)  (c)  (d)

(a) **Size.** (Blade) L. 3 in. (75 mm).
**Material.** Carbon steel blade, wooden handle.
(b) **Size.** (Blade) L. $3\frac{1}{4}$ in. (82 mm).
**Material.** Stainless steel blade, wooden handle.
(c) **Size.** (Blade) L. $3\frac{1}{2}$ in. (90 mm).
**Material.** Stainless steel blade, wooden handle.
(d) **Size.** (Blade) L. $3\frac{1}{4}$ in. (82 mm).
**Material.** Surgical steel blade, plastic handle.

Paring knives should be small and light enough to seem like an extension of your hand. They should be held high up on the handle with a forefinger crooked over the back of the blade to give precise control when paring.

The little cook's knife (a) is small and light enough to work its way round the most knobbly vegetable and is easily sharpened. It is probably the most useful shape if you wish to do elaborate turning as well as paring and trimming.

All vegetable knives should have sharp points so that pips and "eyes" can be picked out easily. The "granny" (b), upturned (c) and "sheep's foot" (d) blade shapes are a matter of personal preference. Knife (d) has a wire attachment that can be clipped to the blade to convert it into a peeler. It is fixed by two strong spring coils to either side of the blade, so suits both left-handed and right-handed users.

# Turning knives

(a)  (b)

(a) **Size.** (Blade) L. 2 in. (50 mm).
**Material.** Stainless steel blade, wooden handle.
(b) **Size.** (Blade) L. 3 in. (75 mm).
**Material.** Stainless steel blade, wooden handle.

These are likely to be the smallest knives in the kitchen, but to be really useful they need to be among the sharpest.

They are used for cutting vegetables into "turned" or decorative shapes – fluted mushrooms, carrots carved into identical ovals, tomatoes cut like roses and radishes like water-lilies.

## Scallion flowers

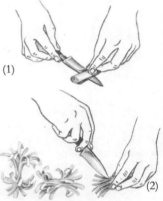

(1)

(2)

*Trim off the bulb of a scallion (spring onion) and cut the stem into short lengths. Then cut into the sections, horizontally (1) and vertically (2), at both ends keeping the middle intact. Put the sections into cold water to open up.*

## Fluting mushrooms

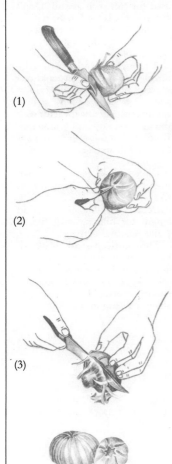

(1)

(2)

(3)

If you are serving mushrooms as an hors-d'oeuvre or as a special dish, you can decorate them attractively by fluting them. Choose very white, firm mushrooms and wash and dry them quickly, but thoroughly. Take a small turning knife. Hold the blade at a slight angle to the mushroom and, using the heel of the blade, cut into the cap, twisting the blade with a flick of the wrist as you do so to make the flutes (1). Press the flat tip of the knife against the top of the cap to indent a star (2). Now take a larger knife and cut through the edge of the cap to trim off any loose flutings and the stalk (3). The caps can be fluted closely or sparingly.

## Lemon baskets and garnishes

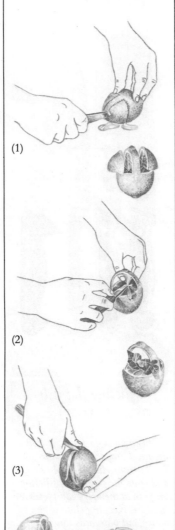

(1)

(2)

(3)

Cut sections from both sides of the upper half of a lemon, leaving the centre whole (1). Cut away the flesh at the centre, leaving the peel. Fill the basket with parsley sprigs and radishes, or watercress (2). Cut narrow strips of peel from a lemon, using a turning knife. Slice the lemon and dip half of each slice in chopped parsley (3).

## Turning carrots

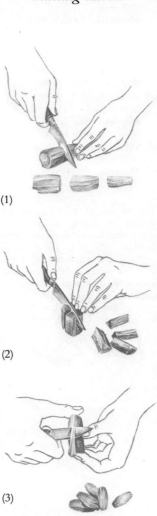

(1)

(2)

(3)

There is a knack to turning carrots into regularly shaped ovals. One way to acquire the even, paring technique required is to practice on an egg. Hold the egg lengthways between finger and thumb and scrape the blade lightly down the shell. This will teach you the correct wrist action.
Peel the carrots and cut them into lengths (1). Cut very large carrots into halves or quarters (2) and trim each piece into seven-sided ovals of equal size (3).

29

(a) **Size.** (Blade) L. 10 in. (255 mm).
**Material.** Stainless steel blade, wooden handle.

(b) **Size.** (Blade) L. 8 in. (204 mm).
**Material.** Stainless steel blade, wooden handle.

(c) **Size.** (Blade) L. 6¼ in. (160 mm).
**Material.** Stainless steel blade, wooden handle.

(d) **Size.** (Blade) L. 5 in. (127 mm).
**Material.** Stainless steel blade, plastic handle.

The blades of filleting knives should be strong, thin-backed and pointed, very sharp and very flexible.

Sharpness and flexibility help to avoid waste, as the blade must follow the bones of a fish very closely. The point is useful when cutting through the skin. A light knife is easier to work with.

# Filleting knives

(a)    (b)    (c)    (d)

The larger the fish, the larger the knife used. Knife (a) is the length used for fish such as cod. Don't cut off heads and tails with a filleting knife because the blade, however large the knife, is much too flexible.

Although intended primarily for filleting fish, the larger knives make good cooked-meat carvers and can be used equally well to cut thin slices of raw meat for such things as escalopes or paupiettes. Knife (b) is a useful size both for filleting fish and slicing cooked or raw meat.

Knife (c) has a pin tang, which makes it relatively light for its size, only 1½ oz (42·5 g). It is extremely flexible and a good length for filleting such fish as plaice, sole and herring.

The short, narrow blade of knife (d) is strong, but very flexible. It is a good knife for filleting, but its bulky handle and cut-away blade make it unsuitable for slicing meat.

## Filleting flat fish
(TWO FILLETS)

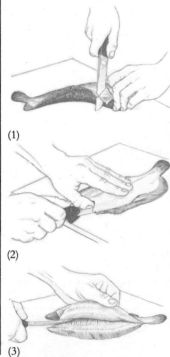

(1)

(2)

(3)

1. Using a rigid knife, cut off the head and scrape out the gut.
2. Turn the fish white-side up and slide the point of a filleting knife in at the belly cavity, above the ribs. Keeping close to the bones, cut outwards towards the fins.
3. Lift the freed half of the fillet and cut along and over the ridge-like spine. Keep the knife close to the bone to avoid damaging the fillet.
4. Replace the fillet and with a knife, now on the far side of the backbone, slice outwards toward the fins.
5. Free the fillet at the tail. Turn the fish over and do the same to free the second fillet.

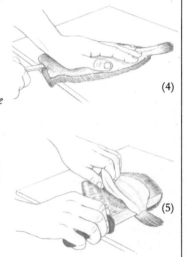

(4)

(5)

## Filleting a round fish

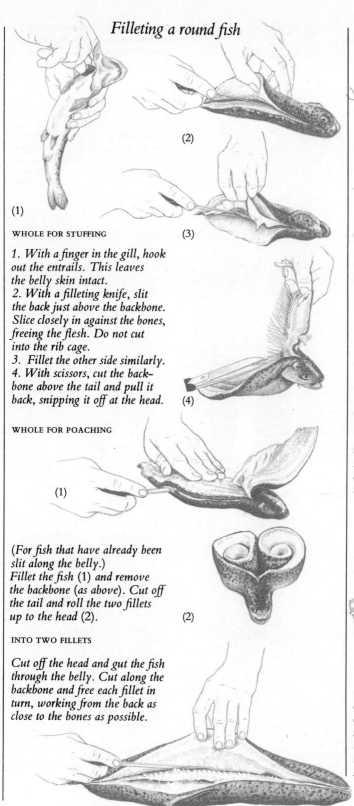

**WHOLE FOR STUFFING**

1. With a finger in the gill, hook out the entrails. This leaves the belly skin intact.
2. With a filleting knife, slit the back just above the backbone. Slice closely in against the bones, freeing the flesh. Do not cut into the rib cage.
3. Fillet the other side similarly.
4. With scissors, cut the backbone above the tail and pull it back, snipping it off at the head.

**WHOLE FOR POACHING**

(For fish that have already been slit along the belly.)
Fillet the fish (1) and remove the backbone (as above). Cut off the tail and roll the two fillets up to the head (2).

**INTO TWO FILLETS**

Cut off the head and gut the fish through the belly. Cut along the backbone and free each fillet in turn, working from the back as close to the bones as possible.

## Skinning a fillet

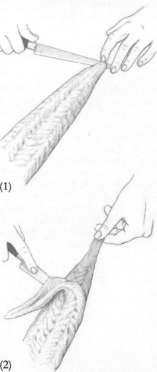

Work with the flesh of the fillet uppermost. Start at the tail (1). Pull the skin with one hand while cutting and pushing the flesh off the skin with a knife (2).

## Slicing escalopes

Use a long filleting knife to cut escalopes. Slice across the grain of the meat, as this makes it much more tender. If the piece of meat is rather flat, you can obtain larger slices by cutting it on the slant.

# Fishmonger's knives

(a) **Size.** (Blade) L. 14 in. (355 mm).
**Material.** Stainless steel blade, plastic handle.

(b) **Size.** (Blade) L. 6 in. (152 mm).
**Material.** Stainless steel blade, plastic handle.

Fishmonger's knives are designed to cope with the heavier work of fish preparation. They have strong, rigid blades and considerable weight, so that they can chop through the backbones of fish and cut off tails and heads.

Knife (a) with its impressive scalloped blade is a baby in the range that includes fish knives with blades up to 20 in (508 mm). It is a beautifully balanced, heavy knife with its tang completely encased in the handle. This makes it

very hygienic. The strong edge, deeply and sharply scalloped, can cut through the backbones of any large fish. It is rather too large for the average, domestic kitchen, but might be useful if your household contains a keen fisherman, who frequently brings home large fish.

The smaller knife (b) is lightweight, yet rigid, with sharp teeth on the back of the blade, for scaling fish. (Always use the back, never the edge, of a fish knife for this operation, as scaling fish makes knives very blunt.)

The edge of this knife is firm and sharp and can be used both as a filleter and fin-trimmer. Fishmongers prefer a firm knife for trimming fins as a flexible blade curves under pressure, however applied.

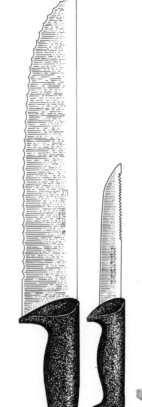

(b)

(a)

## Scaling a mullet

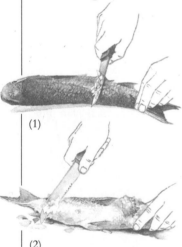

(1)

(2)

Using the back of a firm knife, work against the scales, that is, from the tail to the head of the mullet. You will find the whole process quicker and easier if you scale the back of the fish on one side first.

1. Scrape the back of the knife firmly up the mullet.

2. Turn the fish round and scale the belly.

3. Then turn it over and do the back on the other side.

4. Finish with the belly on that side.

(3)

(4)

## Cutting steaks from fish

First cut off the head, using the largest, strongest, serrated knife you have to saw through the tough backbone. Scrape out the gut cavity, then put the fish on its side with its back away from you. Keep a firm grip on it as you cut against the backbone. To avoid squashing the flesh, hold the fish so it keeps its rounded shape.

## Choppers

## Freezer saws

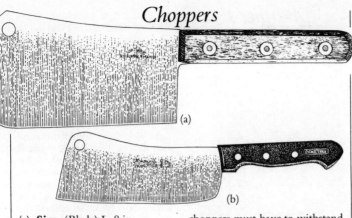

(a)

(b)

(a) **Size.** (Blade) L. 8 in. (204 mm).
**Material.** Carbon steel blade, beechwood handle.

(b) **Size.** (Blade) L. 7 in. (178 mm).
**Material.** Stainless steel blade, plastic handle.

Choppers have heavy, rectangular blades with strong edges for delivering blows that would nick chunks out of lighter knives. The blade should account for at least five-eighths of the total weight of a chopper. If you pick up a good one, you will feel how it wants to drop forward and down, practically doing the job for you, without any exertion on your part.

The heavy meat chopper (a) weighs 2¼ lbs (1 kg) and will go through most joints and bones. It is beautifully balanced at a point about a quarter of the way along the blade from the handle. The beechwood handle is firmly attached to the full tang, which all

choppers must have to withstand the shocks of chopping.

The lamb chopper (b) only weighs 11 oz (312 g) but is well-balanced and strongly made. The plastic handle has been textured to give it grip and completely covers the tang, thus eliminating crevices that could trap dirt. It is a good chopper for general domestic use and would come in handy for flattening escalopes.

Choppers will cut through most small bones, but they tend to splinter them. If you want a neat edge, or are faced with a big bone, it is better to use a saw.

It takes practice to hit the right spot first time. The trick is to use your forearm, rather than your wrist and keep your eye on the target and not the chopper. You can assist it on its way with a blow on the back of the blade delivered with the palm of the hand, or less painfully, with a wooden mallet. This is more accurate than letting the tool fall where it will.

### Chopping up oxtail

*This can be done with a chopper, or a very strong butcher's knife. Do not attempt to cut through the actual bones, but between each joint. Feel along each vertebra as you go, to locate where each ends. Flexing the tail also helps to reveal the position of the joints.*

(a) **Size.** (Blade) L. 10½ in. (267 mm).
**Material.** Stainless steel blade, ashwood handle.

(b) **Size.** (Blade) L. 8¾ in. (223 mm).
**Material.** Stainless steel blade, rosewood handle.

(c) **Size.** (Blade) L. 8 in. (204 mm).
**Material.** Stainless steel blade, ashwood handle.

The dual-purpose knife (a) has scallops on one side for slicing bread or meat, and saw teeth on the other for cutting through solid blocks of frozen food. It does not have suitable teeth for sawing through bones.

The freezer saw (b) is toothed and shaped like a miniature rip saw. It can be used for most frozen food and will cut up small bones.

The long pointed teeth on saw (c) are most efficient on frozen bread. The other side of the blade, which has fine and broad scallops, is for slicing thawed food.

33

(a) **Size.** (Blade) L. 5¼ in. (133 mm).
**Material.** Carbon steel blade, beechwood handle.

(b) **Size.** (Blade) L. 8 in. (204 mm).
**Material.** Stainless steel blade, plastic handle.

(c) **Size.** (Blade) L. 8 in. (204 mm).
**Material.** Stainless steel blade, plastic handle.

(d) **Size.** (Blade) L. 10 in. (255 mm).
**Material.** Carbon steel blade, rosewood handle, brass collar.

Butcher's knives usually have fairly long, firm blades. They are used for slicing through meat and trimming and finishing joints, so they do not need the weight given by a full tang. They usually have a three-quarter tang. Most have handles shaped with "shoulders" where they meet the blade, to give the hand extra leverage when making lengthy cuts into meat.

## Butcher's knives

(a)     (b)     (c)     (d)

Knife (a) is a blend of cook's knife and boning knife and can be used as either, although it is too small and light to chop like a cook's knife.

The butcher's supple knife (b) conforms to the most stringent rules on hygiene and can be sterilized. The blade is broad and well balanced, but the knife is light and is used for filleting and fine slicing. The sharply pointed tip is flexible and is useful for scraping out awkward cavities.

The scimitar-shaped knife (c) is completely rigid, strong and heavy. It is ideal for cutting the soft, meaty parts of a carcass into joints. It is shaped like an American butcher's knife and is made to stringent hygiene specifications.

A similar knife of more traditional pattern, knife (d) is used to slice thick steaks from the rump; divide large chunks of meat and cut between ribs to make chops. The upward curve of the rigid blade is useful when working close to the bone as it extends the cutting edge.

## Saws

(a) **Size.** (Blade) L. 9¼ in. (235 mm). 10 teeth to 1 in. (25 mm).
**Material.** Stainless steel blade, chromed steel frame.

(b) **Size.** (Blade) L. 12 in. (305 mm). Nine teeth to 1 in. (25 mm).
**Material.** Carbon steel blade, plastic handle.

Saws are used for dividing carcasses into quarters and are the only tool that will cut through bone satisfactorily. The kitchen hacksaw (a) will saw through small poultry or cutlet bones, but balks at anything much larger. It can cut through blocks of frozen food, if they are not too bulky. The blade cannot be sharpened or

replaced, but the saw is very inexpensive and should be regarded as disposable, not renewable.

You only need the butcher's bow saw (b) if you cut up large carcasses yourself. It has a detachable, sharpenable and replaceable blade, which is held at the correct tension by a lever just under the handle. It will cut through any bone, even the biggest beef bones.

Make sure when sawing through bone that you remove any bone dust from the meat, as this goes off quickly and will discolour the flesh.

Saws should be sharpened and re-set by experts. Your butcher can probably advise you where you can get this done.

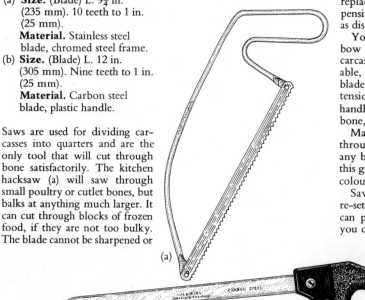

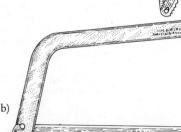

(a)

(b)

1. (Skin up) Use a large butcher's knife and then a saw to cut off the jowl (neck) where the shoulder begins.
2. (Skin down) Mark with a knife between the third and fourth ribs and saw through, finishing off with the knife.
3. Next remove the ham by sawing at right angles to the hind leg 2½ in. (65 mm) in front

## Cutting up half a pig

of the aitchbone. Finish with a knife.
4. Saw off the shank just below the hock joint.
5. You next divide the central part into loin and belly by sawing across the ribs, where the curve is greatest.
6. Finish cutting through with a knife. Then trim scraps and surplus fat from the joints.

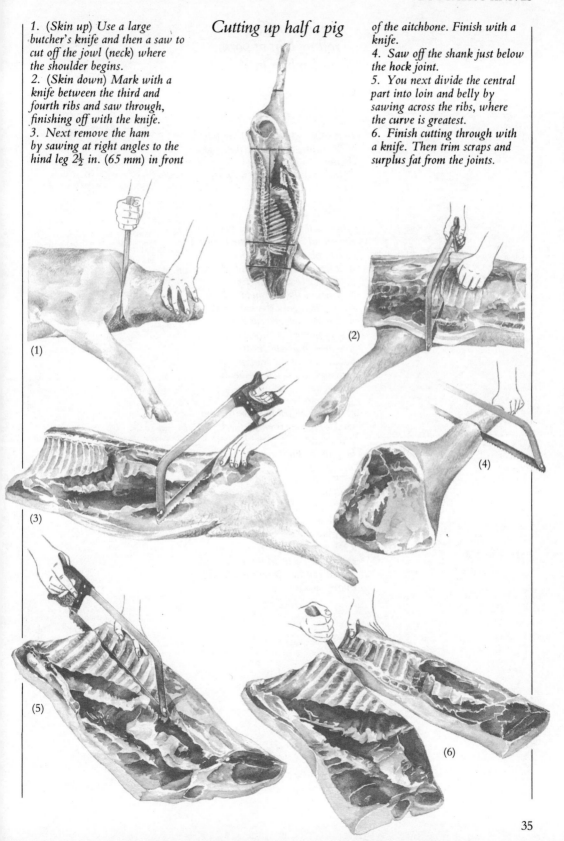

(1)

(2)

(3)

(4)

(5)

(6)

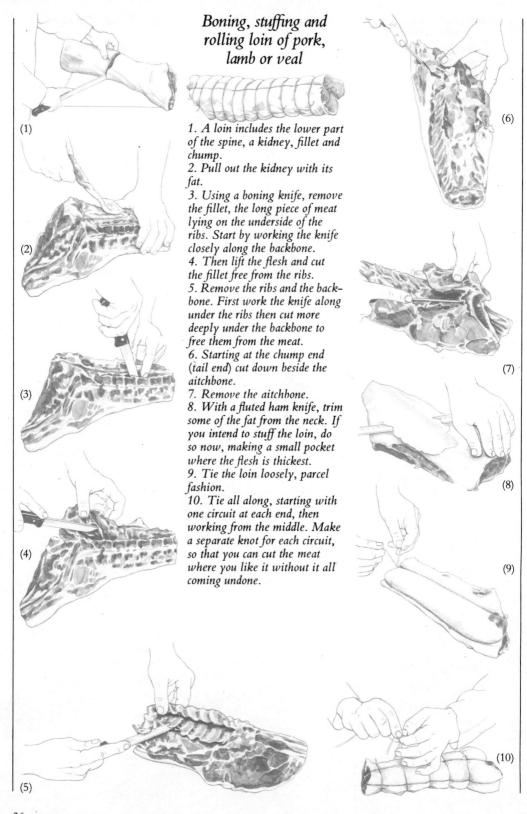

## Boning, stuffing and rolling loin of pork, lamb or veal

(1)

(2)

(3)

(4)

(5)

(6)

(7)

(8)

(9)

(10)

1. A loin includes the lower part of the spine, a kidney, fillet and chump.
2. Pull out the kidney with its fat.
3. Using a boning knife, remove the fillet, the long piece of meat lying on the underside of the ribs. Start by working the knife closely along the backbone.
4. Then lift the flesh and cut the fillet free from the ribs.
5. Remove the ribs and the backbone. First work the knife along under the ribs then cut more deeply under the backbone to free them from the meat.
6. Starting at the chump end (tail end) cut down beside the aitchbone.
7. Remove the aitchbone.
8. With a fluted ham knife, trim some of the fat from the neck. If you intend to stuff the loin, do so now, making a small pocket where the flesh is thickest.
9. Tie the loin loosely, parcel fashion.
10. Tie all along, starting with one circuit at each end, then working from the middle. Make a separate knot for each circuit, so that you can cut the meat where you like it without it all coming undone.

1. *Using a butcher's saw cut through the ribs close to the spine.*
2. *Do both sides similarly.*
3. *Use a sharp boning knife to cut down, round and under the spine to remove it.*
4. *Cut through the flesh to divide the meat into two racks.*
5. *Trim off loose fat and gristle.*

## To make a rack of lamb

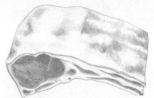

6. *Cut out the piece of cartilage (part of the tip of the blade bone) that lies behind the ribs.*
7. *Score across the skin on the outer side of each rack, halfway down the ribs.*
8. *Loosen the skin on either side of this scored line and tear both sections of skin completely off.*

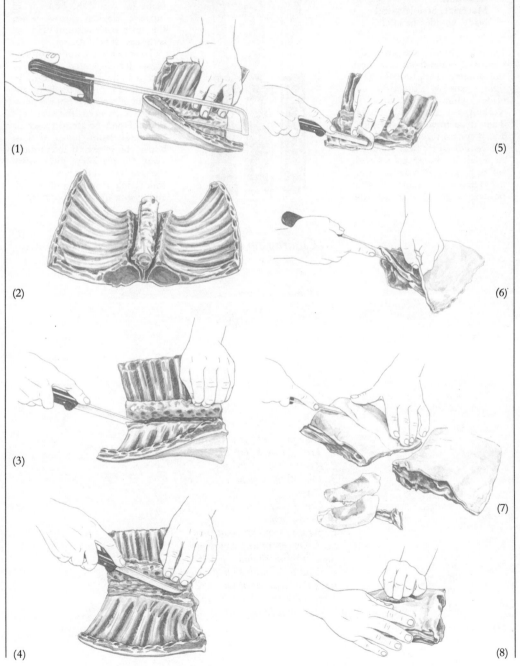

(1)

(2)

(3)

(4)

(5)

(6)

(7)

(8)

(a) **Size.** (Blade) L. 7 in. (178 mm).
**Material.** Stainless steel blade, wooden handle.

(b) **Size.** (Blade) L. 6 in. (152 mm).
**Material.** Carbon steel blade, wooden handle.

(c) **Size.** (Blade) L. 5 in. (127 mm).
**Material.** Stainless steel blade, wooden handle.

These knives are used solely for removing bones from raw meat and poultry. They usually have rigid, narrow, broad-backed blades with sharp points for working round knobbly bones. They need frequent sharpening, as they constantly encounter bone.

Strength rather than weight is required, so choose knives with full or three-quarter tangs. Boning knives are made without bolsters or guards, although the

## Boning knives

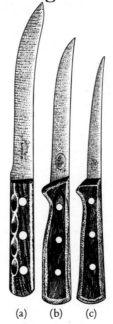

(a) (b) (c)

handles are usually shaped to prevent your hand slipping on to the blade.

Some cooks like very short, rigid, boning knives, others prefer longer, wider blades with a degree of flexibility. Your choice will also depend on whether you are boning a large, simple joint of meat – when the longer, wider blade (a) would be best – or an intricate chicken carcass, when the short, narrow, rigid blade (c) is the easiest type to use.

To use a boning knife economically and efficiently, always cut towards the bone, never away from it. This is particularly important if you are boning anything which needs the skin kept intact. Don't be afraid to scrape the flesh from long, straight bones; this is easier than cutting it away. On reaching a joint, work the free bone about, severing the connecting tendons, rather than attempting to cut through it.

## Quartering a duck

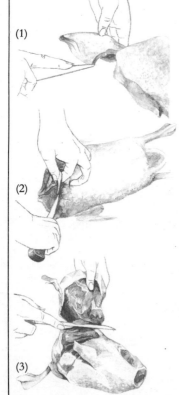

(1)

(2)

(3)

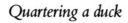

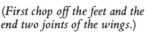

(*First chop off the feet and the end two joints of the wings.*)
1. *Trim the neck flap.*
2. *Remove the wish-bone.*
3. *Cut off the legs at the tops of the thighs.*
4. *Cut closely along one side of the breast bone.*
5. *Scrape the breast meat from the bone, continuing down over the ribs to the shoulder joint.*
6. *Detach the joint so that you have the breast meat with the large wing bone in one piece. Do the same to the other breast.*

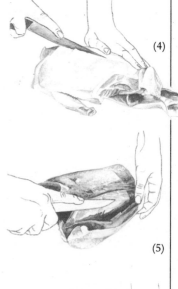

(4)

(5)

(6)

## Boning a chicken

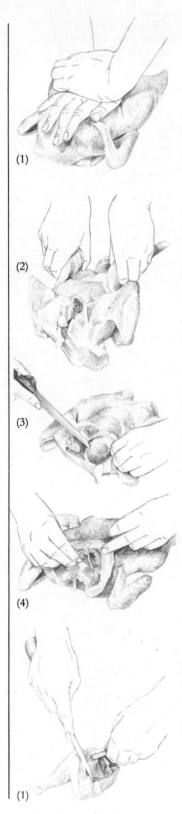

(1)

(2)

(3)

(4)

1. *Push down on the breast bone to flatten the bird.*
2. *(Breast down.) Dislocate the legs by levering them up and inwards, while pressing a thumb on the ball and socket joint.*
3. *Push back the flesh at the neck. Cut through the wing joints when they are exposed.*
4. *(Breast up.) Work the flesh from the breast bone by pushing with your fingers. Remove the wish-bone.*
5. *(Breast down.) Loosen the flesh from the backbone with a knife and lever the shoulder blades free when exposed.*
6. *Loosen the breast meat with your fingers and continue cutting the flesh from the backbone. Then pull on the wings to strip the flesh back from the carcass cutting through the ligaments on the dislocated legs to free them.*
7. *Pull the flesh completely off the carcass and cut it away at the tail. Scrape the flesh down the thigh bones until you reach the joints. Sever the tendons, remove the thigh bones and leave the drumsticks in place. If you like, work the flesh away from the upper wing bones, but leave the wing tips in place.*

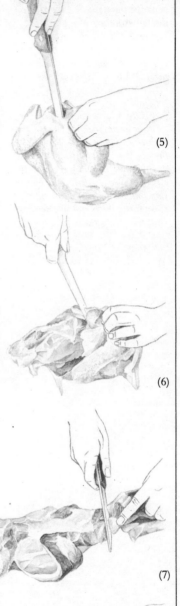

(5)

(6)

(7)

## Boning a chicken leg

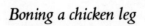

*Scrape the meat from the thigh bone (1), until you reach the joint. Free the thigh bone at the joint and cut out the little knee-cap. Then scrape the meat from the drumstick until you reach the next joint. Pull the bone free, turning the flesh inside-out (2), before reversing it over your thumb (3).*

(1)

(2)

(3)

1. *Work your boning knife between the flesh and the ribs on the lower halves of a pair of best ends (racks) of lamb.*
2. *Don't cut off the loosened flap of meat and fat. Fold it back on itself and trim the meat from between each rib, as far as this fold.*
3. *Using a large cook's knife or carving knife, trim the meat from each end of both racks so that they will join neatly together.*
4. *Thread a trussing needle with string and pierce through the flap and between the last two ribs on the thick end of one rack. Pull the string through.*

## Preparing a crown roast

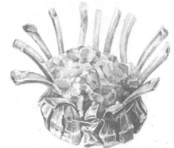

5. *Join the two thick ends by taking the trussing needle and string similarly through the second one. Place the thick ends side by side and pull the string taut, tying them together.*
6. *Turn the racks over and cut the meat half through, between the bases of the ribs, using a boning knife. This makes the racks more flexible.*
7. *Form the racks into a circle with the folds of meat inside and the ribs outside, joining the thin ends with a trussing needle and string as before. Put the stuffing in the centre.*

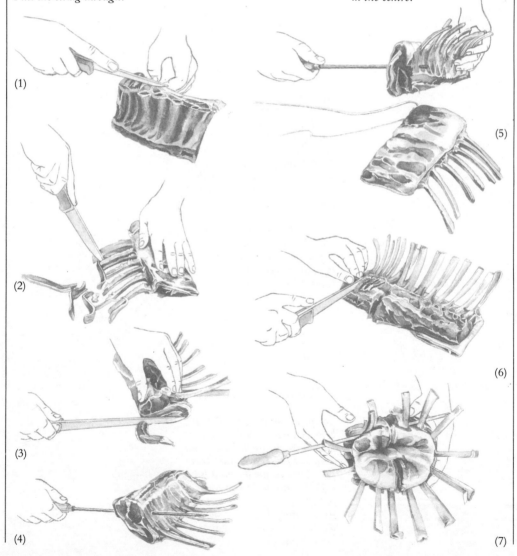

(1)

(2)

(3)

(4)

(5)

(6)

(7)

## Preparing a guard of honour

(1)

(2)

Use a boning knife to cut away the meat from the tips of the ribs on a pair of racks of lamb (1). Keep these trimmings for any stuffing or stock. Stand racks on end so that the ribs interlock. Tie string round the racks between each rib. Roast and serve with a cutlet frill on each rib (2).

## Boning a breast

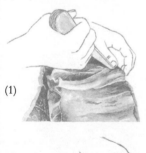

(1)

(2)

With the point of a boning knife score through the flesh between the ribs, taking care not to cut through to the outer skin (1). Scrape the knife around and under each piece of bone and gristle to free the flesh (2).

## Butterflying a leg of lamb

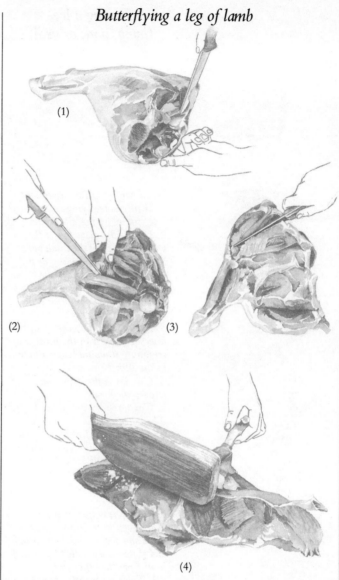

(1)

(2)

(3)

(4)

By removing all the bones, except the shank, you can grill or barbecue the meat on a leg of lamb all in one piece.

1. After trimming most of the fat from the outer side of the leg with a fluted ham knife or filleting knife, turn the leg inside up and remove the aitchbone.

2. Cut down the line of the thigh bone until you reach the knee. Take out the thigh bone, but leave the knee-cap in place.

3. After scraping the flesh from the upper side of the shin bone (leaving it attached on the underside and leaving the tendon also attached), cut deep slits into the thickest parts.

4. Flatten the meat as much as possible by bashing it with a mallet. The shape now resembles a butterfly, hence the name of the technique. The shank bone serves as a handle.

# Boning a leg
## (lamb, pork or veal)

(1)

(2)

(3)

(4)

(5)

(6)

(7)

(8)

(9)

(10)

(11)

(12)

Use a boning knife throughout.
1. With the leg lying on its outer side, cut away the aitchbone.
2. Loosen the meat round the ball on the top of the thigh bone.
3. Working from the top of the leg, cut carefully round the length of the thigh bone.
4. Sever the tendon behind the knee.
5. Detach the knee-cap from the knee, leaving it in the meat, as removing it would leave a hole in the skin.
6. Cut down the shin bone, freeing the meat.
7. Cut carefully round the knee. Then scrape down the thigh bone, twisting it free of the meat.
8. When the thigh bone is freed completely, pull both thigh and shin bones out, holding the meat back with the flat of the blade.
9. Neatly reshape the meat. Then tuck in the flap of shin meat and sew up the hole at that end if necessary. Stuff the boned joint from the other end.
10. Tie it up loosely, parcel fashion, as shown.
11. Feed the string round the meat in a spiral, turning the joint over and over and regulating the tension with your thumb, to form it into a neat oval.
12. With the point of the knife, tuck the end in a loop under the last circuit. One tug on this end before carving will then release all the string.

# Boning a shoulder
## (lamb or veal)

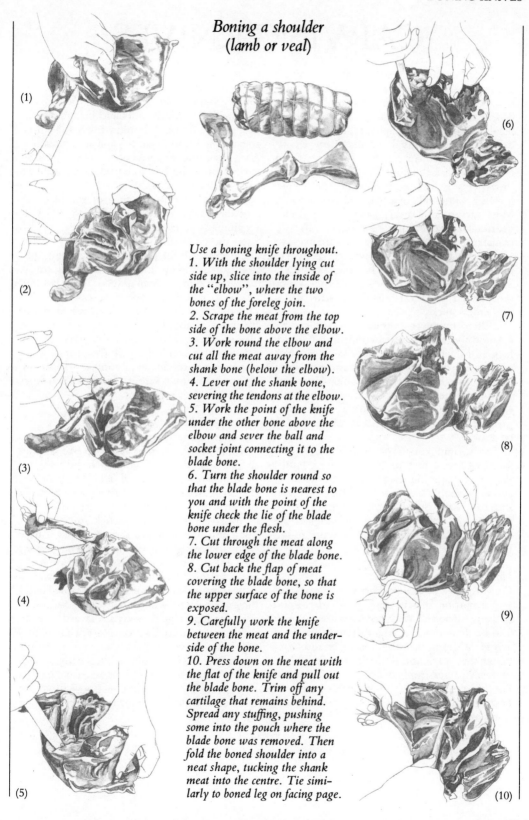

(1)

(2)

(3)

(4)

(5)

(6)

(7)

(8)

(9)

(10)

*Use a boning knife throughout.*
1. With the shoulder lying cut side up, slice into the inside of the "elbow", where the two bones of the foreleg join.
2. Scrape the meat from the top side of the bone above the elbow.
3. Work round the elbow and cut all the meat away from the shank bone (below the elbow).
4. Lever out the shank bone, severing the tendons at the elbow.
5. Work the point of the knife under the other bone above the elbow and sever the ball and socket joint connecting it to the blade bone.
6. Turn the shoulder round so that the blade bone is nearest to you and with the point of the knife check the lie of the blade bone under the flesh.
7. Cut through the meat along the lower edge of the blade bone.
8. Cut back the flap of meat covering the blade bone, so that the upper surface of the bone is exposed.
9. Carefully work the knife between the meat and the underside of the bone.
10. Press down on the meat with the flat of the knife and pull out the blade bone. Trim off any cartilage that remains behind. Spread any stuffing, pushing some into the pouch where the blade bone was removed. Then fold the boned shoulder into a neat shape, tucking the shank meat into the centre. Tie similarly to boned leg on facing page.

# CARVING KNIVES

You can demolish most of the mystique attached to carving with a rudimentary knowledge of anatomy and a good knife.

Carving knives need to be sharp, slightly flexible, and the right shape for the job. Pointed carving knives are used on cuts of meat with the bone in; the tip can free the meat from bones and make incisions in the meat along them. Knives with rounded tips are for carving boneless joints and are usually called "slicers". Most carvers and slicers have full or three-quarter tangs and some have brass collars to enhance their appearance. Handles are made in a variety of materials—wood, silver, ivory, plastic and stainless steel—but the most traditional is stag horn. For the sake of appearance most people prefer carving knives with blades of stainless steel.

When buying a carver don't be seduced by a handsome, showy outfit consisting of knife, fork and steel, unless the blade is of superior quality. Expensively decorated and matching handles may look good at table, but your guests will be far more impressed by neat, elegant slices of meat. So choose a good, taper-ground blade suited to the type of carving to be done.

Fairly rigid knives are used to carve hot joints of meat, such as beef, pork or lamb; slightly flexible knives are used for poultry; and very flexible knives are used for cold meat, such as ham. Some carving knives curve upwards at the tip; this curve extends the cutting edge and makes it easier to work round bones.

## How to carve

Carving must be done expertly to give everyone a portion that is both good to eat and pleasing to look at. With hot roast meat it must also be done quickly. Meat should be carved across the grain. It both looks nicer and tastes better that way—and there are no long fibres of meat to get trapped between your teeth. For this reason too the tougher cuts of meat are best carved as thinly as possible, so that the fibres are extremely short.

Ham, tongue, pot roasts and tinned meats, such as corned beef, should be sliced very thinly—about $\frac{1}{8}$ in. (3 mm) or less—as this enhances delicate flavours and brings out the best in savoury ones. Poultry breasts also need to be carved as thinly as possible if you want to give a serving to everyone. Pork is usually carved fairly thinly while beef, lamb and veal can be cut more thickly.

Never alter the direction of the blade in mid-slice when carving—if you do you will inevitably cut ragged, uneven slices. Try to keep the edge moving forward at the same angle and push the prongs of the carving fork deeply enough into the meat to hold it steady. When the joint has been reduced to the last 1 in. (25 mm) it will become progressively more difficult to carve. If you hold the remainder of the joint steady by reversing the fork and pressing the curve of the prongs down on it you can continue slicing beneath the prongs without bringing the blade in contact with them. By doing this it is possible to carve several more good slices from the joint.

## Carving various types of meat

An unpressed tongue is sliced downwards across its width, starting at the tip and keeping the slices parallel until you reach the root.

Chicken, guinea fowl and pheasant are carved in the same way as turkey (see overleaf). Goose is carved as duck (see overleaf).

Small game birds, woodcock, snipe, grouse, quail and partridge are served whole if they form the main course. They can be divided into halves by cutting lengthwise down the back and the breastbone with poultry shears.

Rabbit and hare are usually casseroled but if they are roasted whole they must be trussed with the hind legs skewered forward and the forelegs pinned backwards. The roast is jointed before it is served at the table, with the saddle left intact. To carve the saddle steady it with the carving fork and cut long narrow boneless slices parallel to the backbone. Carve first from one side and then carve the remaining meat on the other side.

# Carving forks

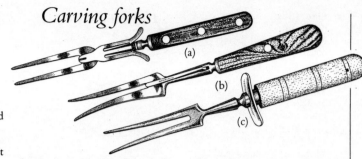

(a) **Size.** L. 10½ in. (267 mm).
**Material.** Stainless steel prongs, plastic handle.
(b) **Size.** L. 11 in. (280 mm).
**Material.** Stainless steel prongs, rosewood handle.
(c) **Size.** L. 12 in. (305 mm).
**Material.** Stainless steel prongs, brass guard, varnished beechwood handle.

It is very difficult to carve without some means of keeping the meat from skidding about on the dish and highly dangerous to try holding it still without a fork. Carving forks are all made with a guard of some sort to protect the hand from an accidental slip of the carving knife.

The guard on fork (a) is wishbone-shaped and designed to form a stand for the knife, while keeping its own curved prongs off the table between servings. Fork (b) has the traditional style guard which snaps in position, up or down, and fork (c) is a simple, straight-pronged fork with a hilt-style guard.

# Meat carvers

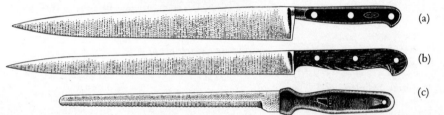

(a) **Size.** (Blade) L. 12 in. (305 mm).
**Material.** Carbon steel blade, plastic handle.
(b) **Size.** (Blade) L. 12¼ in. (310 mm).
**Material.** Carbon steel blade, wooden handle.
(c) **Size.** (Blade) L. 9½ in. (242 mm).
**Material.** Surgical steel blade, plastic handle.

As the meat to be carved is (it is hoped) tender, a carving knife need not be as weighty as a cook's or butcher's knife. Indeed, for many carving jobs a filleting knife is quite suitable. Blades for carving joints of meat with the bone in are of medium width and are 8 to 14 in. (204 to 355 mm) long.

Carver (a) is a perfect knife for carving large joints of meat. It is very flexible towards its point but the rest of the blade is quite firm. This makes it an ideal knife for negotiating the bones in a joint.

Carver (b) is narrower than carver (a) and more flexible along its entire length. It would serve much the same purpose as the wider bladed knife.

Carver (c) is a mass-produced knife with a flat-sided, scalloped blade cut from a strip of steel. It is lethally sharp, dishwasher proof and corrosion resistant. It does not have the flexibility of the other two carvers, which are taper-ground—but is very much cheaper.

# Electric carving knife

**Size.** (Blade) L. 7 in. (178 mm).
**Material.** Stainless steel blades, plastic body.

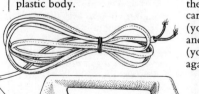

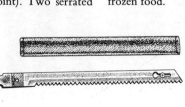

If the whole business of carving and knife-sharpening appals you the best answer is an electric carver. It never needs sharpening (you merely replace the old blades) and no effort is required to use it (you just press the blades lightly against the joint). Two serrated blades oscillate very rapidly against one another and make short work of anything that needs carving. They are sharp enough to halve an uncooked chicken, but should not be used to cut through meat bones or blocks of frozen food.

(a) **Size.** (Blade) L. 8½ in. (215 mm).
**Material.** Stainless steel blade, plastic handle.

(b) **Size.** (Blade) L. 8 in. (204 mm).
**Material.** Carbon steel blade, rosewood handle, brass collar.

(c) **Size.** (Blade) L. 8 in. (204 mm).
**Material.** Stainless steel blade, plastic handle.

## Poultry carvers

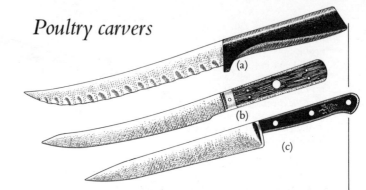

These knives are not so flexible as meat carvers and have shorter blades, but otherwise are much the same shape.

Carver (a) is one of a good quality mass-produced range and has flutes staggered on each side of its edge. It is not taper-ground but does cut beautifully. The lightweight, dishwasher-proof handle may not appeal to lovers of traditionally made knives, but it is standard for all the knives in this particular range.

Another variation in the shape of carving knives is seen in carver (b) which has a pleasantly flexible blade with an upswept point. The brass collar and rivets make it a very pretty knife.

Carver (c) can be used on all kinds of poultry, though you might prefer a slightly longer blade for a turkey.

(a) **Size.** (Blade) L. 10 in. (255 mm).
**Material.** Stainless steel blade, rosewood handle.

(b) **Size.** (Blade) L. 10 in. (255 mm).
**Material.** Stainless steel blade, rosewood handle.

(c) **Size.** (Blade) L. 9 in. (230 mm).
**Material.** Carbon steel blade, plastic handle.

(d) **Size.** (Blade) L. 12 in. (305 mm).
**Material.** Stainless steel blade, rosewood handle.

(e) **Size.** (Blade) L. 10¼ in. (260 mm).
**Material.** Stainless steel blade, wooden handle.

## Meat and fish slicers

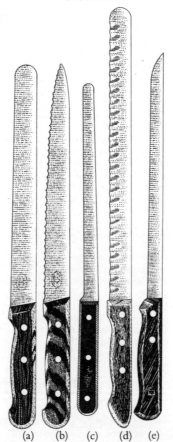

(a) (b) (c) (d) (e)

Slicers are used to carve things that need to be sliced very thinly and for this reason usually have long, fairly narrow, very flexible, round-ended blades. They can be straight-edged, fluted or scalloped. The beef slicer (a) is designed to carve large, boneless joints and performs particularly well on hot, tender meat, unlike the scallop-edged slicer (b) which tends to tear it to shreds and is best kept for use on firm, cold meat. This knife, however, being scalloped, does not need frequent sharpening and the pointed tip — unusual in a slicer — would make it suitable also for carving cold meat on the bone.

The blade of the salmon slicer (c) is most flexible just where it should be, in the centre. It tapers from just under ¾ in. (20 mm) at the heel to just over ½ in. (12 mm) at the tip. It would also do for slicing small joints of ham, though ham slicers should have blades a little wider.

The flutes on the blade of the ham slicer (d) have been ground on both sides and are staggered so that those on one side lie exactly between those on the other. This makes for maximum thinness and flexibility in the blade. This knife can be sharpened on a steel as the actual cutting edge is straight. The advantage of this type of blade can be felt when carving a dense, soft meat like ham; there is just enough friction to help the blade on its way, but no sharp points (as on serrated or scalloped edges) to rip the slices to bits. It is highly recommended as a slicer.

Another beautiful knife is the ham and salmon slicer (e), which like slicer (b), is unusual in being pointed. It is extremely flexible and easy to use.

## Carving a turkey

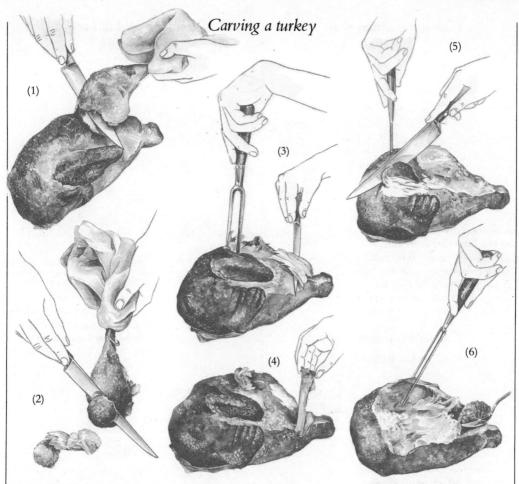

1. Lay the turkey on its side with its back towards you. Grip the end of the drumstick and pull it forward cutting through the joint to separate it from the thigh.
2. If the bird is very large carve slices from either side of the drumstick.
3. Cut slices of meat from the thigh until you reach the bone.
4. Lift the thighbone and disjoint it from its socket, then continue to slice the meat, finally removing the "oyster" from its pocket.
5. Remove the wing and make diagonal slices at 45° across the breast meat until you reach the keel bone. Either remove each slice separately or loosen and remove them all together.
6. Slit the thin skin under the thigh to make an opening and spoon out the stuffing. Next turn the plate round, put the bird meaty side up and carve it similarly on the other side.

## Carving a duck

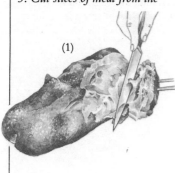

It is easier to carve a duck if you remove the wishbone before cooking (see COOK'S KNIVES). Lay the duck on its breast and remove each leg (1). Separate the thigh from the drumstick. Turn the duck breast up and starting just above the wing, cut long, vertical $\frac{1}{4}$ in. (6 mm) thick slices parallel to the keel bone on each side (2).

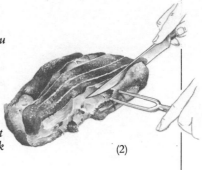

## Carving a crown roast

Cut vertically between each rib
so that each slice represents a
chop with its bone. If the roast
has a meat stuffing, cut through
it (as if it were a cake) at the
same time. Spoon out a vegetable
stuffing.

## Carving a standing (or wing) rib

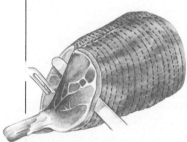

Remove the chine (if the butcher
left it on) before you start
carving. This joint is sometimes
sold with a covering of back fat
and without the chine, as shown.
Stand the joint on its wide end
and cut across it towards the
ribs, freeing each slice by cutting
down close to the bone.

## Carving a loin of lamb, veal or pork

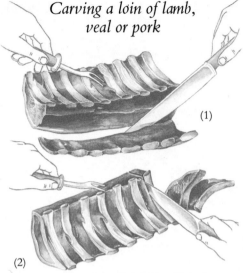

(1)

(2)

Cut off the chine (1) before
starting to carve. Stand the joint
on the flat part where the chine
was removed and slice down
between the ribs (2), including
a rib in alternate slices.

## Carving a blade cut of beef

This American cut is taken from
across the chuck and is usually
pot roasted. It falls easily into
distinct sections which are
separated from the bone for
carving. Turn each on its side
and slice down across the grain.

## Two ways of carving a ham

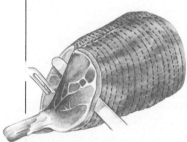

(Both rounded side up.)
English. Remove one slice at
the shank end. Then work along
the bone carving slices from
either side alternately.
American. Cut a vertical wedge
from the shank end. Then cut
vertically along the bone. Detach
the slices by running the knife
beneath them along the bone.

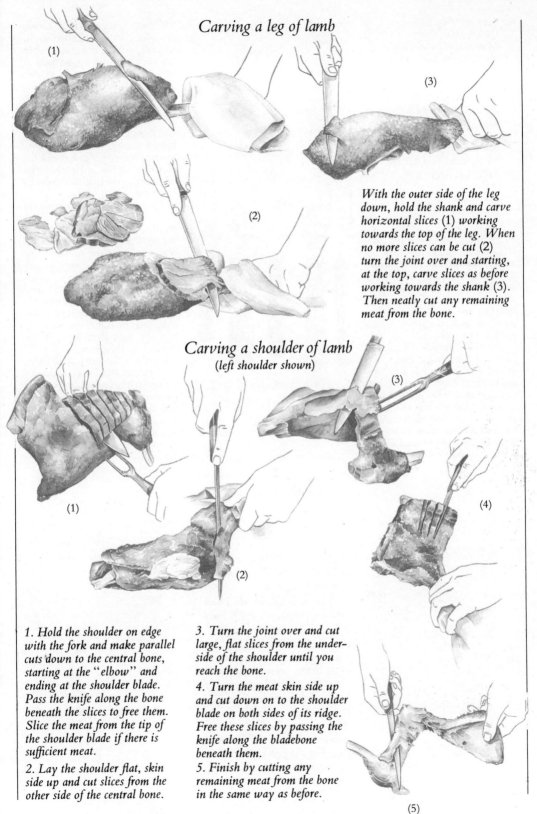

## Carving a leg of lamb

(1)

(2)

(3)

With the outer side of the leg down, hold the shank and carve horizontal slices (1) working towards the top of the leg. When no more slices can be cut (2) turn the joint over and starting, at the top, carve slices as before working towards the shank (3). Then neatly cut any remaining meat from the bone.

## Carving a shoulder of lamb
### (left shoulder shown)

(1)

(2)

(3)

(4)

1. Hold the shoulder on edge with the fork and make parallel cuts down to the central bone, starting at the "elbow" and ending at the shoulder blade. Pass the knife along the bone beneath the slices to free them. Slice the meat from the tip of the shoulder blade if there is sufficient meat.

2. Lay the shoulder flat, skin side up and cut slices from the other side of the central bone.

3. Turn the joint over and cut large, flat slices from the underside of the shoulder until you reach the bone.

4. Turn the meat skin side up and cut down on to the shoulder blade on both sides of its ridge. Free these slices by passing the knife along the bladebone beneath them.

5. Finish by cutting any remaining meat from the bone in the same way as before.

(5)

49

(a) **Size.** (Blade) L. 8 in. (204 mm).
**Material.** Carbon steel blade, rosewood handle.

(b) **Size.** (Blade) L. 6 in. (152 mm).
**Material.** Carbon steel blade, rosewood handle.

(c) **Size.** (Blade) L. 9 in. (230 mm).
**Material.** Stainless steel blade, rosewood handle.

(d) **Size.** (Blade) L. 4 in. (100 mm).
**Material.** Carbon steel blade, rosewood handle.

The words palette knife and spatula are interchangeable. Spatula means "broad blade" in Latin. Cook's palette knives are so called because they are the same shape (flat and broad) as those used by artists to mix powdered pigment with oil and to spread colour thickly on canvas.

The main purpose of kitchen palette knives is to fold, mix, spread and scrape soft mixtures and to flip and lift thin, flat things like pancakes. They are not used so much for cutting, although some have serrated edges for slicing and serving shallow pies or quiches. They can be used too, to slice soft sponge cakes into halves before filling.

## Palette knives

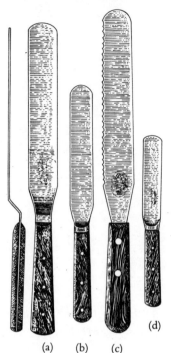

(a)  (b)  (c)  (d)

The crank at the end of the handle on palette knife (a) lifts it up by an inch, which is helpful when taking food from lipped pans. It also allows your fingers to curl under the handle without hitting the work surface when the length of the blade is flat. It is invaluable when trying to remove delicate things, like meringues, from baking sheets without breaking them at the edges and useful for blending stiffish mixtures. The blade is ground to give flexibility at the tip.

The handle of palette knife (b) can be held at a right angle to the tip and the whole blade will spring back straight as soon as it is released. This extreme flexibility makes it perfect for pancake turning.

Palette knife (c) has a scalloped edge, useful for cutting and serving flans and for making decorative marks on butter-cream icing. It is also very flexible, so it can flip and lift things too.

Use the miniature palette knife, or spatulette, (d), for spreading icing and fillings on small cakes and pastries and for buttering bread. It is slightly flexible at the tip, so because of its size, is particularly useful when forming marzipan rosettes and decorations. It is handy too for lifting biscuits and pastries off baking sheets.

## Making rosettes

1. Roll the marzipan into a thin sausage shape and then cut it into small sections.

2. Roll each section into a ball between the palms of your hands.

3. Flatten each ball with the tip of a small palette knife and then work it to a paper-thin petal shape, pressing it with the tip of the palette knife. (Professional cooks often use the rounded end of a light bulb for this.)

4. Form each flower by first rolling a thin "stem" of marzipan. Fix the petals to it, starting with the inner ones, curling each slightly to make the flower more realistic.

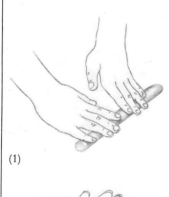

(1)

(2)

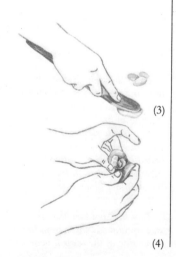

(3)

(4)

## Assembly of a Black Forest cherry cake

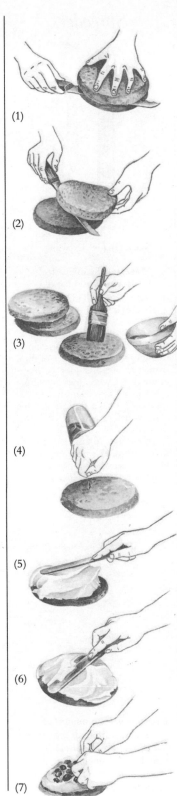

(1)
(2)
(3)
(4)
(5)
(6)
(7)

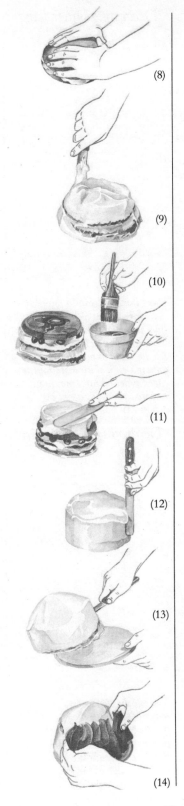

(8)
(9)
(10)
(11)
(12)
(13)
(14)

1. Using a firm, scalloped-edged palette knife, gently slice a chocolate sponge-cake into three layers.

2. Lift off each layer with the palette knife.

3. Brush the surfaces of the lower two layers with brandy syrup.

4. Sprinkle the bottom and the middle layers with kirsch. Place the middle layer temporarily on the top layer, so that surplus liqueur can seep into it.

5. Using a palette knife, cover the base thickly with whipped cream.

6. Shape the cream into a mound.

7. Put stoned black cherries all over the cream mound.

8. Set the middle layer on this mound of cream and cherries.

9. Cover the middle layer with cream similarly, sweeping the palette knife round the sides to remove surplus cream. Decorate with cherries.

10. Place the top layer in position and brush it with brandy syrup.

11. Cover the top layer with cream.

12. Finish the sides neatly, smoothing the cream thickly with the palette knife.

13. Slide the palette knife beneath the cake. Tilt the cake slightly and slip a plate or silver board beneath.

14. Carefully press chocolate flakes all over the cake. Finish with a dusting of icing sugar, a rosette of whipped cream and one black cherry.

## Decorating butter icing

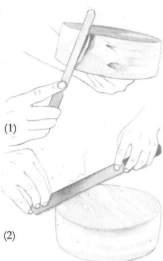

(1)

(2)

*Turn the cake slowly towards you, spreading the icing on the sides in the opposite direction with a large palette knife (1). Ice the top and make zigzag patterns on it with a scalloped-edged palette knife, moving it towards you with a sawing action (2).*

## Decorating mayonnaise

(1)

(2)

*Smooth the surface of mayonnaise with the edge of a palette knife, turning the bowl the opposite way to the knife (1). Then dent the surface at intervals with the edge of the knife to make a pretty pattern (2).*

## Bread knives

(b)

(a)

(a) **Size.** (Blade) L. 10 in. (255 mm).
**Material.** Carbon steel blade, wooden handle.
(b) **Size.** (Blade) L. 7 in. (178 mm).
**Material.** Stainless steel blade, rosewood handle.

A bread knife should be fairly rigid and long enough to slice across the largest of loaves – but otherwise the choice of knife is very much a matter of personal preference.

Scalloped, serrated and fluted edges are found on many bread knives. These give a good initial purchase on the crust. Some people prefer plain-edged knives, believing that they result in fewer crumbs. The long, finely serrated edge on knife (a) is ideal for slicing large flat Italian-type loaves. Bread knife (b) has pronounced scallops. This edge cuts easily through tough crusts, avoiding the heavy pressure on new bread that produces uneven squashed-down slices.

## Spreaders

(b)

(a)

(a) **Size.** (Blade) L. 3½ in. (90 mm).
**Material.** Stainless steel blade, rosewood handle.
(b) **Size.** L. 6 in. (152 mm).
**Material.** Ashwood.

The importance of a thick, smooth layer of butter reaching to the very edges of a slice of thin, firm, rye bread cannot be over-emphasized when making smør-rebrød. The Danish butter spreader (a) has a slightly flexible blade which can do this job better than any table knife. The edge is sharp enough to cut the slices to the traditional smørrebrød size, unlike spreader (b) which is charming but less practical.

## Buttering smørrebrød

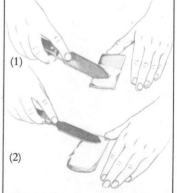

(1)

(2)

*Take a generous amount of butter and, starting at the far end of a slice of rye bread (1), spread it thickly and smoothly in one sweep so that it entirely covers the surface (2).*

(a) **Size.** (Blade) L. 5 in.
  (127 mm).
  **Material.** Carbon steel
  blade, rosewood handle.

(b) **Size.** (Blade) L. 6 in.
  (152 mm).
  **Material.** Carbon steel
  blade, rosewood handle.

(c) **Size.** (Blade) W. 5 in.
  (127 mm).
  **Material.** Carbon steel
  blade, beechwood handle.

(d) **Size.** W. 4½ in. (107 mm).
  **Material.** Plastic.

Painters and decorators remove old paint and fill cracks in plaster with tools identical to the rigid scrapers (a) and (b). In the kitchen cooks mix and cut pastry or bread dough and scrape mixtures off hard surfaces with them. They use them too for cleaning jobs—such

## Scrapers

as scraping wooden chopping blocks clean, and (in commercial kitchens) removing baked-on food from metal hot-plates.

Pastry cooks and bakers cut the ingredients into the dough and divide dough into portions, with the dough scraper (c). Also called a Scotch scraper, it cuts loaves decoratively and is useful for scraping the remains of flour and dough from work surfaces. The rounded corner fits against the curve of a mixing bowl when cleaning mixtures from it. Some versions of this scraper have both corners either square or rounded.

The plastic scraper or "corne" (d) is found in most French kitchens, where it is used as a scraper or scoop. It is flexible enough to be curved in your hand against any shape of bowl, pan or sieve. They are sold in sets.

(a)  (b)

## Preparing fondant

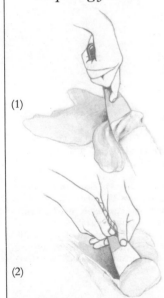

(1)

(2)

Pour the fondant mixture on to a marble slab and let it cool to body temperature. With a rigid scraper, fold the edges in to the centre (1). Continue working the mixture, using two hands if necessary. It will gradually whiten, thicken and get very smooth (2). If it becomes hard and crumbly knead it with your hands and add a little sugar syrup.

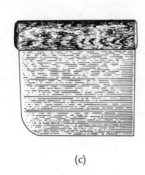

(c)

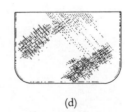

(d)

## Cutting dough

You can cut dough into portions with the dough scraper.

## Making pastry

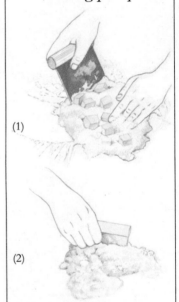

(1)

(2)

Sift the flour on to a pastry board and cut the fat into it with the dough scraper (1), scooping the flour from the edges of the heap into the middle with the flat of the blade and cutting through the mixture with the edge. Add water and continue turning the heap (2) and chopping through it until the right consistency is reached.

53

# Grapefruit knife

**Size.** (Blade) L. 3½ in. (90 mm).
**Material.** Stainless steel blade, wooden handle.

This curved, double-edged, serrated blade is for preparing grapefruit halves. You can also use it to hollow out onions and small melons.

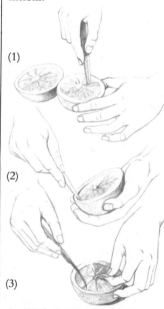

(1)

(2)

(3)

1. With the tip of the knife, detach the flesh of each section from the membrane encasing it.
2. Slide the whole blade between the outer peel and the flesh and go right round the semi sphere, fitting the knife neatly to the curve of the fruit.
3. Cut through the base of the centre core and lift it out with all the membranes still attached.

# Decorating knife

**Size.** (Blade) L. 4 in. (100 mm).
**Material.** Stainless steel blade, pearwood handle.

This type of knife has been used by French chefs for hundreds of years. After a little practice you can get quite quick at turning vegetables with it. One inch of the edge, from the tip, is straight and sharp. The rest is corrugated and not sharpened.

The decorated vegetables garnish roasts and other entrées. The trimmings are used for soups or stock. Carrots look nice with spirals; turnips can have their lower halves ridged one way and their tops the other. Fresh crisp young vegetables are easier to work on than tired old flabby ones.

Work slowly and cautiously, if you are not practised at turning vegetables. Use a peeling action making sure that you cut deeply enough to obtain a truly corrugated surface. Let the shape of the trimmed vegetable determine the direction of the ridges.

# Chestnut knife

**Size.** (Blade) L. 1 in. (25 mm).
**Material.** Stainless steel blade, rosewood handle.

The tiny, hooked blade of this knife is specially designed to score chestnuts across the rounded side of their shells before roasting. This prevents them bursting.

# Parmesan knife

**Size.** (Blade) L. 3 in. (75 mm).
**Material.** Stainless steel blade, wooden handle.

This Italian cheese cutter prizes pieces out of very hard cheeses, such as Parmesan or Pecorino Sardo, prior to grating.

Smaller versions of this knife are made for cutting and serving new Parmesan (which is softer) at table.

Pierce the cheese with the point. Then prize and twist with the blade to break off a piece.

# *Oyster and clam knives*

(a) **Size.** (Blade) L. 2 in. (50 mm). **Material.** Stainless steel blade and guard, wooden handle.

(b) **Size.** (Blade) L. $2\frac{1}{2}$ in. (65 mm). **Material.** Stainless steel blade and guard, wooden handle.

(c) **Size.** (Blade) L. 3 in. (75 mm). **Material.** Carbon steel blade, brass guard and collar, varnished beechwood handle.

Shutting like a clam means shutting very tightly indeed. Clams, like oysters, hold their hinged shells together with very powerful muscles. When cooked they open wide. Perversely, they taste best eaten alive and raw.

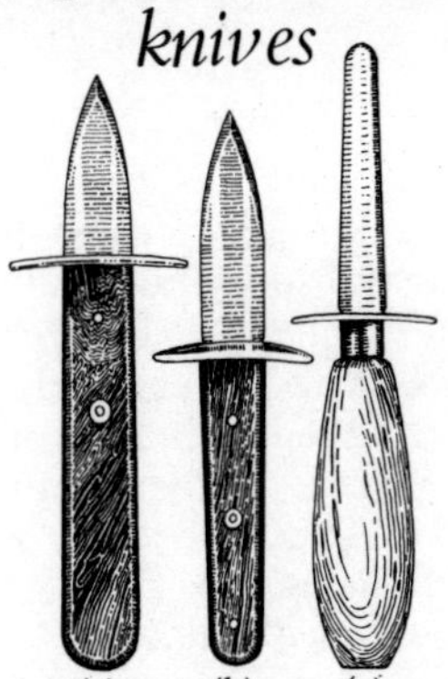
(a) (b) (c)

These knives are designed to open them alive. They are sharp, strong and stubby. Some have guards to protect your hand from the sharp edges of the shell but it is advisable to use a cloth for complete protection.

Of the two short oyster knives, knife (a) transmits more power with its stubby blade, but knife (b) has cutting edges, not only on both sides of its point, like the shorter knife, but also right down one side of the blade. This makes it more useful for cutting oysters from their shells.

The narrow, round-ended blade on knife (c) is sharp all the way round and its length makes it suitable for opening clams as well as oysters.

## *To open an oyster*

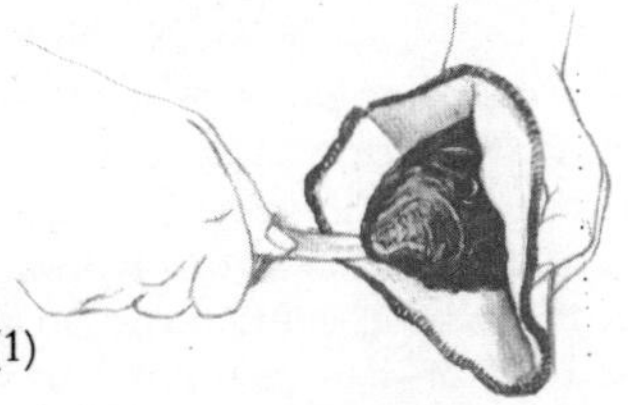
(1)

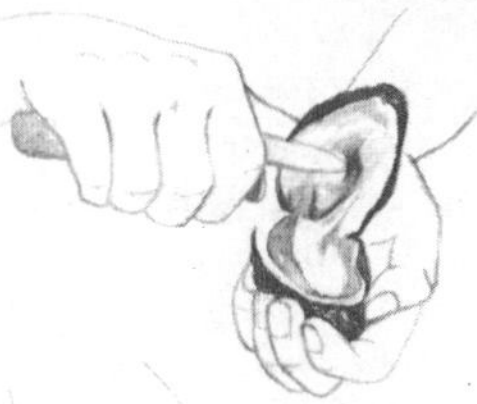
(2)

(3)

OYSTER *1. With the flat shell up, insert the point of the knife into the hinge.*

*2. Push the knife point between the shells and twist it at the same time. As the hinge breaks, slide the knife under the upper shell, lift it and cut through the muscle. Discard the upper shell.*

*3. Scoop the knife under the oyster meat. When it is all loosened, flip it over to give it a better appearance and serve it in its half-shell, with all its juice.*

CLAM *1. Insert the knife into the join between the shells on the side opposite the hinge. Squeeze the blade with the fingers of the hand holding the clam.*

## *To open a clam*

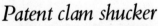

(1)

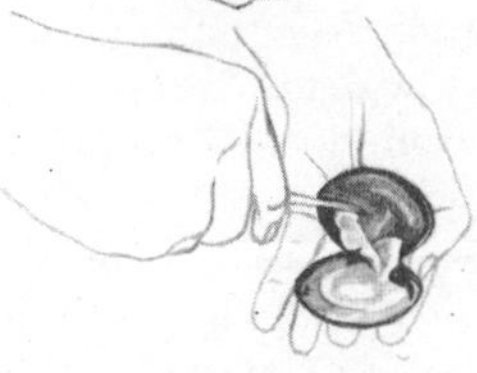
(2)

*2. When the shell parts slide the knife up and around the top shell, cutting through the muscles. Twist off the top shell, loosen the meat and serve with its juice in the lower shell.*

# *Patent clam shucker*

**Size.** (Blade) L. $5\frac{3}{4}$ in. (146 mm). (Base) $7 \times 5$ in. (178 × 127 mm).
**Material.** Stainless steel blade, maplewood base and handle.

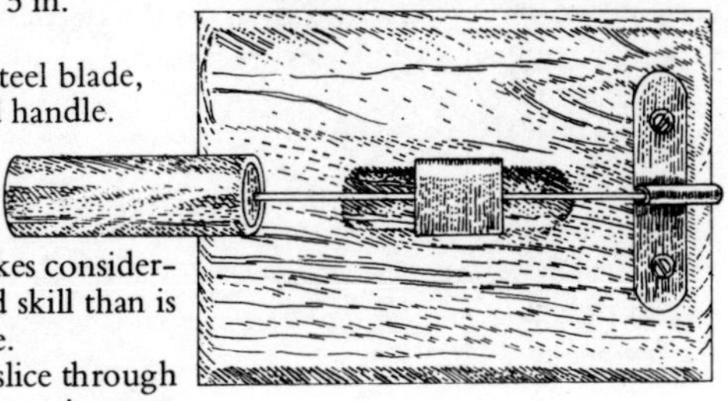

This clam shucker takes considerably less strength and skill than is required with a knife.

It does, however, slice through the body of the clam, as it opens the shell. This spoils their appearance if you wish to serve them raw in the half-shell, but would not matter if you were using them for chowder.

*Put the clam hinge-down in the groove and position the blade carefully on the shell's join. Press down on the handle to open the clam. The juices spill into the groove.*

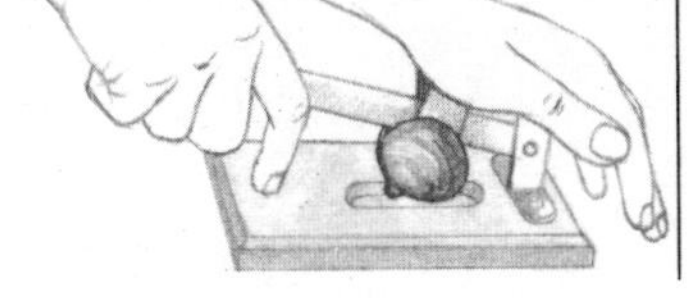

# SCISSORS AND SHEARS

Scissors and shears are not only used for dress-making, embroidery, hedge-trimming and rose-pruning, they also have their uses in the kitchen. Scissors are basically little more than two knives joined together with their cutting edges facing one another – and good, sharp, kitchen scissors are almost as useful as good knives. Shears operate in the same way as scissors, but they can cut through much tougher things, such as small bones or lobster shells. Their extra strength or "muscle" is provided by a powerful spring set either in the pivot itself, or between the handles.

### The advantages of scissors
Apart from the additional leverage given to cutting by using your hand in an opening and shutting movement, scissors cut by dividing things cleanly between two cutting edges – so the material is not pressed upon, or torn jagg-edly. This makes scissors better than a knife for some jobs, such as cutting decorative marks on pastry or dough. Scissors are essential, of course, for cutting paper (lining cake-tins, for example) and a robust pair of scissors or shears waste less juice when used in place of a knife, for disjointing cooked poultry or lobster.

Ideally, there should be two, or even three, pairs of scissors in the kitchen. One long-bladed pair for cutting paper; one heavy, shorter-bladed, general-purpose pair for trimming meat or fish and severing poultry joints; and one small, pointed pair, possibly with curved blades, for finicky work. Shears are not so generally useful as scissors, but you may prefer them for certain jobs.

Kitchen shears work like gardener's secat-eurs, but have longer, curved blades. The best are made of stainless steel. One blade is usually serrated and sometimes notched as well, to help grip small bones. They deal with these exactly as if they were cutting through small twigs. A catch on the end of the handles keeps the shears closed. When it is released the blades and handles fly apart. The pressure needed to bring them together is transmitted from your hand, through the closing spring, to the blades. As the strength of the spring is largely responsible for their efficiency, it is not so important to keep the cutting edge of shears as sharp as those of knives or scissors. Always make sure when buying shears that the handles do not spring beyond the span of your finger and thumb when the catch is released. If they do, you will find them difficult to use and control.

### How to care for good scissors
Like good knives, good scissors are fully ground. The best scissors are made of stainless steel. They will not tarnish or rust like the next best, which are made of carbon steel. These are sometimes chrome-plated, but as this plating is removed from the cutting edge in the final sharpening, plated scissors can rust along this edge and the plating can peel off.

The blades of good scissors are bowed slightly inwards so that the whole length of each blade presses against the other as they cross and cut. This makes the correct setting of the blades very important. Tightening the little screw at the pivot will increase the pressure of one blade against the other.

Make sure when you buy scissors that they are easy to clean. Always dry them carefully after washing and hang them up wherever they will be most useful and where you can see at a glance if they have gone missing. Scissors should not be heavily oiled, but a little drop now and then on the pivot screw helps to keep the blades well set.

## Sharpening scissors

*To sharpen draw an oilstone along the angle of the cutting edge (1). Then run the oilstone along the inner face of the blade to remove any burrs (2).*

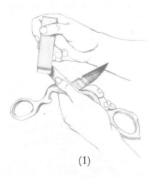

(1)

(2)

(a) **Size.** L. 7 in. (178 mm).
**Material.** Carbon steel.
(b) **Size.** L. 8½ in. (215 mm).
**Material.** Chromed steel.
(c) **Size.** L. 7½ in. (190 mm).
**Material.** Stainless steel.

The pretty, pointed Chinese scissors (a) are suitable for any fiddly, snipping job in the kitchen. They can even be used to bone a chicken. You need to be quite dextrous to do this, but it is no more difficult than using a boning knife; in fact, you are less likely to pierce the skin with these scissors.

The pair of scissors (b) has more to it than just two blades. Between the handles are ribbed edges with which to open jam jars and bottles with screw-top lids. They also incorporate a crown-

## All-purpose scissors

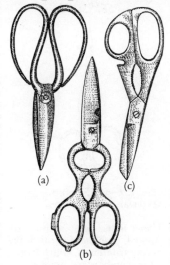

(a)  (c)

(b)

cap bottle opener. The painted handles also have protuberances for cracking nuts and crushing sugar lumps or ice-cubes. There is even a screwdriver head on one, but it is cast too thick to be of much use. More useful is the serrated blade with a notch in it near the pivot, for cutting through small bones.

The heavier and stronger all-purpose scissors are, the better quality they are likely to be. Painted or plastic-coated handles may add to the gaiety of your kitchen, but after a while they are liable to chip or peel. The stainless steel scissors (c) are particularly well designed for kitchen use, nice to look at and easy to keep clean. They have one serrated blade and comfortable handles.

## Trimming rinds

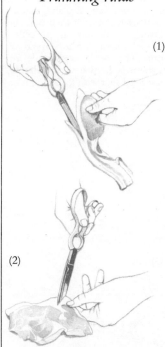

(1)

(2)

Trim rinds from uncooked bacon rashers (1) with sharp scissors. Snip through the rind on pork chops to prevent them curling up when grilled (2).

## Making humbugs

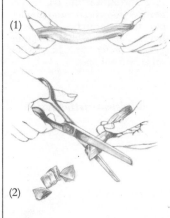

(1)

(2)

Pull a warm sugar mixture into a strip (1) and, with oiled scissors, snip it into sections, alternately horizontally and vertically, to form humbugs (2).

## Decorating dough

Snip bread dough with scissors to make a herring-bone pattern.

## Opening sea urchins

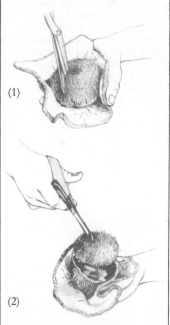

(1)

(2)

Hold the sea urchin in a thick cloth and pierce the top of the shell with the scissor points (1). Then cut round the top and lift this off like a lid, using the scissors as a pair of tongs (2).

## *Paper cutting scissors*

**Size.** L. 9 in. (230 mm).
**Material.** Chromed steel.

To keep these scissors sharp, try not to use them for anything except cutting paper, which is what they are designed to do. The long blades make long, straight cuts, useful when making linings for cake tins, paper frills for ham or cutlet bones, piping bags, funnels or confectionery wrappings.

## *Small trimming scissors*

**Size.** L. 6 in. (152 mm).
**Material.** Chromed steel.

These neat, light scissors are pointed, enabling them to make finicky trimmings, which larger, more cumbersome scissors are unable to do. Use them to cut up green herbs, top and tail runner beans or gooseberries and to snick out the undesirable bits from liver, kidneys or hearts. Some people prefer straight blades, others curved ones.

## *Kitchen cutters*

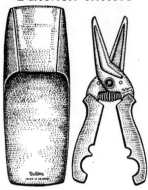

**Size.** L. 7 in. (178 mm).
**Material.** Chromed steel, plastic handles and holder.

These cutters have a spring just behind the pivot, which makes them more like shears than scissors. The New Zealand manufacturer claims that they will cut through anything from cellophane to honey jar lids—and they can. The blades are made of extremely hard steel and should not need sharpening.

## *Making cutlet frills*

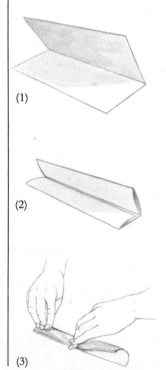

(1)

(2)

(3)

(4)

1. Fold the paper in half lengthways.
2. Open it out and fold the edges in to the centre crease.
3. Re-fold the crease, keeping the edges in, then fold lengthways again to make a guide line.
4. Open out this last fold and make snips towards the centre fold, stopping at the guide line.
5. Open the sheet out and re-fold it, reversing the creases.
6. Pin at intervals.
7. Cut into appropriate lengths, unpin, and wind each length round your finger. Secure the frills with pins or tape.

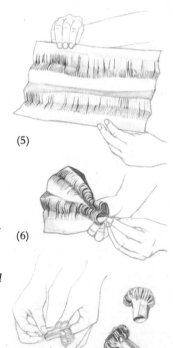

(5)

(6)

(7)

# Fish scissors

**Size.** L. 8½ in. (215 mm).
**Material.** Stainless steel.

These scissors are used for gutting flat fish. Both blades are serrated and the lower is longer than the upper. The projection on the point of the lower blade is designed to scrape blood from inside the fish. The scissors trim fins and slit open fish, but are also strong enough to cut through backbones. They make excellent scissors for general kitchen use.

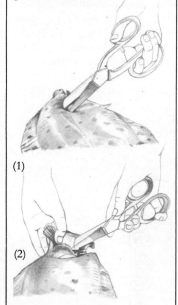

(1)

(2)

*Cut a slit on the belly side behind the head and remove the guts (1). Shut the scissors and scrape out the gut cavity with the projection on the blades (2).*

# Poultry scissors

**Size.** L. 8½ in. (215 mm).
**Material.** Stainless steel with painted handles.

The upward curving blades of these scissors have a bevel on the serrated edge, just by the deep notch near the pivot, which lets them slide tightly against each other from pivot to point. This provides the pressure you need to cut through poultry bones with the minimum of effort. The blades take apart for washing.

# Egg shell cutter

**Size.** L. 4½ in. (115 mm).
**Material.** Stainless steel blades, plastic body.

Squeezing into the scissor category by the skin of its little stainless teeth, this ingenious cutter is made to slice the tops from boiled eggs. Just the gift for people who can't decapitate eggs with a knife or don't approve of picking off the shell; or can't resist gadgets.

# Grape scissors

**Size.** L. 5 in. (127 mm).
**Material.** Electro-plated nickel silver, mother-of-pearl inlays.

You select a sprig of grapes and snip them from the bunch with these scissors, which are designed solely for use at table. They are more decorative than functional and are delicately engraved.

# Shears

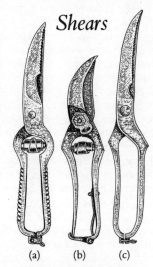

(a)    (b)    (c)

(a) **Size.** L. 9½ in. (242 mm).
**Material.** Chromed steel.

(b) **Size.** L. 8 in. (204 mm).
**Material.** Carbon steel.

(c) **Size.** L. 10 in. (255 mm).
**Material.** Stainless steel.

Poultry shears (a) have a deep notch in one blade to hold small bones firmly when cutting. The open spring between the handles is very strong, but can become a dirt trap. Shears (b) have a similar spring, which gives a kick like a donkey when the catch is released. They are extremely robust. The hidden spring in the pivot of shears (c) makes these the most hygienic but least powerful of the three.

59

# OTHER CUTTING TOOLS

Apart from basic cleaning, peeling, trimming and paring, the preparation of vegetables and other foods often involves slicing, shredding, dicing and cubing, as well as elaborate decorative turning.

All this can be done perfectly well with ordinary cook's knives, but there are several devices on the market – some worth having, some not – which have been designed to make these tasks easier and less time-consuming. Some of these tools are quite simple, others are most ingenious and elaborate.

*Tools which really help*
There are some jobs which are much more efficiently and quickly done with special tools – coring apples or grating cheese, for example. Should you wish to reduce a quantity of firm fruit or vegetables, such as potatoes, cucumbers or apples, to a mass of shreds, strips or wafer-thin discs, the various blades of a tool like a mandoline will help you to do it faster than any knife.

It is just possible to grate small, hard things like nutmegs with the edge of a knife; a very sharp blade will remove the zest from an orange or lemon; but when it comes to grating cheese, shredding potatoes for "latkes", reducing raw onion to a mush, or turning soft bread into crumbs, a grater is by far the best tool.

Some cooks find that non-fibrous foods, such as semi-soft cheese, hard-boiled eggs and raw tomatoes, can be more easily sliced with taut wires or rows of thin, serrated blades, than with an ordinary cook's knife – although, if this is really sharp, it should pose no problems.

It is certainly quicker and easier to cut decorative pastry shapes with specially made stamps or cutters.

As with all tools, kitchen gadgets last longer and work better if they are properly cared for. Very cheap tools may work well for a short time, but then need replacing, because they are so flimsily constructed that their life expectancy can be only brief. Better quality tools may rust or warp if not properly washed and carefully dried before they are put away.

Direct heat distorts and splits wood, so dry wooden implements, such as mandolines (which are particularly susceptible to warping), in a cool, airy place. Tinned steel rusts easily, so graters and intricate metal objects, which are not easy to dry with a cloth, should be put in a warm place to dry off – a cooling oven is ideal. Plastic handles are liable to melt if subjected to extreme heat, however, so make sure the temperature is quite low if the utensil has plastic fittings.

*Choosing a gadget*
Few gadgets on display in the shops are genuinely indispensable. Most are fun to play with, but are strictly speaking rather frivolous. In order to find out if any piece of equipment is worth having, ask yourself these questions:

Is it truly time and labour saving, simple to assemble and work; easy to clean and maintain?

Is it well designed, sturdy, pleasing in appearance and not too bulky to store when not in use?

Is it worth its cost in terms of the amount of work you hope to get from it?

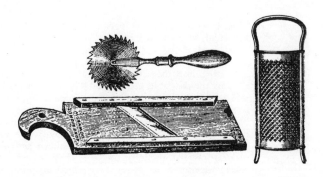

# Peelers

(a)  (b)  (c)  (d)

(a) **Size.** L. 6 in. (152 mm).
**Material.** Stainless steel blade, alloy steel head with plastic screw and handle.

(b) **Size.** L. 6¼ in. (160 mm).
**Material.** Stainless steel blade, wooden handle.

(c) **Size.** L. 2 in. (50 mm).
**Material.** Carbon steel blade, plastic handle.

(d) **Size.** L. 6¾ in. (172 mm).
**Material.** Carbon steel blade, alloy steel handle.

Practical and economical, peeler (a) has a replaceable, convex blade which cuts a wide strip and is reversible for left-handed use.

The traditional English peeler (b) has a blade bent in a V-shape with a sharpened slot, 1¼ in. (32 mm) long, down the centre for peeling. The point is sharpened for picking out blemishes.

The swivel-action peelers (c) and (d) pare very thinly and follow the contours of the bumpiest potato . quite closely. The blade of peeler (c) has a little loop on the side to pick out blemishes. A bean slicer with three blades is fitted on the handle of (d).

## Trimming celery

*Trim the strings from celery with a peeler. Work from the base up, peeling towards you.*

# Making chocolate curls

*Using a sharp peeler, shave a block of chocolate to make chocolate curls.*

## Forming carrot rolls

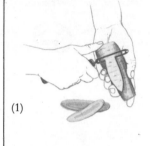

(1)

(2)

(3)

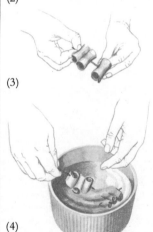

(4)

*Peel a large carrot thinly length-wise (1). Roll the peelings round your finger (2) and spear each roll with a toothpick (3). Put the rolls in iced water to set in decorative curls (4).*

# Asparagus peeler

**Size.** (Blade) L. 5 in. (127 mm).
**Materials.** Stainless steel blade and peeling attachment, plastic handle.

This long-bladed German peeler pares the skin from the thick ends of asparagus stems. It has an angled attachment held in place on the blade with brass screws. By sliding this along the blade you can regulate the depth of the cut, thus avoiding the risk of cutting too deeply into the stalk. Without the attachment, the peeler makes an excellent vegetable knife. The blade can be sharpened.

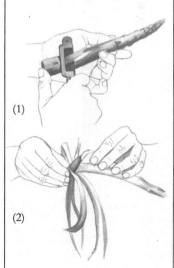

(1)

(2)

*Peel away the hard, white skin at the base of the stem (1). Then snap the peeled stem off at its thickest point, near the base (2).*

## Patent peeler

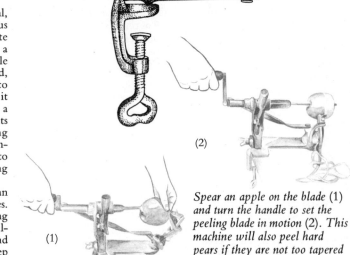

**Size.** L. 14 in. (355 mm).
**Material.** Carbon steel blade, stainless steel shaft, cast iron structure, wooden handles.

Push an apple on to the central, spear-like shaft of this ingenious machine and turn the appropriate handle. The shaft rotates and a tiny blade shaped like a little finger-nail poised on a jointed, spring-loaded arm moves up to the apple. On touching it, it starts peeling the skin away in a continuous ribbon, working its way from one end of the spinning apple to the other. Peeling completed, press the release lever to return the blade to its starting position.

This German machine has an adjustment for soft or hard apples. It works extremely fast, peeling an apple in ten seconds, so although rather specialized and expensive, it could earn its keep in a glut.

(2)

(1)

*Spear an apple on the blade (1) and turn the handle to set the peeling blade in motion (2). This machine will also peel hard pears if they are not too tapered towards the stalk.*

## Canelle knife

**Size.** L. 5¾ in. (146 mm).
**Material.** Stainless steel blade, wooden handle.

The cutting-edge on this oddly shaped blade is on a V-shaped tooth which lies within the horizontal slot near the tip. It pares ¼ in. (6 mm) strips of peel from citrus fruits and can also be used to cut thin grooves or channels lengthwise down cucumbers and carrots. This gives the slices a pretty, flower-like appearance. It is often called a "lemon dresser".

*Draw the blade of the canelle knife upwards in a paring action. If you wish to slice the lemon, remove the strips completely. The slices will then have attractively notched edges. If the strips are left attached at the top of the lemon, the fruit can be carefully halved. The long strips are then looped over and the ends tucked into the grooves where the strips are attached. The lemon half is then used as a garnish.*

## Zester

**Size.** L. 5½ in. (140 mm).
**Material.** Stainless steel blade, wooden handle.

Five little holes punched in the downward-curving end of the zester's blade form the cutting-edge. Draw it firmly across the skin of an orange or lemon to pare just the skin or "zest" and no pith. It produces attractive and tasty wisps for flavouring cakes, desserts and ices and works best on fresh, firm-skinned fruit.

# Mushroom fluter

**Size.** L. 6 in. (152 mm).
**Material.** Stainless steel blade, plastic handle.

Like the little canelle knife, the mushroom fluter cuts decorative grooves. Choose firm, button mushrooms for fluting in straight or curved lines.

*Flute mushrooms by drawing the blade down the cap.*

# Corers

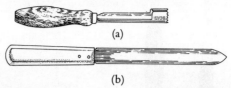

(a)

(b)

(a) **Size.** (Blade) L. 3½ in. (90 mm).
**Material.** Stainless steel blade, wooden handle.
(b) **Size.** (Blade) L. 6 in. (152 mm).
**Material.** Stainless steel blade, wooden handle.

The cutting edge of apple corer (a) is on the end of the cylindrical blade and is ¾ in. (20 mm) in diameter. This tool is indispensable for coring apples and pears, but it is not long enough to core any deeper than 3½ in. (90 mm). For longer cores you need the zucchini (courgette) corer (b).

This has a blade shaped like an elongated, pointed scoop, which hollows out the seed-filled cores of zucchini, tiny marrows or cucumbers, as long as they are not too curved. These can then be stuffed with soft cheese and herbs. Firm the stuffing by chilling in the refrigerator, then serve sliced, as an hors d'oeuvre.

# Cherry stoners

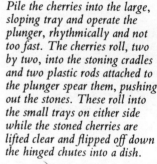

(a) **Size.** L. 5½ in. (140 mm).
**Material.** Tinned steel wire, porcelain cradle.
(b) **Size.** H. 7 in. (178 mm).
**Material.** Cast aluminium frame, steel spring, plastic handle.
(c) **Size.** H. 11½ in. (292 mm).
**Material.** Cast aluminium and plastic structure. Stainless steel chutes, rubber suction-pad base.

Stoning fruit is a fiddly business when done with a knife. Patent stoners speed the process up and leave the fruit whole, which looks more attractive.

These three stoners work on the same principle. The fruit, be it damson, cherry or olive, is placed end-up in a little, hollowed-out holder. A rod is then pushed through it ejecting the stone.

Stoners (a) and (b) work quite efficiently, but as each cherry is put individually into the holder for stoning, they are rather slow. Stoner (c) does a neat job considerably faster and is fun to use.

*Pile the cherries into the large, sloping tray and operate the plunger, rhythmically and not too fast. The cherries roll, two by two, into the stoning cradles and two plastic rods attached to the plunger spear them, pushing out the stones. These roll into the small trays on either side while the stoned cherries are lifted clear and flipped off down the hinged chutes into a dish.*

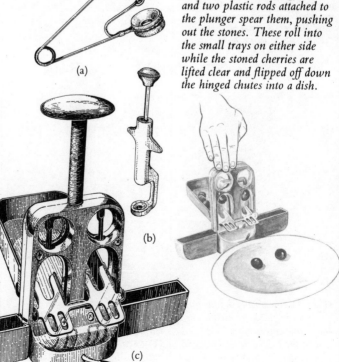

(a)

(b)

(c)

# Ballers

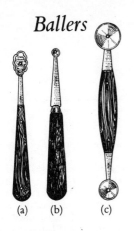

(a)    (b)    (c)

(a) **Size.** (Cup) ¾ in. × 1¼ in. (20 × 32 mm).
**Material.** Stainless steel cup, wooden handle.

(b) **Size.** (Cup) D. ¼ in. (6 mm).
**Material.** Stainless steel cup, wooden handle.

(c) **Size.** (Cups) D. ¾, 1 in. (20, 25 mm).
**Material.** Stainless steel cups, wooden handle.

Although called melon ballers, these cut potatoes, root vegetables, apples, butter and cheese too and can also gouge the cores from halved apples and pears. The tiny baller (b) makes pea-sized carrot balls to serve with peas.

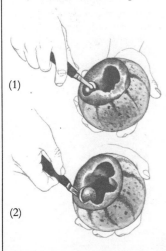

(1)

(2)

*With the cup upside down, push the top edge into the melon until the whole cup is buried (1). Twist the cup completely round, cutting deeply, and bring it out (with ball) right side up (2).*

# Crinkle cut chipper

**Size.** (Blade) L. 3 in. (75 mm).
**Material.** Stainless steel blade, wooden handle.

Chips with wavy edges have a larger surface exposed to the fat than do plain chips—this makes them crisper, as any expert chip-maker will tell you. This crinkle chip cutter is designed to cut wavy-edged chips. The blade is slightly angled so that the chipper cuts gradually and easily through.

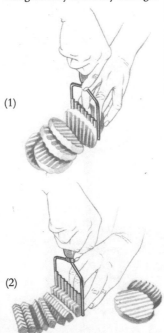

(1)

(2)

*Push the corrugated blade of the chipper down through the potato (1) to cut grooved slices. Then cut the slices into wavy-edged chips (2).*

# Gaufrette cutter

**Size.** (Blade) L. 3 in. (75 mm).
**Material.** Stainless steel blade, plastic handle.

This Italian cutter is not as easy to use as a mandoline for making pommes gaufrettes (latticed potato crisps) but it is far cheaper. The cutting edge is on the corrugated blade attached to the rectangular head. As this is only 2¼ in. (57 mm) wide you must trim the potato to size first. The potato is given a quarter turn with each slice to achieve the lattice pattern every time.

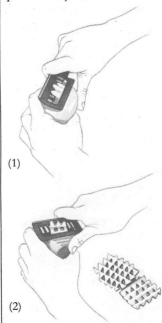

(1)

(2)

*Use the cutter with a paring action to produce a thin, ridged slice (1). Turn the potato and cut it again across the ridges to make a latticed slice (2).*

(a) **Size.** (Blades) L. 3¾, 4 in. (95, 100 mm).
**Material.** Stainless steel blades, beechwood frame.

(b) **Size.** (Blades) L. 3¾ in. (95 mm).
**Material.** Stainless steel.

(c) **Size.** (Blades) L. 3 in. (75 mm).
**Material.** Stainless steel blades, beechwood frame.

Apples and firm vegetables, such as potatoes, beet, courgettes and cabbage, can be sliced very rapidly on a mandoline. Some have blades for cutting julienne strips and chips. These can be cut on mandolines without special blades, by slicing a vegetable one way, gathering up the pieces and slicing them through again with the original cuts running at right angles to the blade.

Mandoline (a) is the simplest, but least satisfactory, of these three mandolines. It has two fixed blades set centrally in the frame. The width of the slices is determined by the angle at which the wooden beds facing the blades are set. These are pivoted by adjusting wing-nuts on either side of the frame, but the beds tend to slip out of position with the pressure of slicing. This mandoline has to

## Mandolines

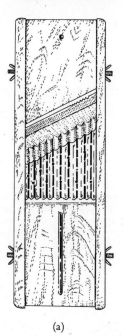

(a)

be held at a slope as it has no supporting struts. Placing the end against a stop prevents it sliding.

The professional mandoline (b) is robust, reliable and versatile. It has four blades, two of which are selected by moving a handle on the side of the frame. One cuts julienne strips (29 at a time), the other chips (nine at a time). The thickness of the slices is adjusted by levers at the back. It has a guard to hold the food being sliced.

A less sophisticated version, (c), has blades set in the movable beds, plus two extra blades with rows of narrow, sharp teeth (15 on one, seven on the other), which can be fitted to project beyond the edge of the straight blade. These cut julienne strips ⅛ in. (3 mm) wide, and chips ½ in. (12 mm) wide. The struts at the back can be reversed when the mandoline is used upside down, for corrugated slices. The slice thickness on this mandoline is easier to adjust and remains more constant than does that of mandoline (a).

All three mandolines have corrugated blades for making latticed potato crisps (pommes gaufrettes). Give the potato a 90° turn with each succeeding slice, cutting across the previous ridges, with the blade set at ⅛ in. (3 mm).

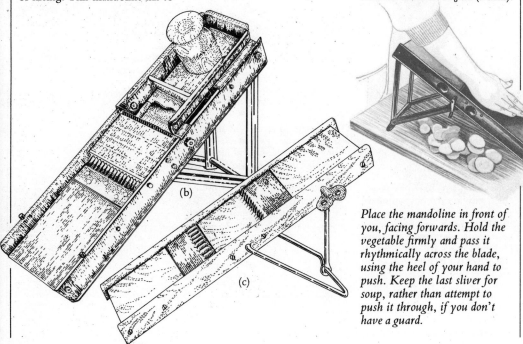

(b)

(c)

*Place the mandoline in front of you, facing forwards. Hold the vegetable firmly and pass it rhythmically across the blade, using the heel of your hand to push. Keep the last sliver for soup, rather than attempt to push it through, if you don't have a guard.*

## Vegetable slicer

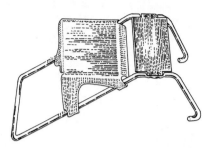

**Size.** (Blade) L. 3½ in. (90 mm).
**Material.** High carbon blue steel blade, stainless steel frame.

This simple tool is well designed for slicing things like cabbage, onions, smoked sausages, fruit and root vegetables. It works very fast.

The platform facing the extremely sharp cutting-edge rests on notches on the frame. It can be adjusted to make slices ranging in thickness from ⅛ in. (3 mm) to ½ in. (12 mm). It will stay firmly in the notches if you rest your thumb on the hook at the back.

When slicing soft-centred things such as oranges, lemons or tomatoes, use a sawing action from side to side and press lightly against the cutting-edge.

## Spin slicer

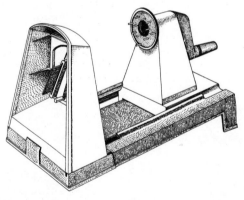

**Size.** 11 × 6½ × 5 in. (280 × 165 × 127 mm).
**Material.** Stainless steel blades and pins, plastic body.

Should you wish to reduce vegetables, such as carrots, cucumbers, potatoes or onions, to a mass of hair-like shreds or one continuous, paper-thin spiral, this odd-looking gadget will do it simply and quickly. It has two 2¼ in. (57 mm) blades, one straight, the other toothed, set in a plastic framework. The toothed blade is removable and slightly awkward to fix, but the mechanism itself is so simple nothing can go wrong.

Peel a vegetable and cut the end straight across. Push it on to the spikes of the sliding holder and push this up against the blade of your choice. Then just turn the handle. The last ½ in. (12 mm) of vegetable is liable to be wasted, however, as it does not reach the blade. The slicer is easy to clean.

*As you turn the handle the spiked food holder spins the vegetable against the blade.*

## Cucumber slicer

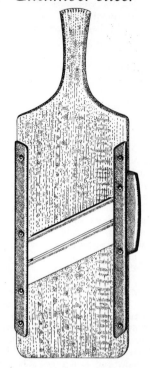

**Size.** (Blades) L. 4 in. (100 mm).
**Material.** Stainless steel blades, beechwood frame, plastic trim, brass pins.

Cut wafers of cucumber and fine shreds of cabbage and potato with this sharp slicer. It is German made and has two blades fixed to a plastic handle, so you can remove them for cleaning.

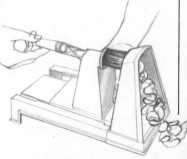

# Slicing machine

**Size.** 12 × 9 × 7 in.
(305 × 230 × 178 mm).
**Material.** Stainless steel blade,
enamelled alloy steel, plastic and
nylon body.

A slicing machine is rather an
extravagant piece of equipment
unless you frequently make large
quantities of sandwiches filled
with thin slices of cold meat,
salami, ham or cheese, or like
preparing salads garnished with
equally elegant slices of cucumber, tomato, lemon, onion or
cabbage.

This slicer is efficient, with a
simple, foolproof mechanism and
is easy to clean. It has four rubber
suction-pads on the base to hold it
steady on smooth surfaces and
two stops on the front to prevent
it sliding backwards on rougher
ones. Other models have clamps.
The 6¾ in. (172 mm) diameter
blade has extremely sharp teeth
and is geared to the detachable
handle by nylon cogs.

Slices up to ¾ in. (20 mm) wide
can be selected by turning a num-
bered disc. This moves a gauge
(which is fitted on the far side
with a narrow, transparent plastic
shield) nearer or further from the

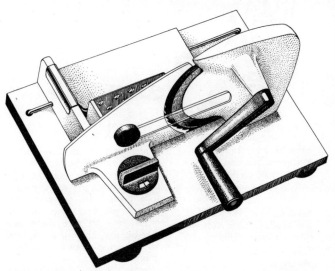

blade. A plastic carriage feeds the
blade, sliding to and fro along a
steel bar on the base of the
machine. A toothed, steel gripping-guard slots on the carriage
and holds the food against the
blade. Neither carriage nor guard
need be used when starting to
slice something large, like a loaf

of bread, but they should be fitted
as a safety measure before your
fingers are within striking distance
of the blade. The gripping-guard
is rather shallow, however, and
does not shield the blade completely. Some models have a
plastic tray to catch the slices; this
one lets them pile up in a heap.

# Electric food slicer

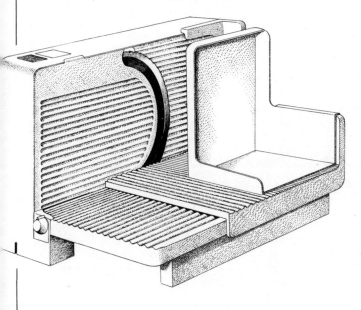

**Size.** (Open) 14 × 10½ × 8½ in.
(355 × 267 × 215 mm).
**Material.** Stainless steel blade,
plastic body.

This beautifully designed electric
food slicer has good safety provision. The 6¾ in. (172 mm)
diameter blade will not rotate
without its shield. The starter
button is a safe distance from the
blade and there is a neat storage
space for the flex, so that no more
than necessary need be exposed.

The well-guarded food holder
fits into a carriage which slides
to and fro on a grooved plastic
bed to feed the blade. Slices can
be selected to any width up to
¾ in. (20 mm) by turning a knob.
The whole bed folds up for storage making the machine only
4 in. (100 mm) wide. It is easily
dismantled for cleaning. It slices
such things as roast meat, bread,
ham, cheese and vegetables.

# Bean slicers

# Tomato slicer

(a)

(b)

(c)

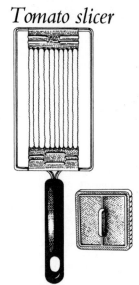

(a) **Size.** H. 6 in. (152 mm). **Material.** Stainless steel cutter, enamelled cast iron body, rubber suction pads on base.

(b) **Size.** L. 1¾ in. (45 mm). **Material.** Carbon steel blades, plastic frame.

(c) **Size.** L. 5 in. (127 mm). **Material.** Carbon steel blades, plastic handle.

If you grow your own beans and freeze them, slicer (a) is invaluable in the green bean season. This solid little machine weighs 1½ lbs (675 g) and is simple and efficient. It chops beans into slices; not quite as long and narrow as those made by slicers (b) and (c), but elegant enough.

Wide enough to take prize-winning runner beans, but fortunately not strong enough to take those past their prime, bean slicer (b) is possibly the cheapest available. If you have large, straight beans you can turn them into shreds as long and fine as spaghetti with this tool; but you have to string them first with a small vegetable knife. Hold the slicer with finger and thumb beneath the lipped edge. Push a trimmed bean down from the top, across the blades, pulling it right through to complete the shredding.

The Australian bean slicer (c) is a more sophisticated version of (b). It works on the same principle but catches and removes the strings of the beans before they pass through the cutters.

**Size.** (Blades) L. 4¼ in. (107 mm). **Material.** Stainless steel blades, alloy steel frame, plastic handle and pusher.

If you have neither a finely serrated salad knife nor a good cook's knife and want thin, even slices of tomato for a salad or sandwiches, the eleven, thin serrated blades of this slicer will cut them for you – provided the tomato is firm.

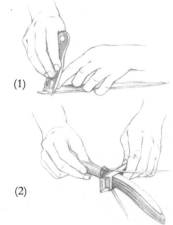

(1)

(2)

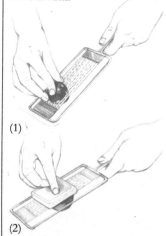

(1)

(2)

*Top, tail and string the beans with a knife, then feed them one by one into the hopper behind the cutting disc. Turn the handle to chop the bean into sections.*

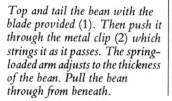

*Top and tail the bean with the blade provided (1). Then push it through the metal clip (2) which strings it as it passes. The spring-loaded arm adjusts to the thickness of the bean. Pull the bean through from beneath.*

*Push the tomato to and fro across the blades (1), pushing it through finally with the plastic pusher to avoid slicing your fingers (2).*

# Patent slicing knife

**Size.** (Blade) L. 8¼ in. (210 mm).
**Material.** Stainless steel blade, plastic handle, stainless steel and plastic gauge.

This knife is much cheaper than a mechanical slicer and does exactly the same tasks with comparable efficiency. It is essentially an ordinary knife with a scalloped edge, but just beneath the handle there is a screw, holding a beak-shaped gauge parallel to the blade and just below it. Turn this screw to fix the gauge at various distances, up to ½ in. (12 mm) from the blade, to determine the width of your slices.
Place the food to be sliced under the knife edge and against the flat inner side of the gauge, then slice downwards with a sawing motion. When you reach the board, pull the knife backwards, point downwards. This has a fairly ruinous effect on the board but makes lovely even slices of bread, meat or vegetables. The gauge can be removed if you want to use the slicer as a general-purpose knife.

# Egg slicer

**Size.** L. 3½ in. (90 mm),
**Material.** Stainless steel wires. Aluminium frame.

Ten fine wires on this egg slicer are stretched across a frame hinged to a hollowed, slotted base. A peeled, hard-boiled egg placed lengthways or sideways in the hollow is sliced as the wires are pushed down upon it.

# Apple corer

**Size.** L. 6¾ in. (172 mm).
**Material.** Stainless steel blades, cast aluminium frame.

This patent apple corer and cutter has blades set like the spokes of a wheel with a corer as the hub. The frame is strongly made with comfortably designed handles.

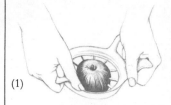

(1)

(2)

*Press the cutter down on an apple (1) to divide it neatly into twelve cored segments (2).*

# Radish cutter

**Size.** L. 7 in. (178 mm).
**Material.** Stainless steel blades, cast alloy handles.

To make a radish look like a flower trim its ends and place it root-end up in the holder of this tool. Bring the cutting blades down on it, pressing the handles together and forcing the blades through. A beak-like blade on the end of the cutting wheel also nips V-shaped pieces from the rims of hollowed-out citrus skins.

# Potato chip cutter

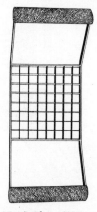

**Size.** (Grid) 3¼ in. (82 mm) square.
**Material.** Tinned steel, plastic covered handles.

By pressing this cutter down on a peeled potato you should get a neat little pile of chips. Trim the potato to fit the grid first and press hard. Don't waste time trying to pull the chips right through—push the cutter down on another potato to free them. This is a simple tool, amusing to use.

# Salad cutter

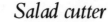

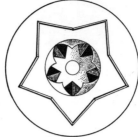

**Size.** D. 5½ in. (140 mm).
**Material.** Stainless steel blades, plastic body.

This cutter will deal with anything (provided it's soft enough) up to 2¼ in. (57 mm) in diameter.

By twisting the bottom half of the case, the five V-shaped blades move inwards and outwards, like the petals of a flower. They cut salad ingredients like cooked beetroot, hard-boiled eggs, cooked new potatoes and tomatoes into halves with vandyked edges. (Strictly for people who like vandyked food.)

This sort of decorative cutting is just as easy with a small vegetable knife – and some practice.

(1)

(2)

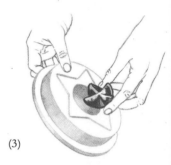

(3)

*Starting with the blades retracted, place a tomato in the centre and twist the case top, clockwise (1).*

*Push the top half of the tomato loose with your thumb and lift it free (2). Turn the top of the case anti-clockwise to retract the blades and tip out the other half (3).*

# Potato chippers

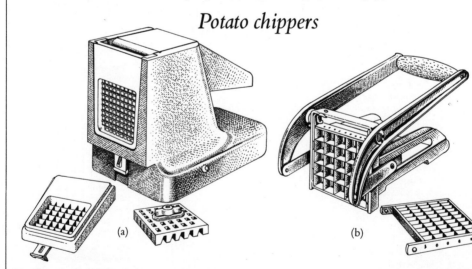

(a)

(b)

(a) **Size.** L. 9 in. (230 mm).
   **Material.** Stainless steel cutters, plastic body and pusher, suction-pad base.

(b) **Size.** L. 10 in. (255 mm).
   **Material.** Stainless steel cutters, chromed steel frame, wooden handle, plastic pusher.

Both these chippers work in the same way – forcing a potato through a cutting grid when the handle is pressed down firmly.

You need a little strength to operate them.

Described as multi-purpose, chipper (a) slices carrots, celery, apples, pears, peppers and onions as well as potatoes. It is made of robust plastic and has a strong suction pad on the base. Two cutting grids, easily fitted, give a choice of chips ½ in. (12 mm) or ¼ in. (6 mm) square in section.

The plastic pushers (one for each grid) are attached to the handle. They are designed to press the chips right through the grid. In practice you may find that you can only clear the chips completely by pushing another potato through.

Chipper (b) also has a choice of cutting grids. One cuts chips ½ in. (12 mm), the other ½ × ¼ in. (12 × 6 mm) in cross section. It has one fixed pusher fitting both grids. The handle is slightly stiffer to push than that of chipper (a). Large potatoes have to be cut into pieces for chipping.

# Cheese slicers

(a) **Size.** L. 5 in. (127 mm).
**Material.** Hardened and tempered tinned steel wire, wooden handles.

(b) **Size.** (Cutter) L. 4 in. (100 mm).
**Material.** Stainless steel wire and roller, plastic handle.

(c) **Size.** (Cutter) L. 4 in. (100 mm).
**Material.** Stainless steel wire and lever, teak board.

(d) **Size.** (Cutter) L. 2 in. (50 mm).
**Material.** Stainless steel head, teak handle.

The domestic cheese wire (a) is not even half as long (or strong) as those used by cheesemongers, but will serve to cut up pieces of Cheddar or Stilton cheese. It will not cut up very large pieces, though, for having no point of anchorage, it has to be looped round the cheese. It is, therefore, rather restricted in its use.

It is difficult (if not impossible) using a knife, to slice cheese as widely and thinly as the rolling cutter (b) does. The thickness of the slice depends on the angle the handle is held at as you pull the roller towards you across the cheese; the more acute the angle, the thinner the slice. It is intended for slicing semi-firm cheeses, such as Gouda, Edam, Samsoe and Maribo, and is exactly the right width for the standard smørrebrød: 4 × 4 in. (100 × 100 mm) or 4 × 2 in. (100 × 50 mm). The cutting wire is replaceable and two spares are provided.

The Danish cheese cutter (c) does the same job as cutter (b), but in a more sophisticated way. The cutting wire is carried on a lever mounted on one side of the cheese board. This lever carries an eccentric gauge, which is twisted round it to select slice thickness. It is a neat cheese slicer for kitchen or table use.

The slicing edge on cutter (d) is on a slot cut into the blade-shaped head. It has a slightly corrugated edge and cuts thin, lightly ribbed slivers from semi-firm cheeses. The blade acts as a lifter and server. The width of the slot fits the smaller smørrebrød.

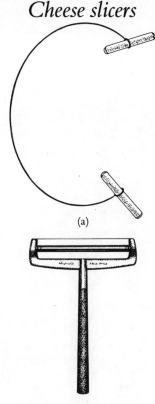

(a)

*Loop the wire round the cheese. Hold the cheese firmly and draw the wire through.*

(b)

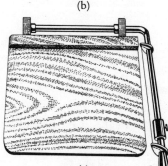

(c)

*Place the cheese with the edge against the gauge and bring the lever and wire down to slice it.*

*Hook the wire cutter over the end of the cheese and draw the roller towards you. The wire will slice evenly through.*

(d)

*Draw the blade firmly across the top of the cheese. The sharp slot will slice a thin sliver from it.*

# Biscuit cutters

(a) **Size.** H. 2 to 5 in. (50 to 127 mm).

(b) **Size.** L. 2 to $3\frac{1}{4}$ in. (50 to 95 mm).

(c) **Size.** L. $2\frac{1}{4}$ to $3\frac{1}{4}$ in. (57 to 80 mm).

(d) **Size.** H. 3 to $6\frac{1}{2}$ in. (75 to 165 mm).

(e) **Size.** L. 3 to $4\frac{1}{2}$ in. (75 to 115 mm).

(f) **Size.** H. $4\frac{1}{2}$ in. (115 mm).

(g) **Size.** W. $1\frac{1}{2}$ to $2\frac{3}{4}$ in. (38 to 70 mm).

(h) **Size.** W. $1\frac{3}{4}$ in. (45 mm).

**Material.** All tinned steel.

These fancy cutters will shape all kinds of animals, birds, gingerbread men and will make pretty, iced biscuits for children's parties.

The Swedish cutters (a), which include a Christmas tree, a reindeer and Santa Claus, are used to cut pepparkakor (spiced ginger biscuits) which are traditionally made there during the Christmas season. They are often given as presents, packed in tins decorated with the sames shapes.

The set of eight assorted cutters (c) make shapes that look particularly pretty when iced in strong bright colours; they also cut unusual canapé shapes or small sandwiches for buffets.

The king, queen, little princess and baby prince in set (d) make a change from the more usual gingerbread men.

Farmyard animal biscuits go down very well at children's parties; the set of cutters (e) are large enough to cut fried bread into interesting shapes. They will certainly make a change from the usual squares or rectangles hidden under a couverture of baked beans. The bird set (b) can be used similarly but the shapes (an odd mixture of wild and domestic fowl) are less interesting.

No collection of biscuit cutters would be complete without a gingerbread man (f). This one has a handle, useful for lifting the cutter cleanly from the dough.

Heart-shaped cutters like set (g) and the lonely heart (h) come into their own on St Valentine's day, when they can be piped with loving messages in icing. Cutter (h) is strongly made and almost as deep as a pastry cutter. It can be used for cutting tough things like slices of potato or pineapple. The disc on the back makes it rigid.

(a)

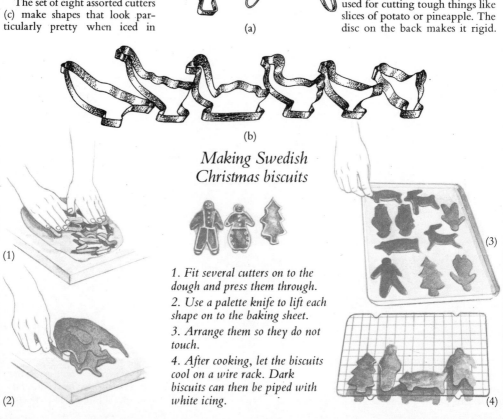

(b)

## Making Swedish Christmas biscuits

1. Fit several cutters on to the dough and press them through.

2. Use a palette knife to lift each shape on to the baking sheet.

3. Arrange them so they do not touch.

4. After cooking, let the biscuits cool on a wire rack. Dark biscuits can then be piped with white icing.

(1)

(2)

(3)

(4)

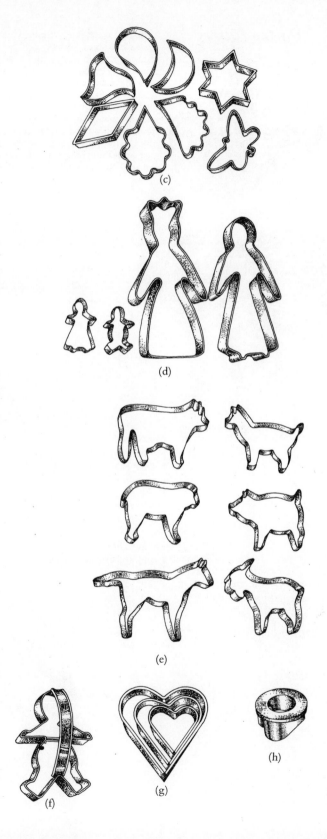

(c)

(d)

(e)

(f)

(g)

(h)

# Multi-sided cutter

**Size.** H. $2\frac{1}{4}$ in. (57 mm).
**Material.** Chromed steel.

Six different shapes, including all the playing card suits, make this six-sided cutter particularly useful. It is strongly made, but the cutters are shallow and cut only to a depth of about $\frac{1}{4}$ in. (6 mm). So make sure you roll out your dough thinly, and evenly. The cutting edges are not as sharp as those made of tinned steel.

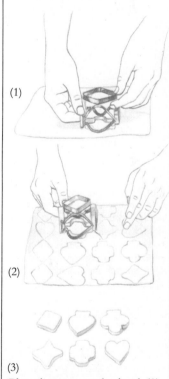

(1)

(2)

(3)

*Place the cutter on the dough (1) and press out one shape. Then turn the cutter over and round, pressing out shapes, until every side has been used (2). You should make sure you have at least one example of each shape (3).*

(a) **Size.** D. 3¾ to 1½ in.
(95 to 38 mm).
Tin of six plain.
**Material.** Tinned steel.

(b) **Size.** D. 3½ to 1 in.
(90 to 25 mm).
Tin of seven crinkled.
**Material.** Tinned steel.

Pastry cutters are versatile tools.
They cut not only pastry, but
such things as beetroot, aspic,

## Pastry cutters

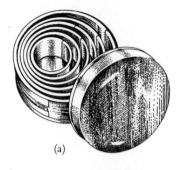

(a)

hard-boiled eggs or, with heavier
pressure, potato. When used for
cutting dough they must be
floured. They can be greased and
used to contain eggs for poaching
in a pan. The larger ones will act as
a trivet for a bowl inside a saucepan of water, if you have no
double-boiler and are making egg
sauces, fruit curds, or steaming a
suet pudding. You can also buy
sets of plastic pastry cutters.

## Cutting pastry fish

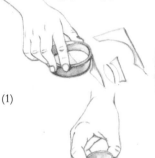

(1)

(2)

(3)

Cut an oval from pastry with a
large, plain cutter (1). Then
mark a scale pattern, pressing
lightly alternately to left and
right (2), using a small cutter.
Finish the fish by cutting out a
V at the tail and marking in an
eye and mouth at the head (3).

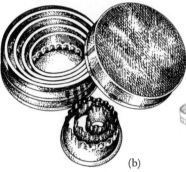

(b)

## Coring pineapple slices

Position a small cutter over the
core and press it firmly through
the slice with the palm of your
hand to remove the core.

## Making ravioli

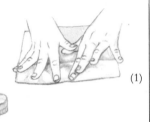

(1)

(2)

Place portions of filling on a
sheet of fresh pasta dough, far
enough back from the edge to
allow the dough to be folded back
over them. Having folded the
dough over, press lightly between
the portions (1) to seal them.
Then cut out each section of
ravioli using half a pastry
cutter (2).

## Forming chocolate whirls

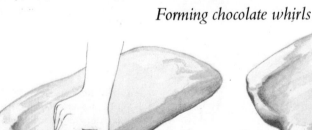

(2)

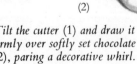

(1)

Tilt the cutter (1) and draw it
firmly over softly set chocolate
(2), paring a decorative whirl.

# Doughnut cutter

**Size.** D. $2\frac{1}{2}$ in. (65 mm).
**Material.** Tinned steel.

This doughnut cutter is useful if you make quantities of doughnuts fairly frequently, but the job is just as easily done with two pastry cutters, or even a wine glass and bottle cap.

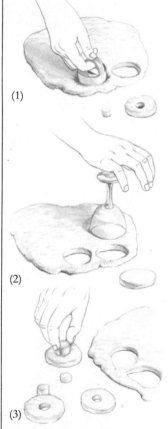

(1)

(2)

(3)

1. *As the floured cutter is pressed into the dough its two circular blades cut out the doughnut shape in one operation.*
2. *An ordinary wine glass cuts circles out of dough very easily.*
3. *The screw-cap of a bottle can then be used to cut the holes in the middle.*

# Small cutters

**Size.** L. 1 to $1\frac{3}{4}$ in. (25 to 45 mm).
**Material.** Tinned steel.

You can decorate pie crusts most expertly with pretty leaflets and lozenges shaped from pastry dough with these small cutters. This set contains six different patterns, but for more variety you can buy little tins containing as many as twelve. Flour them first before using them to cut the dough and fix each shape securely to the raw crust with a little water.

# Aspic cutters

**Size.** L. $\frac{1}{2}$ in. to $\frac{3}{4}$ in. (12 to 20 mm).
**Material.** Tinned steel.

These tiny cutters are used when decorating aspic dishes. They cut shapes from thin slices of carrot, radish, cucumber peel, tomato, capsicum, jelly or egg. They are also handy for cutting cake decorations from marzipan. The top edge of each is neatly turned down for comfortable use. The little tin – only 2 in. (50 mm) in diameter – keeps them all neatly together.

# Square vol-au-vent cutter

**Size.** 4 in. (102 mm) square.
**Material.** Stainless steel.

Most attractive vol-au-vent cases can be made very simply with this triple-bladed cutter. The outer blade cuts a square from puff pastry dough while the two L-shaped blades cut a smaller square joined to the outer one at two corners. The two free corners are overlapped forming a rim.

(1)

(2)

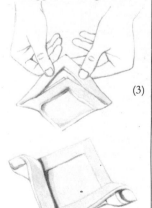

(3)

(4)

*Start with the cut-out square (1). Brush the edges with water and lift one free corner (2), folding it back. Lift the other over it (3) to make the vol-au-vent case (4).*

(a) **Size.** (Wheel) D. 1¼ in.
(32 mm).
**Material.** Wood, steel pin.

(b) **Size.** (Wheel) D. 1½ in.
(38 mm).
**Material.** Stainless steel
wheel, plastic handle.

(c) **Size.** (Wheel) D. 1½ in.
(38 mm).
**Material.** Stainless steel
wheel, wooden handle.

(d) **Size.** (Wheel) D. 1¾ in.
(45 mm).
**Material.** Wood, brass pin.

(e) **Size.** (Wheel) D. 1½ in.
(38 mm).
**Material.** Plastic wheel,
stainless steel and plastic
handle.

(f) **Size.** (Wheel) D. 1¾ in.
(45 mm).
**Material.** Tinned steel
wheel, painted wood handle.

## Pastry cutting wheels

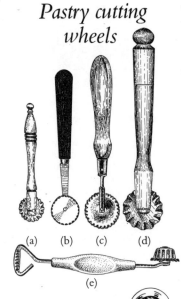

(a)   (b)   (c)   (d)

(e)

(f)

The fluted wheels of cutters (a)
to (d) carve decorative strips of
pastry for lattices on tarts and cut
ravioli from thin sheets of
pasta. The pie-trimmers (e) and
(f) seal and flute the edges of pie-
crusts. Trimmer (e) incorporates
a pastry crimper on the handle.
The deep-rimmed wheel on trimmer (f) simultaneously flutes and
trims pie-crusts, which trimmer
(e) does not.

*Run the ridged boss of a pastry
trimmer round a pie crust to seal
and decorate. The rim trims off
surplus dough.*

## Lattice cutter

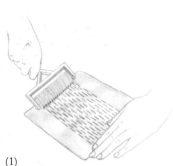

(1)

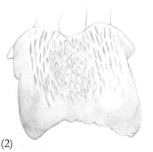

(2)

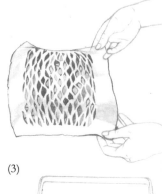

(3)

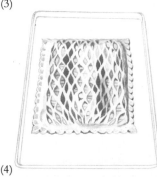

(4)

**Size.** (Cutter) W. 4¾ in.
(120 mm).
**Material.** Nylon cutting
wheels, cast aluminium handle.

Nineteen toothed nylon wheels
1½ in. (38 mm) in diameter and
mounted on one axle are the
cutting device on this tool. It is
used to make latticed tops for
large jam or treacle tarts and is
great fun to use. The wheels cut a
pattern of broken lines which can
be stretched out gently to give the
pastry top a net-like appearance.

*1. Roll the cutter the length of
the dough, pressing firmly to
make sure that the teeth cut
through.*
*2. Gently pull the lattice open,
resting the dough on your hands
and starting from the middle.*

*3. Lift it carefully on to the tart,
spreading the mesh evenly.*
*4. Knock up the edges and crimp
them with the back of a knife
(see* COOK'S KNIVES*).*

## Pizza cutter

**Size.** (Cutter) D. 2½ in. (65 mm).
**Material.** Stainless steel cutter, wooden handle.

There are finger guards on the handle of this pizza cutter, as the cutting wheel has a sharp edge. With it you can first cut out a circle of pizza dough (using a plate, or pizza tin, as a guide) and then, when the pizza is cooked, use it again to cut neat wedges for serving individual portions.

## Croissant cutter

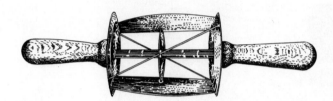

**Size.** (Blades) L. 5½ in. (140 mm).
**Material.** Tinned steel blades, wooden handles.

The four blades set on a slant and rotating round an axle are reminiscent of those on a lawnmower, but this tool is designed to carve neat triangles from croissant dough, not to cut grass. As this is its sole purpose it will only earn its keep if you make croissants regularly and can't cut neat triangles of identical size in any other way. This cuts them 5½ × 5½ × 5¼ in. (140 × 140 × 133 mm).

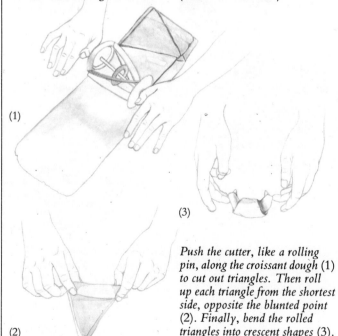

(1)

(3)

(2)

*Push the cutter, like a rolling pin, along the croissant dough (1) to cut out triangles. Then roll up each triangle from the shortest side, opposite the blunted point (2). Finally, bend the rolled triangles into crescent shapes (3).*

## Ravioli cutters

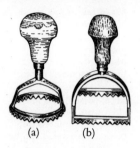

(a)       (b)

(a) **Size.** (Cutter) D. 2½ in. (65 mm).
    **Material.** Chromed steel, wooden handle.

(b) **Size.** (Cutter) 2¾ in. (70 mm) square.
    **Material.** Chromed steel, wooden handle.

Both these cutters make larger ravioli than is usually sold in shops, allowing plenty of room for the filling. The edges of the cutters are thick and bevelled to stamp a wide border with a decorative, zigzag pattern.

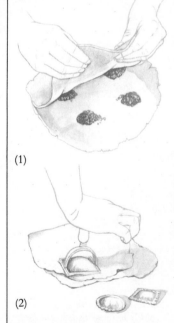

(1)

(2)

*Space the filling evenly in spoonfuls on a sheet of pasta and place a second sheet on top (1). Press the cutters over the mounds of filling (2) to cut out and seal the edges of ravioli.*

# Mezzalunas and hachoirs

(a) **Size.** (Blades) L. 5½ in. (140 mm).
**Material.** Stainless steel blades, wooden handles.

(b) **Size.** (Blade) L. 9½ in. (242 mm).
**Material.** Carbon steel blade, wooden handles, brass collars.

(c) **Size.** (Blade) L. 5 in. (127 mm).
**Material.** Stainless steel blade, beechwood handle and bowl.

Mezzalunas (half-moons) have larger blades than hachoirs and are used with a board to chop up meat and vegetables. Once you have mastered the knack of using one, you will find that you can chop things very quickly to various degrees of fineness.

The double-bladed mezzaluna (a) chops twice as fast as the single-bladed (b). There are also triple-bladed mezzalunas, which should chop three times as fast.

The French hachoir (hash-maker) and bowl (c) make the fine chopping of small quantities of herbs quick and easy. The curve of the bowl keeps the herbs together in the bottom and the blade fits snugly to the curve. These bowls wear away with use, so buy a thick-walled one, which will last longer, be more stable and less likely to split.

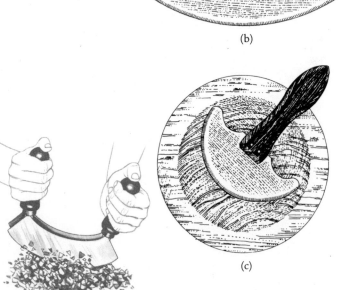

(a)

(b)

(c)

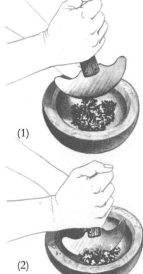

(1)

(2)

*The rocking movement used with a cook's knife to turn herbs and vegetables into a fine hash is employed with a mezzaluna. This two-handled mezzaluna reduces anything choppable to a mince. Use it with a good, thick chopping board.*

*Place a small quantity of herbs in the bowl and chop up and down holding the blade straight (1). Continue until the herbs are chopped as finely as you wish, turning the bowl from time to time as you work (2).*

(a) **Size.** L. 7 in. (178 mm).
**Material.** Stainless steel construction, plastic handle.

(b) **Size.** H. 8¼ in. (210 mm).
**Material.** Stainless steel blade, perspex dome, stainless steel and plastic body.

(c) **Size.** L. 5¾ in. (146 mm).
**Material.** Stainless steel blades, nylon, stainless steel and plastic body.

(d) **Size.** L. (6½ in. (165 mm).
**Material.** Tinned steel cutters, wire handle.

Four rows of teeth set at right angles to one another on a single axle rotate in the bottom of the hopper of the parsley cutter (a) as the handle is turned. This is a popular tool, but it does nothing that can't be done just as well with a good cook's knife. It minces parsley, mint, garlic and onion very finely, but wastes a fair proportion of the gratings which remain in the teeth.

The strong, stainless steel blade of the bouncing chopper (b) is

# Vegetable choppers and mincers

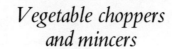

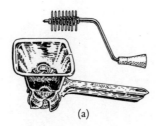

(a)

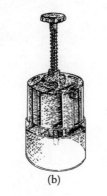

(b)

bent in a zigzag, making six sharp edges inside the plastic dome. As the food being chopped is kept inside the dome throughout the process, this tool is particularly useful when chopping onions. It deals with more food at one time than can parsley cutter (a) but it does tend to be noisy in use. Cut potatoes and onions and other large vegetables into chunks before chopping them.

The German universal mincer (c) is rolled to and fro over food on a board. It will mince nuts, candied peel, meat, fish, fruit and vegetables and cuts hard-boiled egg-whites into neat slices. It dismantles easily for cleaning when the axle of the five cutting wheels is pulled out.

Like all rotary mincers parsley cutter (d) should be used with a board. A hinged guard slots between the ten wheels of this little mincer to prevent bits of parsley flying all over the place. It can be used to mince other fresh herbs too.

Put some herbs into the parsley cutter and turn the handle. Four rows of teeth mince them up.

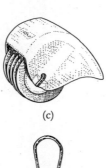

(c)

(d)

Roll the rotary mincer over fresh herbs to chop them up finely.

Place fruit, vegetables, meat or fish beneath the dome of the bouncing chopper and press the spring-loaded handle down sharply. The blade bounces up and down and rotates, chopping to a fine hash quickly and efficiently.

# Box graters

(a)

(b)

(c)

(d)

(e)

(a) **Size.** H. 7¾ in. (197 mm).
**Material.** Stainless steel.

(b) **Size.** H. 7½ in. (190 mm).
**Material.** Stainless steel.

(c) **Size.** H. 8 in. (204 mm).
**Material.** Stainless steel.

(d) **Size.** D. 8 in. (204 mm).
**Material.** Stainless steel.

(e) **Size.** H. 8½ in. (215 mm).
**Material.** Tinned steel.

Graters are basically little more than metal sheets punctured with rows of small holes. Graters (a), (b) and (c) give a choice of at least three surfaces, from fine to coarse and (a) and (b) also have slicing blades for things like cucumber. The broad base of (b) makes it steady in use. The round grater (d) has a useful bowl beneath for holding cheese raspings. The half-moon grater (e) has three types of surfaces (one on the back) and is difficult to clean without a long-handled brush.

*Clean graters under running water, brushing the food out from the back rather than the front.*

# Nutmeg graters

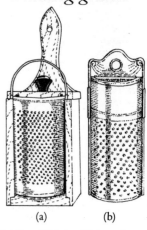

(a)

(b)

(a) **Size.** H. 8 in. (204 mm).
**Material.** Tinned steel, beechwood holder and drawer, plastic handle.

(b) **Size.** H. 6½ in. (165 mm).
**Material.** Tinned steel.

Both these nutmeg graters have drawers to store the nutmegs. In grater (a) the drawer stands vertically in a beechwood holder. You can slide the slightly curved grater out of the holder and grate directly over a dish; or leave it over the drawer, grating into it to collect the powder. The whole thing hangs up by the hole in the handle of the holder.

A secret drawer slides open at the back of grater (b) to reveal the stored nutmegs. The grating surface is also slightly curved.

# Cheese mill

**Size.** H. 3¾ in. (95 mm).
**Material.** Stainless steel grater, plastic body.

A double-walled cylinder with a grater fitted across the top has a domed lid that slots down between the walls. Twist the lid to and fro to grate cheese on to food at table.

## Flat graters

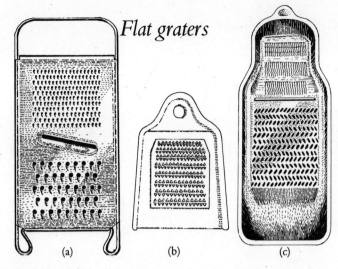

(a) **Size.** H. 10 in. (255 mm). **Material.** Stainless steel.

(b) **Size.** H. 6 in. (152 mm). **Material.** Porcelain.

(c) **Size.** H. 8¾ in. (223 mm). **Material.** Anodized aluminium.

Flat graters take up little space and are easier to clean than other types.

Grater (a) has two types of surfaces, with a slicing blade between them on the reverse side. It has wire feet and a handle.

The Japanese grater (b) is made of ¼ in. (6 mm) thick, white porcelain. It has eight rows of teeth, shaped like tiny pyramids, ranged in double lines with one line grating upwards and one downwards. It is intended for grating fresh ginger, Japanese radish (daikon) and nutmeg.

The oriental grater (c) has very sharp teeth and a lip at the base to catch the juice, when grating such things as fresh ginger.

Use a pastry brush to clear oily or sticky raspings, such as lemon zest, from the teeth of a grater. A quick brush over the surface, back and front, will salvage a considerable quantity.

## Corn cutters

(a) **Size.** L. 5 in. (127 mm). **Material.** Tinned steel.

(b) **Size.** L. 17 in. (430 mm). **Material.** Stainless steel.

The spade-shaped corn cutter (a) has five teeth projecting from the back of the blade and its edge is bent over to form a scraper. The teeth score and split the soft

kernels for cream-style corn and, if reversed, the edge scrapes them off the cob whole.

Corn cutter (b) is made to deal with large quantities of corn. This gutter-shaped tool has teeth and a 1 in. (25 mm) wide blade set two-thirds of the way along its length. You take the guard off the teeth to make cream-style corn. If you want to strip whole kernels, you cover the teeth with the guard and raise the blade.

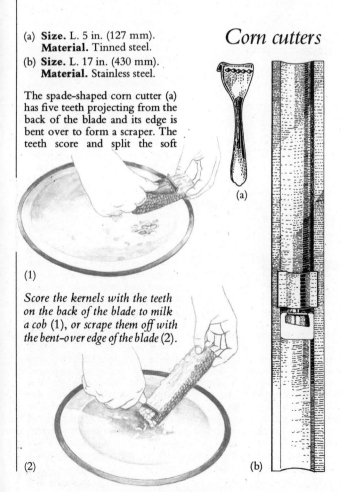

*Score the kernels with the teeth on the back of the blade to milk a cob (1), or scrape them off with the bent-over edge of the blade (2).*

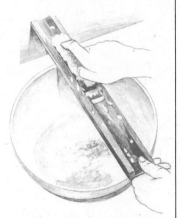

*Lay the cutter over a bowl and push the cob to be milked, small end first, into the channel and down over the teeth and blade.*

**Size.** H. 7 in. (178 mm).
**Material.** Stainless steel cutter, alloy steel body, wooden handle.

Eight toothed discs riveted to a central core form a spiky, seg-mented ball 2 in. (50 mm) in diameter on this grater. The ball is fixed to a shaft turned with a bright red handle. Made in India, where freshly shredded coconut is often required to complete a dish, this is a delightful tool to use. It produces quantities of milky shreds very quickly. You have to clean these from between the blades at intervals, using the point of a knife, as they tend to clog.

## Coconut grater

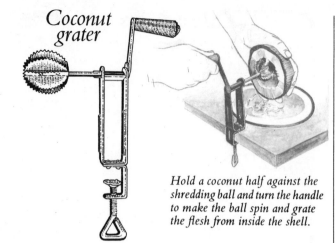

*Hold a coconut half against the shredding ball and turn the handle to make the ball spin and grate the flesh from inside the shell.*

## Rotary graters

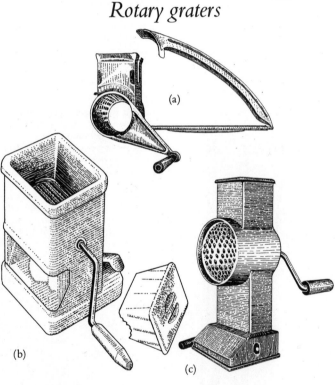

(a)

(b)

(c)

(a) **Size.** L. 7½ in. (190 mm).
   **Material.** Tinned steel.
(b) **Size.** H. 8 in. (204 mm).
   **Material.** Stainless steel teeth, plastic case, rubber suction-pad base.
(c) **Size.** H. 7½ in. (190 mm).
   **Material.** Stainless steel grater and handle, plastic body, rubber suction-pad base.

Rotary graters are extremely useful if you like to use up scraps of food by grating them for garnishes or flavourings. As the grating surface is inside a hopper and the food is pressed upon it with a pusher, there is no risk to your fingers and very tiny pieces of food are grated away almost completely. They are also a safe type of grater for children to use when helping with the cooking.

Grater (a) is invaluable for grating cheese, particularly hard cheese, or small scraps of cheese, but it will also grate nuts and chocolate. Put the food to be grated in the hopper and press it in place with the curved, spade-like arm. Hold the grater over a bowl – or directly over the dish to be garnished – and turn the handle of the grating cylinder. Cylinders for slicing and grating more coarsely are available as extras and there is also a version with a plastic body.

The cheese grater (b) excels at rasping parmesan and other hard cheese, and it will also grate apples, stale bread, nuts, raw carrot and chocolate. The grater takes the form of rows of shark-like teeth set in a plastic drum 2½ in. (65 mm) in diameter, which is turned by a handle. The raspings fall through into a transparent drawer beneath the drum. The body is made of strong plastic and is easily dismantled for washing, as removing the handle releases the axle and the drum. The lid of the hopper acts as a pusher for small scraps of food and also as an airtight container for little bits of hard cheese. The suction pad is very strong.

Not only almonds, but other nuts, hard cheese and chocolate can be rasped finely in the Swedish almond grater (c). It is attractive to look at and well made. The barrel-shaped grater 2 in. (50 mm) in diameter is turned by a detach-able handle. The plastic lid forms a pusher for scraps as well as a small storage box.

# Vegetable shredders

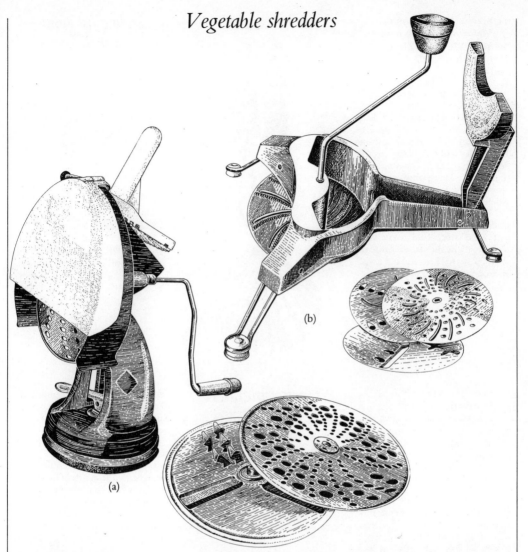

(b)

(a)

(a) **Size.** H. 12 in. (305 mm).
**Material.** Stainless steel
cutting discs, plastic body,
rubber suction-pad base.

(b) **Size.** L. 10½ in. (267 mm).
**Material.** Tinned steel
cutting discs, plastic body.

These vegetable shredders have all
the advantages of rotary graters,
but can deal with far larger pieces
of food. They also have a choice
of grating surfaces – something
not always offered by the smaller
graters. They are the manual
forerunners of electric food-
processors and have become a
standard piece of equipment in the
kitchens of those who dislike (or
can't afford) electric machinery.

Shredder (a) is made in Italy of
robust plastic. It is simple to use
and easy to clean. It works beautifully for fine shreds but not so
well for larger pieces, making
ragged slices of cucumber and
somewhat uneven chips. It also
tends to spray bits to both sides
rather than dropping them all
into a neat heap.

Good features of this tool are
the hinged cutting-guard which
holds all three cutting-discs when
not in use; the hopper, which is
large enough to take a biggish
potato without having to cut it up
first; and the suction base, which
is strong enough to hold the tool
firmly on a smooth surface while
considerable pressure is being

exerted on the cutter and handle.
There is a choice of six cutting
edges as each disc is reversible.

The vegetable shredder (b) is
simple to operate, inexpensive,
strongly made and quick. Four
slotted discs give a choice of slices,
or three thicknesses of shred. They
slide into the base of the
hopper and are turned by the
plastic-handled crank, which acts
as an axle and fixes the selected
disc in place. The food is pressed
on to the cutting discs by the
hinged lid of the hopper.

This machine takes one medium-sized potato at a time; anything larger must be cut to fit the
hopper. It is easily dismantled for
washing and storing.

(a) **Size.** L. 8 in. (204 mm).
**Material.** Cast aluminium.
(b) **Size.** W. 5 in. (127 mm).
**Material:** Shell.

The reverse of the pretty pike-shaped scaler (a) is studded with metal pegs set closely together. The whole thing is curved slightly to follow the contours of any largish fish which needs scaling. The scales collect between the pegs and need to be carefully rinsed out. Hang this scaler up where it will look decorative when not in use.

The sharp, crinkled edge of the scallop shell (b) makes an excellent (and free) fish scaler and scraper. It fits the hand comfortably, is easy to clean and has a nice appropriateness for the job.

## Fish scalers

(a)

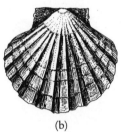

(b)

## Scaling fish with a shell

*Grip the fish firmly by the tail and use the scaler like a brush, working from the tail towards the head against the scales.*

(a) **Size.** H. 4¾ in. (120 mm).
**Material.** Nickel-plated cutters, wooden handle.
(b) **Size.** H. 5 in. (127 mm).
**Material.** Stainless steel wires, wooden handle.

These tools quickly and coolly reduce cut-up fat and sifted flour to the desired consistency for pastry making (a mixture resembling fine breadcrumbs). They can, of course, be used for any recipe where fat has to be rubbed into flour.

Blender (a) is robustly made and efficient. As its five steel cutters are inflexible, you can exert heavy pressure to cut through the hardest lumps of cooking fat. Some users might wish for a thumb-rest on this blender as the handle is rather short.

Six steel wires form the cutters on blender (b). They slice through softened fat very efficiently but, being flexible, constant use can make the wires spring from the handle – releasing retaining nuts

## Pastry blender

(a)

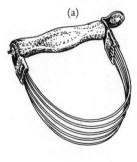

(b)

and washers into the mixture. This blender has a thumb-rest but as the handle is comfortably wide it is not strictly necessary.

With a pastry blender you can deal with interruptions while pastry making without having to first clean your hands of flour and fat. They can be useful tools particularly if you have very warm hands, although lacking a pastry blender you can make do with two table knives or a large fork.

*Use the pastry blender with a bouncing action, mixing the ingredients with it and cutting into the larger pieces of fat as you do so.*

(a) **Size.** L. 7 in. (178 mm).
**Material.** Stainless steel
blade, rosewood handle.
(b) **Size.** L. 8 in. (204 mm).
**Material.** Boxwood.

Butter curls may have rather
strong associations with seaside
boarding-houses and pretentious
restaurants for some people, but
they are quite fun to make (if you
have time) and are a pretty way of
serving butter for a special occasion.

Butter curler (a) has a deeply
serrated blade, curved like a shepherd's crook. It curls butter into
little ribbed cowrie-shell shapes.

The wooden curler (b) makes
long, deeply ribbed rolls of butter.
It is used on the wide side of a
block of butter. Lay the whole
length of the ribbed blade across
the block and draw it towards you.

The butter should be chilled
(not rock hard) for making butter
curls. Dip the curler in a glass of

## Butter curlers

(a)

(b)

hot water from time to time as
you work, but keep the block of
butter and curls cool. In hot
weather the curls can be served
on a bed of crushed ice.

*Turn a block of butter on edge to
make butter curls with the crook-
bladed curler. Draw the blade
towards you, toothed side down,
along the length of the block.*

(a) **Size.** 9¾ in. (248 mm).
**Material.** Nickel-plated
steel ends, plastic handle.
(b) **Size.** L. 6 in. (152 mm).
**Material.** Cast aluminium.
(c) **Size.** L. 5 in. (127 mm).
**Material.** Cast aluminium.
(d) **Size.** L. 8 in. (204 mm).
**Material.** Stainless steel.

These tools have more than one
use and will appeal to people who
like spending their money on
gadgets. However all too often
with tools like these the more
multi the purpose the less well
they work. Most kitchen drawers
contain at least one of these tools
– it usually comes irritatingly to
hand just when you are hurriedly
seeking a completely different
implement of similar size.

Gadgets like these tend to do
the same kind of work–butter
curling and bottle opening being
the most common combination.
Those shown here are more
versatile than most.

Gadget (a) curls butter, scoops
out tomatoes, cuts little balls out

## Multi-purpose gadgets

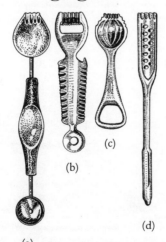

(a)

(b)

(c)

(d)

of melon or cheese and gouges the
cores from halved apples or pears.
Unlike the other gadgets in this
group it has a comfortably shaped
plastic handle and is pleasant to
hold.

Gadget (b) curls butter into
long rolls or little shells, makes
butter or melon balls and cuts
decorative grooves in butter or
icing. It also takes off bottle caps
and opens cans.

The less versatile gadget (c)
just curls butter, scoops out tomatoes and opens bottles.

Use them both as butter curlers
or bottle openers–the jobs they
do best. With the multi-purpose
tool (d) you can core apples–and
peel them if you are left-handed
(the peeling slot only works that
way). With the other end, by
turning the blade on its back, you
can shred vegetables; by turning
it on its side you can scale fish and
with the end you can curl butter.
As you are gripping some kind of
cutting edge, whichever way you
hold this gadget, it is not a very
comfortable tool to use–but it is
versatile and cheap.

# POUNDING, PRESSING AND PURÉEING TOOLS

These manual tools can reduce most food, hard or soft, cooked or raw, to a hash, mince, purée, paste or powder. Some break up and flatten fibrous foods and extract juices. They change the texture of food by pounding it between two hard surfaces, by pressing it, or by passing it through some sort of cutter, grid or mesh.

There are plenty of occasions calling for food to be processed this way – you may want to make baby food, a smooth vegetable soup, a powder or a paste of freshly roasted spices or a mound of pale pink chestnut purée. There are dozens of tools designed for any of these jobs.

Some, like sieves or pestles and mortars, have been in use in the kitchen for hundreds of years; others, like food mills, were among the first mechanical tools. These tools have remained virtually unchanged in design, proving that they are ideally suited to their work.

## Sieves and pestles and mortars
Not only are these tools ancient in origin, but they are also found throughout the world – even in the most primitive and simply furnished kitchens. The materials from which they are made differ according to the natural resources available. In parts of Africa sieves are most delicately woven of grass and grain stems, while in Central America palm leaf fibres and reeds are used. The shape and design of all these tools are always remarkably similar, having evolved slowly to the same pattern as generations of cooks produced and modified tools to meet the same specific purposes.

While electrical food processors have taken much of the drudgery out of food preparation, especially where sieving and chopping need to be done, manual implements still have certain advantages over electrical gadgets. They cost less; are less likely to go wrong; they are easier to control (one second too long with an electric blender and your rough pâté becomes an irretrievable cream); and they still work in a power cut.

## The kitchen basics
Of the tools in this section the following are possibly the most useful: a lemon squeezer, a pestle and mortar, a potato masher, a food mill and a tamis or a chinois. Others are not so essential. If you are thinking of buying some of them, keep a sharp look-out for them on second-hand stalls and at jumble sales. Often when someone buys a modern electric food processor, a good old-fashioned masher, food mill, sieve or chinois gets thrown out. These rejects, often very well made with lots of useful life left in them, are well worth having.

*An old-fashioned method of pressing the whey from curds in cheese-making. The curds were put in a tammy cloth which was then twisted to wring out the whey.*

# Pounders and tenderizers

(a) **Size.** L. 12½ in. (317 mm).
**Weight.** 1 lb (453 g).
**Material.** Wood.

(b) **Size.** L. 10 in. (255 mm).
**Weight.** 1 lb 10 oz (737 g).
**Material.** Carbon steel.

(c) **Size.** L. 13 in. (330 mm).
**Weight.** 7 oz (198 g).
**Material.** Wooden head, chromed steel face.

(d) **Size.** L. 9½ in. (242 mm).
**Weight.** 14 oz (397 g).
**Material.** Chromed steel, with stainless steel teeth.

(e) **Size.** L. 6 in. (152 mm).
**Material.** Stainless steel blades, plastic body.

Affectionately referred to as "bashers" by most cooks, these tools deal with foods that need to be beaten flat, crushed or cracked. They are therefore heavy, strongly made and smooth on one side if not actually flat. They tenderize meat by breaking up and bruising the tough fibres.

Pounders and tenderizers, used to flatten and enlarge escalopes or fillets of meat, are particularly liked by restaurateurs wishing to give customers an impression of generous helpings. These tools should never be used on really tender meat. If you want thin escalopes, ask the butcher to cut them that way; or if the meat is so tough that it actually needs beating, cook it differently. There is a slower, but culinarily superior, method of tenderizing the very tough cuts of meat—a long, care-ful marinading, followed by leisurely cooking.

The rectangular pounder (a) is really efficient and will serve generations of cooks in a kitchen with very little wear to show for it. It is weighty enough to tackle any pounding job—yet it is balanced so well that it can also be used, like the smaller mallet-style pounders, for cracking nuts and crab claws and shattering ice.

The meat bat (b) has one flat face and two sharp edges, useful for trimming meat after it has been flattened. It is ideal for tenderizing and flattening scal-lopini of steak, veal or chicken.

You can also flatten meat with the fluted steel face on one end of the hammer-shaped head of mallet (c) and bruise and break the fibres of tough steak with the toothed, wooden end. The flat side of the head is good for cracking nuts or crushing ice.

A fairly barbaric instrument, heavy for its size and relatively expensive, the steak hammer (d) is designed to flatten steak with its pyramid-shaped studs, then ten-derize it with its sharp, steel blades. It should be reserved for very tough or thick cuts of steak.

Five viciously toothed wheels do the work of the rotary tender-izer (e). It is rolled to and fro across any steak, escalope or slice of liver, minutely cutting into the fibres. Useful only for the very toughest cuts of meat, this ten-derizer can reduce tender meat to a bleeding mess.

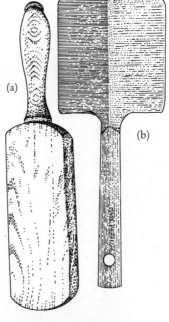

(a)

(b)

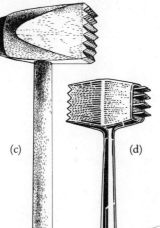

(c)

(d)

*Tenderize steak between sheets of waxed paper by bashing it with a pounder. The paper prevents the meat fibres sticking to the pounder.*

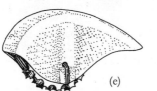

(e)

*Put ice cubes in a polythene bag before crushing them with a heavy pounder. This keeps the chips together and makes them easy to transfer to an ice bucket.*

(a) **Size.** (Mortar) D. 8 in.
(204 mm), (Pestle) L. 9 in.
(230 mm).
**Material.** Wood.

(b) **Size.** (Mortar) D. 3½ in.
(90 mm), (Pestle) L. 5½ in.
(140 mm).
**Material.** Beechwood.

(c) **Size.** (Mortar) D. 6¾ in.
(172 mm), (Pestle) L. 9 in.
(230 mm).
**Material.** Unglazed
porcelain, beechwood
handle on pestle.

(d) **Size.** (Mortar) D. 5¾ in.
(146 mm), (Pestle) L. 6¼ in.
(160 mm).
**Material.** Porcelain.

(e) **Size.** (Mortar) D. 4¼ in.
(107 mm), (Pestle) L. 5¾ in.
(146 mm).
**Material.** Glass.

(f) **Size.** (Mortar) D. 4¼ in.
(107 mm), (Pestle) L. 8 in.
(204 mm).
**Material.** Brass.

(g) **Size.** (Mortar) D. 2¾ in.
(70 mm), (Pestle) L. 5½ in.
(140 mm).
**Material.** Stainless steel.

(h) **Size.** (Mortar) D. 7¼ in.
(185 mm), (Pestle) L. 7 in.
(178 mm).
**Material.** Porcelain mortar,
wooden pestle.

(i) **Size.** (Mortar) D. 10¼ in.
(260 mm), (Pestle) L. 14¼ in.
(362 mm).
**Material.** Stone mortar,
wooden pestle.

(j) **Size.** (Curry stone) L. 13¾ in.
(350 mm), (Roller) L. 7 in.
(178 mm).
**Material.** Stone.

For grinding small quantities a
pestle and mortar are hard to beat.
Don't be tempted to over-fill the
mortar, it works best when it is
less than half full. Put the mortar
either in your lap or on a firm
surface which is low enough to
let you get the right amount of
pressure on the pestle. Then work
the pestle round and round until
you have a paste or powder of the
right consistency. You can speed
up the process by adding some
gritty substance, either coarse salt
or granulated sugar – the recipe is
bound to call for one or the other.

The wooden mortars (a) and (b)
have a good texture for pulveri-
zing hard, brittle foodstuffs that

# Pestles and mortars

## Japanese mortar

*With the pestle, press the seeds
against the pattern of sharp ridges
inside the mortar. Work the
pestle round and round as you
do so to crush them.*

## Curry stone

*Push the roller across the spices,
with a grinding action. With a
flick of your wrists pull the roller
back over them. Don't roll it
over them like a rolling pin.*

cannot be easily milled or grated –
such things as bay leaves, cinna-
mon sticks, coriander seeds, dried
chillies and tamarinds. The disadvantage of wooden mortars is
that some oily or juicy substances
– garlic or parsley for example –
tend to penetrate the wood, and
their smell, flavour and colour
may linger even after the most
thorough scrubbing.

Glass and porcelain pestles and
mortars can be much more easily
cleaned than wooden ones and
once the pounding is done, the
mortar can be used to take other
liquid additions, if you want to
make a paste or a sauce. The
unglazed porcelain mortar (c) has
a fine, rough surface, is imperme-
able and non-staining. The mortar
is lipped for easy pouring. This
type of mortar, with its rough
texture can be used to grind dry
foods as well as moist ones, unlike
the glazed porcelain mortar (d),
which is much too smooth for
grinding hard, dry things. Like
the glass mortar (e) it is best kept
for such jobs as pounding small
quantities of ham, poultry, salmon
or smoked fish into pastes with
lemon juice or melted butter.
Pounding in this way breaks
down the fibres of these foods.

The Indian pestles and mortars
(f) and (g) are used to process small
quantities of spice when a recipe
only requires a little addition. For
masala – the combination of spices,
herbs and seasonings which is
ground daily and is basic to Indian
cookery – the large stone mortar
(i) or the curry stone (j) is used.

The bowl of the Japanese pestle
and mortar (h) is glazed only on
the outside and, unlike other
mortars, its shape is open and
shallow. The pestle is wooden.
This combination works very
well for grinding small oily seeds
such as sesame. The fine, sharp
ridges on the inside of the bowl
hold the seeds against the pestle.

The heavy stone mortar (i) and
curry stone (j) are used in India to
make masala using water (either
fresh or salted), coconut or
tamarind water, vinegar or lime
or lemon juice – according to the
recipe. The ingredients are
crushed with a roller to a paste of
spices and herbs for curries. A
roasted masala can also be dry-
ground on the stone.

# Tamis and champignons

(a)

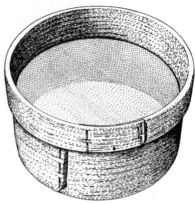

(b)

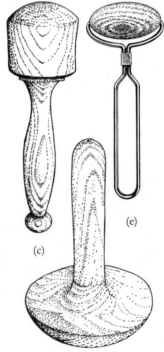

(c)

(d)

(e)

(a) **Size.** D. 11½ in. (292 mm).
**Material.** Wooden rim, nylon mesh.

(b) **Size.** D. 8¼ in. (210 mm).
**Material.** Wooden rim, tinned wire mesh.

(c) **Size.** L. 9¼ in. (235 mm).
**Material.** Beechwood.

(d) **Size.** L. 8 in. (204 mm).
**Material.** Beechwood.

(e) **Size.** L. 8½ in. (215 mm).
**Material.** Wooden ball, tinned wire handle.

If you want to make a purée of fibrous or seed-filled fruits or vegetables, you need a tool that is strong enough to allow the soft parts to be pushed through its mesh, but fine enough to retain any firm or stringy bits.

Wooden, drum-shaped sieves with a flat mesh, like sieves (a) and (b), are known by their French name, tamis (drum). Wooden champignons (or mushrooms, so called because of their shape) are used to press the food through them. Tamis range in size from 6 in. (152 mm) to 16 in (405 mm) and the mesh, which can be wire or nylon, comes in different gauges.

The mesh is stretched like the skin of a drum over the inner deeper hoop and held in place by the outer, shallower hoop. A tamis should be used with the inner hoop uppermost, firstly because it holds more and secondly so that the bowl below will rest on the hoop rather than the mesh.

Some chefs prefer to stand the tamis on a tray (if the food is not too liquid) when making a large quantity of purée. This is much more stable than putting it over a pan or bowl and is one of the advantages of using a tamis. It can also be used as a steamer, if you can find a pan and lid that will fit it exactly, and as a strainer.

A nylon mesh is more resilient than wire and keèps its shape better. It is the best mesh to use for fruit purées, which are discoloured and tainted by wire. A wire mesh is sharper and stronger than nylon, but will rust if not dried carefully. A medium coarse mesh is best for purées.

Champignons like (c) and (d) can be used as mashers to reduce food to a pulp, as well as pestles to press food through a tamis. The drum-headed champignon (c) fits particularly well round the edges of a tamis, while the broad, flat head of champignon (d) makes a useful press when straining cooked cabbage in a colander. Both of these wooden champignons can be used to flatten fillets of meat, steak or chicken breasts.

The wooden roller (e) is used solely with bowl sieves. You roll it in every direction until everything that will go through the mesh has done so.

# Chinois and ladle

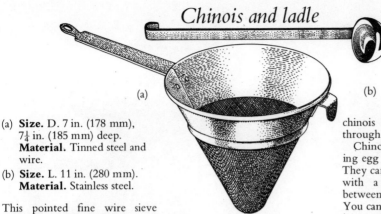

(a)

(b)

(a) **Size.** D. 7 in. (178 mm),
7¼ in. (185 mm) deep.
**Material.** Tinned steel and
wire.

(b) **Size.** L. 11 in. (280 mm).
**Material.** Stainless steel.

This pointed fine wire sieve
is called a chinois, because of
its supposed resemblance to a
Chinese coolie's hat. The one
shown here (a) has an extremely
fine mesh woven in a twill of
tinned steel wire. It strains as
finely as cheesecloth.

A chinois will serve to make
purées of vegetables, as long as
you have a tapered or cylindrical
pestle, or a ladle, such as (b), small
enough to fit the very bottom of
the sieve. You stand the chinois
over a tall pan, pour the food to
be puréed into it and work the
ladle up and down inside the

chinois so that the food passes
through slowly.

Chinois are used also for straining egg custards and fine sauces.
They can be helped on their way
with a balloon whisk rolled
between the palms of your hands.
You can strain gravy very neatly
into a gravy-boat through a
chinois, as the conical shape directs
the liquid to run from the bottom.

If you want a very clear stock,
don't be tempted to hurry the
process up, but let the liquid drip
slowly through a fine chinois. All
solids will sink to the bottom of
the sieve and the liquid will filter
through the mesh above.

This chinois has a hook to
steady it on the rim of a large
bowl or pan. It is best, for ease and
efficiency, to use a chinois over a
pan which is at least 2 in. (50 mm)
deeper than the sieve itself.

# Rotating ball sieve

**Size.** D. 7¼ in. (185 mm),
3½ in. (90 mm) deep.
**Material.** Tinned steel body,
sieve and fittings, plastic handle,
wooden roller.

This bowl-shaped wire sieve
comes with a patent mashing
attachment, which can be easily
clipped on when required. It is
used for making purées of cooked
vegetables.

The mashing attachment consists of an egg-shaped wooden
roller and a tinned steel blade
which rotates inside the sieve as

you turn a crank. The roller
squashes the food and presses it
through the mesh, while the blade
scrapes up whatever is left on the
sides of the sieve, returning it to
the roller. This only works well
with soft foods. It is not good
for processing vegetables with a
lot of fibre, as the stringy bits tend
to wrap themselves round the
central spindle on the attachment.

Also designed for use with bowl
sieves, the wooden roller (opposite) does the same work as the
mashing attachment with far less
bother.

# Food mills

(a)

(b)

(a) **Size.** Mill D. $9\frac{1}{2}$ in.
(242 mm), $6\frac{1}{2}$ in. deep.
**Material.** Tinned steel body
and sieving discs, wooden
handle.

(b) **Size.** H. $9\frac{1}{2}$ in. (242 mm).
**Material.** Plastic body and
bowl, stainless steel blades
and crank, rubber suction
pad base.

The food mill (a) could be described as a mechanical sieve. It is
time-saving when preparing
soups and all sorts of purées and is
easy to assemble. You just fit one
of three sieving discs (coarse,
medium and fine) into the open
base of the bowl-shaped hopper.
There are several versions of this
mill, some with plastic bodies,
including one designed especially
for preparing baby food.

The food is pushed through the
sieve by a spring-loaded, semi-
circular blade of tinned steel,
which is clipped in place to press
down hard on the sieve. It revolves on the surface of the sieve
as the central crank is turned.
Three corrugated feet on the base
keep the mill in place on top of a
pan. You hold it steady with the
handle on the side.

*This well-designed food mill
sieves the pulp and ejects the
waste fibre through a spout on
the side of the hopper, as the
crank is turned. The waste can
be processed again to extract as
much pulp as possible.*

This is a very popular piece of
kitchen equipment, of proved
efficiency, bridging the gap between the tamis and the electric
blender. It is easier to use than a
tamis and because you can select
sieves of different coarseness you
can make purées of exactly the
right texture for your purpose.

The Italian food mill (b) is
designed to purée tomatoes – its
makers claim that it can process
40 to 60 lb. (18 to 27 kg) in one
hour. With it you can make a very
good – rich, pulpy and seedless –
tomato sauce.

It works rather like an old-
fashioned mangle, with a roller in
the hopper feeding the sieve. As
you turn the handle the food is
pushed down against the sieve
and forced through it by the
spring-loaded blades on the roller.
The pulp runs out into a shallow
bowl. The waste is flicked out
through a spout at the side of the
mill, where it is caught in a basin.
It can then be returned to the
hopper for further pressing.

A strong suction pad on the base
of the machine holds the mill
firmly in place so long as the work
top has a very level (preferably
laminated plastic) surface.

# Mashers and ricers

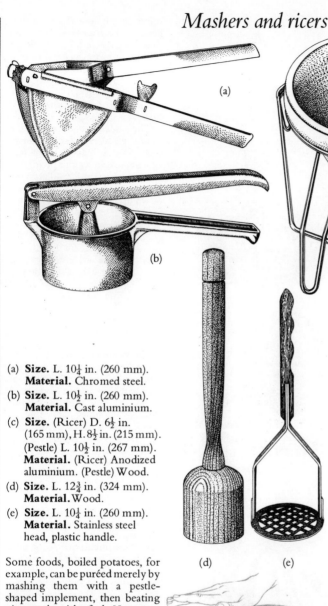

(a)

(b)

(c)

(d)          (e)

(a) **Size.** L. 10¼ in. (260 mm).
**Material.** Chromed steel.
(b) **Size.** L. 10½ in. (260 mm).
**Material.** Cast aluminium.
(c) **Size.** (Ricer) D. 6½ in.
(165 mm), H. 8½ in. (215 mm).
(Pestle) L. 10½ in. (267 mm).
**Material.** (Ricer) Anodized
aluminium. (Pestle) Wood.
(d) **Size.** L. 12¾ in. (324 mm).
**Material.** Wood.
(e) **Size.** L. 10¼ in. (260 mm).
**Material.** Stainless steel
head, plastic handle.

Some foods, boiled potatoes, for
example, can be puréed merely by
mashing them with a pestle-
shaped implement, then beating
vigorously with a fork. However,
lighter, fluffier results are achieved
if the food is pressed through a
mesh or cutting grid.

Ricers are useful for making
this kind of dryish purée. Not just
potatoes but peeled, cored and
cooked apples and other fruit, or
peeled and cooked root vegetables, such as parsnips, carrots and
turnips, can be pressed through
potato ricers, emerging like little
grains of soft rice, hence the name
of this tool.

The V-shaped bucket on ricer
(a) is the most finely perforated

*Force cooked potato through the
holes in the conical ricer, by
rolling the pestle round the rim,
keeping the end in the point.*

of the three ricers shown. This
makes the ricing process slow as
more effort is needed to process
the potato which is shot out
sideways, rather untidily, as well
as downwards. Ricer (b) has a
hinged pusher attached to the
upper handle, which unlike the
press on ricer (a) bears directly
down on the potato, forcing it
quickly through the holes in the
base of the bucket. This is the
neater ricer of the two, and
would be useful when making a
Mont Blanc as the chestnut purée
falls straight down from the ricer.

The conical ricer (c) should be
used with a three-legged stand
which can be placed over a pan or
on a dish. You use a pestle with this
ricer and it works very efficiently
producing very fine grains.

An advantage of the mashers
(d) and (e) is that the vegetables
can be quickly mashed in the saucepan in which they were cooked.
The wooden masher (d) can also
be used as a pounder or as a pestle
in conjunction with a tamis. The
patent masher (e), like masher (d),
is used for puréeing potatoes and
other root vegetables. Neither are
as efficient as a ricer for making
purées, but both are cheap, easy
to use and to clean and likely to
last a lifetime.

(a) **Size.** L. 6 in. (152 mm).
**Material.** Beechwood.

(b) **Size.** D. 6 in. (152 mm).
**Material.** Glass.

(c) **Size.** H. $6\frac{3}{4}$ in. (172 mm).
**Material.** Plastic press,
glass storage jar.

(d) **Size.** H. 10 in. (255 mm).
**Material.** Plastic body,
electric motor.

(e) **Size.** L. $7\frac{1}{2}$ in. (190 mm).
**Material.** Wood.

(f) **Size.** L. $7\frac{1}{2}$ in. (190 mm).
**Material.** Cast aluminium.

(g) **Size.** L. 10 in. (255 mm).
**Material.** Cast aluminium.

(h) **Size.** H. 8 in. (204 mm).
**Material.** Stove enamelled
aluminium body. Nylon
press.

A citrus press should extract the juice from the fruit without giving you a good measure of pulp, pith and pips as well. They come in various shapes. Some have a ridged dome on which the halved orange, lemon, lime or grapefruit is pressed cut-face down to squeeze out the juice. Others press the dome shape into the half-fruit itself.

The traditional wooden citrus reamer (a) is not the most efficient of juicers, but it is an attractive tool of centuries' old design. You cut off the end of a lemon or orange and, holding it over a basin, press the reamer into it, twisting it this way and that to extract the juice.

The glass lemon squeezer (b) is another juicer of traditional pattern. The halved fruit is pressed on to the dome of the squeezer and is twisted to and fro. Pointed teeth prevent the pips joining the juice in the gutter below the rim. The juice is poured off through the lip on one side.

The simple design of juicer (c) incorporates a storage jar for the juice, which holds $\frac{3}{4}$ pt (0·4 ℓ). You put a citrus half—this press can manage a small grapefruit— on to the squeezer and press the top down, turning it back and forth. The juice strains into the jar. It can be poured straight from the container, or be kept in the jar in the refrigerator until needed.

The electric press (d) works exactly like the traditional squeezer (b), except that once

## Citrus juicers

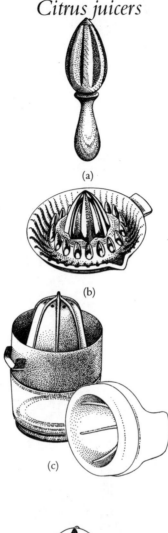

(a)

(b)

(c)

(d)

switched on, the dome rotates beneath the fruit as soon as you press down on it. It has a gutter to trap any pips and a choice of two containers. The large basin holds just under $1\frac{1}{2}$ pt (0·8 ℓ). The smaller tray-shaped one allows the juice to flow directly into a glass.

The Indian lime press (e) is rather primitive, but performs well. Put a halved lime, face downwards, over the perforated recess on one handle and press the smooth dome on the other handle down upon it. This turns the lime inside out as it presses out the juice. It is too small for lemons.

Similar in its action to the Indian squeezer, but larger, the Mexican lime and lemon press (f) has two ladle-like handles hinged together. Once again the halved fruit is put in the perforated lower half, cut-side down. It can also deal with small oranges.

Citrus press (g) works slightly differently from presses (e) and (f), but looks rather similar. There is a ring of spikes in the bottom of the lower cup. The halved fruit fits in here, cut-side up. When the fruit is pressed, the juice flows out through the holes pierced in the peel by the spokes below. With the handles held together you can pour the juice out through the spout on the lower cup. This press works very well on lemons and oranges, but it is too small for large grapefruit.

Impressive in appearance, but rather disappointing in action, the robot-like press (h) takes considerable manual effort to operate. The halved fruit is placed on the squeezer and you pull the handle forward to bring the upper press down upon it. This gadget is fiddly to dismantle and wash and less efficient than the cheaper, more old-fashioned squeezers shown here.

## Small juicers

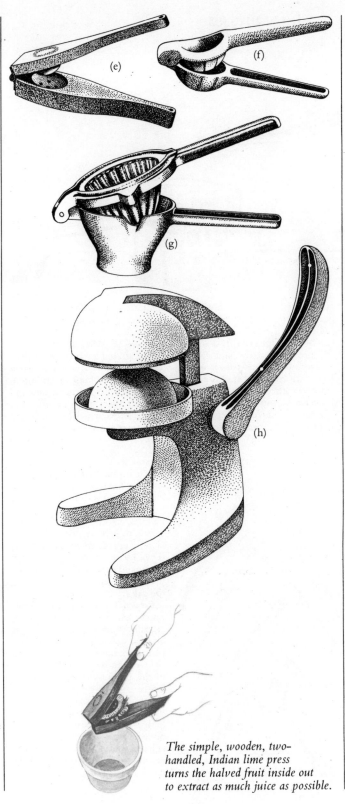

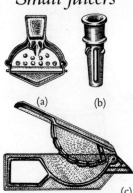

(a)          (b)

(c)

(a) **Size.** L. 2½ in. (65 mm).
**Material.** Stainless steel.

(b) **Size.** L. 3 in. (75 mm).
**Material.** Cast aluminium.

(c) **Size.** L. 5¾ in. (146 mm).
**Material.** Plastic.

Useful in their way but not exactly essential, these gadgets are designed to extract one or two drops only of lemon, lime or orange juice.

Juicer (a) takes one lemon segment, which fits neatly between its two studded pressing faces. As you squeeze these together the juice runs from a lip below. It is an economical way of providing lemon juice at table – and prevents the guests getting their fingers sticky.

The spouted reamer (b) can be screwed into a lemon or orange, which, when squeezed, will exude its juice down the spout. You can safely leave it in the fruit until you need it again.

Juicer (c), of clear plastic, presses half a slice of lemon very efficiently. The juice pours from a spout at one end. It is not so compact or attractive as juicer (a).

*The simple, wooden, two-handled, Indian lime press turns the halved fruit inside out to extract as much juice as possible.*

*Place the slice, peel down, in the grooved handle and bring the notched press firmly down on it.*

95

# Juice presses

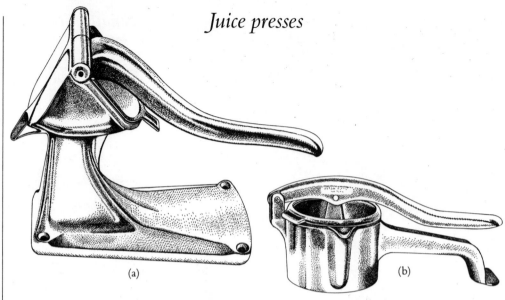

(a)

(b)

(a) **Size.** L. 10½ in. (267 mm).
**Material.** Cast aluminium.

(b) **Size.** H. 8½ in. (215 mm).
**Material.** Cast aluminium.

These juice presses look like potato ricers without perforations. Any kind of juicy fruit can be pressed in them, though large stones should, of course, be removed first. Apples and pears

and other hard fruits should be peeled, cored and grated before pressing.

The large juicer (a) is designed for professional use and can be screwed to a work-top. It works best with citrus fruit, although it can press other fruit. Put the citrus halves into the bucket face first against the ridged sleeve. Because the peel of the fruit is also pressed,

the juice has a rather bitter tang. It is however easier to use than juicer (b).

Juicer (b) extracts juice from finely grated carrots and celery and from meat, if it is still warm after light poaching or grilling in one piece. It is a neat, strong and efficient juicer, with a perforated, ridged sleeve which can be turned to extract more juice.

# Garlic presses

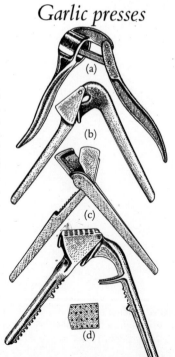

(a)

(b)

(c)

(d)

(a) **Size.** 6 in. (152 mm).
(b) **Size.** 6 in. (152 mm).
(c) **Size.** 6¼ in. (160 mm).
(d) **Size.** 6 in. (152 mm).
**Material.** All cast aluminium.

Garlic presses look rather like potato ricers, and work in much the same way. A garlic clove can be pressed, peeled or unpeeled. A gentle first press with the skin attached to the garlic clove will give you only its juice, useful if you want just a hint of that flavour or if you find raw garlic indigestible; further pressing forces the garlic through the holes in shreds.

A hinged pusher, attached to the upper handle of garlic press (a) acts like a little piston, driving the clove with even pressure through the fine holes in the container. In press (b) the square pusher is cast in one with the upper handle. The holes in the container of press (a)

are smaller than those of press (b), which means that the garlic can be very finely crushed, but also makes the press difficult to clean.

Press (c) has a pivot between the handles, so that it works rather like a pair of scissors. You can clear every shred of garlic from the holes by reversing the handles – little spikes below the pivot then push neatly through the holes in the press.

Press (d) has extra mouldings on the handles for pitting olives, cracking nuts and scaling fish. It also has a detachable tinned steel plate with holes of smaller bore to fit over the unusually large ones in the press. As this press has a larger container than the others and holes with sharpened edges you can mince onion, soft green herbs, cheese, carrots and hard boiled egg in it. It is not a very efficient garlic press, however, as much of the garlic remains in the depth of the holes.

# CRACKERS
# AND CRUSHERS

Cracking nuts is a leisurely job, which is why nutcrackers are usually found in the dining-room rather than the kitchen. However, they are quite handy to have in the kitchen. Apart from cracking nuts, they can be used to crack the legs, if not the claws, of crabs, crayfish, crawfish and lobsters. This job can also be done with a hammer or mallet or – if you run a really well equipped kitchen – with special lobster pincers.

## Nutcrackers

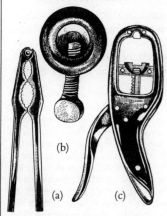

(b)

(a)          (c)

(a) **Size.** L. 7 in. (178 mm).
   **Material.** Chromed steel.
(b) **Size.** D. 3 in. (75 mm).
   **Material.** Plastic.
(c) **Size.** L. 7½ in. (190 mm).
   **Material.** Chromed steel.

Good nutcrackers crack the shell gently and neatly keeping the contents intact. Even the best do not work really fast – so if you plan to make a dish which requires a large quantity of nuts, buy them ready shelled.

The traditional hinged nut-cracker (a) gives some control over pressure as it has two grips, large and small, for different sizes of nut. However, crackers (b) and (c) have a much more precise and effortless action.

The screw on the bowl-shaped cracker (b) slowly increases the pressure on a nut until it cracks. The patent cracker (c) works equally well on shellfish claws or ice. You work the ratchet up until the nut is held in the head of the gadget. Continue working the ratchet until the shell disintegrates.

## Lobster crackers

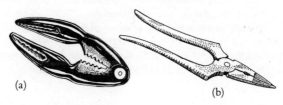

(a)

(b)

(a) **Size.** L. 6 in. (152 mm).
   **Material.** Chromed steel.
(b) **Size.** L. 7¼ in. (185 mm).
   **Material.** Stainless steel.

Made in the shape of a lobster's claws, the lobster crackers (a) work in the same way as hinged nutcrackers. The inside edges of the handles closest to the hinge are ridged so that you can grip hard, shiny lobster or crab claws firmly to crack them.

The elegant looking lobster pincers (b) can crush the legs of any large crustacean in the grooved part of the jaws above the pivot. The flattened points are for pulling the meat from the shell and the cutting edges behind the points are for splitting the softish shell on a lobster's body.

## Ice crushers

(a)

(a) **Size.** L. 6½ in. (165 mm).
   **Material.** Cast aluminium.
(b) **Size.** H. 8¼ in. (210 mm).
   **Materials.** Plastic body, alloy steel cutters.

The efficient little ice-crusher (a) will crush cubes of ice into small pieces, admittedly not much at a time, but enough for one or two cold drinks. The upper handle does the crushing, pushing nine vicious teeth into the lower shovel-shaped one as the handles are closed together. The handles unhook at the hinge so that you can serve the ice directly from the lower one.

The electric ice crushing mill (b) must be the noisiest tool in the book. It crushes ice beautifully. Feed ice cubes into the hopper and nothing more than ½ in. (12 mm) square emerges.

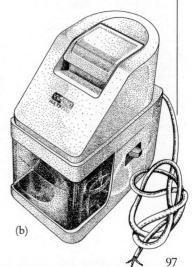

(b)

# MINCERS

Raw and cooked meat, fish or vegetables can be chopped to a hash by an expert cook with a really sharp chef's knife (see COOK'S KNIVES), but patent mincers or grinders are considered by most cooks to save a good deal of time, energy and trouble, especially if large quantities are needed. Minced meat does not stay fresh for very long, so if you use it a lot, it is well worth while owning a mincer. Also, unless you have an excellent butcher, you can never be sure of the quality of the mince you are buying.

Mincers are made with cast iron or plastic frameworks which can be firmly attached to a worktop or table by suction pads, screws or clamps. Food to be minced is dropped into a hopper and falls on to a large revolving screw which is turned by hand with a crank handle. The screw forces the food towards cutting blades or perforated cutting discs. In some mincers the cutting blades rotate against stationary discs, in others, two perforated discs, one stationary, one rotating, mince the meat. These discs are made to give mince of varying textures, from coarse to very fine, depending on the size of the perforations.

The cutting plates and threads for the screw rings and wing nuts are not tinned or plated, which means that they will eventually rust. They must be carefully dried after washing, then given a protective coat of cooking oil.

(a) **Size.** H. 9 in. (320 mm).
    **Material.** Stove enamel and plastic body, tinned steel drums, mild steel discs, rubber suction-pad base.

(b) **Size.** H. 9½ in. (242 mm).
    **Material.** Cast iron body, mild steel cutters.

(c) **Size.** H. 10 in. (255 mm).
    **Material.** Cast iron body, mild steel cutters.

(d) **Size.** 6½ × 11½ in. (165 × 292 mm).
    **Material.** Cast iron body, mild steel cutters.

A good mincer should work fast and effortlessly. Of the mincers shown here the smallest one (a), although cheap, light in weight and attractive, is far slower and harder to work than the bigger ones. They all take the same amount of trouble to put together and dismantle, so if you are looking for efficiency buy the biggest mincer you can afford and accommodate.

When preparing meat for the mincer, trim all gristle, bone and rind off first, then cut it into strips that will fit easily into the top of the mincer.

The small mincer (a) has attachments for slicing and grating as well as mincing. The stove enamelled base has a suction-pad

for fixing to smooth worktops and both the pad and the worktop should be wiped with a damp cloth before use to give greater suction. The handle, the screw and both the hoppers of this model are made of plastic. This mincer works very well as a slicer for such things as cucumber and citrus peel, and makes a good cheese grater, but it is a little flimsy for mincing meat.

The larger mincer (b) has a clamp, protected by rubber pads, which fixes the machine to the edge of the table or worktop. It has three cutting discs. One remains stationary, one is for coarse mince and one is for fine mince. When fixing the cutters in place, be careful to fit the stationary cutter first, fitting it into the slot in the mincer barrel so that it cannot rotate. The second revolving cutter is secured by a wing nut. This mincer works well and efficiently, the only drawback being that the outer disc can slip whilst you are operating the machine, causing scraps of meat and meat juices to escape from around the cutters.

The greater weight and larger size of the mincer (c) makes it far more efficient than mincers (a) and (b). The cutting arrangement is also more effective as the outer disc is stationary and held in place

by a screw ring, and the cutting is done by a four-armed blade which fits on to the central revolving shaft. This model has a choice of five perforated discs and also has a sausage making attachment – a 4 in. (100 mm) long nylon tube which is held in place outside the cutters by the screw ring. This mincer is easy to assemble and operate and produces fine, long shreds of meat. Its only drawback, if it can be termed as such, is that some proportion of the meat remains in the barrel at the end of the mincing process. You must therefore make sure (by feeding a piece of bread through the barrel) that all the meat has been minced.

Designed to be screwed to the work surface, the mincer (d) is capable of dealing with large quantities of meat, especially tough meat. It has a moving rotary knife which works against a stationary perforated plate. Like mincer (c), it has a sausage making attachment and a choice of four plates. The long handle on this model gives considerable extra leverage, making it much easier to operate than any of the others. However, unless you want a mincer permanently screwed to your work surface, you might prefer to use the equally efficient mincer (c) although it is not quite so effortless in use.

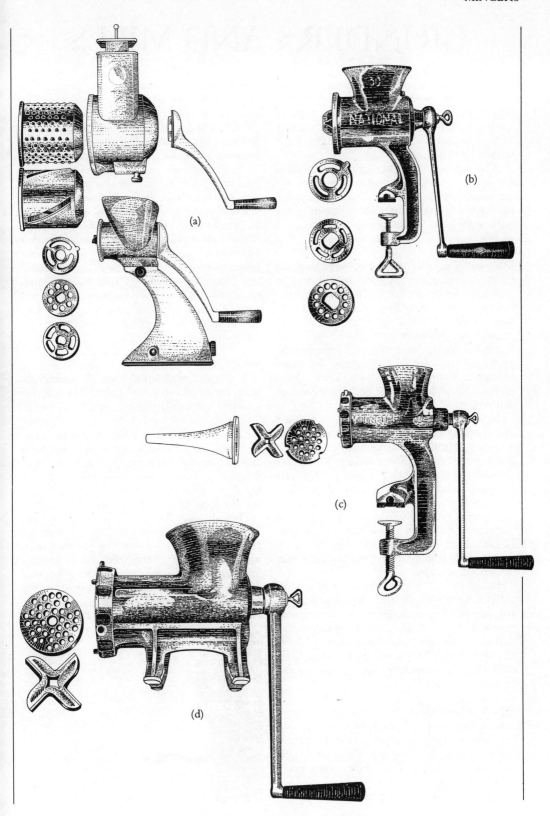

(a)

(b)

(c)

(d)

# GRINDERS AND MILLS

Both coffee beans and peppercorns taste best when freshly ground. Coffee grinders and pepper mills are among the most popular kitchen tools for this reason and an advantage of both is that the fineness of the grind can usually be varied.

This regulation of the grind is achieved simply by varying the space between the grinding surface to allow larger or smaller particles to drop through. This is usually done with a wing-nut adjustment.

## Coffee mills

Most coffee grinders can be adjusted to grind to the coarseness or fineness appropriate to particular coffee machines. There are various grades of ground coffee. Starting with the finest, they are: Turkish, filter-fine and Espresso-fine; medium (percolator, jug and vacuum systems); and coarse. The finer the grain, the stronger the coffee and the more difficult it is to make it clear. (Turks don't worry, the thick sediment is characteristic of that coffee.)

If you like Turkish coffee don't be misled into thinking that you can grind it at home in a domestic grinder. Turkish coffee must be ground as fine as talcum powder (Turks traditionally grind it with stone pestles and mortars) and the only mechanized grinders that can approach this degree of fineness are commercial ones. Neapolitan coffee pots and vacuum systems take grounds about as coarse as granulated sugar. Straight infusions in a jug need slightly coarser grounds than that (see COFFEE MAKERS).

Good electric grinders have gauges with which to set the wheels to the degree of fineness you require. This is the greatest advantage of a grinder. The blades found in the coffee "grinding" attachments of electric liquidizers cut and chop rather than grind, making it difficult to get evenly ground grains of the exact size you need.

## Pepper and salt mills

The excellence of freshly milled pepper (white or black) is clearly apparent if you compare it to the ready-ground variety sold in cardboard cylinders. As with most spices, what gives pepper its pepperiness is a very volatile oil, which quickly loses its pungency once the peppercorns are ground. With a pepper mill you can adjust the size of the grounds for use in the kitchen or at table. Most food benefiting from the flavour of pepper tastes better if the grounds are coarse, leaving some of the grinding to be done between your teeth.

As there are no precious oils to be released by milling salt crystals, and various grades, ranging from the huge, fragile flakes of Maldon salt to the finest "free running" powder, can be bought easily, the grinding of salt is far less important. It is surely more useful to keep a selection of salts in the kitchen for various purposes and to place crystals of an acceptable size on the table in a little dish with a spoon. Maldon salt is best simultaneously crushed and sprinkled between your fingers – and anyway tends to slip past the grinding mechanism of a salt mill.

## Caring for mills

Other mills designed for domestic use include herb, spice and cereal mills, as well as mills for grinding particular seeds, spices or nuts. Whatever the mill, it is best to use it only for the food for which it is intended. Seeds, grains and nuts vary considerably in size, hardness and oiliness and although it is possible to grind wheat or spices in a coffee mill it will not be as speedy or satisfactory as using the proper mill for the job. You will also have to wash it to banish one flavour before you release another – and cast iron grinding mechanisms rust very easily. It is really best not to wash a mill, for the oil in the seeds being ground lubricates the mechanism and washing removes this oil. Surplus powder can be brushed away if you want to keep the grinding mechanism clean; other parts should be wiped with a damp cloth.

(a) **Size.** H. 7¾ in. (197 mm).
**Material.** Cast iron grinding
mechanism, tinned steel lid
and crank, stained wooden
body and handle.
(b) **Size.** H. 8 in. (204 mm),
without clamp.
**Material.** Cast iron grinding
mechanism, crank and body,
wooden handle.
(c) **Size.** H. 8¼ in. (210 mm).
**Material.** Cast iron grinding
mechanism, chromed steel
crank, wooden handle,
painted tinned steel and
wooden body.
(d) **Size.** H. 6½ in. (165 mm).
**Material.** Cast iron grinding
mechanism, crank and body,
wooden handle.

To make really good coffee the
beans should be freshly roasted
and freshly ground. Most of the
aroma of coffee is contained in its
essential and very volatile oils.
Some of this is lost during roasting, more if the roasted beans are
kept too long, or stored in a non-
airtight container, and it vanishes
fastest of all once the beans are
ground. This is why, if you want
to make the best coffee, you should
grind the beans immediately
before you make it.

These mills have grinding surfaces of grooved cast iron which
rotate against each other. They
can be set to grind very finely for
use in a filter or up to the size of a
pin head, if you wish to use a
vacuum system.

The traditional French grinder
(a) is slow to work, but pleasing
to look at. It has a drawer below
the grinding mechanism to re-
ceive the grounds. It is easier to
use on your lap than on the
table, and grinds quite efficiently.
Unless you have long, thin
fingers and thumbs it is awkward
to turn the screw that regulates
the coarseness of the grounds. You
have to remove the drawer and
reach inside the box under the
grinding mechanism to do this.

Made of black cast iron with
gold, hand-painted trimmings,
the design of the English coffee
grinder (b) is unchanged since it
was first made in the mid-nine-
teenth century. It can be clamped
to a table top, but it is more stable
and the handle easier to turn when
screwed to the worktop or wall.

## Coffee mills

(a)

(b)

(c)          (d)

It cannot be adjusted for finely
ground coffee. It is, however,
lovely to look at, reminiscent of a
steam engine.

Grinder (c) mills much more
finely than the other three. The
handle turns smoothly and easily
and the grinder is comfortable to
grip. The ground coffee falls into
the cylinder and you simply
untwist the top, handle and all, to
recover it. This model is Italian
and is commonly used in Mediterranean countries. What could
be nicer than sitting in the sun on
your balcony or doorstep turning
away at the handle of one of these
old-fashioned mills?

The ultra-modern looking
grinder (d) has an open hopper.
This should not be filled too full
as any jolt while grinding will spill
the beans. The grinder must be
held upright in use and is best
placed on a table. The ground
coffee collects neatly in the base,
which unscrews to form a dis-
pensing tray. The grinding mechanism is adjusted by turning an
easily accessible screw.

(a) **Size.** H. 10 in. (255 mm).
**Material.** Plastic and
perspex.
(b) **Size.** H. 7 in. (178 mm).
**Material.** Plastic and
perspex.
(c) **Size.** H. 6 in. (152 mm).
**Material.** Plastic and
perspex.

Grinding coffee by hand is a
leisurely but somewhat time con-
suming job. Electric mills work
much faster than their manual
counterparts and with some it is
possible to adjust the grind with
far greater precision.

The large grinder (a) is similar
to grinder (b) but has the advantage of a simple clockwork mechanism which allows you to select
by number of cups the exact
amount of coffee that you want
to have milled. The ground coffee
falls into a beaker-shaped container and can be poured directly
into your coffee maker. This type
of machine provides a beautifully
quick, precise and tidy way to mill
coffee—and you don't have to
refill the hopper each time you
want to use it. It should not be
run for more than three minutes
at a stretch—but it works so fast
that this time limit should never
be reached.

The Italian coffee grinder (b)
has an airtight hopper which can
be used to store the coffee beans,
and a gauge ranging from 1 to 8
for regulating the coarseness of
the grind. The ground coffee falls
into a clear perspex container—
when you think you have enough,
turn the machine off.

## Electric coffee grinders

(a)

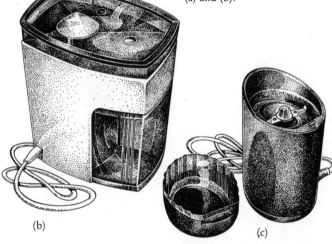

(b)

(c)

The mechanism which reduces
coffee beans to powder in the
small electric mill (c) is not a pair
of crushing wheels as in mills (a)
and (b), but a chopping blade,
rotating very fast. The blade,
located in the base of the mill, is
activated when the perspex lid is
pushed down. The blade stops
rotating as soon as pressure is
released on the lid. The machine
should not be operated for more
than 20–30 seconds at a time.
There is no device for regulating
the coarseness of the grind, so this
must depend on guesswork—a
reasonably effective method as
long as you know for how long to
"whizz" the machine, but for the
serious coffee drinker this process
is obviously less than perfect. The
main advantage of this machine
is that it is very compact and
takes up far less space than mills
(a) and (b).

(a) **Size.** H. 3½ in. (90 mm).
**Material.** Beechwood.
(b) **Size.** H. 3½ in. (90 mm).
**Material.** Beechwood.
(c) **Size.** H. 5½ in. (140 mm).
**Material.** Perspex.

The grinding mechanism of a
pepper mill is metal, while that
of a salt mill is usually nylon,
wood or other material unaffected
by moisture. Otherwise a salt mill
can be made to look (and sometimes work) exactly like a pepper
mill.

The grinding mechanism of
pepper mill (a) is in the base of

## Pepper and salt mills

(a)

(b)          (c)

the mill and is turned by an axle
attached to the lid. The fineness of
the grind can be adjusted by
tightening the screw on the top of
the lid. To fill it with peppercorns,
loosen the screw and remove the
lid.

The matching salt mill (b) has
a nylon ball and peg at the top of
the mill to grind the salt. The mill
is filled from the bottom and the
ground salt comes out of a hole at
the top.

Made of clear perspex so you
can see when it is empty, pepper
mill (c) works exactly like the
wooden mill (a).

# Herb and spice mills

(a) **Size.** H. 4½ in. (115 mm).
**Material.** Perspex, nylon grinder.
(b) **Size.** H. 3½ in. (90 mm).
**Material.** Beechwood.
(c) **Size.** H. 12 in. (305 mm).
**Material.** Cast iron, wooden handle.
(d) **Size.** H. 11 in. (280 mm).
**Material.** Cast iron, plastic handle.

The herb mill (a) is made of clear perspex and will grind salt as well as dried herbs. The container holds about ½ oz. (13 g) of dried herbs and is airtight. If you want to use the herbs as they are, pressure on the spring-loaded lid will release them unground.

Less versatile than the herb mill (a), the nutmeg grinder (b) is designed specifically for mincing whole nutmegs. It can be used for grating chunks of Parmesan cheese (and possibly individual hazel-

(a)

(b)

nuts) but is of little use for other herbs or spices.

The spice mill (c) and the poppy seed mill (d) both work like mincing machines and need to be clamped to a worktop.

Made in a country where a great deal of pounding, milling, and grinding forms a part of the preparation of any meal, the Indian spice mill (c) will grind chillies, spices and grains in generous quantities. The crank is light and easy to turn and the large size of the machine helps it to work fast and efficiently.

Grain as small as poppy seed can be quickly reduced to a soft oily powder in mill (d), which has grinders set extremely close. The mill will also deal with other small grains and seeds, such as coriander, mustard and peppercorns. The mill is made in Austria, where it no doubt comes in handy for strudel containing dried fruit and crushed poppy seed.

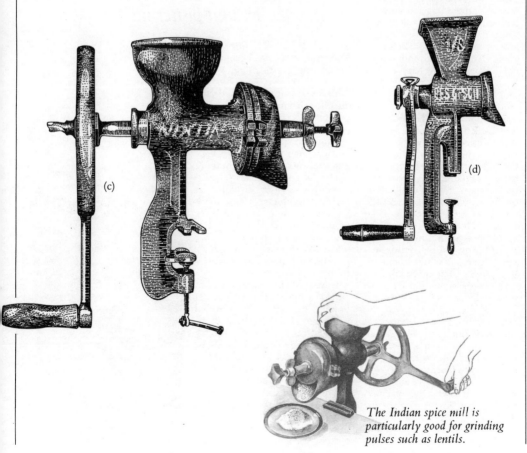

(c)

(d)

*The Indian spice mill is particularly good for grinding pulses such as lentils.*

# Cereal mill

**Size.** D. 11 in. (280 mm).
**Material.** Composition millstones, steel spindles and fittings, wooden handles.

If you are self-sufficient and regard anything resembling a sliced and wrapped loaf as sheer poison, you will like this mill, which can grind wheat (whole, of course) as well as other grain.

The wheat germ and bran in wholewheat flour contain fat, which goes rancid after about three months' storage, souring the flour and reducing its nutritional value. (White flour lasts for at least six months without deterioration.) However, this mill would only really be necessary if you have no easy access to a shop or mill selling freshly ground, wholegrain flours.

The mill has a large stone base with a central spindle on which a smaller grindstone revolves as the handle is turned. The grain is fed through a cup-shaped hopper in the top of the smaller stone. The fineness or coarseness of the flour can be regulated by turning the nuts locking the stones.

The mill is very heavy and should be secured firmly with the clamps provided to a stable surface (if possible) where it will not be in the way. The knob at the side regulates the flow of grain on to the grinding faces. Once you have adjusted the mill to suit you the work can be pleasant, rhythmical and soothing, and not at all arduous. The ground flour falls from between the stones into the bowl-shaped base.

This mill should never be washed as it can take several days for the grinding stones to dry thoroughly; using the mill when it is at all damp will turn your flour into paste.

# Peanut butter mill

**Size.** D. $10\frac{1}{2}$ in. (267 mm).
**Material.** Alloy steel grinding mechanism, plastic body.

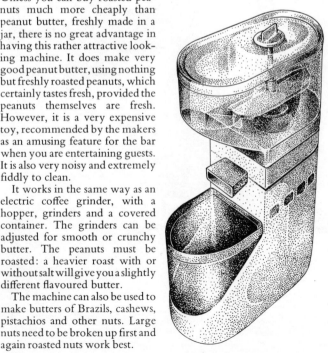

Unless you can buy roasted peanuts much more cheaply than peanut butter, freshly made in a jar, there is no great advantage in having this rather attractive looking machine. It does make very good peanut butter, using nothing but freshly roasted peanuts, which certainly tastes fresh, provided the peanuts themselves are fresh. However, it is a very expensive toy, recommended by the makers as an amusing feature for the bar when you are entertaining guests. It is also very noisy and extremely fiddly to clean.

It works in the same way as an electric coffee grinder, with a hopper, grinders and a covered container. The grinders can be adjusted for smooth or crunchy butter. The peanuts must be roasted: a heavier roast with or without salt will give you a slightly different flavoured butter.

The machine can also be used to make butters of Brazils, cashews, pistachios and other nuts. Large nuts need to be broken up first and again roasted nuts work best.

# BOARDS

The work surface chosen for a particular job can often be as important as the tools that you use to do it. Chopping boards should always be made of wood, which is a relatively soft material, as knife edges quickly become blunt if they strike laminated plastic, ceramic, marble or enamelled steel surfaces. These hard, cool surfaces, however, work very well for pastry or confectionery making.

*Wooden boards*
Hardwoods, such as iroko, teak, beech, elm, ash and sycamore make good chopping boards, pastry boards and bread boards. Avoid using boards made of softwood. They will split, splinter and dent easily.

Some chopping boards are made like butcher's chopping blocks, from strips of hardwood laminated together so that the cross cut ends form the surface of the block. Butcher's chopping blocks are bound with steel to keep the strips firmly in place. Domestic versions, with steel corners, are available, 18 in. (458 mm) square, for those with space enough in their kitchens and there are smaller cutting boards made in the same cross cut way, but not braced with dowling rods or steel.

Wooden boards should never soak in water for any length of time. If they do, they will swell and then warp or split on drying, and the bonded sections of unbraced cross cut boards will loosen and eventually fall apart. They should not be dried near direct heat, nor be put in dishwashers for the same reason. Remove dry flour or slight stains with a damp cloth and clean off food particles with scouring powder on a nylon scourer or scrubbing brush. Dry the board with a cloth and leave it to air before putting it away.

The surface of a board can also soften if it is allowed to soak in water as moisture inevitably seeps down through the grain. This can be hardened again by scattering table salt thickly over the board and leaving it on overnight to absorb the moisture from the wood. Salt has a slightly abrasive cleaning action if rubbed on to the board dry and it will also take away the smell of onion fairly successfully. Lemon juice can be used to bleach out light stains on chopping boards.

*Marble slabs*
Marble slabs become pitted if water is left lying on them and they should always be dried thoroughly. Slight stains can be removed with a mild abrasive, lemon juice or vinegar, after which the marble should be rinsed with water and dried.

## *Caring for boards*

Scour wooden chopping boards with salt and lemon juice to clean them and remove light stains. First pour the salt on to the board and then use half a cut lemon as a scouring pad to rub the crystals into the surface. Wipe the board with a damp cloth after treatment and leave standing on edge to dry.

The surface of a Chinese chopping board should be scraped clean after use with the edge of a cleaver. Draw the upright blade firmly across the block several times, so that the edge scrapes off all food particles and greasy residues. Then scoop up the scrapings on the flat of the blade to discard them.

# Chopping boards

(a) **Size.** 18 × 15 in.
  (458 × 380 mm).
  **Material.** Iroko.
(b) **Size.** 15 × 7¾ in.
  (380 × 197 mm).
  **Material.** Ashwood.
(c) **Size.** 10 × 12 in.
  (255 × 305 mm).
  **Material.** Plastic.
(d) **Size.** D. 12 in. (305 mm).
  **Material.** Wood.

These boards are used when chopping meat and vegetables. They are made in various sizes, but to act as good shock absorbers they should be twice as thick as pastry boards. Because their thickness makes them unlikely to warp, they are usually made in one piece.

The large chopping board (a) is made of iroko, which is closely grained like teak and does not absorb stains from meat as boards made of lighter, less densely grained woods do. It is very heavy and thick enough, 2 in. (50 mm), to take the heaviest blows from a domestic cleaver and stand up well to the teeth of butcher's saws. This is the sort of chopping board you need if you cut up carcasses for the freezer.

Board (b) should only be used for light chopping and cutting. It is made like a butcher's chopping block from strips of wood glued together and then sawn across so that the end grain forms the working surface. This looks very pretty but with use and constant washing the board can come apart. To be really solid it needs to be as thick as a butcher's block and braced with steel or dowling rods.

The plastic chopping board (c) is made of polyethylene and can be sterilized. Its surface is not hard enough to blunt knives and it cannot crack, warp, chip, absorb moisture or taint. This type of board is used in commercial kitchens where public health regulations forbid the use of wooden boards.

The Chinese chopping block (d) is a cross section from a small tree trunk. Splitting is the main hazard with this type of block and thorough seasoning, plus sometimes a metal band, are the ways to avoid it. New blocks should be allowed to absorb a liberal dose, ¼ pint (0·14 litres), of cooking oil on both sides – two days for each side – before being used. Cover the oiled surface with aluminium foil while it seasons. After treating both sides, blot the surface with absorbent paper, sponge the block with soap and water and dry it thoroughly. These blocks are pretty, but rather too cumbersome for use in very small kitchens since they need to be at least 12 in. (305 mm) in diameter and 5 in. (127 mm) thick to be of any real use.

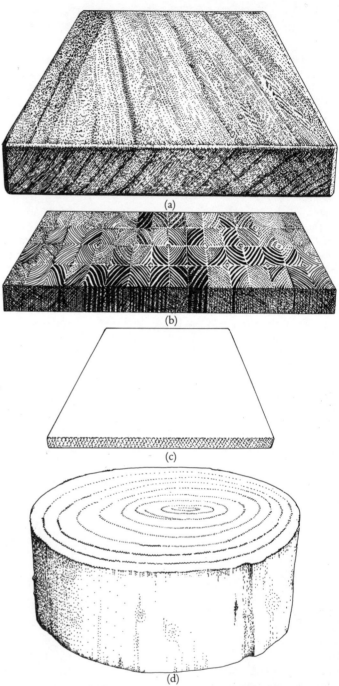

(a)

(b)

(c)

(d)

# Pastry boards

(a) **Size.** 20 × 15 in.
(508 × 380 mm).
**Material.** Ashwood.
(b) **Size.** 14 × 20 in.
(355 × 508 mm).
**Material.** Marble.
(c) **Size.** 19 × 19 in.
(482 × 482 mm).
**Material.** Canvas, wood
frame, metal clamps.

The boards used for pastry
making should be flat, smooth,
ample, free of cracks and crevices and easy to clean. Pastry
boards come in a variety of sizes
and materials – wood, laminated
plastic, and marble are the most
popular. Because they are only
used to mix, knead and roll out
various doughs, the boards and
slabs need not be more than 1 in.
(25 mm) thick.

Unlike many wooden boards
which are made up of three pieces
of wood jointed together, pastry
board (a) is made from one large
smooth piece of wood with
narrow cleats screwed to the ends
to prevent it warping. It is large
enough to deal with most home
baking and with proper care it is
unlikely to split or crack.

The marble slab (b) is the best
board of all for pastry making.
Being a good conductor of heat,
it takes the warmth from your
hands, and from the pastry, at a
touch. Should you have very hot
hands, or a warm kitchen, you
can chill the surface of the marble
even more by putting ice-cubes
in a baking tin on top of it, just
before you start to roll out your
pastry. This board is also perfect

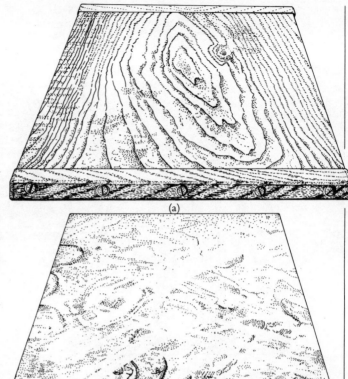

(a)

(b)

for making fondants, pulled sugar
or praline, when you need a very
smooth, impervious, tough, heat-
resistant surface. Slate or stone
slabs are good alternatives.

The pastry cloth (c) makes the
job of rolling out pastry and
lifting it about far less sticky as
the cloth's soft surface, when
heavily floured, does not adhere
to the dough. These cloths can be
used on any flat surface and after

use are scraped clean of flour and
stored. The canvas is weighted to
prevent it from slipping. For
more vigorous tasks, such as
kneading dough, it should be
fastened to the work top with
clamps. The canvas can be slipped
from its frame for washing when
necessary. As canvas tends to
absorb moisture and fat, the pastry
cloth will require frequent and
thorough washing.

(c)

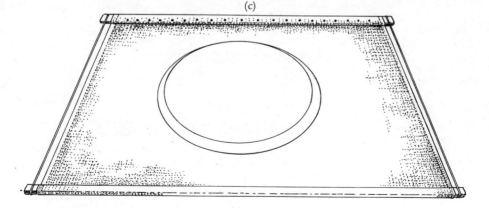

# Carving boards

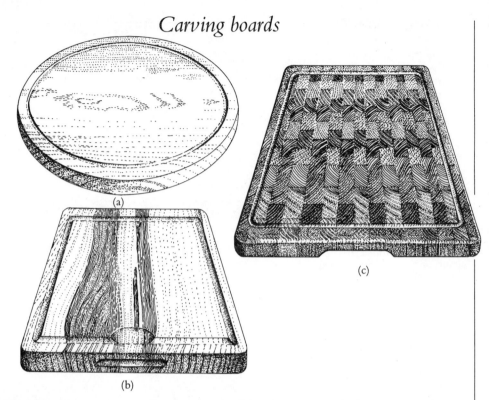

(a)

(b)

(c)

(a) **Size.** D. 11 in. (280 mm).
   **Material.** Beechwood.

(b) **Size.** $14\frac{1}{4} \times 9\frac{1}{2}$ in.
   $(362 \times 242$ mm).
   **Material.** Wood.

(c) **Size.** $16\frac{3}{4} \times 11$ in.
   $(245 \times 280$ mm).
   **Material.** Ashwood.

With a wooden board a carver is in no danger of blunting the knife, which is always a risk when carving on metal or china dishes.

In Europe, the round wooden board (a) is used for carving meat.

It has a groove round the edge to catch the meat juices. In Britain, however, it is generally used as a bread board; the round shape suiting a cob or cottage loaf nicely. It is made of four strips of wood glued together and should not warp, unless treated very badly.

Board (b) is made from three strips of wood and is $1\frac{1}{4}$ in. (32 mm) thick, which gives it weight and stability. It also has a groove round the top for juices and a well at one end to spoon them from. There are grooves

carved into the edge of this board at each end for lifting and carrying. Because the surface of this board runs with the grain, it will score more easily than the cross-grained board (c).

The larger carving board (c) is prettily patterned with the cross-cut ends of the ashwood squares of which it is composed. It has a groove all round the top near the edge for meat juices and recesses at each end on the underside to lift it by. It would be a decorative board for buffet use.

# Slicing boards

(a) **Size.** $10\frac{1}{4} \times 4\frac{3}{4}$ in.
   $(260 \times 120$ mm).
   **Material.** Beechwood.

(b) **Size.** $14\frac{1}{4} \times 7\frac{1}{4}$ in.
   $(362 \times 185$ mm).
   **Material.** Beechwood.

You can slice salami, egg, tomato or lemon on these useful slicing boards and then carry the boards straight to the table. They are not intended for heavy use, as they are only $\frac{1}{2}$ in. (12 mm) thick.

The smaller board (a) could be used as a noodle board, although

(a)

(b)

it is not tapered in thickness from the handle as many noodle boards are. Board (b) is too large and heavy for noodle making and

should be used solely for slicing. These boards are easily stored as they can be hung up by the holes in the handles.

# ROLLING PINS

As long as you work on a smooth, even surface which is reasonably cool, you can produce a thin sheet of dough with nothing more elaborate than a milk bottle, a length of broomstick or even a short piece of curtain-pole. There are however certain drawbacks to these makeshift arrangements – bottles tend to be too short, broomsticks and curtain-poles can be warped, scratched or too thin.

Rolling pins are neither expensive nor bulky, and as they are designed specifically for the job it is worthwhile having at least one – and possibly more if you intend making pasta or noodles or chapattis, all of which require special pins.

Professional chefs use pins without handles made of one straight piece of wood. This enables them to "feel" the pastry more closely. A pin with fixed handles at either end may appear to roll more smoothly and evenly, but with a little practice you can roll a plain, professional pin just as easily, using the tips of your fingers and the palms of your hands.

The choice of the size and shape of pin to use depends entirely on the type of dough to be rolled. Thick, heavy pins are best for rich, lightly textured shortcrust or puff pastries;

long, thin, tapered pins for Chinese noodles or Italian pasta; ribbed or chequered pins for the dimpled flatbreads and oatcakes of Scandinavian and Celtic countries; and for the early stages of making the paper-thin, almost transparent Greek filo pastry or Austrian strudel dough a long medium-heavy pin is called for.

"Cool" pins, designed for rolling pastry, are made of china, marble or glass. Some, made of glass or plastic, are hollow and can be filled with ice or cold water. These have no real advantage over the traditional wooden rolling pins. The china pins, though they may look pretty, are too fragile to be really practical, while hollow ones tend to produce condensation.

All pins should be lightly floured before use to prevent sticking and should be cleaned immediately after use with a slightly damp cloth. Always air and dry the pins thoroughly before stowing them away.

Besides rolling out dough, pins can be used to crush breadcrumbs and crispbread, to shape tuiles (little, curved, almond biscuits) or to beat and flatten escalopes or steaks; though when doing this be careful not to dent the rolling surface of the pin.

## Shaping

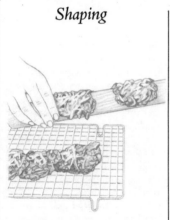

*Take tuiles (biscuits made with flour, butter, sugar and almonds) from the baking sheet a few seconds after they come out of the oven. Then lift them with a palette knife on to a rolling pin to set like curved tiles (or tuiles, in French).*

## Lifting

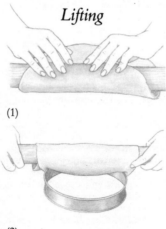

(1)

(2)

*Transfer pastry from board to dish by folding it gently over the rolling pin (1). Turn the pin so that the pastry can be carried over it without stretching. Position the pin carefully over the dish and unroll the pastry so that it falls where you want it (2).*

## Crushing

*Bake slices of stale bread in the oven until they are hard and dry but not coloured. When cool, crush them to fine breadcrumbs with a rolling pin. Cornflakes, oatcakes, digestive biscuits and matzos can be crushed similarly.*

# Rolling pins

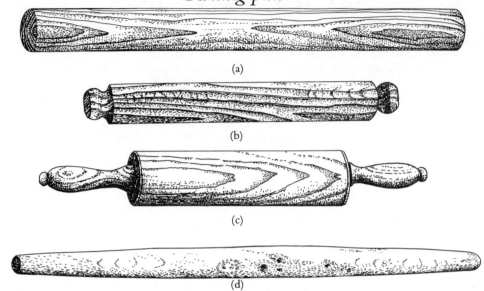

(a)

(b)

(c)

(d)

(a) **Size.** L. 20 in. (508 mm),
   D. 2 in. (50 mm).
   **Material.** Beechwood.
(b) **Size.** L. 14 in. (355 mm),
   D. 1½ in. (38 mm).
   **Material.** Beechwood.
(c) **Size.** L. 18½ in. (470 mm),
   D. 2¾ in. (70 mm).
   **Material.** Beechwood.
(d) **Size.** L. 21 in. (533 mm),
   D. 1¼ in. (32 mm).
   **Material.** Beechwood.

The best pins for all purposes are made of plain, unpolished hardwoods, sanded and rubbed as smooth as possible. Most professionals choose rolling pin (a) as it can be used for all sorts of rolling, and is beautifully smooth and straight. It is also a good weight, 1¼ lbs (567 g), and needs only the lightest of touches to roll it across the pastry. Some straight pins are much wider in diameter than (a) and it follows that the larger the diameter the fewer revolutions a pin will have to make when rolling, thus speeding up the work. Also, a larger curve makes a smoother sheet of pastry.

Although rolling pin (b) is a handy size for most domestic pastry work it is less weighty than (a) and therefore needs slightly more effort when used. The danger with this type of pin

is that a heavy hand will press out the air when rolling, resulting in slightly tougher pastry. However, if space is a problem, the size of this pin makes it easier to stow away in a kitchen drawer. The ends of the pin have been shaped to make small handles, but it is best to ignore these when making pastry and to use the pin in exactly the same way as (a).

Rolling pin (c) has handles which are fixed to the ends of a rod running through the centre of the pin. The rod is of wood, but in some pins it may be of metal and may also incorporate nylon bearings. The rolling technique with this type of pin is slightly different from pins (a) and (b) as the roller is pushed forward by holding both handles (as if you were rolling a lawn, but pushing, not pulling). This type of roller may demand less effort than the others but there is correspondingly less contact with the pastry.

Because of its shape, pressure in the tapered rolling pin (d) is concentrated in the centre, making it extremely useful for rolling out very thin pastry. It is also helpful if you are rolling out little discs or long strips for a specific purpose. It is not, however, a good idea to use this pin with thick pastry as it tends to leave the middle thinner than the edges.

## Using spacers

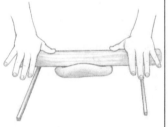

*To be certain that your millefeuilles and vol-au-vents all rise to the same height; that the bases of your pastry shells cook evenly; and that each slice of wedding cake reveals an equally thick, level layer of marzipan beneath the icing, it is essential to roll your pastry or marzipan to a uniform thickness. As an aid to this end professional cooks use spacers—a pair of square sectioned nylon rods, about 15 in. (380 mm) long by ¼ in. (6 mm) square. These are placed at right angles to the rolling pin and just beneath each end. They keep the pin and with it the thickness of the pastry or paste at a constant level. Smooth, straight pieces of wooden batten make cheap alternatives to professional spacers.*

## Making noodles

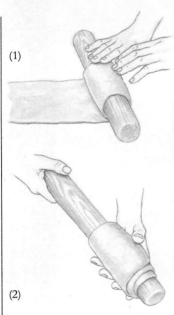

(1)

(2)

1. Roll the pasta dough into a long strip and then roll the strip round the floured pin.

2. Slide it off the pin.

3. Roll the flattened cylinder of pasta into a longer, wider and thinner strip than previously. Continue this procedure until the dough is the thinnest imaginable. (Divide it, if you are short of space.)

4. After letting the dough dry a little over the back of a chair (this prevents the noodles sticking together), roll it up fairly loosely. Then cut it crossways into narrow ribbons. The width depends on the size you like your noodles.

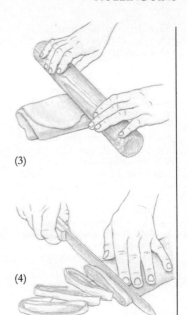

(3)

(4)

## Lining bateau moulds

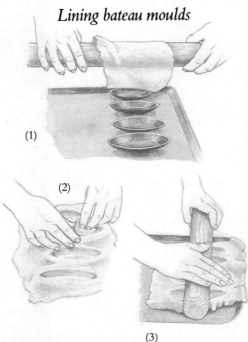

(1)

(2)

(3)

Place the moulds close together and lift the pastry on the pin (see preceding page) and lay it carefully over them (1). Encourage the pastry to sink into the moulds by placing a little ball of pastry in each (2). Roll the pin across the tops of the moulds (3) so that their sharp edges cut through it.

## Preparing herb bread

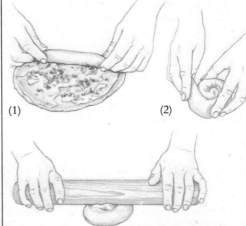

(1)

(2)

(3)

1. Roll out a circle of dough made to a quick bread recipe. Spread it lightly with fat and sprinkle it with salt and chopped green herbs. Then roll it into a sausage shape.

2. Coil it up.

3. Roll the coil flat again to a circle about 10 in. (255 mm) in diameter and $\frac{1}{4}$ in. (6 mm) thick.

4. The herbs are now encased in dough. Cook for one minute in oil in a frying pan, turning once. Drain and cut into wedges.

**Size.** L. 35 in. (889 mm),
D. 1½ in. (38 mm).
**Material.** Beechwood.

Pasta dough should be rolled into
paper-thin sheets, the wider the
better. For this you need a rolling
pin that is at least 24 in. (610 mm)
long. You can of course make pasta
with an ordinary pin, but each
sheet of pasta (sfoglia) will be
much smaller and the whole process more time-consuming. This
very long Italian rolling pin
(matarello) is designed for pasta
making. You need to use a table
that is wide enough to accommodate a large sheet of pasta and
low enough for you to exert
plenty of pressure on the pin.

# Pasta rolling pin
## (MATARELLO)

(1)

(2)

(3)

*1. Flour the table, your hands
and the pin, then flatten a ball
of pasta and roll it out until it is
about ¼ in. (6 mm) thick. With
the pin lying across the pasta on
the edge furthest away from you,
fold the pasta over the pin,
pressing it down with your hands.
2. Push the pin to and fro,
gradually rolling up more and
more pasta, and at the same time*

*slide your hands lightly over
it to stretch it out sideways as
you roll it round the pin. Flour
each part as it is stretched and
rolled.
3. When it is all rolled on the
pin, turn the whole thing at right
angles, unroll the pasta and
repeat the procedure until the
dough is paper thin and almost
transparent.*

# Ribbed pin

**Size.** L. 9½ in. (242 mm),
D. 1¾ in. (45 mm).
**Material.** Sycamore.

This deeply ridged pin can be
used either for making Welsh siot
(a crushed oatcake dish eaten with
buttermilk), or for marking
griddle cakes and flatbreads with
a striped or diamond pattern.

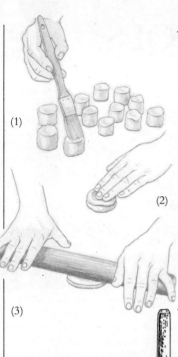

(1)

(2)

(3)

## Rolling Chinese pancakes

(*These little pancakes – Peking doilies – are eaten with Peking duck.*)
1. Roll the well-kneaded dough into a sausage and cut it into 1 in. (25 mm) lengths. Stand these on end and brush the tops of half of them with oil.
2. Press the oiled top of one on to the un-oiled top of another.
3. Roll the two together into a double pancake about 6 in. (152 mm) in diameter.
4. Bake each pair very briefly on both sides on a hot griddle. The steam between the layers will make it puff up.
5. Peel them apart.
6. Fold each in half and steam for five minutes before serving.

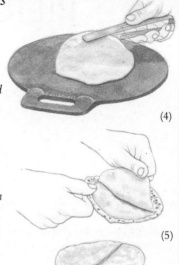

(4)

(5)

(6)

## Indian rolling pin

**Size.** L. 15½ in. (394 mm), D. 1 in. (25 mm).
**Material.** Wood.

A slender rolling pin and round board are used when baking chapattis. The pin is tapered at the ends so that you can exert maximum pressure on the dough, which must be rolled very thinly. To form it into perfect circles you need to change the direction of the pin several times. This is best done by turning the chapatti board – its three little feet make it easy to manoeuvre.

*The ball of dough can be flattened by a mushroom-shaped press.*

## Making chapattis

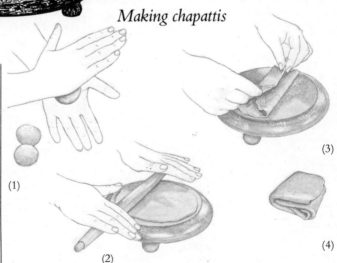

(1)

(2)

(3)

(4)

1. Take pieces of chapatti dough and roll them into balls about 1 in. (25 mm) diameter.
2. Roll these out thinly to 7 in. (178 mm) diameter.
3. Spread them lightly with fat and flour them. Fold them up, edges to middle, to make a square.
4. Roll the folded chapattis out again as thinly as before either as squares or circles. Bake the chapattis on a lightly greased griddle (tava), turning them once.

113

# PIERCING TOOLS

There are certain small but indispensable tools that a cook needs on the many occasions when food needs to be pierced, pricked, trussed, decorated or lifted.

Some piercing instruments, such as skewers, are versatile and can be adapted to deal with a number of small or large jobs – from pricking pastry to spiking baking potatoes. In the past hâtelets (decorative skewers) were used to increase the attractiveness of hot or cold dishes served in the grand style. They were threaded with garnishes such as truffles, crawfish, cocks' combs and turned vegetables and used as ornaments to make a dish more impressive.

A table fork was not considered necessary (fingers as is well known were invented long before them) until the seventeenth century, but kitchen forks have a far longer history. In the past, as now, strong two-pronged forks were used to lift and turn heavy joints of meat or whole poultry, long-handled tridents to toast bread or smoke fish over a fire and wooden forks to scrape out pots and stir sauces. Today forks both as eating implements and holding tools are so much a part of the kitchen that the cook takes them for granted, using them for such diverse tasks as decorating pastry, pricking sausages and moulding pasta.

## *Boning cooked sole*

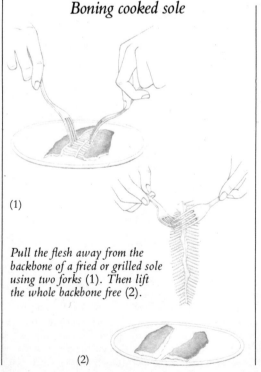

(1)

(2)

Pull the flesh away from the backbone of a fried or grilled sole using two forks (1). Then lift the whole backbone free (2).

## *Making conchiglie*

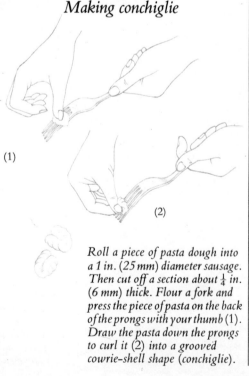

(1)

(2)

Roll a piece of pasta dough into a 1 in. (25 mm) diameter sausage. Then cut off a section about $\frac{1}{4}$ in. (6 mm) thick. Flour a fork and press the piece of pasta on the back of the prongs with your thumb (1). Draw the pasta down the prongs to curl it (2) into a grooved cowrie-shell shape (conchiglie).

(a) **Size.** L. 11¼ in. (285 mm).
   **Material.** Stainless steel
   prongs, plastic handle.
(b) **Size.** L. 11¾ in. (298 mm).
   **Material.** Stainless steel
   prongs, plastic handle.
(c) **Size.** L. 14 in. (355 mm).
   **Material.** Stainless steel.

These very strong, long-tined
stainless steel forks with two
prongs should not be confused
with carving forks. They are
intended primarily to lift and turn
heavy joints of meat when roasting and will also lift a whole fowl
without bending under the
weight. You can use them to
steady a joint while it is being
carved, but take care that the
knife doesn't slip, as some of the
handles are unguarded.

Once you get used to using
them these forks will soon prove
invaluable. With them you can

## Forks

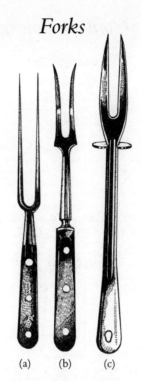

(a)     (b)     (c)

lift boiled puddings from the
steamer, or balance a row of
cooked leeks across the prongs to
drain. They will act as harpoons
for practically any soft boiling
object, from a sausage to an
artichoke, and, with a little twist
of paper on the prongs, can be
used to run butter round a hot pan.

The dishwasher-proof handles
of forks (a) and (b) are secured
with stainless steel rivets to full
tangs, in the same way as good
quality knives. Fork (b) has flat,
curved prongs and is very strong,
but as it has shorter prongs it is
not as versatile as fork (a). Fork (c)
is made of one piece of strong
stainless steel, with a useful guard
if you want to use it for carving
either at table or in the kitchen.

The points of these forks are
extremely sharp and should be
embedded in a cork when they
are not in use.

(a) **Size.** L. 12 in. (305 mm).
   **Material.** Beechwood.
(b) **Size.** L. 11½ in. (292 mm).
   **Material.** Beechwood.
(c) **Size.** L. 12½ in. (317 mm).
   **Material.** Ashwood.

The two long wooden forks (a)
and (b) are not survivors from a
depleted salad set but are made
as single items. They are useful
for swirling the spaghetti about
while it's cooking; for digging
and draining sauerkraut from its
pickle barrel; for whisking a
little lightness into a thick sauce,
or simply for scraping out a pot
without scratching it. The fork
half of a pair of salad servers, if
shaped like one of the forks shown
here, would be just as efficient as
long as it was strong enough.

Fork (a) is four-pronged and
has a hole in its handle for hanging. Fork (b), which has three
prongs, has a plain handle. Both
of these forks are strong and
serviceable.

The spaghetti fork or rake (c)
has eight 1 in. (25 mm) prongs
projecting from its paddle-shaped
back like the bristles from a rather
worn hairbrush. Instead of strug-
gling to tip the contents of a very

## Wooden forks

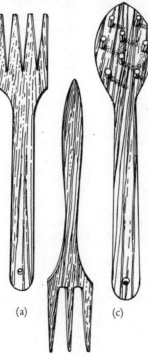

(a)         (c)

(b)

hot, full, heavy pan of cooked
pasta into a colander which all too
often is not big enough, use a
spaghetti fork. If you have one of
these implements you can twirl it
round inside the pot and the
spaghetti will entangle itself on
the fork. It then needs only a
little draining before serving.

## Raking spaghetti

*Place the spaghetti rake in the
pan and swirl it round to
entangle as much spaghetti as
possible. Then lift it out with the
spaghetti. Drain the spaghetti
in a colander before putting it
in a serving dish.*

## Pickle forks

(a)        (b)

(a) **Size.** L. 6¼ in. (160 mm).
**Material.** Bamboo.
(b) **Size.** 5 in. (127 mm).
**Material.** Chromed steel
prongs, dark stained wooden
handle.

Pickle forks are invaluable for
taking firm, slippery pickles from
tall narrow jars. The bamboo
fork (a) has three prongs which
are very sharp and slightly flexible.

The pickle fork (b) has three
short, sharp prongs set in a triangular pattern to give the firmest
hold on the hardest pickle. This
fork can also be used to hold a hot,
boiled potato whilst the skin is
being peeled.

## Onion fork

**Size.** L. 5 in. (127 mm).
**Material.** Tinned steel tines,
wooden handle.

This onion fork looks exactly like
a vicious comb for long-haired
dogs with its wooden handle and
ten close-set, very sharp tines.
Insert the fork into a peeled onion
or whole tomato, and slice them
by cutting between the prongs.
This is a handy tool, but the job
can be done just a well with a
sharp knife – and a little skill.

## Corn cob holders

**Size.** L. 3 in. (75 mm).
**Material.** Tinned steel prongs,
wooden handles.

These corn cob holders are sold in
pairs and are meant to be inserted
at each end of a hot, freshly
boiled corn cob so that you can
hold the cob easily while eating.
Small skewers make quite adequate substitutes if you do not
have these special forks.

## Toasting fork

**Size.** L. 13¼ in. (336 mm).
**Material.** Tinned steel.

This traditional trident-shaped
toasting fork has an extending
handle so that you can hold a
slice of bread near enough to the
fire for toasting while at the same
time keeping your hand far
enough away to avoid getting it
burned. Bread, teacakes and
crumpets can all be toasted with
this fork, preferably over an open
fire of logs or coal.

## Snail forks

(a)      (b)      (c)

(a) **Size.** L. 5¾ in. (146 mm).
**Material.** Stainless steel.
(b) **Size.** L. 5 in. (127 mm).
**Material.** Stainless steel.
(c) **Size.** L. 5½ in. (140 mm).
**Material.** Stainless steel.

These forks are used for nothing
but prizing cooked snails from
their shells. Special tongs are used
to hold the shells securely (see
TONGS). Snails are cooked and
served in little dimpled metal or
china dishes, the forks, tongs and
dishes making a complete set.
These sets are more often found
in restaurants, but if you eat snails
often at home it is difficult to
cook, hold and extract them with
any other tools. Fork (a) is the
most efficient fork as it has long,
closely spaced tines, whereas fork
(b) with its three broader prongs
is only suitable for the very large
snails found in France. The
smaller fork (c) is a good size for
small, wild snails.

## Egg pricker

**Size.** H. 2 in. (50 mm).
**Material.** Plastic.

The heat of boiling water frequently causes an egg to crack as
the air inside it expands. An egg
pricker prevents this by making
a tiny hole in the wide end of the
shell (where the air sac is), allowing
the air to escape as the egg heats
up in the water. It is not a very
vital piece of equipment, but if
you or your family eat numerous
boiled eggs, then it can prevent a
lot of wastage.

# Cake testers

(a)    (b)

(a) **Size.** L. 7 in. (178 mm).
  **Material.** Tinned wire,
  plastic-coated handle.
(b) **Size.** L. 6 in. (152 mm).
  **Material.** Straw, tinned
  steel wire.

The cake tester (a) is a very thin, perfectly straight piece of wire with the end twisted into a plastic-coated handle. When testing a cake, insert the wire into the middle of the mixture, pull it out and examine it. If it comes out clean the cake is done but if mixture still clings to the wire then the cake needs more baking. This wire is so fine that the cake is unharmed by your probing—which is not the case if you use anything thicker like a skewer or a knitting needle.

The straw cake testers (b) tied in a bundle with a metal band, are meant to be used once and then discarded. Simply twist off one of the strands near the band and use in the same way as the cake tester (a).

# Ice pick

**Size.** L. 10½ in. (267 mm).
**Material.** Carbon steel pick, wooden handle.

This ice pick is a fairly lethal weapon and is intended primarily for breaking up large blocks of ice. It is also useful for killing live crabs and lobsters. (Do this with a stab at the back of the head just before you plunge them into boiling water.) Use them too as a holding device while carving large, hot, boneless pieces of meat. When the pick is not in use, the point should always be protected with a cork.

# Crab and lobster picks

(a)  ·(b)

(a) **Size.** L. 8 in. (204 mm).
  **Material.** Stainless steel.
(b) **Size.** L. 7½ in. (190 mm).
  **Material.** Stainless steel.

To obtain every shred of precious crab or lobster meat, particularly from the long, narrow cavities in the legs, you need picks like these. One end is forked, and in pick (a) very sharp, for grabbing hold of the meat and pulling it out. Lacking such a pick you can always messily suck at the legs, or you can improvise a pick by bending the end of a butcher's skewer. Lobster picks will also deal with winkles and snails.

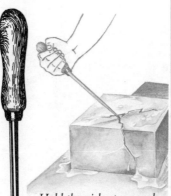

*Hold the pick at an angle of 45° and stab it into the block of ice to break it up. Continue until you have chips the size you want.*

# Pastry prickers

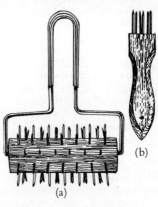

(b)

(a)

(a) **Size.** L. 7¾ in. (197 mm).
  **Material.** Wooden barrel, steel nails, plastic and alloy steel handle.
(b) **Size.** L. 5¼ in. (133 mm).
  **Material.** Tinned steel prongs, wooden handle.

Use pastry prickers to make tiny holes in the bases of tarts and pastry cases before baking. This procedure ensures that the pastry stays level, rising without blisters, as the holes allow the steam to escape evenly. The large pricker (a) has a number of spikes set in a roller and is excellent when pricking large batches of pastry. The pricker (b) is a much smaller version and has six sharp wire prongs set in a handle. It is more useful for home baking than (a) which is used more by professional bakers. Pastry prickers are not essential—a fork or a needle will do the job almost as quickly.

# Sausage pricker

**Size.** L. 8¼ in. (120 mm).
**Material.** Stainless steel blade and pins, rosewood handle.

This may seem a very specialized tool, but the blade can pare vegetables as well as sever the links of a sausage chain. The pins prick sausage skins to prevent them bursting. They are very sharp and should be stuck into a cork when not in use.

(a) **Size.** L. 5 in. (127 mm).
   **Material.** Tinned steel.
(b) **Size.** L. 7 in. (178 mm).
   **Material.** Stainless steel.
(c) **Size.** L. 4 in. (100 mm).
   **Material.** Stainless steel.
(d) **Size.** L. 8¾ in. (223 mm).
   **Material.** Stainless steel.
(e) **Size.** L. 13¼ in. (336 mm).
   **Material.** Stainless steel.
(f) **Size.** L. 14¼ in. (362 mm).
   **Material.** Stainless steel.
(g) **Size.** L. 12¾ in. (324 mm).
   **Material.** Stainless steel.

Meat and poultry sometimes need to be held firmly in shape while cooking–heat has a way of making fibres contract, spread-eagling an untrussed roasting bird or causing the stuffing to spill from carefully folded but un-skewered paupiettes. With skewers and thread these disasters can be avoided. Both wooden and metal skewers are made in various lengths and thicknesses and, if they are made of stainless steel, they can be used again and again. Wooden skewers are cheap but they lack the advantage of a ring handle which can act as an eye for lacing string and make the skewer easier to remove.

Skewer (a) is the type found in meat prepared in butcher's shops.

## Skewers

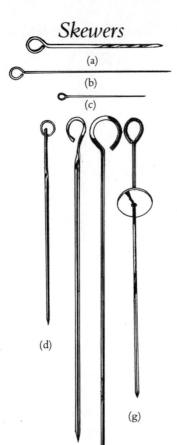

(a)

(b)

(c)

(d)

(e)

(f)

(g)

It is square in section, but twisted to help when inserting it into meat and to make it stay there once it is in place. This skewer is excellent for securing large cuts of meat but it is too thick for small skewering jobs or for testing cakes. It will also rust eventually.

Skewers (b) and (c) are made in various lengths of strong but thin steel with ring handles which act as lacing eyes for string when closing poultry cavities. They are also thin enough to be used to fasten small parcels of food, pau-piettes of fish or meat, or angels on horseback, as they leave only the tiniest holes once they have been removed.

The kebab skewers (d) to (g) are made of flat strips of steel, so that food impaled on them doesn't swing about on the skewer while being grilled. All these skewers have very sharp points with the blunt end curved round to form a handle–except for skewer (d) which has a ring threaded through the blunt end. Skewer (g) is slightly twisted at the pointed end and has a metal disc which is used to push the cooked food off the skewer. Kebab skewers some-times have decorative ends reminiscent of the elaborate hâtelets (ornamental skewers) be-loved by Edwardian cooks.

## Potato bakers

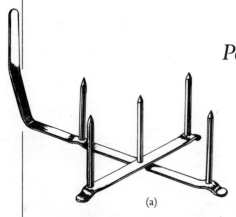

(a)

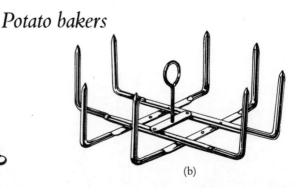

(b)

(a) **Size.** L. (spike) 4 in.
   (100 mm).
   **Material.** Aluminium.
(b) **Size.** L. (spike) 3 in. (75 mm).
   **Material.** Aluminium.

Potatoes impaled on aluminium spikes will bake faster than those laid on an oven rack, as the spike conducts heat to the centre of the potato. The main disadvantage with this implement is that the potatoes need to be fairly small.

Baker (a) holds a maximum of five medium sized potatoes and

has a handle at one end. The slightly smaller baker (b) has shorter spikes which are fixed closer together. It will hold eight rather small potatoes.

These baking spikes can also be used to hold apples and onions as well as pieces of meat or poultry. Alternatively, use skewers.

# Toothpicks

**Size.** L. 3½ in. (90 mm).
**Material.** Wood.

Flat wooden toothpicks, which are pointed at one end, make ideal fastening pins for paupiettes, croques-monsieur and caramelized oranges. They save the trouble of fiddling about with little bits of string and can be easily removed before serving.

## Making candied oranges

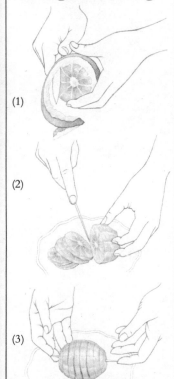

(1)

(2)

(3)

Peel the orange thickly, removing all the pith and membrane (1). Slice it thinly (2). Reassemble it and secure it with toothpicks (3). It can then be marinaded in liqueur or coated in a caramelized sugar syrup. To serve, remove the toothpicks, letting the slices fall in a neat row.

# Larding needles

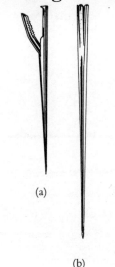

(a)

(b)

(a) **Size.** L. 7¾ in. (197 mm).
 **Material.** Stainless steel.
(b) **Size.** L. 10 in. (255 mm).
 **Material.** Stainless steel.

Larding needles have sharp points and long hollow bodies and are designed to thread small strips of fat through very lean meat to lubricate and enrich it as it cooks. Cavities at the end of these hollow needles are used like needle eyes. When choosing a needle, make sure that it is long enough to pass through the piece of meat which you intend to lard. To use the needle thread it with a strip of fat and push it along—rather than across—the grain of the meat. As you pull the needle out, the meat closes over its path, taking the fat as it does so.

The larding needle (a) holds fat in a hinged, shark-like jaw. The longer needle (b) has a petal arrangement for holding the fat, which is slightly less efficient than the strong jaw of needle (a).

Today animal fats tend to be avoided rather than encouraged in our diet, and larding meat has gone rather out of favour. Instead of larding lean meat with fat you can keep it moist through very fast cooking, paper or foil wrappings or hermetic sealing, or by the addition of fine vegetable purées.

## Larding lean beef with pork back fat

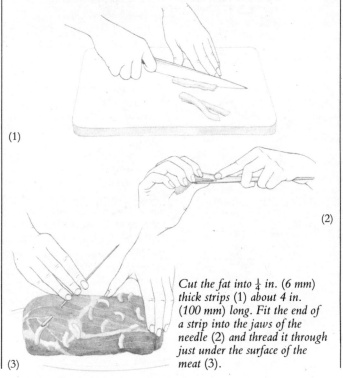

(1)

(2)

(3)

Cut the fat into ¼ in. (6 mm) thick strips (1) about 4 in. (100 mm) long. Fit the end of a strip into the jaws of the needle (2) and thread it through just under the surface of the meat (3).

(a) **Size.** L. 5½ in. (140 mm).
   **Material.** Stainless steel.
(b) **Size.** L. 17 in. (430 mm).
   **Material.** Stainless steel.

Looking like giant darning needles with eyes large enough to take a thin gauge of string and with very sharp, spear-like points, these needles help to make a neat and efficient job of trussing poultry or sewing up stuffed joints. Needle (a) is made in varying lengths – make sure it is long

# Trussing needles

(a)

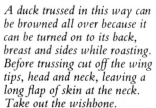

(b)

enough for the bird or meat you are trussing. (A 12 in. needle should cope with a medium-sized turkey.)

Butchers use the long, wooden-handled trussing needle (b). With this needle, the eye is at the point, which means that the string can be threaded and pulled through as soon as the point emerges. The needle is then withdrawn. This makes for quick trussing of large and resistant joints and carcasses for the freezer.

# Trussing a duck

(1)
(2)
(3)

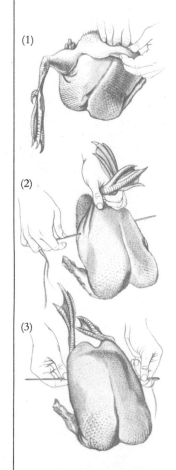

*A duck trussed in this way can be browned all over because it can be turned on to its back, breast and sides while roasting. Before trussing cut off the wing tips, head and neck, leaving a long flap of skin at the neck. Take out the wishbone.*

*1. With the bird resting on its shoulders, break the backbone by forcing the parson's nose forward into the cavity. Tuck it inside and press the two little bones on either side of the cavity inwards.*

*2. With the bird on its back, lift the legs. Draw the needle through the thighs just below the leg bones.*

*3. Push the legs down and stretch the flap of skin from the belly out over the legs. Then bring the needle back again, drawing it (through the flap) above the leg bones. Knot the ends of string.*

*4. Sit the bird on its neatly trussed tail-end and stretch the flap of skin from the neck over the back and around the wings.*

*5. Secure this skin by drawing the needle through the duck under the wing bones. Bring the needle back again, this time going over one wing bone, through the back, then over the other wing bone. Knot the ends.*

*6. Cut off the feet. You now have a neat, brick-shaped trussed duck.*

(4)
(5)
(6)

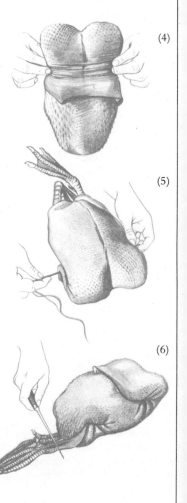

# PASTRY BRUSHES

Pastry brushes are most often used to apply washes of beaten egg, milk or syrup to dough, pastry, cakes and fruit tarts, either before or after baking. The best sizes for this have heads between 1 in. (25 mm) and 1½ in. (38 mm) wide. However, there are plenty of jobs for pastry brushes in the kitchen and one or two extras of other sizes will be found quite useful.

The best brushes are either flat or round headed and made of sterilized hog's bristle, set firmly in plain wooden handles. Flat brushes are constructed exactly like house painter's brushes with the bristles set into a tinned steel band with non-toxic glue. Round brushes usually have the bristles glued directly into a cavity in the handle. Nylon brushes may last longer than natural bristle ones but their filaments are square-ended, harder and less resilient than bristle. This makes them likely to mark very soft pastry. They also lack the microscopic barbs found on natural bristle, which means that each dip into your egg glaze will have a smaller charge with a nylon brush. The filaments can also melt.

Brushes should be washed in warm, soapy water, then flicked dry and left to air. Avoid drying the bristles by tweaking them in a towel, as you may loosen them. Brushes which have been used for eggs should be rinsed in cold water before washing.

(a) **Size.** L. 8 in. (204 mm).
    **Material.** Hog's bristle, beechwood handle, tinned steel band.
(b) **Size.** L. 8 in. (204 mm).
    **Material.** Hog's bristle, beechwood handle.
(c) **Size.** L. 7 in. (178 mm).
    **Material.** Goose feathers.

The flat pastry brush (a) is 1 in. (25 mm) wide and a good size for spreading melted jam on to rolled-out marzipan when icing rich fruit cakes, or for brushing surplus flour from pastry. Use it, too, rather than a screw of buttered paper, to apply a beautiful, even film of oil or fat to the insides of tins or dishes that need greasing. (The butter or fat need not be

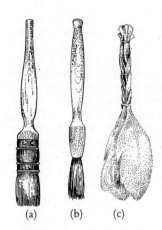

(a)    (b)    (c)

melted, a good brush picks up plenty, if the fat is slightly soft.) You can also use this brush (instead of a spoon) to coat food with melted aspic.

The round pastry brush (b) is not so generally useful, but is ideal for glazing intricate pastry decorations, as it is narrow enough to reach into crevices.

The old-fashioned goose feather brush (c) consists of a bunch of feathers lashed together for about half its length. Like birch twig whisks it is possibly bought more for its old-fashioned "folksy" appearance than for its efficiency; but, in fact, if you need a tool to apply the lightest possible white-of-egg glaze, the traditional goose feather brush is the one to use.

*You can quickly apply redcurrant jelly to the fruit in barquettes, or other tartlets, using a flat brush.*

*A goose feather brush is very flexible and will put a thin, smooth glaze on delicate pastry without leaving a mark.*

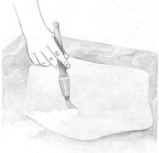

*Brush surplus flour from the surface of rolled-out pastry with a pastry brush. This is more effective than blowing it.*

# SPOONS, SKIMMERS, LIFTERS AND TURNERS

You will need a spoon whenever something needs mixing, tasting, skimming, scooping or measuring.

Spoons for stirring and mixing are usually made of wood, which is strong, inflexible and a poor conductor of heat – factors worth considering if the spoon is needed for vigorous beating or for stirring for any length of time in a pan of boiling jam. These spoons should be made of hardwoods: beech, ash, sycamore, hornbeam and olive are those most frequently used. Softwoods are sometimes resinous and resin is a flavour that can linger for ages, brought out by the heat every time the spoon is used. Flavours, conversely, are absorbed by wood, so make sure that any wooden spoon, whether made of hard or softwood, is washed, dried and aired very thoroughly before being put away.

The clean slicing edge of a metal spoon makes it an ideal utensil for the special cutting action needed when folding light mixtures together. With a large metal spoon you can baste meat, skim fat off gravy, taste cool mixtures (not very hot ones as metal retains heat), mix and measure. A smaller tablespoon (or rather two tablespoons) is useful for shaping soft mixtures like meringue, quenelles or dumplings before cooking. The best but most expensive kitchen spoons are made of stainless steel; cheaper spoons are made of chromed steel. Metal spoons often have wooden or plastic handles to protect your hand from the heat and holes for hanging them up – preferably somewhere near the stove where they will be most handy.

The shape of a spoon is closely linked to its purpose. In England and America wooden spoons with thick scooped-out bowls are used for beating cakes and batters, stirring stews and sauces and making jam. In France, a flat rectangular spatula is more commonly used, as it more closely fits the contours of the flat-bottomed French mixing bowl. The size of the spoon is also important, so it is a good idea to keep a selection of different sized spoons available – a short light spoon is just what you want for a small quantity of sauce or mayonnaise, a larger spoon is needed to mix batters or stir a stew and a really large, very long-handled spoon is necessary when making jams and preserves. Since spoons are usually quite cheap most cooks have a fairly varied collection of these homely tools, either in a jug by the stove or hanging from hooks nearby.

## Ladles

A ladle will help you to transport liquids neatly and safely from the stockpot, saucepan or mixing bowl so that you can safely deposit the contents precisely where you want them. They are also useful, once you know their capacity, for measuring liquids. Scoops, used for portioning out dry ingredients, such as rice or flour, can similarly be used as rough measures.

Ladles are usually made of metal, often with hooks at the end of the handle so that you can hang them either on the wall or on the rim of the pan from which you are ladling.

When choosing a ladle examine the join (if any) between the bowl and handle and make sure it is good and strong. Consider too the slope of the handle: will it allow a full ladle to ascend from the depths of your largest pot without spilling half its contents? And if you are going to use it for napping éclairs with chocolate sauce is it upright enough for the job to be done comfortably?

## Skimmers and strainers

Ladles and spoons used for skimming and straining are usually made of metal with perforated or slotted bowls. For some tasks, such as deep frying batter-coated foods, wire mesh skimmers prove more useful. With these the fat can be thoroughly cleared of small bits and pieces of food which if left behind soon burn and give the fat an acrid taste.

Lifters and turners are usually flat, sometimes flexible, sometimes slotted or perforated. Their shape and size is a matter of personal preference.

(a) **Size.** L. 12 in. (305 mm).
(b) **Size.** L. 18¼ in. (463 mm).
(c) **Size.** L. 12 in. (305 mm).
(d) **Size.** L. 14 in. (355 mm).
(e) **Size.** L. 12 in. (305 mm).

These attractive wooden spoons are made of either beechwood or hornbeam, which is lightweight, strong and pale in colour. Spoons (a) and (b) are general purpose kitchen spoons made in the traditional pattern.

The angled wooden spoons (c) and (d) are used in exactly the same

# Wooden spoons

way as rounded spoons, but have corners on the bowl to help them get into the crevices of sharply-angled pans. Spoon (d) is completely flat with a hole in it and is used to stir thick mixtures like porridge.

The egg-lifting spoon (e) has a large hole in the middle of the bowl which enables you to lift eggs out of boiling water more easily. It also allows them to drain and dry before going into their egg cups. Hardly an essential tool, but like (d) it could be useful for beating air into batters.

## Creaming

*Tip the bowl so that you can exert maximum pressure on the spoon. Use the back of the spoon to crush the sugar and fat against the sides of the bowl.*

## Beating

*Tip the bowl and beat rapidly with the spoon to eliminate any lumps and to incorporate as much air as possible into the mixture.*

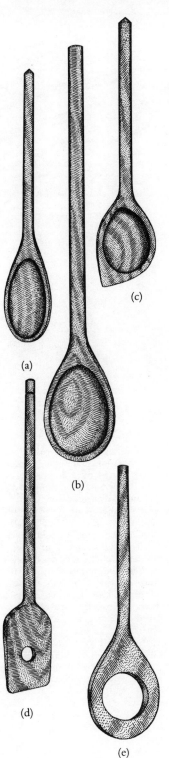

(c)

(a)

(b)

(d)

(e)

## Shaping a cottage loaf

*Divide the dough in two, with one piece twice as large as the other. Flour the handle of a wooden spoon and press it into the centre of the dough; this helps to secure the top piece to the dough below.*

## Brandy snaps

*While brandy snaps are still warm from the oven and pliable, wrap them around the greased handle of a wooden spoon to form cylinders.*

123

(a) **Size.** L. 13¾ in. (350 mm).
(b) **Size.** L. 12 in. (305 mm).
(c) **Size.** L. 11¼ in. (285 mm).
(d) **Size.** L. 11 in. (280 mm).
(e) **Size.** 12 in. (305 mm).

Where English and American cooks use wooden spoons, French cooks use wooden spatulas. A flat-sided spatula is certainly better for folding mixtures together, and it can also double as a turning and lifting tool.

Spatula (a) is the classic shape, its flat bowl, shaped like an exclamation mark, tapers in section at the tip and thickens into a flat, straight, narrow handle. This spatula is quite inflexible, unlike spatula (b) which gives slightly and is angled to scrape corners clean of any mixture. The paddle-shaped spatula (c) is very rigid with tapered sides which make it excellent for vigorous beating and for scraping the straight sides of saucepans.

Shaped like a flattened club, spatula (d), with sharp edges for scraping, makes a good tool for beating or pounding. The slight curve of spatula (e) makes it useful for lifting as well as mixing, and the four slots cut into the blade help incorporate air when beating.

# Wooden spatulas

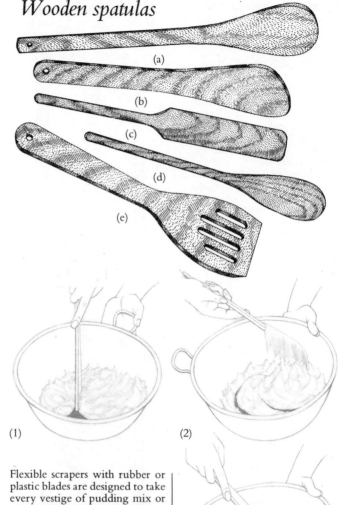

(1)  (2)  (3)

# Scrapers/spatulas

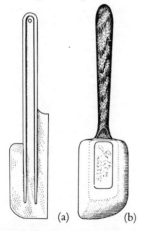

(a)  (b)

(a) **Size.** L. 9 in. (230 mm).
**Material.** Plastic.
(b) **Size.** L. 9¼ in. (235 mm).
**Material.** Rubber blade, wooden handle.

Flexible scrapers with rubber or plastic blades are designed to take every vestige of pudding mix or cake batter from the mixing bowl. (These tools are always popular with children who like to do this with their fingers.) They are also good tools for folding and blending very light aerated mixtures.

The double-edged spatula (a) is cheap, but avoid using it with hot pans as it is made of the sort of plastic that melts in contact with direct heat. Spatula (b) is sturdier, but again is not suitable for use in very hot pans. Both spatulas do a very thorough job of cleaning out mixing bowls and are essential with non-stick pans which will be scratched if scraped clean with wooden or metal spatulas.

*Always add the lighter ingredients to the heavier ones to avoid losing air in the mixture. Do this by "cutting" with the spatula rather than stirring (1). Lift the spatula clear with every turn (2). Move the bowl round as you work until the mixture is well blended (3).*

(a) **Size.** L. 9½ in. (242 mm).
**Material.** Stainless steel.
(b) **Size.** L. 12½ in. (317 mm).
**Material.** Chromed steel bowl, wooden handle.
(c) **Size.** L. 12¾ in. (324 mm).
**Material.** Stainless steel bowl, plasticized wood handle.

Metal spoons, used in the kitchen for stirring, mixing and basting, should be strong and inflexible. Spoon (a) is made of one piece of metal, which means it is less likely to come apart than spoons with

## Small spoons

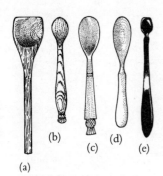

(a)

(a) **Size.** L. 6 in. (152 mm).
**Material.** Wood.
(b) **Size.** L. 4½ in. (115 mm).
**Material.** Boxwood.
(c) **Size.** L. 5 in. (127 mm).
**Material.** Horn.
(d) **Size.** L. 4¾ in. (120 mm).
**Material.** Horn.
(e) **Size.** L. 5¼ in. (133 mm).
**Material.** Stainless steel.

All these small spoons, used primarily for serving rather than preparing food, are designed for specific purposes. Spoon (a) has angled corners specially shaped to get into the corners of jam pots. The carved boxwood spoon (b) and the stainless steel spoon (e) have flat bowls for dabbing mustard on to the side of your plate. Spoons (c) and (d) are made of horn and make very good egg spoons. (Metals can give a nasty taste to a boiled egg and silver tarnishes.) They also make attractive sauce spoons – though not for hot sauces as horn can deteriorate with heat.

## Metal spoons

(a)

(b)

(c)

## Shaping meringues

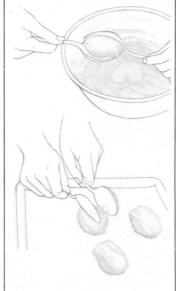

*To form oval meringues, use two metal spoons. One spoon acts as a scoop and the other slides under the mixture to ease it on to the tray. This will give you meringues of the same shape and size each time.*

joins. Although it is sturdy, its metal handle can get very hot if left for any time in a hot pan.

The slightly larger spoon (b) has measurements marked in the bowl (from one teaspoon to two tablespoons) as well as a small lip on the side for pouring. Spoon (c) has a handle guaranteed to be chip-proof and heat resistant, which are advantages not possessed by spoon (b), which has a gaily painted wooden handle vulnerable to every kind of wear and tear, chipping, working loose and burning.

## Making a level spoonful

*To obtain a level spoonful of dry ingredients, draw the edge of a knife across the bowl of a heaped spoonful.*

## Making a biscuit crumb base

*To make a firm base of biscuit crumbs for a cheesecake mix them with melted butter, then press them into the flan tin with the back of a spoon.*

125

## Tasting spoons

(a)                (b)

(a) **Size.** L. 9¼ in. (235 mm).
**Material.** Porcelain.
(b) **Size.** L. 9¾ in. (248 mm).
**Material.** Wood.

Spoons for tasting, where the tasting is to be truly critical and not just a greedy slurp on the sly, are best made of stainless steel or porcelain. A metal spoon tends to retain heat and burn your lips; a porcelain spoon (a) remains cool and allows a clear clean taste. This spoon is very pretty – but also expensive and, being made of porcelain, breakable.

The wooden spoon (b) has a runnel along the handle between the stirring bowl and the smaller tasting bowl. The runnel ensures that the mixture will be sufficiently cool by the time it reaches the taster, but unfortunately it is too narrow to be useful for anything other than fairly thin liquids. This spoon is also awkward to hold and, without a steady hand and some concentration, messy to use.

## Rice paddles

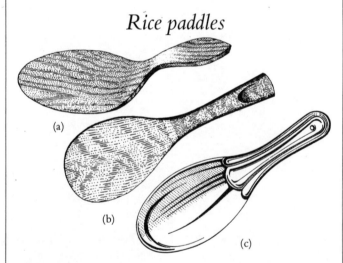

(a)                (b)           (c)

(a) **Size.** L. 9¼ in. (235 mm).
**Material.** Wood.
(b) **Size.** L. 9¾ in. (248 mm).
**Material.** Bamboo with varnished handle.
(c) **Size.** L. 9½ in. (242 mm).
**Material.** Aluminium.

These Oriental rice paddles can be used for serving rice or for mixing cooked rice with meat or vegetables. Both paddles (a) and (b) are made of very smooth wood or bamboo. They are only slightly curved, and taper to a thin but rounded edge so that you can separate a large, soft, grainy mass of rice without cutting or mashing the grains. Their nearly flat bowls hold a fairly generous amount of rice. (To keep the rice from sticking, dip the paddle in cold water first – the rice will then slide off easily.) The metal rice paddle (c) is primarily a serving spoon, the bowl being exactly the right size for one large portion of rice.

## Wooden ladles

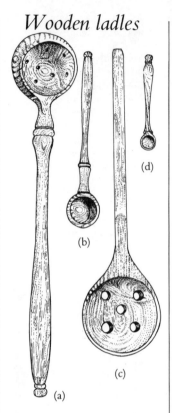

(a) **Size.** L. 16 in. (405 mm).
(b) **Size.** L. 8 in. (204 mm).
(c) **Size.** L. 13½ in. (343 mm).
(d) **Size.** L. 4 in. (100 mm).

Often made of boxwood, olivewood or beechwood, these deep, almost spherically bowled ladles are designed to take pickles, preserves and olives from their jars or preserving barrels.

Ladle (a) has a deep perforated bowl with a very long handle and will reach to the bottom of a very large pickle jar or barrel and scoop out large amounts.

By contrast, the tiny ladle (b) will just about manage to scoop up one cherry or olive at a time, retaining its preserving liquid as the bowl is not perforated.

The flatter, larger ladle (c) is big enough to scoop up whole preserved peaches or candied oranges. It is useful if you are making candied fruit as it will allow the syrup to drain away without cutting into the fruit.

The smallest wooden ladle (d) is unperforated and is suitable for use as a salt spoon.

## Ladles

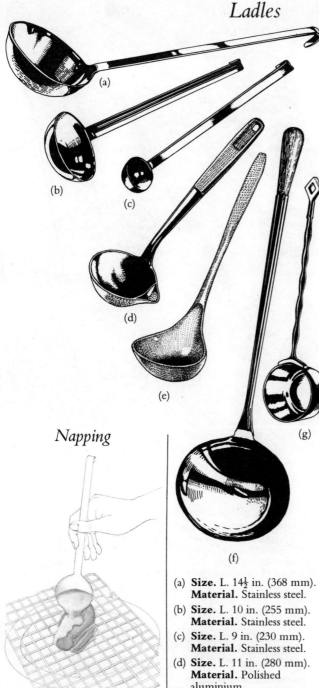

(a)

(b)

(c)

(d)

(e)

(g)

(f)

## Napping

A ladle with a very upright handle is the best tool to use when applying a coating of sauce to food after it has been arranged on a dish. Pass it over the dish, pouring the sauce evenly.

(a) **Size.** L. 14½ in. (368 mm).
**Material.** Stainless steel.

(b) **Size.** L. 10 in. (255 mm).
**Material.** Stainless steel.

(c) **Size.** L. 9 in. (230 mm).
**Material.** Stainless steel.

(d) **Size.** L. 11 in. (280 mm).
**Material.** Polished aluminium.

(e) **Size.** L. 11¼ in. (285 mm).
**Material.** Plastic.

(f) **Size.** L. 18 in. (458 mm).
**Materials.** Stainless steel bowl, wooden handle.

(g) **Size.** L. 8 in. (204 mm).
**Material.** Stainless steel.

Ladle (a) has a long handle so you can reach to the bottom of a deep pan and a small flange or turned-out edge round the rim of the bowl. (Without such a rim a ladle can make a messy job of pouring.) It is made of one piece of stainless steel, which makes it expensive, but gives it the advantages of strength and ease of cleaning.

The smaller ladle (b) has a very long upright handle, making it useful for "napping" (or masking) dishes with sauces. With this ladle your hand is at a comfortable angle for pouring out the sauce and righting the ladle again.

The very small ladle (c) has a tiny bowl and its design makes it ideal for use with a chinois as it is small enough to fit right to the bottom of the sieve.

Gravy ladles are made with very long slanted handles so you can skim off gravy from shallow roasting pans, and oval rather than round bowls with one side forming a spout (these are fine for right-handed cooks, not so good for left-handers). These ladles are also useful for measuring out the same quantity of liquid again and again – which you need to do when making pancakes for example. Ladle (d) has a patent device in the bowl for separating fat from gravy. A bar across the bottom of the ladle with a small hole in it allows the gravy to be poured through, leaving all the fat behind in the ladle.

Ladle (e) is made of brightly coloured melamine, which is heat resistant and very strong. It suits a right or left-handed cook as it has a turned-out edge all round the rim of the bowl.

The Chinese ladle (f) has a handle set at an angle to the bowl which suits the contours of the very wide and shallow wok. A skilful Chinese chef uses a spatula and this ladle at the same time, rapidly stirring, scooping and turning the food as it cooks. The large ladle shown here has a capacity of ½ pt. (0·28 ℓ) and it can also be used for serving soup or skimming fat from broth.

The Indian ladle (g) has a cup-shaped bowl which is riveted firmly on to its decorative handle. It is used for serving curry.

(a) **Size.** L. 9½ in. (242 mm).
**Material.** Stainless steel.
(b) **Size.** L. 12¼ in. (310 mm).
**Material.** Chromed steel bowl, wooden handle.
(c) **Size.** L. 11½ in. (292 mm).
**Material.** Tinned wire.
(d) **Size.** L. 12¾ in. (324 mm).
**Material.** Tinned wire.
(e) **Size.** L. 10½ in. (267 mm).
**Material.** Wire mesh.
(f) **Size.** L. 17 in. (430 mm).
**Material.** Stainless steel bowl, wooden handle.

Both the perforated metal spoons (a) and (b) are designed to lift food from pans of boiling water for serving, or to remove scum or floating pieces from stock or broth. Spoon (a) is a useful shape (like a large perforated tablespoon), a handy size and, as it is made of one piece of the stainless steel, is the stronger of the two spoons.

Skimmers (c) and (d) can both be used to retrieve quenelles or dumplings from broth or boiling water, and to lift chips, fritters or croquettes from deep fat. Skimmer (d) is larger than (c) and saucer-shaped, so that you can take up a number of dumplings or fritters at one time (since once cooked they all tend to rise to the surface together), while allowing all superfluous liquid to drain away. The larger the skimmer the more you can take up at one go, but if the pan is not big a small spoon-shaped skimmer is more useful. Both skimmers (c) and (d) have long handles so that the cook will be at a comfortable distance from the hot fat – the bowl-shaped dumpling ladle (d) is particularly good for fishing doughnuts from deep fryers.

# Slotted spoons and skimmers

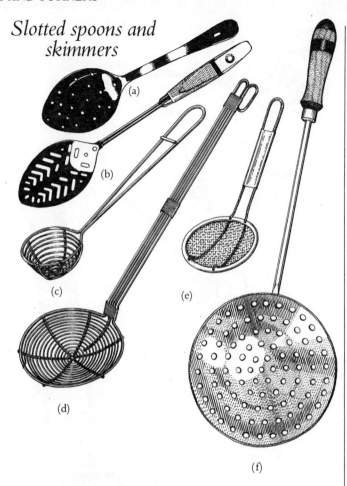

A wire mesh skimmer should be used to remove batter-coated foods from deep fat as the fine wire mesh will clear the fat of small bits of food and particles of fried batter. The Japanese skimmer (e) is especially well made and sturdy: it has a neat light frame, and the mesh is welded rather than stapled to the frame so that the skimmer has smooth edges.

The Indian skimmer (f) is flat and perforated all over, with a wooden handle set horizontally to the bowl. It is designed for use in a large shallow frying pan and is used to remove Indian fried breads from hot fat.

Scoops like these are made in all sizes. Scoop (a) has a flat back, which means it holds more than scoop (b), its handle has a closed welded end and, being made of stainless steel, it is obviously destined for a long and useful life. Scoop (b) is made of tinned steel, but as long as it is used only with dry foods it should not rust, and will serve most purposes while costing much less than scoop (a).

# Flour scoops

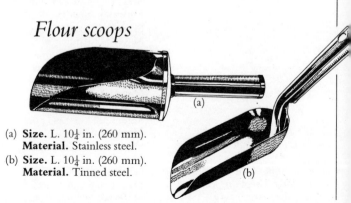

(a) **Size.** L. 10¼ in. (260 mm).
**Material.** Stainless steel.
(b) **Size.** L. 10¼ in. (260 mm).
**Material.** Tinned steel.

## Lifters and turners

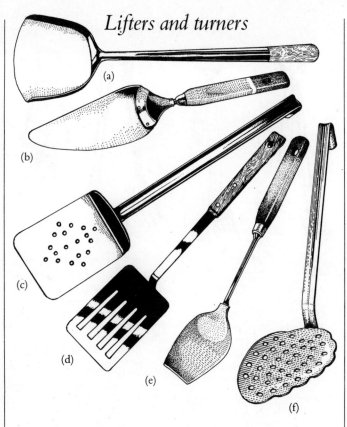

(a)
(b)
(c)
(d)
(e)
(f)

(a) **Size.** L. 14 in. (355 mm).
**Material.** Stainless steel.

(b) **Size.** L. 11½ in. (292 mm).
**Material.** Chromed steel.

(c) **Size.** L. 15½ in. (394 mm).
**Material.** Stainless steel.

(d) **Size.** L. 14½ in. (368 mm).
**Material.** Stainless steel.

(e) **Size.** L. 11½ in. (292 mm).
**Material.** Nylon spoon,
plastic handle.

(f) **Size.** L. 17 in. (430 mm).
**Material.** Stainless steel
bowl, wooden handle.

The Chinese turner (a) is used with a ladle in a wok. The two tools together turn, stir and blend the food as it cooks at top speed. The edge of the turner is curved to fit the rounded contours of the wok and the sides are lipped so that it resembles a little shovel. With it food can be scooped up and turned quickly and easily. It is very well made and nicely balanced, but its long handle limits its use to wok cookery.

The very flexible turner (b) is a useful all purpose utensil, good for lifting and turning rashers of bacon, fried eggs or fillets of fish. Unfortunately, it is so cheaply made that it needs to be replaced every few years – usually the chrome plate wears off or it breaks where the handle is riveted to the blade.

Lifters (c) and (d) are more sturdily made, with long handles welded or riveted to the blades. The slotted lifter (d) has a patented bonded-wood handle, which will not chip, burn or split.

The spoon-shaped lifter (e) makes a nice baster and turner, especially for fried eggs. It has a nylon bowl which won't scratch non-stick pans.

Lifter (f), with a perforated bowl, is designed as a fish lifter. The bowl is scalloped along the front edge and lipped upward at the back, making it a useful strainer, drainer and lifter all in one.

## Ice cream scoops

(a)
(b)

(a) **Size.** L. 9 in. (230 mm).
**Material.** Stainless steel.

(b) **Size.** L. 7 in. (178 mm).
**Material.** Aluminium.

Scoop (a) is the sort of scoop that is used in ice cream parlours and mystifies children with the swiftness and neatness of its action. Plunged into ice cream, it will produce a perfect sphere with one squeeze of the handle as the curved metal blade whizzes across the semi-spherical bowl and back again. The scoop is a handy tool for freezer owners and useful too for shaping mashed potatoes or whipped egg whites.

If you can't wait for the most solid block of ice cream to thaw enough for scoop (a) to work on it, then scoop (b), which is filled with a chemical similar to that used in car radiators, will dig into it for you. The chemical is not toxic and is, in any case, sealed into the handle from which it cannot escape.

## Stilton scoop

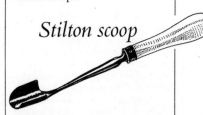

**Size.** L. 9¼ in. (235 mm).
**Material.** Electro-plated nickel silver, ivory handle.

A Stilton scoop like this may still be found in antique shops and on secondhand stalls. In Victorian times, the fashion was to use the scoop to take portions from a whole Stilton cheese without disturbing the rind. Modern Stilton eaters often prefer to cut slices horizontally from the top, rind included.

# Cooking tongs

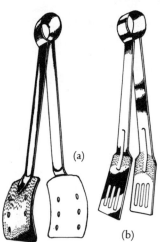

(a) **Size.** L. 13 in. (330 mm).
**Material.** Bamboo.

(b) **Size.** L. 8 in. (204 mm).
**Material.** Stainless steel.

(c) **Size.** L. 9¼ in. (235 mm).
**Material.** Stainless steel.

Hands are the most efficient tools for picking things up, turning them over and setting them down, but they have one great disadvantage – they are not heat resistant. This is what makes tongs like these, designed to deal with food as it cooks, so useful.

The bamboo tongs (a) are beautifully simple in construction, feather-light, with an open span of 2½ in. (65 mm). Although very cheap they work wonderfully well. With them you can turn frying foods, lift and serve spaghetti and pick vegetables out of boiling water. The tapered ends can pinch up tiny particles of food most precisely.

Indian cooks use tongs (b) to turn flatbreads on a bakestone. They do not need a wide span and the tongs open only 1¼ in. (32 mm).

The metal tongs (c) perform similar tasks to tongs (a), but because the ends are inflexible and close only at the extreme edge, they are not as unerringly accurate in their grasp.

# Serving tongs

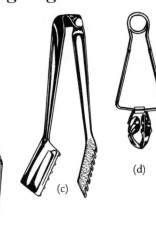

(a) **Size.** L. 9½ in. (242 mm).
**Material.** Stainless steel.

(b) **Size.** L. 8¾ in. (223 mm).
**Material.** Stainless steel.

(c) **Size.** L. 7½ in. (190 mm).
**Material.** Stainless steel.

(d) **Size.** L. 6¼ in. (160 mm).
**Material.** Stainless steel.

If you want to lift escalopes, chops or fish from the frying pan or grill, and transfer them to a serving dish or to plates, the serving tongs (a) with their large, perforated ends are the ones to use. They are strong enough to handle quite large pieces of food and the perforated ends open to 4½ in. (115 mm).

The flat, slotted ends on the sandwich tongs (b) are set at an angle to enable them to rest on the plate, so that sandwiches can be served tidily and hygienically.

As this style of service is rarely experienced in most ordinary families, tongs like these might prove more useful for general lifting and cooking jobs. The ends close flat together making it easy to grasp things firmly. They open to 4 in. (100 mm).

The spaghetti tongs (c) have one comb-like and one spoon-like end angled so that they form a narrow cup when closed together. They could serve other foods, apart from spaghetti, but they only open to 2 in. (50 mm).

The little snail tongs (d) are used to hold the hot, buttery shells in which snails are cooked. They are always paired with special snail forks (see FORKS). Unlike other tongs, you squeeze them together to open them and they snap shut when released, holding the snail shell very firmly.

# Strawberry huller

**Size.** L. 2¼ in. (57 mm).
**Material.** Tinned steel.

If the length of your elegant nails makes strawberry hulling difficult, use these instead. You can also use them to pick out the few bones that always seem to get left in fillets of fish before cooking.

*Hold the shell at its widest point, or the spring will cause the shell to pop out.*

(a) **Size.** L. 7½ in. (190 mm).
**Material.** Tinned steel wire.

(b) **Size.** L. 10¼ in. (260 mm).
**Material.** Stainless steel.

(c) **Size.** L. 9 in. (230 mm).
**Material.** Tinned steel wire, wooden handle.

Pot-lifting tongs are a help when taking heavy pans without handles from the heat. Tongs (a) are made of heavy gauge wire and are simply designed like scissors. Two triangular loops on the ends allow you to use them for lifting food as well as pots. They open very wide, 6¼ in. (160 mm) and can grip the necks of jars.

The long-handled tongs (b) are designed specifically for lifting Indian pots and pans, which are made without handles. They are very strong indeed and can lift the heaviest pots.

The pronged end of the French tongs (c) goes under the lip of a pan and the other looped one clamps firmly on top. You can lift almost any weight with these tongs (which are made of very heavy gauge wire) as long as you can get a good purchase. The fat, wooden handle helps you grip firmly and the wire one fits neatly over it. These tongs interlock most ingeniously and are something of a puzzle to reassemble the first time you take them apart. Like the Indian ones, they work best if the jaws are not opened more than 1½ in. (38 mm).

## Pot-lifting tongs

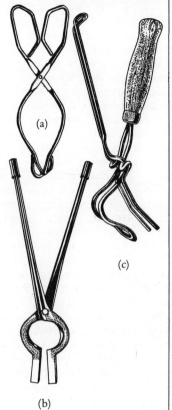

(a)

(c)

(b)

## Pastry crimper

**Size.** L. 4 in. (100 mm).
**Material.** Chromed steel.

These are more likely to be found in professional kitchens than domestic ones. They make the decorative, twisted edges on tarts and flans and can be used instead of marzipan crimpers to decorate simnel cakes and butter balls. They demand some skill in use, simple though the task and the tool may seem. The serrated ends enhance the decoration.

### Decorating marzipan

*Use the crimpers to pinch up the top of a marzipan ring in a herring-bone pattern. This forms the crown of the Simnel cake.*

## Chopsticks

### Whisking eggs with chopsticks

*Use three chopsticks together to whisk eggs. Hold them between your bent fingers with your thumb lying across all three to keep them firm.*

**Size.** L. 12½ in. (317 mm).
**Material.** Bamboo.

Chopsticks work like tongs, with your thumb and forefinger forming the hinge. Kitchen chopsticks are 3 in. (75 mm) longer on average than table chopsticks. Oriental cooks use them to reach into deep pots, pans and bowls and to stir, beat, whisk and lift all sorts of food.

Kitchen chopsticks are usually bamboo, though there are also stainless steel chopsticks, with ridges near the ends for grasping slippery morsels of food.

### How to hold chopsticks

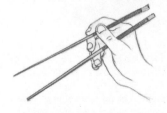

*The lower chopstick rests in the crook of your thumb and on the top joint of your third finger. The upper chopstick is held between forefinger and thumb.*

# WHISKS AND BEATERS

Lightness and volume can be put into cakes and sauces by the skilful incorporation of one of the most useful ingredients in the world – free and invisible air. Tools for putting air into mixtures range from whisking attachments on sophisticated electrical food processors to nothing more than a humble bundle of twigs. There is also a host of patent machines designed to beat air into the thickest of sauces by the rapid rotation of wires, coiled or banded together in various shapes and activated by springs, cogs, gears and ratchets. Yet the most popular tool among professional chefs has always been the perfectly simple balloon whisk made of a bunch of wire loops with the loose ends held together to form a handle.

## Whisks for different purposes

These whisks are made in various weights, with correspondingly different degrees of flexibility to suit the varied types of mixtures in which they can be used. Egg whites, being very light and capable of increasing in volume by many times their original size, need whipping with a large, light, bouncy, round-ended balloon whisk, while a thick, heavy choux pastry, half-set ice cream or dense béchamel sauce is beaten most satisfactorily with a more elongated and rigid whisk made

with thicker, heavier and stronger wires. French chefs, when not using a spatula, prefer to use whisks to blend sauces, where others might more traditionally use wooden spoons. Whisks, if used properly (that is to say, vigorously) will make a very quick and thorough job of obliterating stray lumps, blending ingredients and imparting a final gloss to a sauce.

It is helpful to have a good selection of wire whisks in the kitchen. Once you get used to using them you will find them invaluable; relatively cheap compared with other blending gadgets; easy to clean, because of their simple construction and with no complicated mechanism to go wrong. It is important to fit the size and shape of the whisk to the bowl you are using. If the receptacle is too small the mixture will not have room to expand and incorporate its air and the whisk will be cramped for space in which to move. If the whisk is too small for the pan your work will be doubled and when beating egg whites you may find them creeping up your arm. A rounded whisk suits a round-sided bowl, a slightly pointed whisk gets into the corners of a saucepan. Hence the necessity for plenty of whisks – you will find at least half a dozen in a good kitchen.

## Whisking egg whites

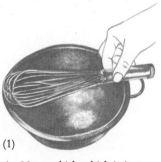

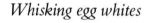

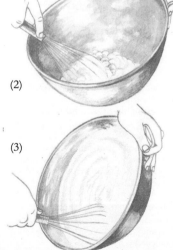

(1)

(2)

(3)

(4)

1. Use a whisk which is just a little longer than the diameter of the bowl. First clean the bowl thoroughly, then stand it on a cloth to avoid scratching it. Add the egg whites – be very careful not to include any yolk.

2. Beat quite slowly at first, turning the bowl and changing hands as you work. (When beating any mixture,

ambidexterity gives one hand a rest while the other takes over.)

3. As the mixture stiffens, beat faster. Finish by whisking really fast with the bowl on its side. This stage is called tightening the whites.

4. The whisking is finished when the foam stands up in peaks and stays put when the bowl is held upside down.

# Egg whisks

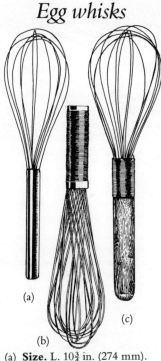

(a)

(b)

(c)

(a) **Size.** L. 10¾ in. (274 mm).
   **Material.** Stainless steel.
(b) **Size.** L. 10½ in. (267 mm).
   **Material.** Tinned steel.
(c) **Size.** L. 12 in. (305 mm).
   **Material.** Tinned steel
   wire, wooden handle.

Because of their lightness, springy wires and bulbous shape all three of these whisks are suitable for beating egg whites to a mountain of foam. To do this they are best used with a copper bowl, as the chemical reaction of raw egg whites to copper makes the foam stronger and larger (see BOWLS).

Whisk (a) is very light, with seven looped strands of wire firmly sealed in the handle. It is the most expensive of the three, but the easiest to keep clean and very strongly made. Whisk (b), with ten wires, is heavier than the others and therefore more tiring to use, although the extra number of very springy wires helps to whip up a foam. The handle is bound round with wire to give a good grip. Whisk (c) has eight wires bound to the handle with a spiral of wire. It is the cheapest, though probably the least hygienic whisk of the three, but is pleasant to use because of its wooden handle and not too heavy.

# Sauce whisks

(a)

(b)

(c)

(d)

(e)

(a) **Size.** L. 6 in. (152 mm).
   **Material.** Tinned steel.
(b) **Size.** L. 9 in. (230 mm).
   **Material.** Tinned steel.
(c) **Size.** L. 10¼ in. (260 mm).
   **Material.** Tinned steel.
(d) **Size.** L. 10¼ in. (260 mm).
   **Material.** Tinned steel.
(e) **Size.** L. 10¼ in. (260 mm).
   **Material.** Stainless steel.

Unlike egg whisks, sauce whisks are rigid and elongated in shape. Their wires are usually held firm—either with a loop on the end of the head (whisk d) or with a perforated ring near the handle (whisks a and b).

Although it is small, whisk (a) is ideal for whipping up a small quantity of cream, blending a vinaigrette or quickly finishing a butter sauce. It is slightly flexible at the tip.

Whisks (b) and (d) have no "give" in them at all. Their wires are thicker than those of egg whisks and their elongated shape makes them useful for beating thick sauces in straight-sided pans. Whisk (c) is slightly flexible, having no device to keep the wires rigid, and its wooden handle makes it very light to use.

The batter whisk (e) is a flat version of a balloon whisk. Its three wire loops are joined firmly by a fourth wire down the middle. A whisk of this shape is excellent for beating batters or any other fairly liquid mixture which needs to be well blended and smooth, as well as slightly aerated.

## How to hold a whisk

*When stirring or folding light mixtures, hold the whisk as you would a pencil, with the balloon end pointing away from you.*

*Hold the whisk with the balloon end facing you when working a stiff mixture. This hold is much less tiring.*

# Birch whisk

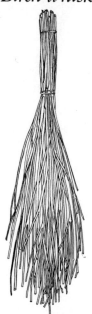

**Size.** L. 11¼ in. (285 mm).
**Material.** Birch twigs.

A bunch of twigs wired together makes a rather primitive – but quite effective – whisk, good for smoothing sauces and beating egg whites. The twigs are flexible and follow the contours of any pan or bowl closely. The delicate young twigs of silver birches are used for such whisks which are quite simple to make. You can collect a bunch from the tips of the branches (in winter when the tree is dormant), trim them and scrape off the bark. Then tie them together tightly with wire. Alternatively use a dampened split twig as a binder. This tightens round the bunch of twigs as it dries, holding them securely.

These whisks need to be replaced fairly frequently as, with use, they tend to shed little twiglets into the sauce or batter being whisked. They are not very easy to clean either as particles of food catch in the twigs.

# Coiled whips

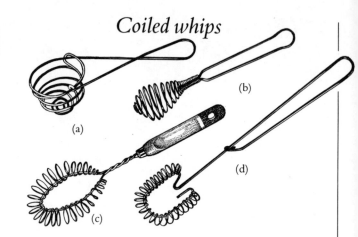

(a) **Size.** L. 8½ in. (215 mm).
   **Material.** Tinned steel.
(b) **Size.** L. 8¾ in. (223 mm).
   **Material.** Stainless steel.
(c) **Size.** L. 11¼ in. (285 mm).
   **Material.** Chromed steel.
(d) **Size.** L. 12½ in. (305 mm).
   **Material.** Chromed steel.

These patent whips made from coiled wire are certainly springy but do not have any other great advantage over the more traditional whisks, unless you are looking for cheapness. Whip (a) is made from one piece of wire, first coiled into a bowl shape and then extended to form the handle.

Whip (b) has a bulb-shaped head which is mounted on a thicker wire handle. Neither whip is as efficient at whisking egg white to meringue consistency as the traditional balloon whisk – or even spiral or rotary whisks. Whip (a) can be used as an egg separator and is also quite handy for fishing boiled eggs out of water. To use them as whisks, hold them as if they were wooden spoons and beat away.

The spiral whips (c) and (d) have coils of very springy wire wound round thicker wire frames. They whisk egg whites quite well, better than whips (a) and (b).

# Sprung whisk

**Size.** L. 12½ in. (317 mm).
**Material.** Plastic body, stainless steel spring.

This whisk rotates rapidly in one direction as you press the handle down and spins equally fast in the other direction as you release it. It beats whipped cream, sauces and batters efficiently, and whisks egg whites speedily when used in a small bowl. It also possesses one advantage over most other whisks; it works in a confined space bounding up and down on the spot, instead of circling the bowl.

*Hold the whisk upright in the bowl and pump the handle up and down like a child's top to make the head of the whisk spin, whipping the ingredients.*

## Rotary whisks

(a) **Size.** L. 12¼ in. (310 mm).
**Material.** Stainless steel beaters, chromed steel structure, wooden handles, nylon pinions.
(b) **Size.** L. 10½ in. (267 mm).
**Material.** Stainless steel beaters, chromed steel structure, Nylon pinions and handles.

The effort of whisking is, in theory, much reduced if you use one of these whisks, which have two four-bladed beaters that are turned by a small handle. You hold the whisk by another handle, which means that these tools require both hands to use them. However, they are speedy and efficient, especially for egg whites, though not noticeably labour saving.

Rotary whisks are most useful when tackling rather heavy mixtures – half-set ice cream for example. As both whisks have beaters suspended in a wire frame, they don't actually touch the sides of the bowl or pan in which they are being used – an advantage when whisking in a non-stick saucepan. The larger whisk (a) is more sturdily made than whisk (b) and, as it has a larger drive wheel, it is slightly less tiring on the wrist turning the crank.

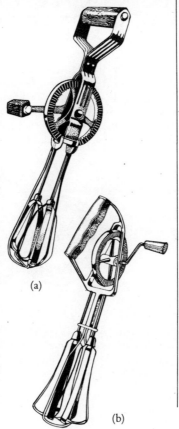

(a)

(b)

## Battery whisk

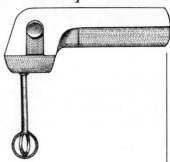

**Size.** L. 7¼ in. (185 mm).
**Material.** Plastic body and whisks, two high-powered 1·5 v batteries.

This little battery-operated whisk is only meant to tackle the light whisking of small quantities. It froths up milkshakes, mixes cocktails, smooths lumps from sauces, makes two-egg omelettes and whips cream.

It would make a good present for an elderly or disabled person, who might have difficulty in using a conventional whisk. It is light to hold – unlike other electric beaters. The beaters are plastic and breakable, but replacements can be bought quite cheaply.

## Molinillos

(a) **Size.** L. 5½ in. (140 mm).
**Material.** Wood.
(b) **Size.** L. 10¼ in. (260 mm).
**Material.** Wood.
(c) **Size.** L. 11¼ in. (285 mm).
**Material.** Wood.
(d) **Size.** L. 13¾ in. (350 mm).
**Material.** Bamboo.

These wooden swizzle sticks are found in Spain and Latin America where hot, frothy chocolate is almost a national beverage. The name means "little mill". Sticks (a) and (b) are made of softwood and come from southern Spain. The smallest one (a) is for use in a small jug or cup, and the similar, larger one (b) in a deep jug or pan. Some, like the Mexican swizzle stick (c), are very intricately carved; others, like (d), which is made from a branch of bamboo, are quite simple.

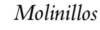

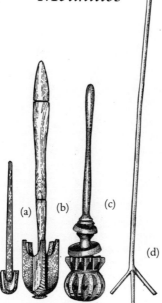

(a)    (b)    (c)

(d)

*Place the molinillo in a pan of melted chocolate and milk. Hold the stem between your palms and rub them together vigorously. The chocolate and milk will be quickly blended into a frothy cream similar to a milk shake.*

# SEPARATORS AND HOMOGENIZERS

Some of the most mundane tasks in cookery demand a great deal of dexterity and precision. One scrap of yolk in egg whites and they become unwhiskable, heavy and lacklustre; a hint of greasiness about the gravy can mar a meal; the correct timing of an addition to a sauce – in the right quantity – is essential for the success of a dish. All these things depend on a well co-ordinated hand and eye. If yours have lost, or never had, this cunning, you can use gadgets that take most of the trial and error out of adding and subtracting in the kitchen.

## Gravy separating dish

**Size.** L. Cap. ½ pt. (0·28 ℓ).
**Material.** Porcelain.

French and typically practical, this double-spouted, double-handled gravy dish can be used at table as well as in the kitchen. It pours lean gravy from a funnel-shaped spout on one side of the dish and the separated fat, which has risen to the surface, from a shallow spout on the other. These spouts are sometimes labelled "M" (for maigre, lean) and "G" (for gras, fat).

*Fat can be poured off the gravy using the "gras" spout. Lean gravy can be then poured from the bottom using the "maigre" spout.*

## Egg separators

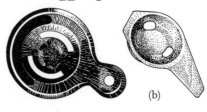

(a)

(b)

(a) **Size.** L. 5½ in. (140 mm).
    **Material.** Tinned steel.
(b) **Size.** L. 4½ in. (115 mm).
    **Material.** Plastic

These egg separators have been invented for those who can master neither of the techniques shown below. They are shaped like round spoons with holes or slots halfway up the bowl.

Balance the separator over a small bowl or cup and crack the whole egg into it. The yolk stays in the little depression at the bottom of the bowl, while the white trickles through the slots into the basin below.

### Two ways of cracking eggs by hand

*Crack the egg on the side of a bowl or with the edge of a knife to divide it in half. Then tip the yolk to and fro from one half shell to the other until it is completely free of white.*

*Break the egg into the palm of your hand and use your fingers as a separator, letting the white slip through between them. This is a particularly efficient way to separate eggs.*

(a) **Size.** H. 8½ in. (215 mm).
**Material.** Plastic and
chromed steel structure.
(b) **Size.** L. 9½ in. (242 mm).
**Material.** Plastic.
(c) **Size.** H. 4 in. (100 mm).
**Material.** Plastic.

The patent homogenizer (a)
works by a simple pumping
mechanism which emulsifies fat
and aqueous liquid by forcing
them through a very small aper-
ture into the lower section of the
machine. It will make mayonnaise and, if you combine the recommended amounts of unsalted
butter and milk, it will make
cream (which it virtually recon-
stitutes from its original comp-
onents in the milk and butter fat).
Most cooks will find that mayonnaise is made more quickly in a
liquidizer or by hand. It takes
about five minutes constant
pumping to make ½ pt. (0·28 ℓ)
of cream or mayonnaise. The
machine is worth having for
cream, which cannot be so simply
reconstituted in any other way.
 The tube-like handle of the
patent spoon (b) releases oil drip
by drip into its shell-shaped perforated bowl making, as you stir
the yolk of an egg with a little
salt, pepper and vinegar, the most
perfect mayonnaise. The handle
will hold ⅕ pt. (0·11 ℓ). The only
drawback is that the little tap at

## Patent homogenizers

(a)

(b)

(c)

the bottom of the tube can work
loose with the oil and the stirring
action inconveniently separating
the bowl of the spoon from its
handle.
 While it is impossible to make
an emulsion strong enough for
mayonnaise in it, the cylindrical
mixer (c) will aerate cream, blend
a vinaigrette and combine the
ingredients for a simple sauce. It
splits into two dimpled halves and
has a capacity of ¾ pt. (0·42 ℓ).

## Adding oil

*Fill the handle with oil and
then use the spoon to blend the
other ingredients for a mayonnaise dressing. As you stir the
oil is added slowly, drop by
drop, through a valve at the
base of the handle.*

(a) **Size.** L. 10¾ in. (274 mm).
**Material.** Rubber bulb,
plastic tube.
(b) **Size.** L. 11 in. (280 mm).
**Material.** Rubber bulb,
aluminium tube, stainless
steel needle.

These syringe-like objects may
strike some cooks as too suggest-
ive of the operating theatre to be
used on a luscious piece of roasting meat; but once such squeam-
ishness is overcome they will
prove themselves to be very
efficient tools.
 The plastic tube of baster (a) is
marked in fractions of fluid
ounces and the tube takes up 1 fl.
oz. (28·41 ml) with one squeeze.
It can be used not only for basting
but also for separating the fat
from the gravy. To do this, fill
the tube with the meat juices by

## Bulb basters

(a)          (b)

squeezing the rubber bulb at the
top then releasing it slowly. The
fat will rise to the top of the tube
if you leave it upright for a
minute or two. The meat juices
can then be slowly squirted from
the bottom. You can also use it to
take the cream from the top of the
milk and even (the manufacturers
suggest) to water small plants and
flowers.
 The needle projecting from the
tube on baster (b) is for injecting
liquid fat into lean meat as you
baste it, an idea not likely to
find favour with cholesterol-con-
scious dieters – and an operation
which will in any case puncture
the meat, causing it to lose juices
that are best retained. You can
also use it to inject a marinade
into large pieces of meat. It holds
slightly less than 1 fl. oz. (28·4 mℓ)
per squeeze.

137

# SIFTERS, STRAINERS, SHAKERS AND SPINNERS

The two main purposes of these tools are to separate or sift fine particles from coarse ones and to strain solids from liquids. They may also be used to sprinkle and scatter light, powdery substances such as sugar and flour. To make them work, a little shake or tap, or simply the force of gravity, is all that is required.

Sifters and strainers are usually bowl-shaped, drum-shaped or conical. Bowl shapes are useful both for straining vegetables and for dry, powdery substances and they fit nicely over other bowls or pans. With dry substances the contents tend to be scattered more or less at random and cannot be directed into a narrow opening. This random sprinkling also occurs with drum-shaped sieves.

Liquids are best strained through conical sieves. The conical shape acts as a funnel and directs the flow of liquid in a manageable stream.

The size of the mesh is an important factor, since it governs the size of every particle that passes through it. Equally important is the size of the sieve or strainer itself – it should fit nicely over the bowls and pans that you intend to use it with. It is also worth having two or three really large ones. You will find that, when boldly tipping potatoes or cabbage from a pan of boiling water, the larger the colander, the easier the job.

Salad shakers and spinners are designed to dry the leaves of salads after they are washed. This can be done by tipping them into a specially designed mesh basket, or even into a tea towel and whirling it about in the open air. But you cannot do this indoors without spraying water all over. The answer to this problem is the salad spinner. The wet leaves are put in a cage enclosed by a lidded bowl. You spin the cage and the water is flung off the leaves into the outer bowl.

## Drum-shaped sieves

(a) **Size.** D. 8 in. (204 mm).
**Material.** Tinned steel frame, tinned wire and nylon mesh.
(b) **Size.** D. 10 in. (255 mm).
**Material.** Stainless steel.

The simple Indian sieve (a) is similar in shape to a French tamis (see PURÉEING TOOLS). It has five interchangeable meshes, which vary in weave from very coarse to fairly fine. The coarsest weave is made of tinned wire; the other four are all made of nylon.

Sieve (b) is a more refined version of the Indian sieve. It has two quick-release meshes – one fine and one medium – which are interchangeable.

(a)

(b)

(a) **Size.** D. $7\frac{3}{4}$ in. (197 mm).
**Material.** Tinned wire.

(b) **Size.** D. 7 in. (178 mm).
**Material.** Tinned wire.

(c) **Size.** D. $6\frac{1}{4}$ in. (160 mm).
**Material.** Nylon.

Sieves (a) and (b) are both made of tinned wire mesh which is held firmly to a tinned wire frame by a rolled rim. The handle and hooks form part of the frame.

The weak points of sieve (a) are the mesh itself, which will, in time, wear out in the centre of the bowl – the point which receives the most pressure if it is used for making purées – and the handle, which with prolonged use may be squeezed out of shape.

These points are reinforced in sieve (b) which has a double mesh with the stronger, more open mesh on the outside, and a piece of wood that holds the two bars of the handle apart. The only trouble with a double mesh is that it is extremely difficult to clean thoroughly.

Sieve (c) is made of nylon, with mesh, frame, hooks and handle all moulded in one piece. It is ideal for straining any food which might be tainted or discoloured by metal.

(a) **Size.** D. $2\frac{3}{4}$ in. (70 mm).
**Material.** Tinned wire.

(b) **Size.** D. $4\frac{3}{4}$ in. (120 mm).
**Material.** Stainless steel.

(c) **Size.** D. $5\frac{1}{4}$ in. (133 mm).
**Material.** Stainless steel.

These are similar in construction to bowl sieves, but the mesh is moulded into a conical shape. This makes them more suitable for straining liquids as the shape funnels everything into the point.

The small sieve (a) is made of tinned wire and is useful for straining tiny quantities of liquid. Sieve (b) is made of stainless steel. This is more expensive than tinned wire but it is longer-lasting and safe to use with acid foods. It has a wooden infill to strengthen the handle. Sieves (a) and (b) are very pointed in shape which precludes their use as puréeing tools unless you have a spoon or pestle which will fit well inside them. They are in any case not very strong. Sieve (c), on the other hand, is more strongly made and it is deeper and

## Bowl-shaped sieves

(a)

(b)

(c)

## Making eggs mimosa

*Bowl sieves can be used to sieve hard-boiled egg yolks to make eggs mimosa for sprinkling on top of stuffed eggs or kedgeree.*

## Conical sieves

(a)

(b)

(c)

does not have such a pointed end. This means that you can use it not only as a straining tool but also as a chinois, for puréeing with a pestle, a ladle, or a whisk (see PURÉEING TOOLS). It is made of perforated stainless steel, with its handle welded firmly to one side and a hook, for resting it on top of a bowl or pan, welded to the other.

(a) **Size.** D. 9 in. (230 mm).
    **Material.** Aluminium.
(b) **Size.** D. 8½ in. (215 mm).
    **Material.** Earthenware.

A colander is exactly like a perforated basin. The holes are large enough to allow water to flow through them fairly rapidly but small enough to retain an object as tiny as a pea. Colanders, like all the other tools in this chapter, are made in a variety of sizes. They are invaluable for draining vegetables and pasta from boiling water and for washing and rinsing fruit and vegetables or large pieces of fish or meat before cooking. A very large colander may be cumbersome to accommodate in a small kitchen but is worth having if you often cook pasta for more than four people or make lots of jam, pickles, wine or preserves. Colanders are not intended for puréeing or for draining fine loose grain such as rice. If you haven't got a proper steamer, you can use a colander over a saucepan for steaming vegetables or couscous. A colander can also be used to make spaetzle (see PRESSES).

# Colanders

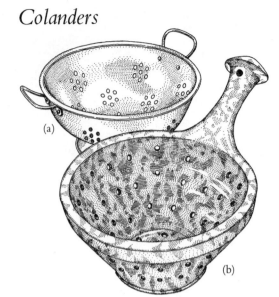

(a)

(b)

Colander (a) is suitable for the everyday needs of a smallish family. It stands on a small pedestal and has two riveted handles.

Colander (b) is Italian and made of earthenware. This kind works just as well as a metal colander and can be found in any country which

is still richly endowed with traditional potteries. It has an ochre glaze splashed with bright green. It is good for straining foods that have a high acid content, though you could equally well use an enamelled colander which is not breakable.

# Pasta strainer

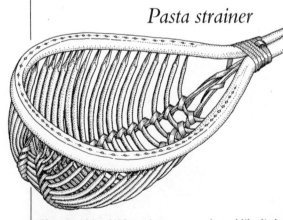

# Coffee and tea strainers

(a)

(b)

**Size.** L. 19 in. (482 mm).
**Material.** Willow frame and ribs, bamboo binding.

There are modern stainless steel and plastic versions of this rustic-looking strainer, but they are no more efficient and not nearly as pretty. The type of pasta for which this strainer is intended is not spaghetti, linguini, tagliatelle, fettucini or any of the other ribbon-like versions; nor is it for any of the smaller kinds of pasta that are

shaped like little bits of rice, stars or letters of the alphabet. The gaps between the rib-like bars are too far apart for any of these. The pasta which it is designed to deal with is the filled kind – ravioli and tortellini – or the medium-size fancy shapes, such as farfelloni (butterflies), conchiglie (shells), ruote (wheels) and gozzetti (pipes). It is used like a scoop rather than like a strainer, and holds a fair amount of pasta in its spoon-shaped basket.

(a) **Size.** D. 2½ in. (65 mm).
    **Material.** Stainless steel.
(b) **Size.** D. 2¼ in. (57 mm).
    **Material.** Chromed steel.

The coffee strainer (a) is conical in shape and small enough to place over a coffee cup. It has a hook as well as a handle so that you can balance it on the cup.

The tea-strainer (b) is designed for use at the tea table. The small, bowl-shaped sieve is hinged to a drip-catching stand which also acts as a handle when pouring tea.

(a) **Size.** D. 9 in. (230 mm).
**Material.** Aluminium,
tinned steel handle.
(b) **Size.** L. 13½ in. (343 mm).
**Material.** Chromed steel,
plastic handle.

These are ingenious space-saving
devices which you can use for
draining the cooking water from
vegetables instead of a colander.
   Pan strainer (a) has hooks on a
sliding handle which means that
it will fit pans of different sizes.
   Strainer (b) consists of a crescent-
shaped piece of perforated metal
with a rim which fits on to the rim

## Pan strainers

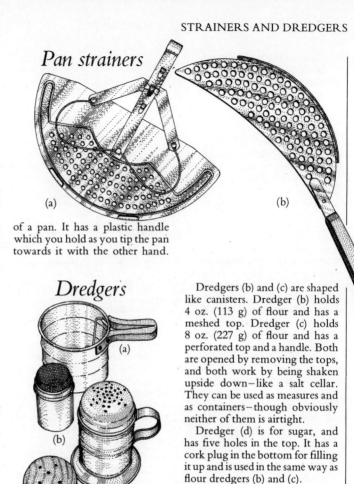

(a)

(b)

of a pan. It has a plastic handle
which you hold as you tip the pan
towards it with the other hand.

(a) **Size.** H. 3½ in. (90 mm).
**Material.** Aluminium cup,
plastic handle.
(b) **Size.** H. 3½ in. (90 mm).
**Material.** Chromed steel.
(c) **Size.** H. 5½ in. (140 mm).
**Material.** Tinned steel.
(d) **Size.** H. 5½ in. (140 mm).
**Material.** Wood canister,
Cork plug.

Dredgers (a), (b) and (c) are all for
flour. Flour should fall lightly and
airily into cake mixtures and on
food that needs coating and should
fall as a fine even dust on worktops
and in baking tins. Poured straight
from a packet or storage jar, it
may come out in a lumpy mass. It
is therefore useful to have a tool
that will act both as a container and
as a sieve or, better still, as a
measure and a sieve combined.
   Dredger (a) holds 12 oz. (340 g)
of flour. It is shaped like a straight-
sided cup with a mesh across its
base rather than a solid bottom.
The flour is sifted, not by shaking
or tapping it as with a sieve, but
by oscillating spokes set inside the
cup just above the mesh. They are
activated by a trigger which forms
part of the handle. (There are also
flour dredgers available with three
mesh screens which means that the
flour is sifted three times.) In
practice this method works very
well for small quantities of flour
(say, 3 or 4 oz. (85 or 113 g) but
it is very slow. For larger amounts,
an ordinary bowl or drum-shaped
sieve is much quicker.

## Dredgers

(a)

(b)

(c)

(d)

Dredgers (b) and (c) are shaped
like canisters. Dredger (b) holds
4 oz. (113 g) of flour and has a
meshed top. Dredger (c) holds
8 oz. (227 g) of flour and has a
perforated top and a handle. Both
are opened by removing the tops,
and both work by being shaken
upside down—like a salt cellar.
They can be used as measures and
as containers—though obviously
neither of them is airtight.
   Dredger (d) is for sugar, and
has five holes in the top. It has a
cork plug in the bottom for filling
it up and is used in the same way as
flour dredgers (b) and (c).

## Dusting a cake

(1)

(2)

(3)

*An easy way of making a
decorative pattern on a chocolate
sponge cake is to scatter icing
sugar through a paper doily as a
stencil. To make your own
pattern, fold a square or circle of
paper into eight and snip out*

*shapes in the two folded sides of
the triangular shape (1). When
you open out the paper, you
should have a perfectly
symmetrical pattern (2). Place
this on the cake, and dust on icing
sugar, using a dredger (3).*

141

(a) **Size.** L. 14½ in. (368 mm).
   **Material.** Felt.
(b) **Size.** L. 12¼ in. (310 mm).
   **Material.** Flannel.

The clear pure juice of fruit, either cooked or raw, is used to make wines and jellies. It should be extracted without pressure or it will become cloudy. The best method is to place the pulped fruit in a cloth jelly bag which is suspended over a bowl and left to drip, preferably overnight. The finer the mesh of the cloth, the clearer the juice will be. These bags are made of very closely woven fabric, the hairy fibres helping to trap the smallest particles of fruit. Both these bags have loops at the top so that you can hang them up over a bowl. They are very strongly made and capable of holding several pounds of fruit without giving way. A jelly bag can also be used to clear calf's foot jellies after they have been clarified with egg whites.

Bag (a) is made of thick white felt. It absorbs a great deal of moisture, but you can avoid losing too much juice by pouring 1 qt. (1 ℓ)

# Jelly bags

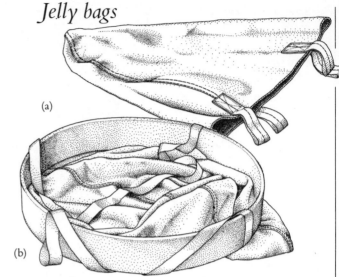

(a)

(b)

of hot water through it before using it. Inevitably it will become stained with fruit juice, but it should not be washed with anything other than hot water. The loops at the top are meant to go through the bars of a special wooden stand. They can equally well be strung to the legs of a chair.

Bag (b) is made of white flannel. It has a round hoop at the top to keep it open and two long tapes to hang it by. Again, some sort of structure needs to be rigged up to support it, and the same pre-wetting rule applies as with bag (a). Wash the bag in hot water.

(a) **Size.** H. 10 in. (255 mm).
   **Material.** Tinned steel.
(b) **Size.** H. 11½ in. (292 mm).
   **Material.** Chromed steel.
(c) **Size.** D. 9¼ in. (235 mm).
   **Material.** Plastic.

Shaker (a) folds completely and space-savingly flat when not in use. It also turns inside out to make a basket with two little feet. The best way to dry salad in it is to perform some arm-swinging exercises out of doors where the water can be flung off without inconvenience. Shaker (b) is not collapsible; it stands firmly on six little feet and can be used to store eggs.

The salad spinner (c) is a more sophisticated version of the salad shaker above and suitable for use indoors. Its main disadvantage is that it takes up quite a lot of room. Geared wheels in the lid rotate the inner plastic basket holding the washed salad. The water is flung out of the lettuce into the outer bowl. Rinsed potato chips can also be dried in a salad spinner before frying.

# Salad shakers

(a)

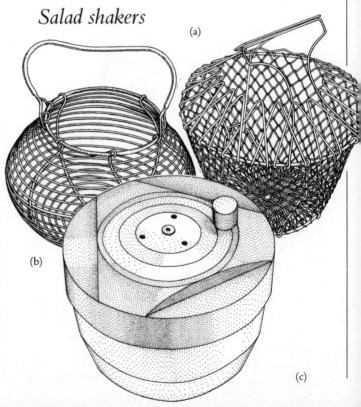

(b)

(c)

# FOOD MIXERS AND FOOD PROCESSORS

This section divides quite simply into four categories: liquidizers and blenders; hand-held whisks and beaters; table mixers and food processors. Some of the tools in the last two categories are supplied with numerous extra attachments—juice extractors, wheat mills, potato peelers, sausage funnels, shredders and slicers and even tin openers—thus earning them the title of multi-purpose appliances.

They all have one thing in common—a small electric motor, which drives blades, shredders, and beaters at high speed. They work many times faster than ordinary knives, graters and whisks. They are particularly useful if you are preparing food for a party, or are processing large quantities for the freezer. All you need is a power point and space to accommodate these wonderful inventions—plus, of course, the necessary cash.

### The "pros" and "cons"

In practice, however, some cooks find that efficiency and speed are gained at the expense of what is best described as an intimacy or closeness with the food being prepared. While a mayonnaise or bread dough made with the help of electric beaters and blades will taste just as good and be ready just that bit sooner than the sauce or bread made laboriously by hand, the cook is just that much further away from the careful watching of important developments or impending failure. Moreover, if you actually enjoy using your manual skill and physical energy, these machines can make you feel quite deprived of that pleasure.

The time and labour saved by using electric tools must be balanced against a few other disadvantages. Firstly, these tools are bulky, complicated and expensive to buy and maintain compared with the manual tools they replace. Secondly, they are more vulnerable to breakage—whether by misuse, wear and tear or accident—and the cost of replacement or repair is relatively high. Thirdly, they rely on electricity and are therefore useless in power cuts or in places without a reliable supply.

When choosing the best appliance for your needs a visit to the kitchen equipment department of the nearest large department store should prove quite helpful. While there are few shop assistants in such places who are capable (let alone paid) to show you the uses of a simple cook's knife or advise you on its purchase, there is usually a very smart salesperson stationed behind each of the latest electrical gadgets, eager to demonstrate its working.

### Care of electrical appliances

Before doing anything with these tools read the instructions (which should be packed with them) and follow them very carefully, especially anything having to do with wiring plugs, the electricity supply and the assembly of various parts. Assembling the machine is sometimes tricky at first, as these appliances can be quite complicated and the instructions are often confusing.

Keep the appliance clean, always bearing in mind that electric motors should never be immersed in water. Those with very sharp cutters need careful treatment if they are to stay sharp; you cannot sharpen them, although you should be able to replace them (another expense). Be careful not to bend whisks and beaters; they follow the contours of their own mixing bowls very closely and once out of true they lose their efficiency.

Find out from the instruction book if the motor has an automatic cut-out when overheated or overloaded. Some do, some don't. Some have a re-set button in the base. If the machine stops for any reason always check the fuse before flying into a panic. Dangerous machines are not manufactured by reputable companies, but the safety factor should be considered and checked occasionally especially if you are using a very old or second-hand machine. Check the insulation of the wires and make sure that the parts that are supposed to be watertight are still effective.

The appliances in this section represent only a fraction of the number currently available. This is not because they are less useful than other kitchen tools, but because (although their purpose remains the same) their design, refinements and styling change almost as often as those of motor cars, with new competitors sending a challenger into the market place every year. Each machine included here is a typical and good representative of its kind.

# Blenders and liquidizers

These tools usually consist of a base containing a small electric motor, upon which sits a goblet fitted with a set of four propeller-like blades. These turn rapidly when the appliance is switched on, chopping up the foodstuffs inside. They can be used for making purées, soups, sauces, frothy drinks, batters, cocktails and baby foods. They can also chop herbs and candied peel; grate cheese; make breadcrumbs (hard or soft) and rub fat into flour. They come to the rescue when you find you are short of ingredients – making caster or icing sugar from granulated; turning rice into rice flour and whole almonds into ground ones.

Blenders are particularly useful for soups and purées, surpassing the old-fashioned sieve or food mill in terms of time and energy saved. You need to watch carefully, however, if you want a grainy or coarse purée, as a second's extra blending can change the consistency irreversibly.

Blenders are inexpensive, compact machines, taking up little space on the worktop and are easy to store. They are often sold with optional attachments, including vegetable shredders, chippers, slicers and peelers.

Some blenders are sold with coffee mills as standard attachments. These small, lidded containers have two blades which can chop tiny, hard objects such as rusks, nuts or coffee beans; they can also be used to grate up cheese or make breadcrumbs. Coffee experts, however, prefer mills which grind rather than chop the coffee beans.

You will probably use a blender most often to make soup. If your family is a large one, bear in mind that four people can easily swallow as much as 2 pt. $(1 \cdot 14 \ell)$ of a delicious thick pea soup at a sitting, so choose the largest goblet available. On the other hand, if you are only going to use it to make purées for the baby, a goblet that holds 1 pt. $(0 \cdot 57 \ell)$ will do. Remember too that the goblet should only be filled about two-thirds full. As the blades whizz round the contents are whirled upwards, and some goblets can overflow if very full even though the lid is on. Choose one

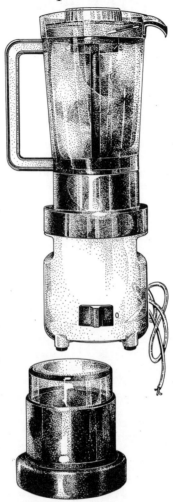

**Size.** H. 14½ in. (368 mm), with goblet fitted. Goblet capacity, 2 pt. $(1 \cdot 14 \ell)$.
**Material.** Plastic, nylon and steel structure, electric motor. (Goblet) Plastic with stainless steel blades.
**Controls.** One speed, on-off switch.
**Standard attachments.** Coffee mill.
*Size.* Cap. 2 oz. (56 g).
*Materials.* Plastic and stainless steel structure, stainless steel blades.

with a lid that fits as firmly as possible, without being tiresome to take on and off. Some models have lids that fit with a locking twist inside the goblet. These leak very little, even when overfilled. Blenders have a removable cap in the centre of the lid through which additional ingredients for mayonnaise, batters and sauces can be added while the blades are spinning.

Goblets are made of plastic, heat-resistant glass or stainless steel. Some of the plastic ones are darkly tinted and like steel ones obscure the state of the contents. Also some types of plastic are stronger and more heat-resistant than others. Most goblets are graduated with combinations of imperial or metric measures. In some models the removable cap on the lid is also a measure, which comes in handy when adding precise amounts through the lid. Some goblets unscrew at the base so that the blades and their hub can be removed. This makes it easier to scrape out thick purées and clean the goblets thoroughly. The best way to clean the goblet after use is to "liquidize" some hot, soapy water in it.

The good thing about blenders is the speed with which they can deal with fairly small quantities of food – but remember that no quantity smaller than the amount required to cover the lowest blades of a blender has any hope of being processed. Also, a certain amount of liquid must be added to make an evenly textured purée. Without it the food at the top of the goblet remains untouched.

Blenders operate in various ways. Some have just one speed, which is controlled with an "on-off" switch; others can spin faster the further you turn a knob; still others have two, three or as many as 16 or 20 speeds. Needless to say, the simple "on-off" type is the cheapest and for most foods quite adequate. The motors required for operating blenders do not need to be very strong or expensive, but they do have one of the disadvantages of cheapness – they are extremely noisy. Also they can only run continuously for a maximum recommended time. This varies between 45 seconds and six minutes.

These portable electric tools are designed to operate a pair of whisks. At the press of a button they will whip eggs, beat omelettes or mix batters. Some of the sturdier, more expensive hand-held mixers have beaters for mixing and creaming thick cake mixtures and hooks for kneading bread dough. All you have to do is put the ingredients in a bowl, fit the appropriate beaters to the mixer, hold it over the bowl with the beaters within and activate the motor.

The great advantage of a hand-held mixer is that it is portable, which means it can be used wherever it is needed – as long as there is a power point within reach. However, this portability is also one of its weaknesses, as you do have to hold the mixer as it works, unless you have a stand for it.

There are some feather-light, hand-held mixers available (some are even battery operated), but they tend to be so feeble that they can hardly manage to whip up a few egg whites without overheating and cutting out. In fact, the more versatile hand-held mixers are usually quite heavy, weighing without any attachments between $2\frac{1}{2}$ and 3 lbs $(1 \cdot 17 - 1 \cdot 36$ kg); but they are well balanced with much of the weight in front of the handle. Most hand-held mixers are designed in such a way that they can be held with the body of the machine resting on the edge of the mixing bowl while they are beating. Some models come with bowls and stands supplied, others only offer these as extras.

The best hand-held mixers can whisk up to ten egg whites at a time and can just about cope with 2 lbs (0·90 kg) of cake mixture. They will deal with creams, sauces, batters and pudding mixtures and can mash or purée soft fruits and cooked vegetables. Those with dough hooks can knead a yeast mixture containing between 1 and $1\frac{1}{2}$ lbs (0·45–0·72 kg) of flour – but for perfect performance most usually seem happier with smaller quantities than the maximum amounts recommended.

The strongest hand-held mixers have three speeds: low for cutting fat into flour; medium for heavy

## Hand-held mixer

**Size.** H. $12\frac{1}{2}$ in. (317 mm).
**Material.** Plastic and steel structure, electric motor.
**Controls.** Three speeds.
**Standard attachments:** Dough hooks, wall bracket.
**Optional attachments:** Liquidizer cap. 1 pt. (0·57 ℓ). Can opener, vegetable peeling bowl, 4-disc shredder/slicer, strainer, cream beaker, splash guard, extra bowl, stand.

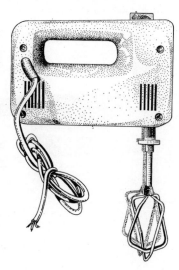

mixtures such as dough, or for creaming fat with sugar; high for blending sauces and beating egg whites. These controls should be on the handle so that you can change speed conveniently while beating. Most hand-held mixers have a maximum recommended operating time of eight to ten minutes, after which they should be rested for twice as long to allow the motor to cool.

Divested of their beaters, some of these machines can be stood on end to accommodate liquidizers, coffee mills and tin openers; they can also be fixed to the spindles of separate attachments to drive slicers, shredders, sieves, mashers and vegetable peelers. These attachments are usually made of plastic, nylon or stainless steel and, while not as tough as the materials of the attachments on more expensive tools, are strong enough if used reasonably carefully. Wall-mounted brackets simplify the problem of where to keep the basic machine with its beaters – but not all manufacturers supply this extra, and storage space has to be considered if you intend to buy all the accessories offered.

Hand-held mixers and their attachments cost very much less than table mixers – the basic machine costing about the same as an electric blender. Their low price is due to their rather limited power. The bigger, stronger table mixers can process larger quantities more speedily, so before buying a cheaper hand-held mixer and adding attachments to it, it is worth considering whether it will be adequate for the work you intend to do with it. If you only expect to use it for mixing, beating and processing small quantities of food, the capacity of a hand-held mixer would probably be sufficient – but then you might also be just as happy with good quality, well designed, old-fashioned manual implements.

Most hand-held mixers are fairly noisy, but not as noisy as blenders. They are easy to keep clean, but some of the attachments are fiddly to assemble and come in shapes which are very awkward to stow neatly.

The work load taken on by this type of electric tool is much more impressive than that of the hand-held mixer, for the simple reason that the motor is more powerful. In terms of strength, size and weight, the table mixer is a cart horse to the hand-held mixer's pony. Because of their bulk, table mixers cannot easily be lifted in and out of cupboards – and this is a drawback. They are best kept ready for use in a convenient position on a kitchen worktop; and this is not always easy to find in a cramped kitchen.

Table mixers are very expensive. The basic machine costs up to six times as much as a hand-held mixer, with most of the more useful optional attachments costing at least half that basic price. However, the quality and performance of these tools is correspondingly good, and the many optional attachments available make them exceedingly versatile. Juicers, shredders, and slicers, coffee grinders and tin openers are frequently offered as extras. The English table mixer shown in the specification has a range of 13 attachments that includes a cream maker, a wheat mill, a potato peeler, a bean and citrus slicer and a sieve. Biscuit presses, noodle makers, ice-cream makers, ice crushers, silver buffers, and sausage-making funnels are available with certain European and American mixers.

However, the possession of every one of these attachments still does not make for the ownership of the most efficient kitchen tool known to man; for somehow, somewhere, all these bulky extras have to be accommodated and you also need to know exactly how to assemble and dismantle them when you change from one job to the next. The only advantages possessed by the table mixer over the food processor are these: mixers are able to make foams incorporating lots of air and they can deal with very large quantities of food at a time. Their bowls are capacious, holding three or four times as much as those supplied with hand-held mixers and nearly twice as much as food processors. They have the power to deal with up to 6 lbs (2·72 kg) of cake or pudding mixture and

## Table mixers

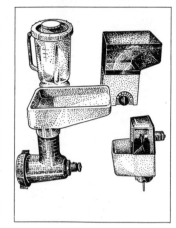

**Size.** H. 12 in. (305 mm).
**Material.** Plastic, nylon and steel structure. Stainless steel beaters.
**Controls.** Slow and high speed outlets, with master control switch with choice of five speeds.
**Standard attachments:** Bowl and stand.
**Optional attachments:**
Mincer, slicer and shredder, bean and peel slicer, wheat mill, can opener, coffee grinder, cream maker, juice extractor, liquidizer, high speed slicer/shredder, juice separator, "K" beater, whisk, dough hook, potato peeler, colander and sieve, stainless steel bowl, sausage filler.

4½ lbs (2·08 kg) of bread dough at one time. The mincing attachments on table mixers are generally excellent, working fast and efficiently, and the coffee mill attachments are usually real mills, fitted with grinders, not chopping blades.

If you already own a blender and a hand-held mixer (with or without attachments) you may well feel that a table mixer is unlikely to provide much that is better, or more useful, apart from its greater strength and capacity – and the mincing attachment. If you are starting from scratch, a speedy, compact food processor could be a better tool to buy; it will cost the same price, or slightly less.

Table mixers, like hand-held ones, are noisy machines. The switches can be adjusted to various speeds; as the speed is increased the purr of the motor changes to a full-throated roar. Because of their weight these machines stay put without "walking" while the motor is dealing with heavy loads and the best do not even vibrate. Most can be run continuously for about five minutes when beating a heavy mixture and correspondingly longer with light ones. Some have automatic cut-outs and re-set buttons should the motor over-load, but usually the required mixing is completed before these are needed.

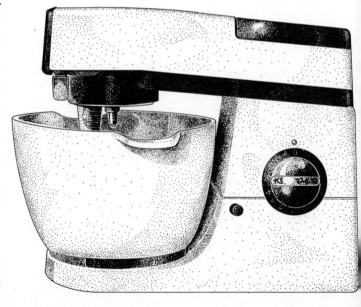

# Food processors

The food processor originally appeared in the kitchens of French restaurants in 1963 and has become popular since in domestic kitchens; often being preferred to its nearest rival, the table mixer, because it is so compact, versatile and free of complicated attachments. It is not just simple to use, it is also strong and (among the better makes) extremely quiet.

In the base of the machine is an electric motor; this turns a central spindle on which a very sharp double-bladed knife is set. A plastic bowl with a lid encloses the spindle and knife. This lid has a "chimney" down which the food to be processed is dropped. The blades whirl very fast, chopping fish, meat, nuts, vegetables or fruit in ten seconds; mincing in 15; puréeing in 20 seconds and reducing these foods to a paste or cream in 30 seconds.

Most models have discs for slicing and shredding fruit or vegetables and some have plastic blades for making and kneading dough. You can also use a processor to make mayonnaise.

It is largely the food processor that has made it possible for chefs and cooks to prepare the Nouvelle Cuisine recipes. Traditionally, stews, soups and gravies are thickened with a roux (a combination of flour and fat). With Nouvelle Cuisine, vegetables such as carrots, onions and celery are reduced to a mush and used instead. While many cooks are quite happy to chop one onion with a knife, these recipes call for far greater amounts. With a food processor, you can reduce a fruit like a lemon to a pulp in less than two minutes; the pulp can then be used to thicken a sauce.

Most food processors are fairly heavy (an advantage that stops them "walking"), but unlike table mixers they take up so little space that it is not difficult to find a permanent position on the worktop for them. As the double-bladed knife is a mixer, blender, mincer and slicer in one, and two shredding discs, plus a dough blade, form part of the basic equipment, optional extras are few and in any case hardly necessary. This is possibly one of the most attractive features of this tool. Some models provide juice

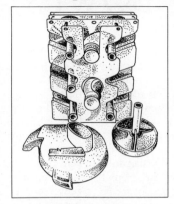

**Size.** H. 15 in. (380 mm).
**Material.** Plastic and steel structure, electric motor. Plastic drum, stainless steel blades and cutters.
**Controls.** One speed on-off switch, operated by turning lid.
**Standard attachments:** Plastic dough blade, shredding and slicing discs.
**Optional attachments:** Machine cover, disc rack, nine grating and slicing discs, including a julienne, a French fry cutter, parmesan grater and ripple cutter. Also a wide feeding funnel and juicer.

extractors with a pulp-ejecting mechanism as well as several extra shredding discs.

The drawbacks – and there are one or two – include the relatively small capacity of the mixing bowl in all but catering models. The bowls of domestic processors hold no more than 1½ pt. (0·85 ℓ), which means, for example, that you can only make 1 lb. (0·45 kg) of mousse, mince or paté at a time. However, the machine works so fast that for large amounts you can easily make several batches. Unfortunately the bowl is unsuitable for whipping egg whites. Covered in as it is, not enough air can be incorporated into the mixture to make a foam of any sort bulk up properly.

The best food processors have very quiet, strong, constant-speed induction motors. This makes them considerably more expensive than cheaper food processors which rely on series motors. These motors are far noisier, tending to vibrate and slow down when they meet with resistance. They also take up more space within the machine making it less compact in design.

The best models have handles on the bowls (a great advantage when emptying them) and "lock-in" blades which do not come out of position when heavy mixtures are being processed.

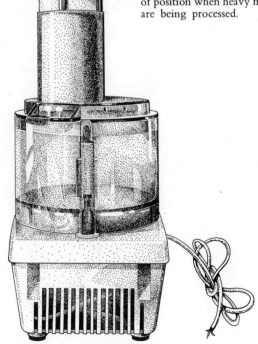

# BOWLS

Bowls and basins are for warming things up, cooling things down, mixing, beating, jelly-fying, marinading, salting, serving and storing things—and, if you make steamed puddings, for cooking in. The enormous variety of uses to which bowls can be put in the kitchen indicates that a good assortment of various shapes and sizes is much more desirable than a set of matching basins all made of the same material and fitting neatly inside one another like Russian dolls.

A busy cook will need a very large bowl, ideally of copper, for beating egg whites; an equally large, preferably straight-sided, earthenware bowl for proving bread dough; a variety of earthenware or steel stacking basins for mixing and storing; white earthenware pudding basins for cooking steamed puddings; wooden bowls for serving salads, and glass, plastic or china bowls for almost all the previously mentioned purposes.

Size, weight, heat resistance, texture and shape are the factors which determine the suitability of one bowl rather than another for a particular task. Copper or steel bowls have a texture that holds the foam of beaten egg white to the sides of the bowl so that it keeps its airy bulk. China and glass bowls, on the other hand, are too smooth; the egg white continually slips down, compressing the foam and losing air, however vigorously you beat. Basins with rims can have covers tied over them; wide bowls are better for the rapid cooling of hot liquids and for skimming fat or cream; deep bowls, if heatproof, can be fitted nicely into saucepans if a double boiler is needed (when making custard, for example); unglazed pottery bowls keep liquids cool.

When mixing something that engages both hands, such as mayonnaise, place the bowl on a folded, dampened cloth to keep it steady.

## Copper egg bowl

**Size.** D. 8 in. (204 mm), Cap. 6 pt. (3·42 ℓ).
**Material.** Copper bowl, brass handle.

The expense of these hammered copper bowls is only justified if you make meringues, soufflés, sponge cakes, zabaglione, sherbets and the like very often; or it could be that if you had one of these bowls you would make all these things very often. They are certainly lovely bowls to work with and beautiful to look at, though being made of copper and having a round bottom rather than a flat base, they are useful for nothing but beating eggs. The chemical reaction set up between raw egg white and copper increases the strength of the protein in the whites, enabling them to stretch further which makes a larger, stronger foam. Always wash the bowl before you use it and make sure too that it is large enough (egg whites when whipped increase four times in volume).

*Scour the bowl with a mixture of salt and either vinegar or lemon juice. This removes all traces of grease and discoloration. Then rinse it in hot water and dry it with a clean cloth.*

The bowl shown here is fairly small—they range from 8 in. (204 mm) to 20 in. (508 mm) in diameter—and is completely semi-spherical, but beautifully balanced so that even without being held it remains upright. The round bottom ensures that all the egg white is incorporated in the whisking and is consistently beaten. It also acts as a pivot when the whisking is in progress, enabling you to turn the bowl as you beat with a minimum of effort. The brass handle is to hang the bowl by, not to hold it by. It has a rolled edge—a necessary feature, as the best way to release the whipped egg from the whisk is to rap the whisk smartly on the side of the bowl, thus giving the edge quite a lot of punishment.

Bowls of a similar shape are also made of stainless steel and these can be used as general mixing bowls. They cost half as much as copper ones, but are not widely available.

# Mixing bowls

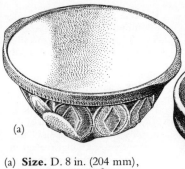

(a)

(a) **Size.** D. 8 in. (204 mm),
Cap. 3 pt. (1·70 ℓ).
**Material.** Earthenware.

(b) **Size.** D. 6½ in. (165 mm),
Cap. 2½ pt. (1·42 ℓ).
**Material.** Stoneware.

(c) **Size.** D. 8 in. (204 mm),
Cap. 3 pt. (1·70 ℓ).
**Material.** Aluminium.

(d) **Size.** D. 7½ in. (190 mm),
Cap. 3 pt. (1·70 ℓ).
**Material.** Stainless steel.

Bowl (a) is a patent English mixing bowl made of yellow earthenware; this yellow shows through the glaze on the bowl's decorated outside. It comes in a range of sizes up to 15½ in. (394 mm) diameter. It has a flattened area just above the base on one side so it can be kept in a tilted position while you beat your cake or pudding mixture—an arm-aching exercise which has almost been forgotten since the invention of electric mixers. However, it is worth making cakes this way once in a while; you have a far better idea of the state of the mixture with the old-fashioned bowl and spoon. Yellow clay is not fired to such a high temperature as white, so these bowls are not as strong or heatproof as white pudding basins (see overleaf). Test them for cracks before buying them. They should give a resonant "ping" when lightly tapped with a pencil.

Bowl (b) is a typical French mixing bowl, heavy, stable and unlikely to crack. It has the straight-sided, flat-bottomed pattern seen in bowl (d), a pronounced rim and a lip for pouring. The range includes bowls up to a massive 15 pt. (7·52 ℓ) capacity. The bowls are glazed on the inside, but unglazed outside, apart from the distinctive dark-brown rim.

(b)

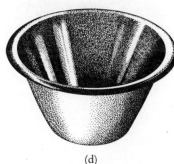

(d)

## Using a stainless steel bowl as a cooler

*Cool mixtures in a stainless steel bowl by standing it in a larger container filled with iced water. To warm food stand the bowl in a pan of hot water.*

(c)

The aluminium chef's bowl (c) costs only a fraction of the price of a copper egg bowl and is similarly shaped; but don't be tempted to use it for whipping egg whites. The result is very unpleasant—a not very well mounted mass of grey foam. This bowl is designed for beating and whipping ingredients for sauces, cake mixtures and creams. However, you must use a wooden spoon or plastic beater, rather than a metal whisk, or discoloration will occur. It is not so well balanced as a copper egg bowl and is, in fact, designed to be held in the crook of the elbow, against the chest with one hand tucked round the handle, rather than used on a table top. This is fine for flat-chested cooks, but not so good for bosomy ones.

Straight-sided, flat-bottomed, stable, unbreakable, hygienic, heatproof and easy to stack, steel mixing bowls, like bowl (d), are found in professional kitchens where all mixing, separating, cooling and temporary storing is done in them. They range in diameter from 7½ in. (190 mm) to 17 in. (430 mm) and are expensive but virtually indestructible. Flat-sided spatulas with angled ends are best used for stirring or beating in these bowls. Steel bowls are excellent conductors of heat and therefore useful for rapid cooling or heating of food. The larger sizes of these bowls are well shaped for the proving of bread dough, their steeply sloping sides keeping the exposed surface area of the dough to a minimum.

A large, dome-shaped bowl that can withstand heat of about 200°C (400°F) can be used as a cover over bread baking in the oven. The steam that collects between the dough and the upturned bowl will create an excellent crisp crust.

(a) **Size.** D. 6¼ in. (160 mm).
  Cap. 2½ pt. (1·42 ℓ).
  **Material.** Earthenware.
(b) **Size.** D. 5 in. (127 mm).
  Cap. 1¼ pt. (0·71 ℓ).
  **Material.** Aluminium.

Basin (a) is the classic English pudding basin, capable of withstanding the heat of steaming. It can be lined with suet pastry and filled with steak and kidney, or filled with syrup and sponge mixture (treacle pudding). Both these boiled or steamed puddings are sealed in the bowl with a lining of greaseproof paper and a cover of cloth, which is tied down securely with string under the deep rim round the top. This basin makes an excellent mixing bowl, its material being heatproof and unscratchable and absolutely unaffected by any type of foodstuff. The curve of its sides perfectly fits the bowl of a wooden spoon, so that no part of a mixture can remain lumpy or unblended. It

## Pudding basins

(a)

(b)

is also useful for storage, shaping a summer pudding, catching the drips from a hanging bag of home-made curd cheese or from a jelly bag filled with fruit pulp. Placed inside a saucepan of slightly smaller diameter, it makes a double boiler.

The polished aluminium basin (b) is specially designed for boiled puddings, but cannot hold fruit unless it is lined with greaseproof paper. It is similar in shape to basin (a) but has a clip-on lid with a handle attached. It makes a useful container, but is not so good for mixing things, as it is light and the metal can cause discoloration. Both basins range from 4½ in. (115 mm) diameter, ½ pt. (0·28 ℓ.) capacity, to 9½ in. (242 mm), 6 pt. (3·41 ℓ). Basins of similar shape are made of polypropylene. These withstand boiling water, but being very light are not so pleasant to use as mixing bowls. They also tend to discolour with use.

## Preparing a basin for a suet pudding

(1)

(2)

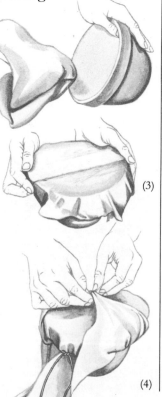

(3)

(4)

1. *Reserve a quarter of the suet pastry for a lid and roll out the rest into a circle 2 in. (50 mm) wider in diameter than the bowl. Fold it in half. Take up a deep pleat and roll a pouch.*

2. *Open out the pleat and, with your fist in the pouch, lift the dough into the tilted basin. Right the basin and line it with the dough.*

3. *Having added the filling, seal the pudding with a lid of dough and a piece of greaseproof paper (pleated to allow for expansion).*

4. *Cover it with a cloth tied securely under the rim. Then knot the opposite corners of the cloth together to form a handle for lifting the basin from the pan.*

## Banneton

**Size.** D. 8 in. (204 mm).
**Material.** Reed.

This little basket made of reeds is used during the second proving of bread dough. It gives a very attractive ridged pattern to the finished loaf. Flour it heavily and place the knocked-back dough inside it to double in size once more. When the dough has risen, turn it out, upside down, on to a baking sheet. The impression of the woven reeds will remain on the loaf after baking.

# Serving bowls

(a)

(c)

(d)

(b)

(a) **Size.** D. 10¼ in. (260 mm),
    Cap. 8½ pt. (4·83 ℓ).
    **Material.** Plastic.
(b) **Size.** D. 8¾ in. (223 mm),
    Cap. 3½ pt. (2 ℓ).
    **Material.** Glass.
(c) **Size.** D. 9 in. (230 mm),
    Cap. 6 pt. (3·41 ℓ).
    **Material.** Teak.
(d) **Size.** (Serving) D. 11¾ in.
    (298 mm),
    Cap. 9½ pt. (5·40 ℓ).
    (Individual) D. 5 in.
    (127 mm),
    Cap. 1 pt. (0·57 ℓ).
    **Material.** Earthenware.

Brightly coloured plastic, which
can be made in any colour and
can be moulded to any shape, is
particularly popular for capacious serving bowls. Bowl (a) is a
light, strong plastic bowl, resistant to staining by acids and to
temperatures below 130°C
(266°F). It is unbreakable, but
sharp tools will scratch it, so take
care to use wooden or plastic
spoons when using it as a mixing
bowl or for salads.
  Bowl (b) of toughened (but
not oven-proof) glass is particularly useful when layered food
needs to be shown off to advantage. Use it for set cold dishes,
trifles, syllabubs, mousses and
jellies. It is also an attractive bowl
for serving salads of all kinds.

## Chapon au salade

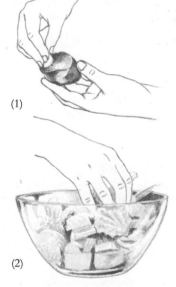

(1)

(2)

*To introduce a subtle flavour of
garlic into a salad, rub a cut
clove of garlic on a piece of
toasted bread (or chapon) (1).
Soak the bread in olive oil, bury
it among the salad leaves and
pour on the dressing (2).*

Wooden bowls, bowl (c), make
very handsome receptacles for
salads, either of fruit or vegetables. Make sure you have a
large enough size for green salads,
as in order to coat all the leaves
with dressing you need plenty of
space to toss them about in the
bowl. Keep garlicky salad to
the same serving bowl each time
for wood absorbs flavours and
these bowls should have only the
minimum of washing if they
are to remain in good condition.
A regular anointing of oily salad
dressing is very good for wood.
If the bowl is not being used for
this type of salad, a dressing of
vegetable oil every six months is
quite beneficial. If these bowls
must be washed, be very brief
about it. Then dry and air them
before putting them away.
  The iced soup of Spain, gazpacho, needs to be kept as cold
as possible, both before and after
serving. The gazpacho bowls (d)
of thick unglazed pottery allow
little or no exchange of temperature between what they contain
and the air outside and act as perfect insulators for hot or cold
liquids. This thick, heavy Spanish pottery is not so porous that
the bowls become impregnated
with the flavour of what has gone
before. The small bowl (for individual helpings) is a miniature
of the larger serving bowl.

# CAKE, BREAD AND PASTRY TINS

The art of baking requires skill all along the line. For success the ingredients need to be the best available; measured out in the right proportions and mixed to the proper consistency; and the heat of the oven has to be set in advance and regulated accurately. Then there are the finishing touches – artistic designs in icing or just a dusting of sugar; rich cream rosettes or a simple glaze of syrup. Yet, even if your recipe demands no more than the addition of one egg to a packet of cake mix, none of this business will be of any use at all without the proper size, shape and weight of tin in which to bake your beautiful concoction.

*Choosing a tin*
Cookery books usually state what size of tin to use; but as a rule, the mixture should fill the tin by no more than two thirds. As it bakes the mixture should rise to the rim or slightly above. If the tin is too large the mixture will still rise, but you will end up with a very squat cake. If the tin is too small, the mixture may overflow and result in a cake with a cracked or wrinkled surface.

Rich, dense bread and cake mixtures should be baked in tins made of strong heavy-gauge steel. They need long cooking and will burn if the tin is too thin. On the other hand, sponge cakes and pastry are cooked much more quickly and need lighter, thinner tins so that the heat can penetrate fast.

For a metal tin to keep its shape, it needs a strong rigid edge. This is simple if the tin is fluted, as the fluting imparts strength, but if it is straight-sided, the edge should be either rolled or lipped. Some tins have dimpled surfaces which impart a little more strength.

*Preparing tins*
Mixtures that are very fat, like pastry, are less likely to stick than mixtures containing mostly flour and water, such as bread. Cake mixtures, which contain a proportion of sugar, are the most likely to stick of all.

Tins manufactured with non-stick linings need only the lightest of greasing, if they need greasing at all. (Their manufacturers recommend greasing only for mixtures that have very little fat or a high sugar content.) Non-stick baking tins are lined with a very smooth slippery water-repellent material. Food cooked in these tins tends to have a smooth crisp crust and turns out very easily indeed, needing none of the digging, scraping, banging and prising that all too often accompanies its removal from ordinary tins. However, even when treated with the greatest care, the non-stick coating does wear off eventually. (One bakery expert calculated that a non-stick pan makes about 200 trips to the oven before reverting to its tinned steel or aluminium beginnings.)

Other tins and dishes should always be greased. With use they will build up a non-stick surface of their own and, provided you don't scour them too harshly, further greasing will be unnecessary. Use your fingers to spread the fat, or use a pastry brush – it gives an even coat and goes into cracks and corners.

*Positioning in the oven*
Old-fashioned ovens made of brick or clay were heated by wood or coal fires, which were swept out before the oven was used. The residual heat could bake several batches of bread, cakes or pies, and was so even that food could be cooked on the floor of the oven. This is not the case with most modern domestic ovens, although some ovens provide even heat by means of a fan and these can be successfully used for "batch baking". In most ovens, because the heat rises, you will not get an even temperature throughout, which is why it is best to bake in the centre of the oven and not to bake one thing above another. In any case, don't overcrowd the oven by putting too many tins in it at one time. It is important that the heat attacks the tin equally from all sides, so make sure that the tin is positioned so that there is enough air space all round it.

**Size.** H. 12½ in. (317 mm).
**Material.** Stainless steel. ·

These tall conical metal tins, shaped like dunces' caps or megaphones, are used to create the festive French confections known as croquembouches. These consist of dozens of small choux buns, which are filled with cream, then dipped in caramel so that they stick to each other. They are

## Croquembouche tin

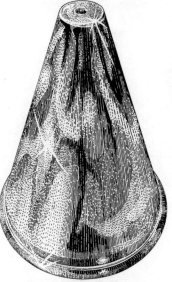

placed inside the tin while the caramel is still warm. As it cools it solidifies to hold the buns together. The tin is then removed.

Croquembouches are made for weddings, birthdays, anniversaries and christenings, and decorated with the appropriate symbol. They should be mounted on pedestals of nougatine caramel, which can be shaped while warm on a tartlet tin or brioche mould.

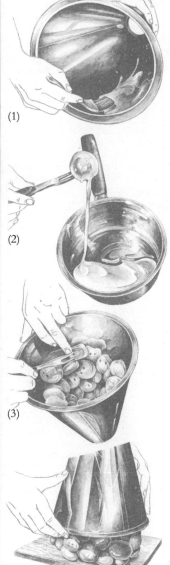

(1)

(2)

(3)

(4)

## Making a Croquembouche

*1. Oil the inside of the tin very thoroughly, using tasteless oil and a pastry brush.*

*2. Dip each cream-filled bun in melted caramel. It is not necessary to completely coat the buns.*

*3. Start at the pointed end of the tin and place the buns closely together and evenly around it. The uncoated parts should face inwards.*

*4. When the caramel is quite cool turn out the croquembouche. It may need some encouragement with a palette knife; it also helps if you first place the tin on its side and press down on it.*

*5. Shape a rose by rolling a small piece of marzipan into a ball.*

*6. Then press it out between your forefingers and thumbs . . .*

*7. . . . to form individual petals.*

*8. Attach the rose to the top of the croquembouche, then decorate the gaps with rosettes of cream.*

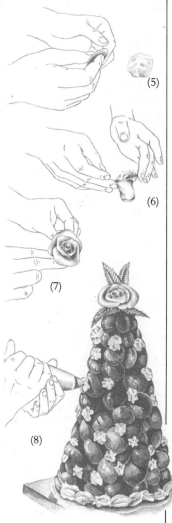

(5)

(6)

(7)

(8)

# Deep cake tins

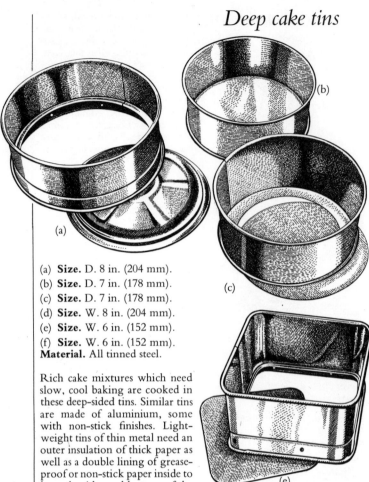

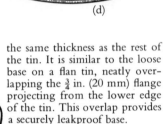

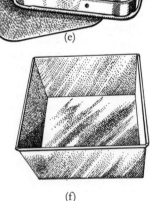

(a)

(b)

(c)

(d)

(e)

(f)

(a) **Size.** D. 8 in. (204 mm).
(b) **Size.** D. 7 in. (178 mm).
(c) **Size.** D. 7 in. (178 mm).
(d) **Size.** W. 8 in. (204 mm).
(e) **Size.** W. 6 in. (152 mm).
(f) **Size.** W. 6 in. (152 mm).
**Material.** All tinned steel.

Rich cake mixtures which need slow, cool baking are cooked in these deep-sided tins. Similar tins are made of aluminium, some with non-stick finishes. Light-weight tins of thin metal need an outer insulation of thick paper as well as a double lining of grease-proof or non-stick paper inside to keep the sides and bottom of the cakes soft and moist. They should also stand on several layers of brown paper or a sheet of corrugated paper while baking. Commercial quality tins are heavier and should not need these measures. The most useful cake tins for domestic use are 6, 7 and 8 in. (152, 178 and 204 mm) in diameter. Loose bases are helpful when it comes to taking the cake out of the tin.

Tin (a) has a loose base made of a double thickness of metal with an air space between for insulation against burning from below. This insulation is only really necessary if your oven gives trouble in this respect.

Tin (b) has a fixed base, tightly and neatly seamed, but this type of tin needs to be well greased and lined to make sure of getting the cake out cleanly once it is baked. The loose base on tin (c) is of

the same thickness as the rest of the tin. It is similar to the loose base on a flan tin, neatly overlapping the $\frac{3}{4}$ in. (20 mm) flange projecting from the lower edge of the tin. This overlap provides a securely leakproof base.

The heart-shaped tin (d) is most likely to be used for baking celebration cakes and is one of a range that includes stars, horseshoes, hexagons, ovals, clover leaves, slabs and numerals. These last, being complicated in shapes, are made without bases and are designed to stand on baking sheets. Like cake rings and other shapes without bases, they are called "hoops" after the old-fashioned wooden hoops which were used before commercial tins became widely available.

The square tin (e) is for baking the kind of rich fruit cake that cuts best into rectangles rather than wedges. It is also a useful tin for children's cakes as a square can be cut into sections which can be arranged to make houses, aeroplanes and so on.

Unlike tin (e) which has rounded corners and is lined like a round cake tin, tin (f) is truly square and must be lined by a different method (see opposite).

If you want to use a square tin when the recipe specifies quantities for a round one, use a tin that is 1 in. (25 mm) less in width than the diameter of the round tin. In other words tin (f), which is 6 in. (152 mm) square, holds the same as a round tin that is 7 in. (178 mm) in diameter.

## Lining a heart-shaped tin

(1)

(2)

(3)

(4)

1. Brush the tin with butter.
2. Turn it over, lay greaseproof paper over it and cut the heart-shape with the back of the knife.
3. Gauge the depth of the tin with the blade, add ½ in. (12 mm) and cut a strip to size.
4. Line the tin, putting the base in first. Brush the paper with butter.

## Lining a square tin

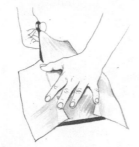

(1)

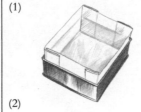

(2)

(3)

Cut a square of greaseproof paper more than twice the size of the tin. Lay it over the base and make two parallel cuts into the corners on two opposite sides (1). Fold the paper into a box shape. Put the box into the greased tin (2). Trim the overlaps (3) and brush the lining with butter.

## Lining a round tin

(1)

(2)

(3)

Using the greased tin as a guide, cut a circle of greaseproof paper (1). Cut a strip 1½ in. (38 mm) deeper than the tin. Fold over the edge and snip it at intervals (2). Line the tin putting the base in over the snipped edge (3). Grease the lining.

## Insulating a large cake

(1)

(2)

Cut a long strip of brown paper three times the depth of the tin. Fold it lengthways and pin it round (1). Stand the tin on a folded sheet of brown paper (2).

155

(a) **Size.** D. 7½ in. (190 mm).
   **Material.** Tinned steel.

(b) **Size.** L. 11¾ in. (298 mm).
   **Material.** Aluminium.

(c) **Size.** W. 7½ in. (190 mm).
   **Material.** Tinned steel.

(d) **Size.** D. 9½ in. (242 mm).
   **Material.** Tinned steel.

(e) **Size.** D. 6 in. (152 mm).
   **Material.** Aluminium.

## Shallow cake tins

(a)

(b)

(c)

(d)

(e)

Light fruit cakes, spiced cakes and seed cakes are baked in tins with sides roughly 2 in. (50 mm) deep, while even shallower, straight-sided tins with sides 1 to 1½ in. (25 to 38 mm) deep are used for sponge cakes and sponge sandwiches (genoises) which are very fragile, egg-based, airy cakes.

The spring-clip tin (a) has a choice of three bases, one flat, one fluted and one a tube. When the clip is unfastened the sides expand by ½ in. (12 mm) freeing the base and making the extraction of very fragile cakes, such as rich tortes or soft cheesecakes, quite simple.

To allow for the baking of a shallow sheet of sponge, the Swiss (jelly) roll tin (b) is only ¾ in. (20 mm) deep. It must be well

greased and the base should be lined with paper to keep the underside of the sponge damp and soft. This makes it easier to roll the sponge up without it cracking, after it has been turned out and spread with jam. This tin is made of aluminium which is a good conductor of heat and an excellent material for baking mixtures which have to be cooked quickly.

If you bake brownies, parkin or gingerbreads, the shallow square tin (c) is a good shape. It is useful too for baking the everyday plain cake that cuts most easily into squares.

The large sponge flan tin (d) has fluted sides and a raised centre. It is used for baking sponges which contain a sweet filling and are left upside-down after being turned out of the tin.

The round tin (e) is used for baking sponge cakes and sponge sandwiches. Grease it well with butter and then flour it to give the cakes a firm crust on the sides. A round of paper in the bottom prevents the base sticking and makes turning out the sponge easier. Non-stick finishes are particularly useful for sandwich tins, but will need greasing just like other tins in this case. It is best to buy sandwich tins in pairs (or even threes) so that you can bake each layer at the same time and match them exactly.

## Smoothing off

*Smooth the surface of a cake mixture before baking. Don't be too vigorous or fussy or you will knock all the air out of the mixture.*

## Turning out a sponge cake

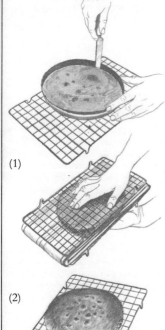

(1)

(2)

(3).

*Allow the tin to cool slightly, then loosen the edges with a palette knife (1). To avoid marking the sponge top lay a folded cloth on the wire rack before turning out the cake (2). Lay another rack on the cake and turn both racks over with the cake in between. Remove the top rack and let the cake cool.*

## Making a swiss roll

*Turn out the sponge on to a sugared sheet of waxed paper. Trim off all crisp edges to make it roll easier. Spread it with melted jam. Make a shallow cut along one of the short sides about 1 in. (25 mm) from the end. Fold this over (1). Using the paper to press against, finish the roll (2).*

## Keeping fruit cakes flat

*A bowl of water on a rack below the cake in the oven produces steam that helps to keep the top of the cake flat. Remove the bowl once the cake is half-way through the cooking time.*

## Balmoral loaf tin

**Size.** L. 6 in. (152 mm).
**Material.** Tinned steel.

This ridged bread tin can be used for baking all sorts of fruit cake as well as plain and fancy bread. The ridges make it easy to cut the cake or bread into even slices. When used for baking bread it can be placed upside down on a baking sheet, with the dough inside it, or be covered with a baking sheet "lid" to make a flat top (see BREAD TINS). This tin is also known as a toast rack tin.

## Dariole mould

**Size.** H. 2½ in. (65 mm).
**Material.** Aluminium.

These little flowerpot shaped moulds can be bought singly or in quantity and come in various sizes. They are used for making small sponge cakes, castle puddings, timbales, savoury or sweet jellies, popovers and little crème caramels. The name dariole refers to an old English type of pastry which was made in this shape. It was made of puff paste and filled with custard. These moulds are also used for baking small rum babas which are served lying on their sides. Fill them less than half way and leave them to rise two-thirds full before baking. Little brioches can be baked in them as well.

(a) **Size.** D. 8 in. (204 mm).
   **Material.** Tinned steel.
(b) **Size.** D. 6½ in. (165 mm).
   **Material.** Aluminium.
(c) **Size.** D. 6½ in. (165 mm).
   **Material.** Tinned steel.
(d) **Size.** D. 7¼ in. (185 mm).
   **Material.** Aluminium.
(e) **Size.** D. 3½ in. (90 mm).
   **Material.** Aluminium.

# Tube tins

Traditionally the cakes baked in these tube tins are flamboyantly lavish and unconscionably rich. They have hollow centres which can be filled with cream and have a large area of surface crust which can be drenched in exotic liqueurs or syrups.

Some authorities recommend leaving the tube in the centre ungreased to help the cake rise − and the dry surface does give the mixture a little extra support as it rises. The tube in the centre conducts the heat to the middle of the cake so that it cooks quickly and evenly.

The Trois Frères tin (a) is designed for a cake created in the 19th century by the three Julien brothers. The cake, a sponge made of rice flour, sugar, butter and eggs, is flavoured with maraschino. When turned out of its tin, it is set on top of a sweet pastry base, soaked in apricot syrup and sprinkled with chopped almonds and angelica. This tin resembles a shallow kugelhopf tin with the tube just a little higher than the outer rim so that when the mixture rises it will not overflow.

Tins (b) and (c) are kugelhopf tins. This cake originated in Austria but is now also found in

France and Germany, thanks to Marie Antoinette who brought a liking for it with her. It is made from a rich sweet brioche-like dough with almonds stuck in each of the swirling flutes. Tin (b) is made of very thin aluminium with a narrow tube just level with the rim. Tin (c) is a weighty professional's tin. The outer bowl is fluted and made without a seam to spoil the pattern. Kugelhopf tins may also be used to bake other cake-like bread and light sponge cakes such as American angel-food cake and chiffon cakes.

Smooth, shallow and seamless, the savarin tins (d) and (e) are designed to bake rings of sweet

yeast dough similar to that used for babas. Before serving, the savarin is soaked in a rum or kirsch-flavoured syrup, either as it is or with an apricot syrup. The hole in the centre is filled with Chantilly cream surmounted by a pile of cherries soaked in a kirsch-flavoured syrup. Tin (e) is for individual savarins or little rum babas which are prepared in the same way as the larger ones.

Savarin tins should be brushed with melted butter and then floured before filling. If the tube is too short and you are afraid the mixture might overflow into it, slip a funnel of greaseproof paper into the tube to extend it.

*1. Stick split almonds into each of the flutes of a very well buttered mould.*

*2. Half fill the mould with dough. Cover it with a cloth and leave it to rise to the top of the tin before putting it in the oven to bake.*

*3. After baking turn the cake out on to a rack. When it has cooled a little dust it with icing sugar. (A goose-feather brush gives the most delicate drift of sugar when shaken over the cake.)*

## Preparing a kugelhopf

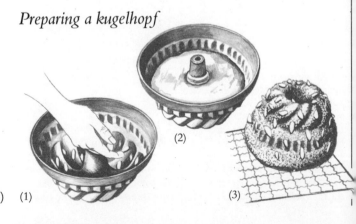

(1)  (2)  (3)

(a) **Size.** D. 7 in. (178 mm).
**Material.** Tinned steel.

(b) **Size.** D. 5½ in. (140 mm).
**Material.** Tinned steel.

(c) **Size.** D. 2¼ in. (57 mm).
**Material.** Blued steel.

Rich, sweet or savoury yeast brioche loaves are traditionally made in tins shaped like these. The fluted and flared sides not only pattern the loaf but allow the dough to spread out amply as it proves. A brioche is glazed and dome-shaped with a little top-knot surmounting it.

Tins (a) and (b) can also be used for baking cakes as well as brioche dough and make pretty moulds for cold puddings or for shaping pedestals for spectacular desserts.

## Brioche tins

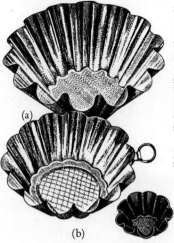

(a)

(b)

(c)

These pedestals are made from caramel with chopped almonds. The liquid caramel is poured on to an oiled marble slab, allowed to cool slightly then lifted as a sheet, moulded into a brioche tin and trimmed. As the caramel cools it hardens and can be lifted out.

The tiny tin (c) is for baking small versions of the traditional brioche; these are often served as a breakfast bread in France. You can also use this little tin for shaping tartlets.

These tins are all made in one piece without seams and with sharp edges.

## Making a brioche

1. Soften the butter by pounding it with your hand.

2. Make a well of flour, putting the yeast and sugar inside and a pinch of salt outside, so that the yeast and sugar are mixed first without salt. Add the rest of the ingredients and knead the mixture, lifting, slapping down and spreading the dough until it is very smooth and elastic.

3. Fold the dough round the softened butter and work it with your hands, squeezing with your thumbs as though trying to strangle it. Work it until the butter is absorbed.

4. Let the dough rise, knock it back and then divide it into one large and one small ball. Hollow out the large one and drop the little one in to it.

5. Put the dough into a buttered tin and snip it round the join of the top-knot with scissors.

6. Make smaller brioches by pinching the top-knot out of the dough with your fingers.

7. Brush the top of the well-risen brioche with egg glaze twice before baking it.

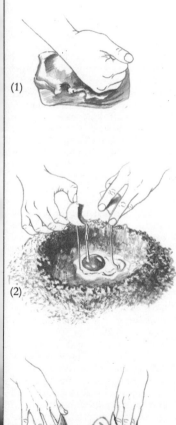

(1)
(2)
(3)

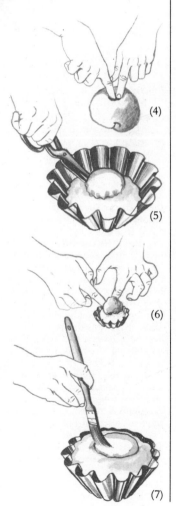

(4)
(5)
(6)
(7)

# Bread tins

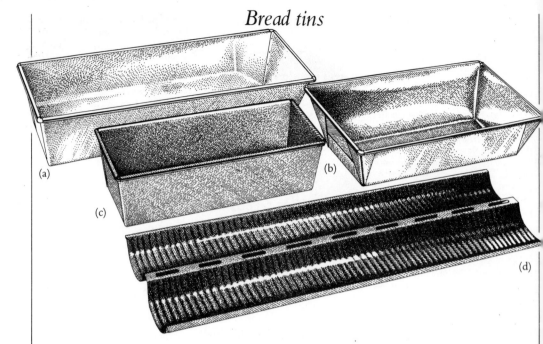

(a)
(b)
(c)
(d)

(a) **Size.** L. $14\frac{1}{4}$ in. (362 mm).
**Material.** Tinned steel.
(b) **Size.** L. $10\frac{1}{4}$ in. (260 mm).
**Material.** Tinned steel.
(c) **Size.** L. $10\frac{1}{4}$ in. (260 mm).
**Material.** Blued steel.
(d) **Size.** L. $17\frac{1}{2}$ in. (445 mm).
**Material.** Blued steel.

Ordinary daily bread, unlike cake, consists mainly of flour and water. It contains no sugar or fruit – or if it does it contains only a very little – and is aerated by yeast rather than eggs. Its consistency, when raw, is firm and malleable, not soft and runny like cake mixture. For this reason it is quite often baked without a tin, being simply shaped into an oblong or round loaf, or twisted and plaited into a fancy shape. For this type of loaf all you need is a flat, firm, heat conducting tray or tile to support it while it bakes.

Bread tins, if used at all, are generally rectangular with plain, sometimes slightly sloping, sides. Decorative flutes and scallops have no place on bread tins; the exception being the barrel-shaped Balmoral loaf tins with their narrow, slice-sized corrugations and the crinkle-ended rectangular tins. Certain cakes, such as Madeira cakes, seed cakes, marble cakes, ginger cakes and fruit loaves are traditionally baked in rectangular bread tins. Round loaves can be baked in shallow cake tins.

The long, narrow French tin (a), has slightly sloping sides and rolled edge reinforced with wire. This is a good tin to use if you want a loaf to cut into regularly shaped slices.

The shorter, wider tin (b) is a large family size tin with an insulated base to prevent burning. English loaf tins, like this one, are traditionally wider than European ones and are measured by the weight of bread they can hold. This is a strongly made tin formed from one flat sheet of tinned steel, with the corners reinforced by their own pleats.

Blued steel, the material of tin (c), is sheet steel that has been heated to a very high temperature until it turns blue or even black by oxidation. This process gives the tin some rust resistance and a smooth, non-adherent surface. This tin has a dimpled finish which helps to give good "baking release". It is made of a heavy commercial quality steel with neatly sealed and trimmed corners and an edge rolled over strong copper wire. The sides are more vertical than those of tins (a) and (b), which makes this a good shape for baking the almost square sectioned "pain de mie". To make this bread either invert the tin over the bread while it bakes on a baking sheet, or place the baking sheet over the tin as a lid and weight it down. Make sure that you fill the tin no more than two-thirds full with dough before you begin proving it. You can buy special "pain de mie" tins made with sliding lids.

Also of blued steel, the baguette tin (d) is designed to hold two loaves of the French stick shape. Anyone who has attempted to bake baguettes on a flat baking sheet would be delighted to own one of these tins; but measure your oven before you rush out and buy one – not all modern domestic ovens can take a tin of this length.

If you make bread regularly it is best to buy commercial quality baking tins. They will be heavy and strong enough to withstand any amount of banging about and should last a lifetime. They will gradually acquire a smooth non-stick patina of their own so that after a while they won't even need greasing. Aluminium and non-stick bread tins are good if you bake bread only on rare occasions.

## Filling bread tins

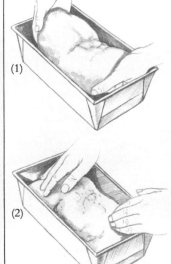

(1)

(2)

Knead the dough into an oval shape and put it into the greased tin (1). Push it into the corners with your fingertips (2).

## Decorating baguettes

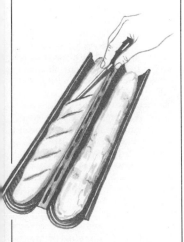

Roll the dough into two long sausage shapes and lay them in the tin. Cut diagonal slashes with a sharp blade along their length.

## Simple bread plait

(1)

(2)

(3)

(4)

1. Roll the dough into three long sausages and start in the centre for a nice oval shape.
2. Lift each outer strip over the middle one in turn . . .

3. . . . and continue plaiting, tucking the outer strips neatly under the centre one at the end.
4. Plait and finish the other half similarly.

## A six-strand plait

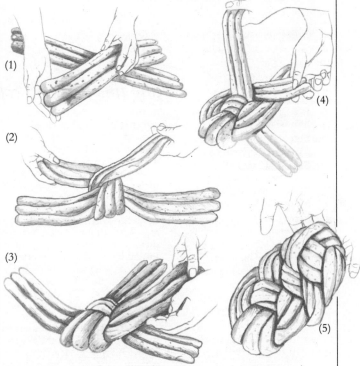

(1)

(2)

(3)

(4)

(5)

For this more challenging plait divide the dough into six pieces and roll them into long sausages, three slightly shorter than the others.
1. Lay the three shorter strips across the others.

2. Loop and cross the larger strips over the shorter ones.

3. Continue plaiting . . .

4. . . . lifting the outer strips over or under, as appropriate.

5. Tuck the ends neatly under.

# Earthenware bread pot

**Size.** D. 6 in. (152 mm).
**Material.** Earthenware.

Made of the same clay as a flower-pot and shaped like a shallow one, this pot bakes bread beautifully – as would a real flowerpot, or any container made of earthenware. It must be seasoned before being used for baking bread. Do this two or three times by oiling it well and leaving it empty in a fairly hot oven, possibly while bread is being baked in other pans. This type of pot, with its some-what rustic character, is almost always used for wholemeal loaves.

## Baking bread in a flowerpot

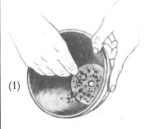

(1)

(2)

(3)

1. *Grease the pot and sprinkle it inside with crushed wheat grains.*

2. *Knead the dough into a ball and place it inside the pot, filling it by two-thirds only.*

3. *Allow it to prove to within $1\frac{1}{2}$ in. (38 mm) of the top, then turn the pot upside-down on a prepared baking sheet and bake it. Turn it out on a rack to cool.*

# Baking tins for small cakes

(a) **Size.** L. $12\frac{1}{4}$ in. (310 mm).
**Material.** Tinned steel.

(b) **Size.** L. $9\frac{1}{4}$ in. (235 mm).
**Material.** Tinned steel.

(c) **Size.** L. 12 in. (305 mm).
**Material.** Tinned steel.

(d) **Size.** L. 14 in. (355 mm).
**Material.** Tinned steel.

(e) **Size.** L. $13\frac{1}{2}$ in. (343 mm).
**Material.** Tinned steel.

(f) **Size.** L. 14 in. (355 mm).
**Material.** Tinned steel.

(g) **Size.** L. 13 in. (330 mm).
**Material.** Cast iron.

(h) **Size.** L. 9 in. (230 mm).
**Material.** Tinned steel.

Small cakes, batters, buns, pies and tarts can be baked in batches in little trays, which are pressed out in various shapes from sheet steel. They are also useful for cooking any surplus cake mixture from a large cake, or making one or two tartlets from scraps of pastry. Like other cake tins they should be made of a fairly heavy gauge of metal, or they will buckle in the heat of the oven, tipping the mixture out of the cups before it is set. They can be made of aluminium and sometimes have non-stick (release) coatings.

The bun tins (a), (b) and (f) are of different patterns, but all can be used for baking little cakes, tarts or pies. Tin (b) has nine shallow moulds which are grooved to represent scallop shells. Scallop shells were and can still be used for baking small cakes, though a very hot oven tends to burn them, making a dreadful smell. The fluted cups in tray (f) produce twelve prettily patterned cakes, tarts or pies.

Two trays with specific uses are the eclair tray (c) and the French Madeleine tray (e). The eclair tray is used, not only to bake choux pastry for eclairs, but also "langues de chat" made of sponge mixture. It is strongly made with a rolled edge. The Madeleine tray is tra-ditionally used for baking the little, paw-like cakes of that name. This tray is of lightweight steel and has the sides turned down to rein-force it and give it a base to stand on. Madeleines, made with runny batter, cook with flat tops; to make the traditional humped Made-leines de Commercy use a thicker batter and allow it to rest in the moulds for an hour before baking.

The tartlet tray (d) is French and strongly made of heavy-gauge tinned steel. It has eight, shallow, flat-bottomed moulds with fluted sides for open tartlets. Cast iron bakewear is very heavy but con-ducts heat excellently. The corn fritter pan (g) has seven moulds shaped like ears of corn. These turn out fritters with deep golden tops and crusty bases. Because the cast iron holds the heat so well, the fritters bake through without the crusts getting burned.

The four flat-bottomed, straight-sided moulds in tray (h) are for baking individual portions of Yorkshire pudding, so that each person gets a nicely risen, saucer-shaped helping to himself. It could also be used for baking small fruit tarts, savoury pies and quiches.

## Baking tins for small cakes

(a)

(b)

(c)

(d)

(e)

(f)

(g)

(h)

## Popover pan

**Size.** H. $2\frac{1}{4}$ in. (57 mm).
**Material.** Aluminium.

Popovers, like Yorkshire puddings, need to be baked in preheated pans containing a little lard or dripping. The batter is then poured into the pans which are placed near the top of a hot oven. These individual pans can be bought singly or set in trays. They are similar in shape to dariole moulds but are a little dumpier.

(a) **Size.** D. 8 in. (204 mm).
(b) **Size.** D. 6 in. (152 mm).
(c) **Size.** L. 14 in. (355 mm).
**Material.** All tinned steel.

Tarts, flans and quiches are rather fragile when cooked, so unless you bake them in dishes that can be brought to the table you must have tins for them that can be easily removed. As pastry shrinks a little when cooked, this manoeuvre need not be too difficult. You can use a ring on a baking sheet or special flan tins with loose bases (see overleaf). If using a ring make sure that it lies flush with the sheet and that the sheet is thick enough not to buckle with heat, otherwise the shell will be misshapen and difficult to detach. You may also lose some of the filling.

The simpler ring (a) has rolled edges which make it very strong. Ring (b) has a fluted sleeve spot welded inside the outer ring. This makes it, and the resulting tart shell, a little stronger. The fluted edge stands proud of the plain rolled edge and is thin and sharp to cut neatly through the pastry dough. Take care when washing this ring that no pastry or dampness lingers in the crevices between the rings.

The rectangular flan form (c) is a good alternative to a flan ring if you already have a round loose-bottomed flan tin. Rectangular flans look particularly nice when filled with slices of fruit.

(a) **Size.** D. 9 in. (230 mm).
   **Material.** Aluminium.
(b) **Size.** D. 10¾ in. (274 mm).
   **Material.** Stainless steel.

Pie plates are, by British tradition, used to bake shallow lidded pies or open tarts with decorated edges. Plate (a) is the typical shape, somewhat deeper than a normal dinner plate, yet shallower than a soup plate. The rim is wide so that an edge can be laid on it and be well sealed if need be. The American pie plate (b) is narrow rimmed and deeper than (a). It is a prettier plate, and would not look out of place among other serving dishes at table. The groove round the rim catches the pie juices and prevents them from spilling and burning messily in the oven.

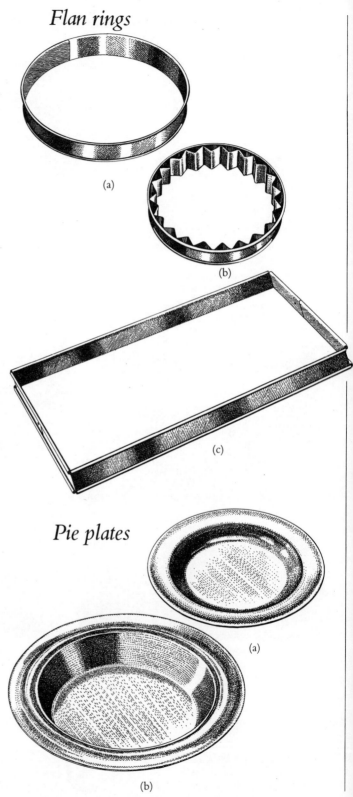

*Flan rings*

(a)

(b)

(c)

*Pie plates*

(a)

(b)

## Decorative pastry edges for open pies and tarts

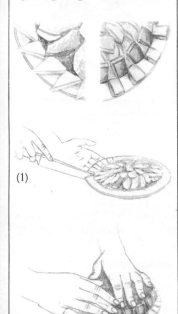

(1)

(2)

(3)

*To make a decorative edge on the pastry laid on a wide-rimmed pie plate, cut the edge at 1 in. (25 mm) intervals (1). Fold alternate pieces back to make little castellations (2), or fold each section diagonally (3) to make a zigzag pattern.*

# Baking sheets

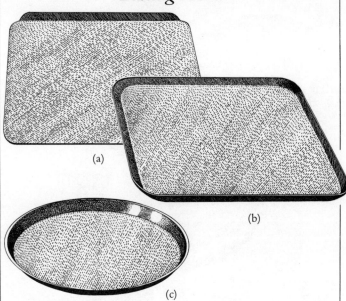

(a)

(b)

(c)

(a) **Size.** L. 14 in. (355 mm).
(b) **Size.** L. 14 in. (355 mm).
(c) **Size.** D. 9 in. (230 mm).
**Material.** All pressed steel.

You need a flat, rigid heat-conducting baking sheet which can be easily slid in and out of the oven when baking pastry shapes, meringues, gingerbread men, shortbread, scones, biscuits, pizzas and bread shaped by hand. These sheets can also support moulds and patty tins while they bake and act as bases for flan rings and cake hoops. Ceramic baking dishes are placed on preheated baking sheets in the oven so that the heat is conducted more directly to the base (see PORCELAIN FLAN DISHES). It is a good idea to buy baking sheets in pairs so that you can fill a second sheet with food while the first batch is cooking; but don't be tempted to slide one above the

other in the oven as they will bake at different speeds, saving very little time.

Sheet (a) is of slightly lighter gauge steel than sheet (b), but both are extremely rigid. The turned-up end on sheet (a) makes it easier to move it around in the oven and to hold it. Sheet (b) has slightly sloped edges for the same reasons.

The round sheet (c) with its sloping rim is intended to hold a shallow disc of pizza dough. It could also be useful for supporting flan rings or for cooking soda breads, tea cakes and scones which are baked as rounds and then divided into quarters.

Pressed steel is not oxidized enough to make it quite rustproof, so these sheets should be washed and dried well after use and lightly greased before being put away in a well ventilated place.

## Preparing a baking sheet

*Brush the surface with butter, first one way and then the other, smoothly and evenly (1). Sprinkle flour along one edge. Tip the sheet so that the flour flows, sticking to the fat (2). Tap it to remove the surplus.*

(1)

(2)

# Flan tins

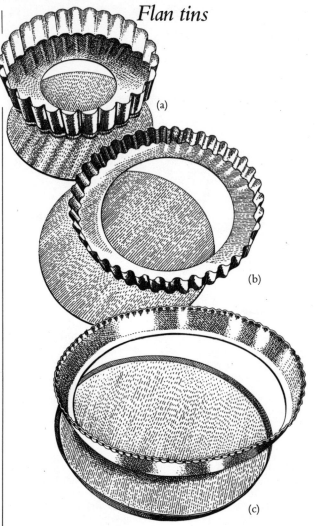

(a)

(b)

(c)

# Baking beans

**Size.** 5½ oz. (150 g) weight.
**Material.** Aluminium

To make sure of well cooked, crisp crusts on the bottom of pastry shells they are usually first baked "blind", that is without a filling in them. The time-honoured method of keeping the base of an empty shell flat while baking is to weight it down with dried peas and beans. After much use these get burnt and smelly and have to be thrown away. The modern solution is to use ceramic or aluminium beans, sold in packets of various weights. They are everlasting, good conductors of heat and washable.

## Blind baking

(1)

(2)

(a) **Size.** D. 9 in. (230 mm).
   **Material.** Tinned steel.
(b) **Size.** D. 9½ in. (242 mm).
   **Material.** Tinned steel.
(c) **Size.** 11½ in. (292 mm).
   **Material.** Aluminium.

These loose-bottomed flan tins make the turning out of fragile flans and tarts easy. Their fluted sides also add strength to the pastry shells.

Tin (a) is strongly made with a loose base which fits over a wide flange. This deeper than average tin is for baking rich custard-filled flans. The shallower tin (b) is also strong and comes in nine sizes. The loose base of tin (c) has a slightly turned-up rim so the flan is best left on the base for serving.

## Removing a flan from a loose based tin

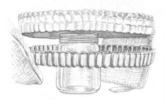

*Allow the flan to cool slightly then stand it on a jam jar. Gently ease the outer ring down. The flan can be left on the tin base or transferred to a serving plate.*

*Line the flan tin with pastry. Prick it all over with a fork or skewer, then line it with foil or greaseproof paper (1). Sprinkle beans all over the surface to keep the pastry flat while it bakes (2).*

## Porcelain flan dishes

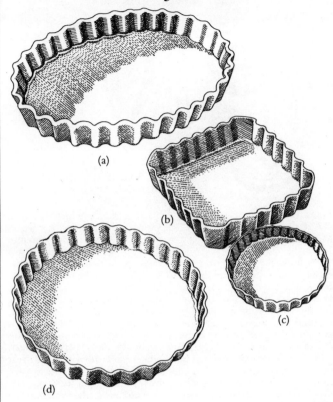

(a)

(b)

(c)

(d)

## Lining a porcelain dish

(1)

(2)

(3)

(a) **Size.** L. 11 in. (280 mm).
(b) **Size.** L. 6½ in. (165 mm).
(c) **Size.** D. 4½ in. (115 mm).
(d) **Size.** D. 9¼ in. (235 mm).
**Material.** All porcelain.

These four flan dishes are all made of vitrified white porcelain with fluted, slightly sloping sides. The underside of the base is unglazed so that the heat can penetrate. To assist this very important process, heat a heavy baking sheet, then stand the dish on it. This helps to

make a crisp bottom crust which is otherwise a problem with pastry made in ceramic dishes as they absorb heat more slowly than metal ones.

Dishes (a) and (b) are English-made of heavier porcelain than the French dishes (c) and (d). Dish (d) is a classic French flan dish. These dishes can also be used to bake gratins, lasagnes and custards, besides making very pretty serving plates for cold food and salads.

*Lay the pastry over the dish and press it lightly in place, folding over a shelf of pastry inside the rim. Then roll the pin over the dish to cut away the surplus (1). With your fingers squeeze the shelf upwards so that it extends a little above the rim. Crimp it using your index fingers to press the dough into each flute (2). Prick the base with a fork (3).*

## Making a lattice top

(1)

(2)

(3)

*To weave a lattice top on a tart, lay parallel strips of pastry on the top (1). Then fold back alternate strips and lay a strip across the remaining ones.*

*Replace the folded pieces, and fold back the others before laying another cross strip (2).*

*Continue weaving until the whole top is latticed. Dampen the pastry to seal the lattice ends to the shell and trim off the surplus (3).*

# Crumpet rings

**Size.** D. $3\frac{1}{4}$ in. (82 mm).
**Material.** Chromium oxide coated steel.

Crumpet batter is much more liquid than that of muffins. You have to use rings for crumpets if you want them nice and thick, but this is less important for muffins, though rings will stop them spreading out and flattening. Put the greased rings on a heated griddle and fill them with crumpet batter, using a ladle. Remove the rings when the underside is done and turn them over to cook on the other side without the rings.

You can use them as egg poachers by buttering them thoroughly, then standing them in a pan of simmering water and cracking an egg into each.

# Tartlet tins

**Sizes.** L. $2\frac{1}{4}$ in. to $4\frac{3}{4}$ in. (57 mm to 120 mm).
**Material.** Tinned steel.

They look like doll's house tart tins, but these little fluted tins are for serious baking in real ovens. Little pastry cakes baked in them can be filled with a couple of mouthfuls of something delicious in aspic or one or two expensive out-of-season strawberries, glazed with slightly alcoholic syrup. Use them to make prettily shaped sponge cakes too. Smaller versions of these tartlet tins are made especially for petits fours.

# Boat moulds

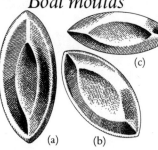

(a) **Size.** L. 5 in. (127 mm).
(b) **Size.** L. $4\frac{1}{4}$ in. (107 mm).
(c) **Size.** L. $4\frac{1}{4}$ in. (107 mm).
**Material.** All tinned steel.

These moulds, which come in various sizes are also known as bateau and barquette moulds. They are for making little pastry cases for hors d'oeuvres or desserts. They can be baked blind in the same way as large pastry shells (see BAKING BEANS) or by placing a smaller one inside sandwiching the pastry. Buy them in two sizes in dozens, for this reason. Mould (c) has sharp edges, which make this type of boat mould easier to line with pastry by the rolling pin technique (see ROLLING PINS) than moulds (a) and (b) which have flat edges.

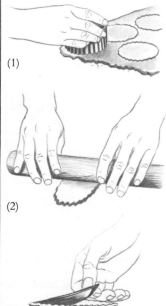

(1)
(2)
(3)

# Making strawberry boats

1. Use a fluted cutter to make the circles of pastry.
2. Roll each circle into an oval.
3. Line the moulds with the ovals of pastry and bake them with a smaller mould inside to keep the shape.
4. Fill the boats with créme pâtissière using a forcing bag.
5. Arrange strawberries on top.
6. Glaze each boat with fruit jelly and decorate them with rosettes of cream.

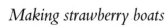
(4)

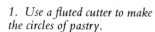
(5)

(6)

# Cream horn mould

**Size.** L. 4¼ in. (107 mm).
**Material.** Tinned steel.

Cones like these are used to form pastry horns. The pastry is baked on them and when the mould is removed the pastry cones are filled with cream. They can also be used to form cornets of biscuit, using the same recipe as for tuiles and bending the warm, freshly baked biscuits round them.

# Cannoli forms

**Size.** L. 3¾ in. (95 mm).
**Material.** Tinned steel.

These little cylinders are greased and used like horn moulds to shape and bake pastry. The little tubes of pastry that result are filled with sweet cream or (by Sicilian tradition) sweetened ricotta (a soft sheep's milk cheese), candied peel and nuts and are sprinkled with icing sugar.

# Patty tins

**Size.** D. 2¼ in. (57 mm).
**Material.** Tinned steel.

These shallow little tins are for making tartlets in the traditional English shape. They are called patty tins—a name derived from the French word pâté, for pie. They are placed on baking sheets.

## Forming cream horns

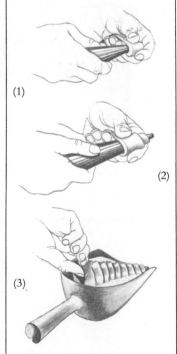

(1)

(2)

(3)

*Dampen strips of puff pastry and, starting at the tip, squeeze a strip (wet side out) on to a greased horn (1). Spiral it up the horn (2). Tweak off any surplus, hold the finishing-point and dip the other side in caster sugar (3). Bake it sugared side up.*

## Making cannoli

(1)

(2)

*Roll circles of sweet pastry dough into ovals the same length as the cannoli forms (1). Wrap each lengthways around a form (2). Seal the join with egg white. Deep fry the cannoli and remove them from the forms while still hot.*

## Filling tartlet shells

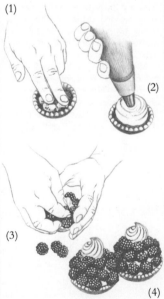

(1)

(2)

(3)

(4)

1. Drop a blob of jam into the tartlet case and cover it with cubes of sponge cake.
2. Drench them with rum and pipe a huge dollop of whipped cream on top.
3. Press black cherries (or other fruit) into the cream.
4. Glaze with hot jam or jelly and finish with a piped rosette of cream.

# Raised pie moulds

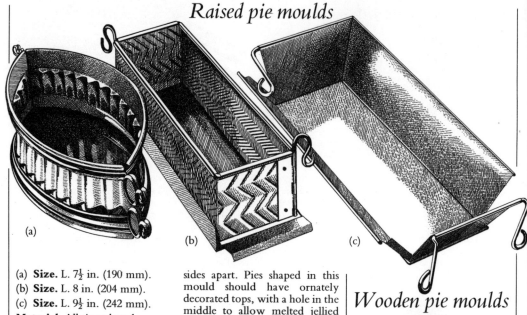

(a)

(b)

(c)

(a) **Size.** L. 7½ in. (190 mm).
(b) **Size.** L. 8 in. (204 mm).
(c) **Size.** L. 9½ in. (242 mm).
**Material.** All tinned steel.

A raised pie with a prettily decorated, golden crust is a beautiful thing to see; these moulds are designed to produce flawless, shapely pies.

Mould (a) is the traditional pattern for savoury meat and game pies. The sides are separate, and can be removed from the base. To take the pie out just remove the clips at each end and pull the sides apart. Pies shaped in this mould should have ornately decorated tops, with a hole in the middle to allow melted jellied stock to be poured in when the pie is cold to fill the gaps between the meat and the crust.

The herringbone pattern and straight sides on mould (b) produce an ideal shape for cutting slices from raised pies and pâtés en croûte. The base slides out easily from the sides.

The sides of the hinged tin (c) open out flat when the catches at either end are lifted.

# Wooden pie moulds

**Size.** H. 6 in. (152 mm).
**Material.** Sycamore wood.

This wooden cylinder is used to make raised pies. A hot-water paste is moulded round it, which is then removed as the paste cools. Its place is taken by pie mixture.

# Using a fluted pie mould

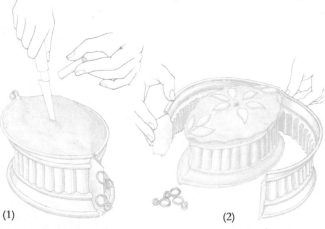

(1)

(2)

Line the mould with dough and strips of pork fat and fill it with a pâté mixture. Cover it with a thin sheet of pork fat and a thick lid of dough. Make a hole in the centre (1) so that steam can escape. Add pastry flowers and glaze before baking. Add aspic once the pie is cold. Remove the mould when aspic has set (2).

If you can't find a wooden raised pie mould, a greased and floured jam jar will do. Mould hot-water paste round the sides of the jar, roll it to smooth the outside wall, let the paste cool and then gently lift out the jar.

# Pie dishes

(a)

(b)

(c)

(d)

(a) **Size.** L. 6½ in. (165 mm).
   **Material.** Earthenware.
(b) **Size.** L. 9¾ in. (248 mm).
   **Material.** Earthenware.
(c) **Size.** L. 12 in. (305 mm).
   **Material.** Stoneware.
(d) **Size.** L. 10¾ in. (274 mm).
   **Material.** Pyrex.

Pie dishes can be square, round or rectangular, made of glass, stainless steel or enamelled steel. The traditional English pie dish, however, for steak and kidney or apple and blackberry pie, is oval and is usually made of earthenware, in white, brown, yellow, blue or green. It is deep enough to hold plenty of juice-smothered meat, fish or fruit and it has a flat turned-out rim so that a pastry lid can be firmly attached to the edge. Tops are sometimes made of mashed potato, in which case the contents are more solid as with the hashed mutton of a shepherd's pie or the fish mixture of a fish pie, and the flat rim is not so important. A pie dish is also used to make traditional English puddings.

Pastry and pie filling are best cooked together. If the filling needs more cooking than the pastry, put the pie into a hot oven to set the lid and then lower the heat to cook the filling. Protect the lid meanwhile with a loose-fitting cover of two or three sheets of dampened greaseproof paper. If you prefer to cook the filling beforehand, make sure that it and the pie dish are quite cold before covering them with pastry or the lid will begin to melt.

The smallest dish (a) is made of glazed earthenware and is just the right size for a pie for one person. Dish (b) is also made of earthenware. It has a good concave rim, better for attaching pastry than the more convex rim of dish (c). This large, heavy dish is made of glazed stoneware. Dish (d), made of Pyrex, is cheaper than an earthenware dish but not as attractive. It has a good flat rim.

(a) to (c) **Size.** H. 3 in. to 4¼ in.
   (75 mm to 107 mm).
   **Material.** Porcelain.

When you make a pie with a pastry lid, the pie dish – unless it is very small – should have a little funnel put in the centre. The top of the funnel pokes up through the pastry, supporting it and letting out the steam from the filling at the same time, thus ensuring a crisp upright lid, not a soggy sagging one.

If you have a variety of pie dishes in several sizes, you will also need pie funnels of different heights to go inside them. These funnels are

# Pie funnels

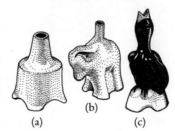

(a)

(b)

(c)

all made of porcelain, with scallops cut out of the base so that the juices of the filling can mingle freely in the bottom of the dish, and hollow centres so that steam can escape from the centre of the pie. All have shoulders of some sort to support the pastry at the point where the funnel pokes through. Funnel (a) is in the traditional style. Funnel (b) is shaped like an elephant and gives immense pleasure to children as the diminishing pie gradually reveals his presence. Funnel (c) represents one of the four and twenty blackbirds that were, according to the English nursery rhyme, baked in a pie.

# MOULDS AND PRESSES

All the tools shown here are designed to shape food – by pouring it into a mould and turning it out when cooked or set, by pressing it between two specially shaped plates, by stamping a design on to it, or by pushing it through holes.

*Moulds*
The richer and more exciting a dish, the more the cook likes to dress it up, adding eye-catching enticement to something which is already wickedly extravagant and irresistible enough. Dishes based on lavish quantities of rich and expensive raw materials such as cream, wine and eggs mixed with fine purées of luscious fruit, fish or fowl are made even more appealing and mouth-watering by being moulded into pretty shapes.

The moulds shown here are all designed to help in this respect. Like the mousses, custards, jellies and creams which they help to create, none of them is absolutely essential in a strictly down-to-earth, healthy regime, but life would be rather dull without the occasional treat. At the very least, a mould can be used to turn a packet dessert into a fantastic turreted castle or an endearing bunny rabbit.

Food is moulded in much the same way as casts are made in bronze, iron or plaster of Paris. The food is poured while liquid into a suitable

shape. It is essential that the mould stands level without being propped up and that the pattern inside it is not too intricate or convoluted for reproduction. Mixtures need to be fairly smooth to reproduce patterns clearly and, unless they are to be solidified by freezing, they should contain enough gelatine, cornflour or eggs to set firmly. Most of the food shaped in these moulds is eaten cold, with the exception of certain sponge puddings, timbales and baked charlottes.

Other simpler foods such as shortbread dough and butter can be made to look very special, moulded into perfectly symmetrical shapes with a pattern stamped on one side, with attractive wooden moulds.

*Presses*
There is some food, quite simple in itself, which relies for its success on being the right shape. Tortillas, beefburgers and cooked ham and meats, for example, will all look far more professional if you use special presses to compress and mould them into the right shape. More complicated mechanical presses and extruders will enable you to make a variety of impressive treats—home-made pasta, spicy, deep fried Indian savouries, Spanish churros and perfectly shaped little cookies.

## *Butter moulds*

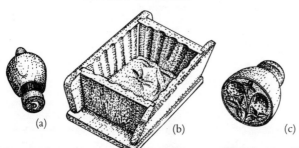

(a)  (b)  (c)

(a) **Size.** H. 3¼ in. (84 mm).
(b) **Size.** L. 7¼ in. (185 mm).
(c) **Size.** H. 2 in. (50 mm).
**Material.** All wooden.

Butter moulds should be wet before use.

Mould (a) has a cylindrical cavity in its cup-shaped container and a plunger patterned with a leaping fish. To make a butter pat

for one, retract the plunger, fill the cavity with butter and push out the butter with the plunger.

Mould (b) is Austrian and patterned with eidelweiss. It takes a good half pound slab of butter. The butter should be soft when it is put in and allowed to harden before being taken out.

Mould (c) is for stamping a strawberry pattern on top of the butter in an individual dish.

## *Shortbread mould*

**Size.** D. 7 in. (178 mm).
**Material.** Beechwood.

This wooden mould, crisply engraved with a thistle motif, looks like a little platter. The mould should be lightly oiled. Scottish shortbread dough is then rolled into the mould and turned out on to a baking sheet to be cooked.

(a) **Size.** Cap. $2\frac{1}{4}$ pt. $(1\cdot3\,\ell)$.
(b) **Size.** Cap. $1\frac{1}{4}$ pt. $(0\cdot7\,\ell)$.
(c) **Size.** Cap. $\frac{1}{4}$ pt. $(0\cdot1\,\ell)$.
(d) **Size.** Cap. $\frac{1}{2}$ pt. $(0\cdot3\,\ell)$.
(e) **Size.** Cap. $\frac{3}{8}$ pt. $(0\cdot2\,\ell)$.
(f) **Size.** Cap. $\frac{1}{2}$ pt. $(0\cdot3\,\ell)$.
(g) **Size.** Cap. $\frac{3}{4}$ pt. $(0\cdot4\,\ell)$.
(h) **Size.** Cap. $2\frac{1}{2}$ pt. $(1\cdot4\,\ell)$.
**Material.** All copper.

All these moulds are for mousses and jellies, both sweet and savoury.

Copper moulds are naturally very expensive. They are lined with tin to prevent any chance of a deposit of verdigris coming into contact with the food while it is in the mould—and although proper cleaning will prevent this, an untinned mould is still inadvisable as prolonged contact with copper can adversely affect certain foods.

Most of these moulds have little rings attached so that they can be hung up on the wall as ornaments when not in use. They may need frequent polishing to keep them bright and shiny; copper moulds are usually sold with a protective coating of lacquer, but this tends to wear off with use.

Copper moulds are made in all shapes and sizes, but of the many available few will stand level without being propped up. Some are sold with little stands, otherwise use a wedge of bread, pastry, marzipan or anything malleable that comes to hand.

The fish-shaped moulds (a), (b) and (c) and the lobster mould (d) all need props if they are to be filled level. Use them for fish mousses and decorate them with cut-out shapes that will accentuate their fishiness and contrast in colour.

The little rosette and turret moulds (e) and (f) both stand level without any help and suit sweet or savoury mousses or jellies. They can also be used as cake tins—as can any of the metal moulds shown here. Similarly, decoratively shaped cake tins may be used as timbale, mousse or jelly moulds.

Mould (g), which has a pineapple design, demands a fruit-based recipe. It needs supporting if it is to remain level while the contents set.

The ribbed mould (h) is for making the traditional Austrian

# Copper moulds

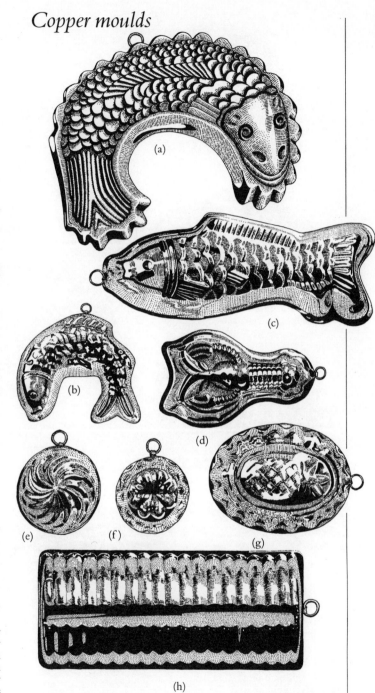

(a)

(c)

(b)

(d)

(e)

(f)

(g)

(h)

rehrücken cake, which consists of eggs, sugar, chocolate and ground almonds. After being turned out, it is coated with a chocolate glaze and decorated with a line of whole skinned almonds along its spine. It looks like a saddle of venison—hence its name. This mould may also be used for straightforward mousses and other kinds of cake, and is a particularly suitable shape for pâtes which are to be turned out and decorated after being cooked. The "spine" helps the mould to stand level so it doesn't need propping up.

# *Porcelain moulds*

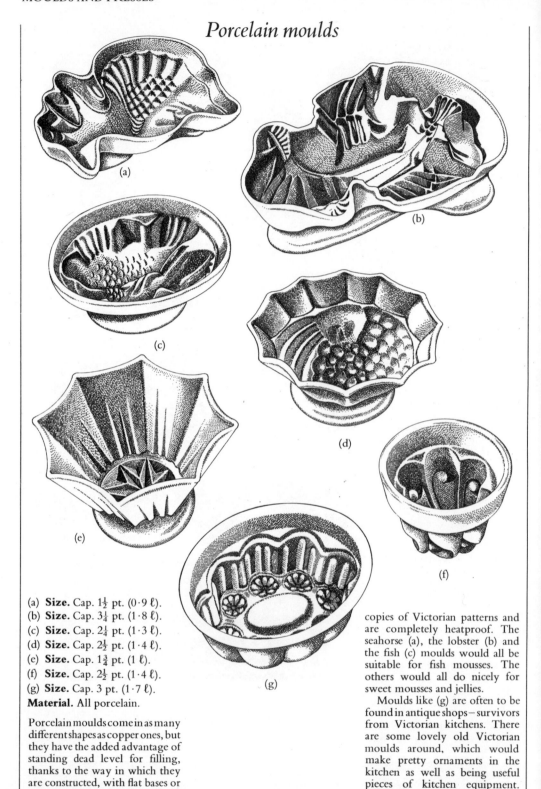

(a) **Size.** Cap. 1½ pt. (0·9 ℓ).
(b) **Size.** Cap. 3¼ pt. (1·8 ℓ).
(c) **Size.** Cap. 2¼ pt. (1·3 ℓ).
(d) **Size.** Cap. 2½ pt. (1·4 ℓ).
(e) **Size.** Cap. 1¾ pt. (1 ℓ).
(f) **Size.** Cap. 2½ pt. (1·4 ℓ).
(g) **Size.** Cap. 3 pt. (1·7 ℓ).
**Material.** All porcelain.

Porcelain moulds come in as many different shapes as copper ones, but they have the added advantage of standing dead level for filling, thanks to the way in which they are constructed, with flat bases or little plinths. Moulds (a) to (f) are copies of Victorian patterns and are completely heatproof. The seahorse (a), the lobster (b) and the fish (c) moulds would all be suitable for fish mousses. The others would all do nicely for sweet mousses and jellies.

Moulds like (g) are often to be found in antique shops – survivors from Victorian kitchens. There are some lovely old Victorian moulds around, which would make pretty ornaments in the kitchen as well as being useful pieces of kitchen equipment. These shouldn't cost much.

# Earthenware moulds

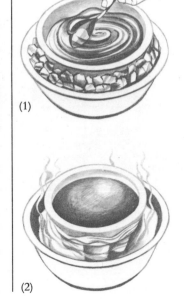

(a)

(b)

(a) **Size.** Cap. 3 pt. (1·7 ℓ).
(b) **Size.** Cap. 2 pt. (1·1 ℓ).
**Material.** Both earthenware.

Earthenware moulds are cheaper than porcelain or copper moulds but less finely incised. They are glazed inside to make the surface smooth and non-porous, while the outside is left unglazed. They are made in simple designs and generous sizes. Mould (a) is ideal for bread or baked puddings as well as for jellies and mousses; a custard, clafoutis (sweet batter pudding) or rice pudding would look very special in it. It has three little feet underneath so that it stands level. Mould (b), which also stands perfectly level, is in the traditional kugelhopf shape and could be used to bake that cake as well as for mousses or jellies.

# Glass moulds

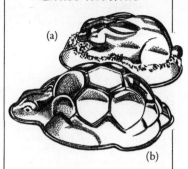

(a)

(b)

(a) **Size.** Cap. 1 pt. (0·6 ℓ).
(b) **Size.** Cap. 1 pt. (0·6 ℓ).
**Material.** Both glass.

The rabbit (a) and tortoise (b) moulds are made of toughened glass. They will withstand moderate, indirect heat, they both stand level, and they are not expensive. Transparent moulds are useful if you want to make desserts with different layers or to fix decorative slivers of fruit in strategic places. Both rabbit and tortoise look very nice on a plateau of green blancmange or jelly.

# Using a mould

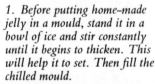

1. Before putting home-made jelly in a mould, stand it in a bowl of ice and stir constantly until it begins to thicken. This will help it to set. Then fill the chilled mould.

2. To loosen the jelly, run the tip of a knife around the inside edge of the mould. Then stand the mould in a bowl of warm water for a few seconds.

3. Invert a plate over the mould and turn over plate and mould in one sharp movement. Lift away the mould.

4. To unmould a thick custard, gently ease the custard away from the sides of the mould by pressing down with the fingertips.

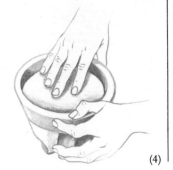

(1)
(2)
(3)
(4)

(a) **Size.** H. 8 in. (204 mm).
**Material.** Earthenware.
(b) **Size.** D. 7 in. (178 mm).
**Material.** Earthenware.
(c) **Size.** L. 3¼ in. (84 mm).
**Material.** Porcelain.

Soft cream or curd cheeses can be moulded, either during the process of making them from curdled milk, or when making them into desserts, mixed with sugar, cream and maybe eggs. Cheese moulds are always perforated in the base and sometimes round the sides so that the whey can escape. Moulds for dairy use are usually made of plastic, aluminium or stainless steel but the domestic moulds shown here are made of earthenware and porcelain. Primitive moulds of basket or wood are also used, but they are not so easy to clean (cheese moulds should be sterilized before use), nor do they last as well. Most moulds have fairly large drainage holes so, in order not to lose too many curds before the cheese is set, it is necessary to line them first with clean, damp muslin.

# Cheese moulds

(a)

(b)

(c)

Mould (a) is made of glazed earthenware and consists of the perforated mould itself as well as a draining jug which fits underneath. The mould holds a fair-sized cheese for moulding as a dessert, or takes just over 1 pt. (0·6 ℓ) of curds before draining. The jug has a wide lip and holds 1½ pt. (0·9 ℓ).

Mould (b) is in fact an ordinary earthenware flowerpot. It is used as a mould for the traditional Russian Easter dessert, paskha. (A flat-sided, wooden, pyramid-shaped mould may also be used to make this dessert.)

Mould (c) is a small version of the traditional French coeur à la crème mould. It has drainage holes in the base and is shaped like a heart. A coeur à la crème is made from a mixture of sieved cream cheese mixed with sugar and stiffly beaten egg white. After draining and setting in its muslin-lined mould, it is turned out, smothered in cream and served with fraises de bois (tiny little wild strawberries), raspberries or a purée of fresh fruit.

## Making a paskha

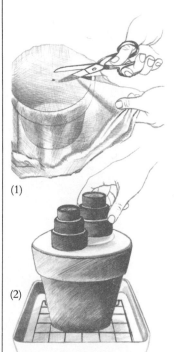

(1)

(2)

1. Sieve well drained cottage cheese and mix it with soured cream, chopped candied peel, eggs and sugar. Drape a large square of muslin over the pot and cut a slit from one edge to the centre. Push the muslin into the pot, overlapping it at the slit, and smooth it against the sides. Fill the lined flowerpot.
2. Cover the top with a saucer, weight it down and place it on a rack on a plate. Let it drain and set in the refrigerator for 24 hours.
3. Turn out the paskha on to your hand and set it upside down on a rack. Peel off the muslin.
4. Invert the paskha on to a serving plate and decorate it with strips of candied peel.

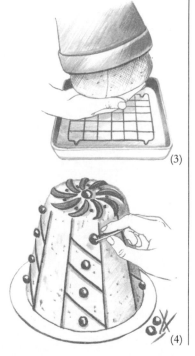

(3)

(4)

(a) **Size.** Cap. 3 pt. (1·7 ℓ).
**Material.** Aluminium.
(b) **Size.** Cap. 3 pt. (1·7 ℓ).
**Material.** Pyrex.

These moulds are traditionally lined with sponge fingers or buttered bread. The slightly outward slope of the sides helps to keep the bread or sponge in place before the centre is filled. Charlottes are usually filled with fruit purée or sweet mousse. They can be either hot or cold, depending on the ingredients. The handles at the sides are to help you to invert the mould and turn out the dessert.

# Charlotte moulds

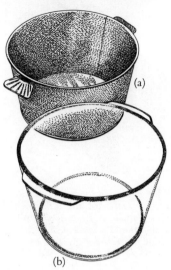

(a)

(b)

Charlottes make very impressive desserts but are actually quite simple to make. Charlotte moulds can also be used to make cakes, straightforward mousses, timbales, trifles, babas au rhum and brioches.

The aluminium mould (a) is not as attractive as the Pyrex one (b) but this is not an important consideration if the pudding is to be removed from the mould. The Pyrex mould is slightly deeper, and so more suitable for boudoir biscuits than the aluminium one which is a better depth for langues de chat biscuits. Both will go in the oven.

## Making a charlotte

*Cut a circle of greaseproof paper to fit the base of the mould. Cut the biscuits to fit the paper (1). Put the paper circle in the mould and arrange the cut biscuits on it wrong side up. Square off one end of the sponge fingers and place them, cut end down and right side facing out, round the side of the mould (2). Fill the mould and square off the fingers so they are flush with the filling (3). Arrange more fingers on the top, in the same way as for the base. When the charlotte has set, turn it out and remove the greaseproof paper.*

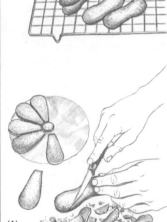

(1)

(2)

(3)

**Size.** Cap. 1½ pt. (0·9 ℓ).
**Material.** Tin-lined copper.

This mould will do for cakes as well as for timbales, ices or jellies. It may be used in the same way as a savarin, charlotte, baba, dariole or kugelhopf mould – all are interchangeable and are suitable for timbales.

A timbale is usually a tall, castle-shaped dish of rice or

## Timbale mould

mousse, sweet or savoury, hot or cold. A suitable sauce, purée or cream can be poured into the centre or around the edges of the timbale.

This mould has a central funnel which makes a hollow in the centre of the rice or mousse for the sauce or cream. It is made of tin-lined copper so that it does not affect the contents and is therefore fairly expensive.

# Ice cream moulds

(a)

(b)

(c)

# Making a bombe

(1)

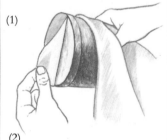

(2)

(a) **Size.** Cap. ¼ pt. (0·1 ℓ).
    **Material.** Aluminium.
(b) **Size.** Cap. 1 pt. (0·6 ℓ).
    **Material.** Tinned steel.
(c) **Size.** Cap. 1½ pt. (0·9 ℓ).
    **Material.** Tin-lined copper.

Once frozen (see ICE CREAM MAKERS), an ice cream can be moulded into any shape as long as the pattern is fairly simple. Ordinary jelly moulds will do but lids need to be improvised. Lids are necessary if the ice cream is to keep its flavour while it solidifies in the freezing compartment of your refrigerator or in the freezer. Moulds made specially for ice creams are all provided with lids and are made of metal rather than glass or ceramic so that the temperatures required for freezing and then unmoulding can be conducted to the contents as quickly as possible.

The conical mould (a) is the proper shape for the Indian ice cream made of evaporated milk and nuts and known as kulfi. It is made of aluminium and has a screw-top lid. It makes one individual ice cream, which is served standing upright on its wide end.

Mould (b) is square with a simple pattern in the base and a flat lid.

Mould (c) is known as a bombe, like the ice cream which is moulded in it, though authorities differ as to whether the name is due to its shape or to the fact that the ice cream contains a centre which is surprisingly different from the outside. The best moulds are made of heavy-duty copper with a tin lining and a little screw in the rounded end which you undo when you want to unmould the bombe. This releases suction so that the ice cream slides out easily.

*Put a chilled bombe mould in a bowl of ice and line it with a layer of ice cream (1). Allow this to harden in the freezer. Add the fillings of your choice, and finish with a layer of ice cream. Put a circle of greaseproof paper on top and put on the lid. Freeze for about four hours. Unmould, removing the greaseproof paper. Wrap a towel, soaked in warm water, round the mould (2). Invert the bombe on to a chilled plate.*

(a) **Size.** L. 3 in. (75 mm).
    **Material.** Tinned lead.
(b) **Size.** L. 7 in. (178 mm).
    **Material.** Plastic.
(c) **Size.** L. 15 in. (380 mm).
    **Material.** Rubber.

Mould (a) is made of lead, and tin-plated for safety. It is cool so that melted chocolate sets quickly on it and heavy so that it stays put while you peel off the chocolate image of a leaf. The same effect can be achieved by pouring melted chocolate over rose leaves.

Moulds (b) and (c) are for fondants. Melted fondant is poured into them and removed when cool and set. The sweets can then be dipped in chocolate.

# Confectionery moulds

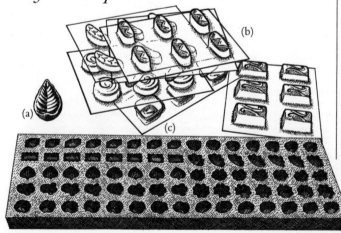

(a)

(b)

(c)

# Chocolate moulds

(a) **Size.** H. 6¼ in. (160 mm).
(b) **Size.** H. 6¼ in. (160 mm).
(c) **Size.** H. 4½ in. (115 mm).
**Material.** All tinned steel.

Made in two parts to ease un-moulding and held together by clips, these moulds of a lamb, a hare and a cockerel really come into their own at Easter time. Chocolate Easter egg moulds are also available.

To make chocolate animals, first clip the mould together. Then hold or stand the mould upside down; moulds (a) and (b) have feet on the clips so that they stand upside down. Slowly pour in melted hot chocolate and swirl the chocolate round the inside until there is an even layer. Repeat this process until you have chocolate walls of about ⅛ in. to 3/16 in. (3 mm to 5 mm) thick. When the chocolate is cold, unclip the two halves and carefully remove the chocolate animal.

These moulds can also be used for making animal-shaped cakes. First butter the moulds, fill with cake batter and cook. When the cakes are unmoulded, coat them in soft white icing and shredded coconut.

# Burger presses

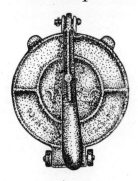

(a) **Size.** H. 4¾ in. (120 mm).
**Material.** Plastic.
(b) **Size.** H. 4¾ in. (120 mm).
**Material.** Aluminium.

These presses are for shaping perfectly flat, round burgers of identical shape and weight, such as you can buy in a packet. The raw minced meat, plus any other ingredients of your choice, is spooned into the space below the plunger, the base is slotted into place over it, the plunger is pressed down and the base is removed to reveal a smooth, neat burger. Both presses work on the same principle.

Press (a) is made of plastic and costs considerably less than press (b) which is made of cast aluminium. Press (a) is sold with a packet of waxed paper discs to put between the burgers if you want to store them in a refrigerator or freezer. These are also available on their own. Press (a) is not as easy to clean thoroughly as press (b) because it has to be completely dismantled before you can get at the moving parts. Press (b) makes slightly larger burgers than press (a)—about 2 oz. (57 g) each.

# Tortilla press

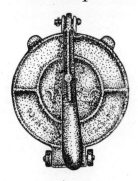

**Size.** D. 6½ in. (165 mm).
**Material.** Aluminium.

A tortilladora or tortilla press consists of two discs hinged together; the lower disc also has a handle opposite the hinge. The tortilla dough is pressed between the two discs of the press to make a flat, paper-thin circle. The alternative is to shape the dough by flipping it between the palms of the hands – a technique which requires much practice in order to perfect it. The tortilla is cooked on a griddle.

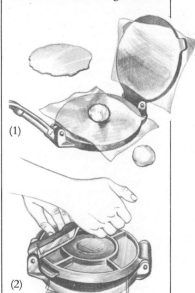

(1)

(2)

*Roll the tortilla dough into small egg-sized balls and put them one at a time into the press, which has first been lined with plastic sheeting (1). Bring down the handle over both discs (2).*

(a) **Size.** L. 9 in. (230 mm).
   **Material.** Aluminium.
(b) **Size.** L. 8¼ in. (210 mm).
   **Material.** Aluminium.

To compress cooked meat while it cools, so that it will be easier to slice, some sort of weight needs to be applied to it. These moulds shape and compress at the same time; any gaps left by the awkward shape of a piece of boned and rolled ham will be filled by the juices that are pressed out and jellify as they cool.

Press (a) is rectangular and has a removable lid and a screw set in a cross bar above to exert pressure on the lid. It is simpler in construction and cheaper than press (b) which has springs, lid and adjustable locking arms.

This type of press can be improvised at home with a deep bowl,

# Ham and meat presses

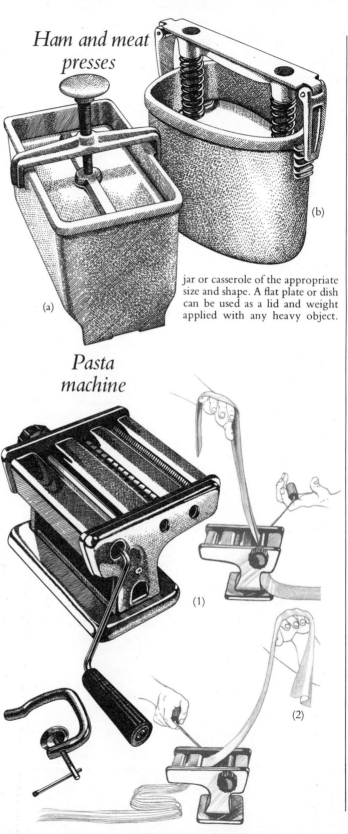

(b)

(a)

jar or casserole of the appropriate size and shape. A flat plate or dish can be used as a lid and weight applied with any heavy object.

**Size.** H. 5¼ in. (133 mm).
**Material.** Stainless steel.

This machine is used both for rolling and for cutting out pasta. It makes long 6 in. (152 mm) wide strips of beautiful 'sfoglie' for stamped-out, stuffed pastas such as ravioli and tortellini, or for cutting into lasagne and pappardelle (wide ribbons). These same 'sfoglie' can be rolled through the cutters on the machine to make wide or narrow tagliatelle. It is very easy to operate and saves much energetic rolling by hand and cutting by eye.

The machine has a clamp to attach it to the edge of a table and a handle which operates all three rollers. There is a gauge at the side to adjust the pressure which dictates the thickness of the pasta.

More sophisticated and extremely expensive machines are also available, including one electric one which mixes the dough and turns out tagliatelle all in one go.

*Make fresh pasta from flour, olive oil, eggs, water and salt. Pass the dough through the machine to roll it into a flat strip (1) and then pass it through again to cut it to the required shape (2).*

# Pasta machine

(1)

(2)

**Size.** D. 5 in. (127 mm).
**Material.** Nickel plated steel machine, hardboard stand.

There are several different ways of making spaetzle, which are small noodles made of a batter of flour, eggs and milk or cream. You can stand a colander over a pan of boiling water and stir the batter through it; you can make firmer batter, more like a dough, and force it through a ricer; you can cut small strips of dough on a noodle board – which is held over water; or you can use one of these machines.

This machine is sold with a board with a large hole in it which holds it over a pan of any size. It has holes in the bottom for the spaetzle to fall through. They are helped on their way by a revolving blade, and the whole contraption

## Spaetzle machine

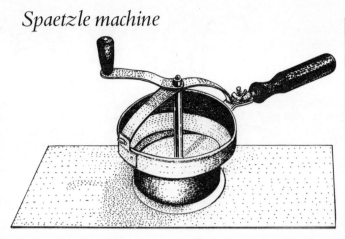

works in much the same way as a food mill. It comes apart for easy cleaning and is very simple to operate. The board which comes with it is not so good as it breaks extremely easily.

## Indian doughpress

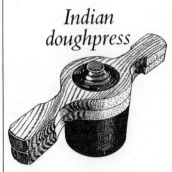

**Size.** H. 4¾ in. (120 mm).
**Material.** Wooden press, brass cutting discs.

This simple press forces a savoury spicy dough made of chickpea flour through a decoratively shaped hole. It has interchange-able cutting discs which produce a variety of shapes. It is held over a pan of deep hot oil; the resulting noodles are crisp and golden and are eaten cold as snacks or savouries. This press is easy to operate and very sturdy as the frame, handles and plunger are all made of thick wood. The cutting disc is held by a brass ring at the base of the machine.

More sophisticated – though not more efficient – presses are made for the same purpose with a turning mechanism to force out the dough. These are usually made of brass and are similar to churro presses.

## Churro press

**Size.** H. 7½ in. (190 mm).
**Material.** Stainless steel.

The favourite teatime snack of Spanish children is a crisp hot churro, smothered in sugar and dunked in hot drinking chocolate. Churros are also made and sold on street corners in Spain.

The press for this delicacy comes with a variety of cutters mounted on a couple of strips; the pattern of your choice is slotted into place at the base of the machine. The dough – which is made of flour and water or milk, sometimes with eggs as well – is dropped in a spiral straight into boiling oil.

## Cookie press

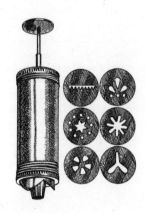

**Size.** L. 7¾ in. (197 mm).
**Material.** Aluminium.

Biscuit dough is shaped into individual cookies and piped straight on to the baking sheet by skilful manipulation of this machine. It looks like an icing syringe (see CAKE DECORATING EQUIPMENT) and works in much the same way. There is a choice of eight different cutters.

# CASSEROLES AND BAKING POTS

In English the word "casserole" has come to mean a heavy, lidded pot which is used either on top of the stove or in the oven. It also describes the rich, substantial stews of meat and vegetables that are cooked slowly and gently inside it, as well as the method of cooking. All of this must be confusing to the French, for whom a "casserole" is either a saucepan or a stewpan. What in English are called casseroles are generally described in France as "marmites" or "cocottes" ("jars" or quite simply "pots"), though there are also special names for pots shaped to suit specific dishes, in which case they take the name of the dish: for example, a pot made for the cooking of daubes is called a daubière and one for tripe is called a tripière. Other pots, like the English "casserole" and the terrine have given their names to the dishes cooked inside them.

Iron and clay cooking pots are among the earliest utensils used by cooks. The versatility of their materials – particularly of clay – allows them to be fashioned to suit the food, the style of cooking and the cooking arrangements of any cuisine, whether primitive or sophisticated. They may be tall and thin, bellied or straight or wide and shallow. They may be carried to a baker's oven, simmered over a gas ring, nestled into a bed of hot ashes or charcoal, packed (once the contents are simmering) inside a haybox, or left all day in a modern domestic oven. But their greatest virtue, whatever their size and shape, is the way in which these pots slowly absorb heat, retain it and evenly transmit it to their contents so that the food at the top of the pot is cooked just as thoroughly as the food at the bottom. Moreover, only a low heat is required, which means that the food is unlikely to burn in them and that there is a considerable economy in fuel.

## Clay pots

Earthenware, stoneware and porcelain pots are all made from clay. All clay pots are brittle, their toughness, density (and cost) increasing with the temperature at which they are fired at the pottery. Thus, earthenware pots, which are fired at the lowest heat – about 1652°F (900°C) – are the most breakable and the cheapest.

Earthenware is usually pink, brick-red or creamy coloured and is relatively porous. It may be shaped by a mould or hand-thrown, the latter process giving each pot its own variations of shape and markings and a homely look that is the very opposite of mass-produced machine-made ware. (These pots may also have less desirable irregularities, such as ill-fitting lids and wobbly bases.) Thick stews which benefit from a little evaporation are best cooked in eathenware pots.

Earthenware pots are intended to be brought to the table. Straight-sided marmites are easy to serve from; bean pots, with their narrower openings are more awkward unless you have a suitably shaped ladle.

Glazes are applied to clay pots to make them non-porous and to make them easier to clean. They may also enhance the look of a pot, brightening its natural colour or bringing another colour to it. Some pots are glazed inside and out, some glazed only partially and some – clay cooking bricks, for example – not at all. Another way of sealing or "curing" a new earthenware pot is to rub it with a cut clove of garlic before using it for the first time. This is meant to impart an oily glaze which will bake into the porous clay.

For pots used on top of the stove it is best if the base is unglazed as this helps the heat to penetrate. Conversely, a glazed pot retains heat better than an unglazed pot. Cracks and crazing will not affect the efficiency of the pot; the cracks close up as the glaze expands with heat.

## Cast iron pots

Stews, terrines and daubes can be cooked just as well in an iron pot as they can be in the more traditional, rustic, pottery pot. Most straight-sided pottery shapes can be reproduced in cast iron and look just as attractive on the table. The heavier the pot, the better it is for cooking. A thick iron pot retains heat better and diffuses it more economically than a lightweight pot. Cheap, thin, enamelled pots heat up more rapidly, and more unevenly, which means that the food is more likely to burn and stick in them. Like pottery pots, cast iron pots work best in cool ovens or over a low heat.

# Casseroles

(a)

(b)

(c)

(d)

(e)

(a) **Size.** Cap. 9 pt. (5·1 ℓ).
(b) **Size.** Cap. 5½ pt. (3·1 ℓ).
(c) **Size.** Cap. 5 pt. (2·8 ℓ).
(d) **Size.** Cap. 5½ pt. (3·1 ℓ).
(e) **Size.** Cap. ¾ pt. (·4 ℓ).
**Material.** All enamelled cast iron.

Cocottes, or casseroles, are straight-sided, round or oval pots with lids. They are usually fairly deep. Meat or poultry to be cooked in these pots is usually floured first and browned in a separate pan before being combined with liquids and vegetables in the casserole. The lids can be hermetically sealed with a strip of dough, or they can be tilted slightly to allow steam to escape.

The large oval pot (a) could easily accommodate two chickens, a goose or a small turkey for braising or pot roasting. The smaller pot (b) is a more useful size for family catering and, being oval, could easily accommodate a large chicken. The round pot (c), comes from a range of cast iron ware that includes shallower dishes that can be used with the lid of this casserole. It is made of the same vitreous enamel as pots (a) and (b).

Pot (d) has a recess in the lid. It is similar in shape to pots used in more primitive kitchens, Indian as well as European, where the cooking was done on charcoal fires. Hot coals were also placed on the lids of these pots so that the heat came evenly from above and below. This pot, known as a "doufeu" (from "doux" meaning gentle and "feu" meaning fire), is designed to work on the same principle. The recess in the lid can be filled with water or ice cubes before being put in the oven. The water heats up of course, but it still cools the lid sufficiently for steam to condense on the inside of lid and drip down to baste the food. The underside of the lid is dimpled, which helps the basting process.

The small pot (e) is intended for serving one portion of stew which has been cooked in a larger pot. Small amounts of leftover stew could be reheated and served in this pot and it could also be used, like a terrine, for making and serving pâtés.

# Slow cookers

(a)

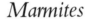

(b)

(a) **Size.** Cap. 5 pt. (2·8 ℓ).
**Material.** Stoneware pot, plastic case.

(b) **Size.** Cap. 2½ pt. (1·4 ℓ).
**Material.** Stoneware pot, metal case.

To an old-fashioned earthmother with her much loved, much used and rather battered collection of Mediterranean daubières and terrines, the idea of cooking in an electrically heated stoneware pot seems all wrong, especially if, like pot (a), it has a transparent plastic lid and is housed in an insulated plastic tub or, like pot (b), it sits inextricably in an enamelled metal cylinder. But the truth is that they work very well, cooking stews (as well as other things) extremely slowly and economically.

Both pots are equipped with very low heating elements – pot (a) works at 70 watts, pot (b) at 55 watts – so that the food is cooked at a temperature which never rises above boiling point. Most food will not suffer if left to cook in this way, and in fact food cooked slowly at a low temperature should taste very good, retaining much of its moisture and bulk as well as flavour and vitamins. No steam or smells escape from these pots, which is an additional bonus if you live and cook in the same room.

(a) **Size.** Cap. 8½ pt. (4·8 ℓ).
**Material.** Earthenware.

(b) **Size.** Cap. 4½ pt. (2·6 ℓ).
**Material.** Earthenware.

(c) **Size.** Cap. ½ pt. (0·2 ℓ).
**Material.** Earthenware.

Marmites are round, tall and straight-sided pots, usually made of earthenware, which are put in the oven and used for composite stews such as cassoulet or pot-au-feu. Pot (a) is a classic and capacious marmite, ideal for large family meals. The outside is unglazed. The clay is traditionally sealed by rubbing it with a cut clove of garlic. The smaller marmite (b) is glazed all over and can simmer on top of the stove as well as in the oven. Pot (c) is a miniature version of pot (a) and is called a "petite marmite". Originally these pots were used as individual tureens for the broth from the pot-au-feu cooked in the giant pot (a).

# Marmites

(a)

(b)

(c)

# Clay cooking pots

(a)

(b)

(c)

(d)

(e)

(a) **Size.** L. 11½ in. (292 mm).
(b) **Size.** L. 11 in. (280 mm).
(c) **Size.** L. 11 in. (280 mm).
(d) **Size.** H. 5¾ in. (146 mm).
(e) **Size.** D. 7½ in. (178 mm).
**Material.** All earthenware.

Clay pots are primitive – similar pots to these were used in Greek and Roman times, and are now enjoying a revival due to the current concern with rich cookery based on too much fat. No water or fats are needed with these pots, which can be used to cook chicken, duck, fish, meat, as well as potatoes.

All these pots are made of porous unglazed earthenware, and all have (or should have) very close-fitting lids. Clay bricks are used in the oven and need to be dampened first. Potatoes and chestnuts are cooked in dry pots – pot (d) or (e) – either in the oven or on top of the stove.

A clay brick should be soaked in water fifteen minutes before it is used. The seasoned food, surrounded with suitable herbs or chopped vegetables, is put in it and the whole thing is placed in a cold oven set to the appropriate temperature. As the oven gets hot, steam condenses on the lid of the pot and bastes the food. At the end of the cooking time the food should be tender, moist and tasty, swimming in its own juices and lightly browned on top. This method of cooking resembles baking foods on a bed of salt or in a pastry crust – the results are also similar, with the flavour, juices and aroma of the food all beautifully conserved.

The shape and size of the brick should follow as closely as possible that of the food cooked inside it. Pot (a) is a chicken brick; pot (b) is a fish brick. The oval brick (c) will accommodate any suitably

sized bird or piece of meat with some vegetables.

By standing pots (a) and (b) up on their flat ends you can see that they have been made in one piece on a potter's wheel, then laid flat and their lids sliced off with wire. This gives them flattened undersides and perfectly fitting lids. Pot (c) has been moulded; the lid has a recessed handle but it is not so close-fitting as those on the hand-thrown pots.

Pots (d) and (e) are known as "diables". The name, which is French for devil or jack-in-the-box, may be due to the fact that originally these pots were bedded down in red-hot charcoal – though certainly if you cook chestnuts without scoring them first they will hop about, exploding in the pot as they cook and expand.

These two pots should never be washed, though like the bricks, they will darken with use.

# Tagine

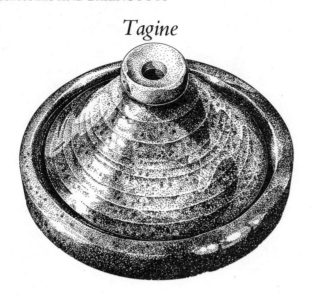

**Size.** D. 12 in. (305 mm).
**Material.** Earthenware.

In Moroccan kitchens, stews are simmered and stirred in a tagine pot over an open fire or bed of charcoal. The stews or "touagens" usually include fresh and dried fruit as well as meat and may be thickened with cooked dried beans or chickpeas and sweetened with honey. They are not as liquid as the stews accompanied by couscous which are cooked in a deeper pot, more like a saucepan (see SAUCE-PANS).

The tagine pot shown here is made of very thick earthenware; some, made of finer earthenware, are elaborately glazed and decorated with beautiful patterns.

(a) **Size.** Cap. 5 pt. (2·8 ℓ).
   **Material.** Earthenware.
(b) **Size.** Cap. 5½ pt. (3·1 ℓ).
   **Material.** Earthenware.
(c) **Size.** Cap. 4½ pt. (2·6 ℓ).
   **Material.** Earthenware.

These pots all have fat, rounded bodies with narrow openings at the top and close-fitting lids. Because of their shape, the food cooked inside them loses very little moisture by evaporation, making them suitable for soupy stews, garbure (a thick béarnaise soup of meat and vegetables) or beans cooked slowly in the oven.

The English stew jar (a) is glazed a rich dark brown, inside and out, except for the base which has been left unglazed so that the heat can penetrate from the floor of the oven.

Pot (b) comes from Béarn and is known as a toupin as well as a daubière. Daubes cooked in this pot retain plenty of moisture, while soups based on dried pulses and vegetables thicken up wonderfully in it. The straight handle is for manoeuvring the pot on the top of the stove, the small handles are for lifting it.

Pot (c) is a Tuscan bean pot. Pots of this shape are traditionally used for making deliciously soft, creamy haricot beans, baked overnight in the oven.

# Bean pots

(a)

(b)

(c)

**Size.** Cap. 1½ pt. (0·9 ℓ).
**Material.** Earthenware

## Sandy pot

The sandy pot can be used on top of the stove or in the oven. It is made from a mixture of sand and clay that is extremely fragile and light, hence its exterior reinforcement of strong wire. The outside of the pot is unglazed. In Chinese kitchens, the sandy pot is used for "clear simmering", which means the long slow cooking of meat or fish with vegetables in a fragrant stock.

## Terrines

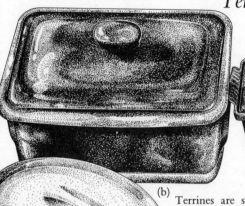

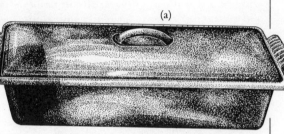

(a)

(b)

(c)

(d)

Terrines are straight-sided clay pots with lids and are used for pâtés or "terrines" of minced or puréed meat or fish. Terrines can also be made of porcelain or cast iron, as well as the traditional earthenware, and the pâté is served directly from the pot.

A terrine should be placed in a bain marie and baked at a low temperature in the oven. The lids of some terrines have holes in them to allow steam to escape, though the use of the lid is optional: if you like your pâté brown on top, leave it off; if you like it pale and moist, leave the lid on.

The long cast iron pot (a) can be used to great effect to make a long thin pâté for a party – but unless you give a lot of parties, or cook for a restaurant, its size and shape rather limit its usefulness, unlike the covered pots (b) and (c), both of which can double as casseroles. Pot (d) is made of porcelain to look like pastry, a culinary joke that is not likely to fool you into thinking that the pâté inside is really pâté en croûte. The partridge on the lid of the pot is indicative of the sort of pâté you might hope to find within it.

(a) **Size.** L. 12½ in. (317 mm).
**Material.** Enamelled cast iron.
(b) **Size.** L. 8 in. (204 mm).
**Material.** Porcelain.
(c) **Size.** L. 8 in. (204 mm).
**Material.** Earthenware.
(d) **Size.** D. 5¾ in. (146 mm).
**Material.** Porcelain.

## Lining a terrine

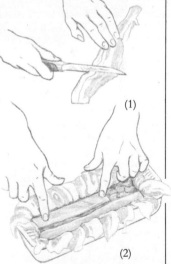

(1)

(2)

To line a terrine with streaky bacon, first remove the rinds then stretch the bacon with the back of a knife (1). Place the bacon in the terrine then press the pâté mixture into it. When the terrine is filled to the top, the pâté can be covered with more bacon (2) or left uncovered with a bayleaf on top.

# SOUFFLÉ DISHES

A soufflé, as the name implies, is a light, fragile, air-filled concoction. It is based mainly on eggs: the yolks are incorporated in a thick, creamy sweet or savoury sauce and the stiffly beaten egg whites are folded in just before the mixture goes into the oven. The heat causes the egg white bubbles to expand, at which point the straight sides of the soufflé dish dictate the direction in which they must go – namely upwards.

The cooked soufflé should be brought in its serving dish straight from the oven to the table, with the top trembling (if it is still soft inside) and well risen. This perfect, slightly underdone soufflé should stay inflated long enough for everyone in the room to admire it, or until it is punctured by a serving spoon. In Eliza Acton's time, when kitchens were miles away from the dining room, the soufflé made its journey with a salamander held over it which kept its top from sinking.

A soufflé dish is sometimes used with a paper collar, which is either fixed with a paper clip or tied round it with string. These collars are only really necessary if you have made too much mixture for the dish and wish to increase its depth. Paper collars can also be used to mould a cold, gelatine-based mousse or a frozen dessert so that it gives the impression of a soufflé.

(a)

(b)

(c)

(a) **Size.** D. 7 in. (178 mm).
**Material.** Stoneware.
(b) **Size.** D. 6 in. (152 mm).
**Material.** Porcelain.
(c) **Size.** D. 6 in. (152 mm).
**Material.** Glass.

Although you could make a soufflé in any round, deep, straight-sided ovenproof dish – a cake tin, charlotte mould or earthenware casserole would do – the results are nicer and possibly better if you use a dish made specially for the job. A soufflé dish is round so that the heat penetrates evenly to the centre, deep and straight-sided so that the mixture can rise to its maximum height, and made of fireproof porcelain, stoneware or glass so that it can be used both as a cooking pot and as a serving dish.

Traditionally, soufflé dishes are fluted so that they look like the pleated paper cases that were once made to hold ramekins. These were little soufflé-like creations made of bread cubes, eggs and cheese. (The name "ramekin" is still used for small soufflé dishes, holding just enough for one portion.) At the top of the dish there is usually a rim, which is useful if you need to tie string around an outer paper collar. The underside of the dish should be unglazed (some are, some aren't) so that as it stands on a baking tray in an oven the heat can quickly penetrate.

A soufflé will continue to cook in its dish after it has been removed from the oven. A soufflé made in a relatively heat-absorbent dish, such as the stoneware dish (a), should be removed sooner, and should be less well done, than a soufflé made in a porcelain dish.

Dish (b) is a classic white porcelain soufflé dish, smooth within and fluted without. The underside of the dish is unglazed. The rim at the top of the dish is also unglazed, again to help the heat to penetrate. Several sizes are available. The largest hold over 4 pt. (2·3 ℓ).

Both dishes (a) and (c) are made in one size only. Dish (c) is made of fireproof glass to the same design as the porcelain soufflé dish. The wide rim is a change from the usual pattern but it makes the dish easy to handle. The stoneware dish (a) is straight-sided and glazed inside and out. This soufflé dish can also be used as a casserole for dishes that do not require a lid.

# Individual soufflé dishes

(a)

(b)

(c)

(a) **Size.** D. 3¾ in. (95 mm).
**Material.** Porcelain.

(b) **Size.** D. 3¼ in. (82 mm).
**Material.** Porcelain.

(c) **Size.** D. 2½ in. (65 mm).
**Material.** Porcelain.

These dishes are miniature versions of the white porcelain soufflé dish shown opposite and can be used for small individual gratins as well as for soufflés. They also can be used for baked custards, baked in the oven with a lining of caramel at the bottom of the dish or, with the top of the custard strewn with sugar, for crème brûlée. To caramelize the sugar, place the dish under a hot grill and set it in a bowl of crushed ice to prevent the custard from curdling.

# Custard cup

**Size.** D. 3 in. (75 mm).
**Material.** Porcelain.

The custard cup can be used for frozen mousses, bread or rice puddings as well as for baked custards. It is made of thick white porcelain and is quite sturdy. It comes in one 6 oz (170 g) capacity size only.

## Preparing a soufflé dish

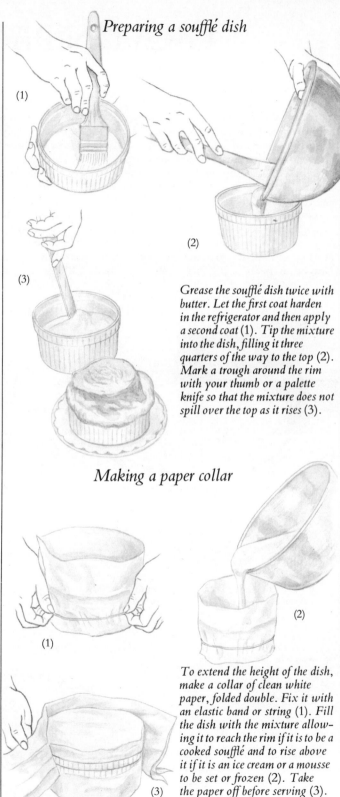

(1)

(2)

(3)

Grease the soufflé dish twice with butter. Let the first coat harden in the refrigerator and then apply a second coat (1). Tip the mixture into the dish, filling it three quarters of the way to the top (2). Mark a trough around the rim with your thumb or a palette knife so that the mixture does not spill over the top as it rises (3).

## Making a paper collar

(1)

(2)

(3)

To extend the height of the dish, make a collar of clean white paper, folded double. Fix it with an elastic band or string (1). Fill the dish with the mixture allowing it to reach the rim if it is to be a cooked soufflé and to rise above it if it is an ice cream or a mousse to be set or frozen (2). Take the paper off before serving (3).

# GRATIN PANS

For most people, food with a crisp, brown shiny crust is irresistible. Caramel-coloured peaks of mashed potato, brown blisters and speckles on a coating of cheese sauce or a crunchy, rocky surface of toasted breadcrumbs spread over the creamy contents of a savoury dish – all these are the trademarks, in French cookery, of a "gratin", or something which is "gratiné" or cooked "au gratin" : meaning, in plain English, "burnt on top".

Gratins are meant to be served in the dishes in which they are cooked. These gratin dishes, or gratin pans, are made of good heat-resisting and heat-conducting materials – copper, porcelain, earthenware or cast iron – as they are used in the oven as well as under a grill. They are shallow rather than deep which means that each serving has a generous proportion of crust; at the same time they will fit under a grill or in the top of an oven. They can be lifted by a small rim or by little handles; these project to the side rather than upwards, again so that the surface of the dish can go as close as possible to the grill.

A gratin dish may have straight or sloping sides. Sloping sides increase the surface area of the gratin, which is fine for sauced eggs lying on a purée of spinach or a gratin of potatoes, but for food which needs to remain upright, such as stuffed vegetables, a straight-sided gratin dish is more useful.

## *Round gratin dishes*

(a)

(b)

(c)

(a) **Size.** D. 10 in. (255 mm).
**Material.** Tin-lined copper, brass handles.
(b) **Size.** D. 6¾ in. (172 mm).
**Material.** Porcelain.
(c) **Size.** D. 6½ in. (165 mm).
**Material.** Enamelled cast iron.

The copper gratin dish (a) is lined with tin and fitted with brass handles, which makes it particularly nice to look at when it comes to the table. The smaller dish (b) is made of porcelain; its small size and very sloping sides make it par-

ticularly suitable for cooking eggs, both on top of the stove or in the oven. Dishes (a) and (c) can both be used for cooking eggs as well as for gratins; their greater depth allows for a bed of diced or puréed vegetables under the eggs.

(a) **Size.** D. 8 in. (204 mm).
**Material.** Enamelled cast iron.
(b) **Size.** D. 4½ in. (107 mm).
**Material.** Earthenware.

Dish (a) will hold twelve snails in their shells; dish (b) will hold six. Both dishes are designed to hold the stuffed snail shells upright while they bake in the oven, and should be brought, sizzling hot, to the table.

## *Snail dishes*

(a)

(b)

# Oval gratin dishes

(a)

(b)

(c)

# Ramekins

(a)

(b)

(c)

(a) **Size.** L. 12 in. (305 mm).
**Material.** Enamelled cast iron.

(b) **Size.** L. 12½ in. (317 mm).
**Material.** Enamelled cast iron.

(c) **Size.** L. 12½ in. (317 mm).
**Material.** Enamelled cast iron.

Gratin dish (a) comes from a range of cast iron ware designed so that lids, dishes and pots can be used interchangeably or in combination. These dishes are often bought in pairs as the lid of one dish fits over the other to form a shallow, lidded casserole. When inverted,

the gratin dish also forms a domed lid for a casserole.

Dish (b) is relatively deep and straight-sided. It is a good size and shape for cooking cannelloni or stuffed cabbage leaves.

The tinned copper dish (c), like the round copper dish opposite, is made in a variety of sizes and can be used in much the same way. Round gratin dishes, however, are better for cooking eggs on top of the stove because the heat can reach all parts of the dish equally. Similar dishes to these are also made in aluminium. These are considerably cheaper, but not so handsome.

(a) **Size.** D. 3¼ in. (82 mm).
**Material.** Earthenware.

(b) **Size.** D. 3½ in. (90 mm).
**Material.** Porcelain.

(c) **Size.** W. 3½ in. (90 mm).
**Material.** Porcelain.

These dishes should always be bought in some quantity so that they can be used as individual serving dishes. They are used for individual custards, pâtés, gratins and the like. Dish (a) has a little handle and is just right for one baked egg. Dish (b) can be used for eggs or, like dish (c), for baked custards or petits pots de chocolat.

191

# ROASTING PANS

Roasting pans have flat bases and slightly sloping sides; they may be rectangular or oval in shape and are usually fairly shallow. Although these pans are designed for roasting meat or poultry, they can also be used as baking tins for batter puddings, slab cakes and pies or as gratin dishes.

Deep roasting pans with lids can make moister roasts and help to prevent fat from spattering on to the walls of the oven. In both open and lidded pans the meat or poultry can be put on a roasting rack (see RACKS) to allow the fat and juices to drip into the pan. The drippings can later be separated and the fat kept for frying and the juices used for gravy.

Roasting pans are made in a variety of materials – tinned steel, aluminium, enamelled cast iron, glass, porcelain and earthenware.

Tins of the latter four materials can be handsome enough to use as serving dishes. Cookers are usually supplied with rather poor quality roasting pans; if you are buying a new roasting pan look for a strongly made pan in a material which conducts heat well and does not warp. If you like to make gravy in the roasting pan, choose a material that will go on the hob. Make sure you pick a size that will fit in your oven, allowing at least 2 in. (50 mm) leeway all round for air to circulate. Roasts can be very heavy so unless you don't mind picking up heavy weights, it is best not to buy a cast iron roasting pan. Choose a pan with good sturdy handles which can be gripped easily so that you do not fumble with a hot pan.

Covered electric cook pans (see FRYING PANS) can also be used for roasting.

---

(a) **Size.** L. 14 in. (355 mm).
    **Material.** Tinned steel.
(b) **Size.** L. 12¼ in. (310 mm).
    **Material.** Tinned steel.
(c) **Size.** L. 14 in. (355 mm).
    **Material.** Aluminium.
(d) **Size.** L. 10¾ in. (274 mm).
    **Material.** Porcelain.
(e) **Size.** L. 13½ in. (343 mm).
    **Material.** Glass.
(f) **Size.** L. 15½ in. (394 mm).
    **Material.** Enamelled cast iron pan, tinned steel handles.

Tins (a) and (b) are both made of tinned steel, without seams and with strong rims. Tin (a) has recesses at either end to act as handles, while tin (b) has wire handles which fold down flat when not in use and open out when the pan is lifted. Both are shaped so that basting can be done easily with a spoon.

Tin (c) is French and is made of heavy-gauge aluminium with two rigid handles in cast aluminium. It is slightly deeper than tins (a) and (b), which helps to cut down on spatter, and makes it useful for batter puddings or slab cakes.

Pan (d) is also French and is made of oven-proof porcelain with the underside left unglazed for better heat conduction. It has no handles, but is small enough

### Deglazing a pan

*Use the fat and juices left in the pan after sautéing or roasting to make a sauce or gravy.*
*First pour off any excess fat, then put the pan over a medium heat. As soon as the juices bubble add a glass of wine or some stock. Stir all the time, using the liquid to dislodge any sediment left on the base or sides of the pan – deglazing the pan. Add enough liquid to make the amount required and let it simmer a little before returning the meat to the pan or straining the liquid into a sauce boat.*

to pick up easily with one hand. It is attractive enough to double as a serving dish, so it would be perfect for roasting and serving a row of little birds wrapped in vine leaves. It is also suitable for other dishes, such as rolls of stuffed cabbage, gratins, stuffed pancakes and custards.

Pan (e), also French, may be used for the same purposes as pan (d). It is made of heat-proof glass, with large rims at either end which act as handles.

Pan (f) is made of vitreous enamelled cast iron. Once heated it transmits heat to the contents with such intensity that it is likely to burn the fat and juices in the bottom. For this reason it is advisable to use a cooler oven than you might with an ordinary roasting tin, and to put some water in it before you begin roasting. It is a useful shape for baking cakes or making gratins, and particularly good for lasagne with its handsome appearance and its straight, fairly deep sides. It has strong tinned steel handles hinged at each end so that they fold down when not in use and out when you lift the pan. This roasting pan is very heavy, and even more so when it holds something like a turkey, so take care when taking it out of the oven.

# Shallow roasting pans

(a) **Size.** L. 11 in. (280 mm).
   **Material.** Tinned steel.

(b) **Size.** L. 12¾ in. (324 mm).
   **Material.** Aluminium.

(c) **Size.** L. 20 in. (508 mm).
   **Material.** Aluminium and
   magnesium alloy pan,
   aluminium rack.

Pan (a) has high sides and a domed
lid which stops fat from spattering
and keeps the roast moist. It will
brown the meat but will not make
it crisp – if you wish to crisp the
top, take the lid off towards the
end of the cooking time. The pan
is very light in weight and its base
is flat and stable. This size is good
for a chicken.

Pan (b) is a self-basting roasting
pan; it has a dimpled lid, so that
when the steam condenses on the
inside of the lid, it drips evenly on
to the roast. It has handles on both
pan and lid.

Pan (c) is similar to (a) but
comes with a rack to keep the meat
off the bottom of the pan and out
of the fat and juices. This size is
large enough to hold a 25 lb. (11 kg)
turkey but there are other sizes
available for smaller roasts. The
pan and lid both have handles.

# Deep roasting pans

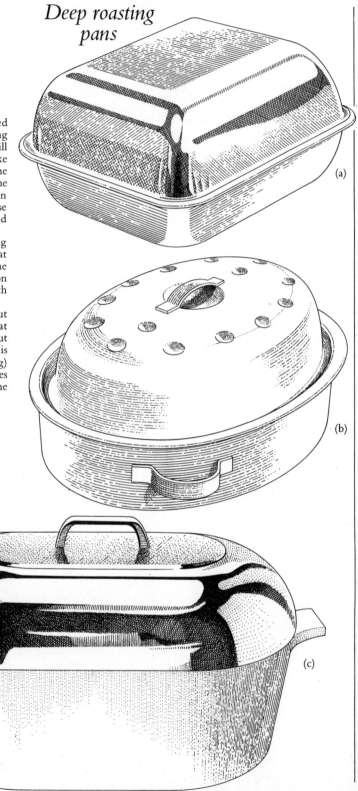

(a)

(b)

(c)

# SAUCEPANS, STEAMERS AND POACHERS

These pots and pans are used primarily for cooking food which needs to be immersed in liquid, or in the steam from that liquid, on top of the stove. Cooking by boiling, simmering, poaching or steaming can be managed quite adequately with a set of cheap light aluminium or enamelled steel pans if you intend to prepare nothing more elaborate than poached eggs, packeted soups, boil-in-the-bag dinners and steamed potatoes. Cheap pans serve well enough if you eat merely to survive and, with care, it should be some time before they are so chipped, dented, distorted and burnt that you have to throw them away and buy new ones. At this point you might well consider buying better pans: by then, perhaps, you will have become a more ambitious cook; with really good pans, your cooking can become more versatile and successful.

*Saucepans*

Good pans are usually expensive, but they will last for generations. Choose them in the shapes and sizes that best suit the type of food you cook and the number of people that you are likely to cater for.

The best pans are made of metals that conduct heat well. They have firmly attached, comfortable handles and, if they have lids, these fit well. Saucepans should be heavy and distribute heat evenly so that you can braise, pot-roast or stew in them with a minimum of liquid. You can also use them to sauté food in fat without the risk of it sticking or burning before adding liquid. The base should be thick; a thin base will buckle with use over high heat, making it inefficient, not to say useless, on electric and solid fuel cooking plates, and likely to cook unevenly over gas. The base should also be smooth. Some bases are slightly concave on the outside, particularly those that are made of two metals sandwiched together, to allow for the different rates of expansion of the two metals. Stainless steel pans, for example, often have copper or aluminium bases. Pans which have been moulded rather than cast or stamped have the advantage of thick bases with thinner sides.

The sides may be straight, curved or sloping and high or low, according to what the pan is for. Straight sides serve best for general pur-poses. Some people prefer curved sides, partly because they look nice and partly because they help with the convection, or movement of heat within the pan. Milk pans have sloping sides with lipped rims. Preserving pans for jam making also have sloping sides to speed up the evaporation of water and lipped rims for pouring out the jam. But the classical saucepan – the casserole russe – is round and is almost twice as wide as it is deep, with straight sides. The point at which the sides meet the base may be curved or angular. Neither offers any problem as long as you have wooden spoons or spatulas which fit nicely into the corners (see SPOONS).

Handles should be firmly attached to the pan with rivets rather than with screws or by welding. They should be placed some distance below the rim so that lifting and pouring are comfortable. Very large pans, and pans made of cast iron, are heavy – especially when full; these should have two handles, either one long one and a small ear-shaped one opposite, or a pair of ear-shaped ones. A plastic or wooden handle will be cool to hold, but unless the plastic handle can withstand a fair amount of heat it will burn easily. These handles are usually shaped so that they are comfortable to hold and are attached to the pan by a long metal core or screw-ended rod which should, for safety's sake, be screwed tight and firmly riveted to the pan at the other end. Professional chefs' pans nearly always have metal handles – usually of a metal that transmits heat less well than the pan itself. Even so, all but those with asbestos hands will find that these handles get painfully hot. You need the protection of a cloth to hold them or, if they are small ear-shaped handles, you could do what the French often do and wrap them around with string. Long handles should be long enough to keep your hand away from the hot pan. (Be careful not to position these saucepans with the handles facing the front of the stove, as you could tip boiling water over yourself by knocking into them.)

Lids are considered essential on English and American saucepans, and so they are if you want to steam, poach or stew food. French saucepans, on the other hand, rarely have them. In French kitchens, cooks make do – if they wish to cover food while it simmers – with a disc of greased paper or a flat, all-purpose lid with a long handle that does not get hot. If you want to steam food in a pan, the lid should fit very well so that as little steam as possible escapes. It should have a rebate so that it fits tightly inside the rim of the pan. If you buy a set of matching pans in various sizes, check whether the lids can be turned upside down so that the pans can be stacked one on top of the other. You can do this well with flat lids, but not so easily with domed ones. On the other hand, condensation from steam runs back into the pot more readily with domed lids, which is why they are shaped like this on poachers and steamers. Plastic handles on lids do away with the need for an oven mitt; metal ear-shaped handles can be made heat-proof with string or with a cork, sliced lengthways.

Special-purpose pans vary in shape to a greater or lesser extent from the classic casserole russe. But a standard saucepan can in fact be used instead of some of the special pans. For example, by lodging a ceramic bowl or pudding basin above simmering water inside an ordinary saucepan, you have a double boiler or porringer. And by skilful use of colanders, aluminium foil and trivets, ordinary pans can easily be converted into steamers and poachers.

## Steamers and poachers

In many ways, steamed or poached food is better than food that has been boiled or stewed. Boiled and stewed food is immersed in liquid and much of its goodness is lost in the process. This does not matter if the cooking liquid is to form part of the finished dish, or is to be used to make stock, soup or gravy, but it is a pity if it is going to be thrown away.

Steaming is slightly slower than boiling, but the process retains more vitamins and flavour. Steamed food also retains its shape, whereas boiling can give it quite a buffeting. Steamed food is cooked in a perforated container which sits over a pan of boiling water. The lower pan sometimes has a spout so that it can be topped up without removing the upper container. The food is placed directly over the holes in the container or, if it is being cooked with a sauce or flavourings, it can be put in a dish or basin inside the steaming compartment. It is important to keep steam in by covering the whole contraption with a tight-fitting lid.

Poaching is half way between boiling and steaming. The food is usually laid on a rack inside the pan with water, court bouillon or stock covering it. The water should stay just below boiling point, gently cooking the food but not destroying it. When it is cooked, it can be lifted from the pan on the rack.

## Materials

Most pans are made of metal – cast iron (plain or enamelled), stainless or enamelled steel, copper or aluminium. The main exception to this is a pan made of porcelain. Saucepans may also be made of glass, which looks lovely but does not conduct heat well.

The materials of which a pan is made will influence the way in which heat is transmitted to the contents. They also have some bearing on the cost. Unfortunately, the best conductors of heat happen to be among the most expensive metals. Silver, an excellent conductor of heat, non-toxic and non-corroding, is the best material, with copper coming next. There are some beautiful pans made of copper and lined with silver, but they cost a great deal. The next best are solid copper, or tin-lined copper. Copper, as long as it is of heavy gauge, gives an instantaneous and even transmission of heat; it also loses heat very rapidly, so that you have perfect control over the temperature inside the pan. Copper makes superb pans for the rapid cooking and crisping of tender cuts of meat or fish, for braises and stews, for sauces that need close guarding against curdling, for sugar and for jam. All except for the last two types of pans are lined with tin; this prevents the adverse effect which copper has on some foods. Pans can be retinned when the lining wears off. Besides making good pans, copper looks handsome and can be kept bright and shiny by polishing it with special metal polish or with a regular application of lemon or vinegar and salt. The handles of copper pans are usually made of brass or gunmetal, neither of which transmits heat as well as copper.

Cast iron is ideal for long, slow cooking as it conducts heat evenly and well (see CASSEROLES), but not as quickly as copper. Large pots and pans made of cast iron are very heavy – make sure you can lift an iron pan before you buy it, bearing in mind it will be even heavier when full. Cast iron, if it is not enamelled, may rust. It is also brittle so should not be dropped. Handles are usually cast in one piece with the rest of the pan, which means they get very hot. Cast iron will cook well over a much lower heat than other metals. It should become almost "non-stick" in time, as long as you do not scour it too harshly.

Enamelled steel is only worth having if it is

of good quality. Poor quality enamelled steel is thin and coated with inferior enamel which chips easily. A cheap pan will become rusty and dented where it has chipped, wobbly in the bottom where it has warped, and possibly irreparably scorched. Good quality enamelled steel is almost as good as enamelled cast iron, heavy and chip-proof, though not quite as good a heat conductor. Like enamelled cast iron, enamelled steel is now available in a wide range of colours and looks good enough to bring to the table. Handles are usually plastic.

Stainless steel is very durable and makes excellent pans provided it is of a heavy gauge. However, it is not such a good conductor of heat as copper, iron or aluminium. For this reason it often has a disc of copper or aluminium on the base, or a core of mild steel sandwiched between two layers of stainless steel. It is tough, handsome and easy to clean, though it does tend to stain – this can be removed with special cleaning stuff, but avoid scouring if you want to keep a shiny, mirror-smooth surface. Handles are usually made of plastic and sometimes of wood. Stainless steel pans are expensive, but as long as they are well made, with provision for the efficient conduction of heat, they will prove economical to use and virtually indestructible.

Aluminium is the cheapest and most commonly used metal for pots and pans. As long as it is made in a heavy gauge it works very well. It is an excellent conductor of heat, although it holds it for longer than copper, it is light, fairly tough and easy to maintain. Its disadvantages are that it can turn certain foods a greyish colour and it can become stained and pitted. These problems can be prevented by lining the pans with silicone or "non-stick" resins and giving the exterior an anodized finish. Aluminium can also be given a shiny, polished finish which will protect the surface. Recent discoveries indicate that the adverse effect aluminium has on some foods is prevented if the metal is hardened electrochemically. It also becomes almost non-stick and a great deal tougher. Pans made of this type of aluminium feel very silky to the touch and are dark grey – they look similar to cast iron pans – and are expensive. Handles on aluminium pans are usually of iron, aluminium or plastic.

Porcelain conducts and holds heat well; it also looks elegant enough to bring to the table. It has the obvious disadvantage of being easily broken, either by being dropped or by being subjected to extreme changes of temperature. Porcelain saucepans are good for making delicately flavoured sauces, cooking fruit and making fondues. The handle is usually porcelain and attached by a separate metal band; this keeps the handle cool. There are also porcelain milk jugs which can go straight from stove top to the breakfast table.

## Hotpan

**Size.** D. 9¾ in. (248 mm).
**Material.** Stainless steel pan and lid, aluminium base, plastic bowl.

The design of this pan enables food to be cooked almost completely in its own juices, without the addition of much (or any) other liquid and with a minimum of fat (or none at all). It is made of heavy-gauge stainless steel with a thick disc of aluminium on the base which conducts heat well and enables you to use very low heat. The base also has an outer skin of stainless steel so that the aluminium does not mark ceramic hobs. The lid, made of two separate layers of stainless steel, fits very closely inside the pan.

Once the food is cooked, the whole pan – which has a wide rim to hold it by rather than handles – can be placed inside the strong plastic bowl; this will keep the base of the pan off the surface of your table. There is an air gap of about 1 inch (25 mm) between the bowl and the pan which insulates the contents of the pan and stays warm for an hour or so.

# *Saucepans*

(a) **Size.** D. $5\frac{3}{4}$ to $8\frac{3}{4}$ in.
(146 to 223 mm).
**Material.** Aluminium pans
and lids, cast iron handles.

(b) **Size.** D. $8\frac{3}{4}$ in. (223 mm).
**Material.** Aluminium.

(c) **Size.** D. $7\frac{1}{2}$ in. (190 mm).
**Material.** Stainless steel
pan, copper base.

(d) **Size.** D. 8 in. (204 mm).
**Material.** Porcelain.

The set of polished aluminium pans (a) has black iron handles and light aluminium lids which are quite flat when reversed so that the pans can be stacked for storage. These pans, which are French, are made of heavy-gauge aluminium, and the base is of the same thickness as the sides. The handles curve upwards from their fixing half-way down the sides, giving a comfortable, well balanced hold on the pan and arching clear of other pans on the stove or at its side. There are holes in the handles so that they can be hung up.

Pan (b) is made of heavy-duty aluminium and is very heavy, especially when full. It is ideal for the slow simmering of stocks, soups and stews. Larger sizes are also available. These usually have small ear-shaped handles opposite the long handles to help you to lift them.

Pan (c) is made of satin-finished stainless steel with a thick copper disc on the base to help with the conduction of heat. It has a strong plastic handle and a plastic knob on the lid, which fits the pan tightly. This is a very expensive pan, but is excellent quality and will last for generations. The rim of the pan curves outwards for easy pouring.

Pan (d) is made of white porcelain. Its handle is protected from the heat of the pan by a band of stainless steel. The pan is lipped for pouring. This is a beautiful, expensive and fragile pan, definitely for "show" and not to be kept like Cinderella in the kitchen.

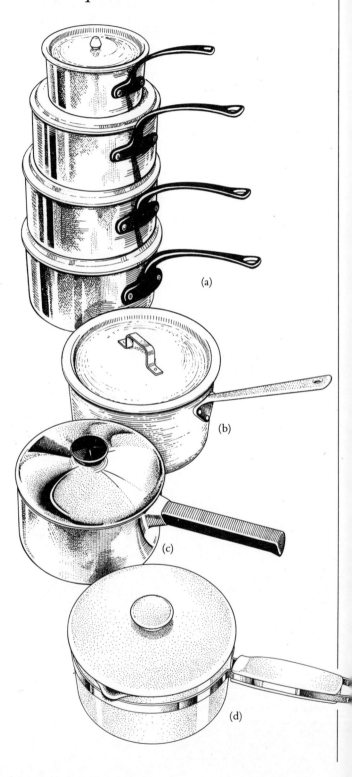

(a)

(b)

(c)

(d)

# Two-handled pans

(a) **Size.** D. 7¾ in. (197 mm).
    **Material.** Aluminium.
(b) **Size.** D. 8¼ in. (210 mm).
    **Material.** Aluminium.

Stockpots like (a) are useful for making large quantities of stock or soup, or pot au feu. Pans similar to this one are known in France as faitouts and are used, as their name suggests, for boiling just about anything and everything. They need to have two handles because they are very heavy when full.

Pan (b) is known as a rondeau. It is wide, fairly shallow, with ear-shaped handles and a flat lid. It makes a useful pan for boiling awkward shaped vegetables like leeks or for poaching fish such as trout. It can also be put in the oven and used to make a "brun" by roasting bones and onions a dark brown before adding the liquid that will make the stock. It is a good shape for braising poultry or meat and is a most useful, professional pan.

Both these pans are made of aluminium which has been hardened electrochemically. This makes them tough, virtually non-stick and safe to use with any foods. It also gives them a silky, dark grey finish, making them attractive enough to bring to the table.

(a)

(b)

# Couscoussier

**Size.** D. 9 in. (230 mm).
**Material.** Aluminium.

This is a special pan for making the North African speciality couscous. The meat and vegetables cook in the lower half and the accompanying couscous – a coarse semolina – cooks in the perforated steamer above it. Unlike other kinds of steamed food, couscous cooks best if some of the steam is allowed to escape, hence the eight largish holes in the lid.

# Sugar boiler     Milk pan     Butter warmers

(a)

(b)

(a)

(b)

**Size.** D. 5 in. (127 mm).
**Material.** Copper.

Sugar boilers are shaped like ordinary saucepans but they have lips for pouring. The best ones are made, like this one, of untinned copper. This is because copper is the best material for rapid heat conduction; the temperature of boiling sugar is critical if you are trying to cook it to a specific stage, and sugar must therefore stop boiling the instant you remove it from the heat. The inside is not tinned because sugar boils at such a high temperature that the tin might melt. The handle is hollow in order that it may be extended by the insertion of a special wooden cylinder; without this it gets very hot, but not as hot as it would if it were solid. Remember when boiling sugar to keep washing down the sides with a wet pastry brush. This pan has straight sides which are easier to keep free of sugar grains than sloping ones.

(a) **Size.** D. 6½ in. (165 mm).
   **Material.** Aluminium pan, plastic handle.
(b) **Size.** D. 3¼ in. (84 mm).
   **Material.** Glass.

This pan (a) has a black non-stick lining and sloping sides to allow rising milk to spread as it gets near to boiling point. It has a lipped rim all round and a plastic handle. Milk pans do not have lids. Use only plastic or wooden spoons with this pan so as not to damage the lining.

A little glass disc (b) in the bottom of any pan helps to stop milk from boiling over by oscillating with the convection of the heat. This has the same effect as stirring the milk, which only boils over because the air bubbles can't release themselves quickly enough from the dense liquid.

(a) **Size.** W. 4¾ in. (120 mm).
   **Material.** Stainless steel pan, copper base, teak handle.
(b) **Size.** D. 3 in. (75 mm).
   **Material.** Porcelain.

Little pans like these may not seem enormously useful until the occasion arises when you need melted or clarified butter, and nothing else, to pour on to your asparagus, poached salmon or seakale. Your smallest saucepan is likely to be too large and unsuitable to put on the table at a dinner party; and if the butter is decanted into a jug or sauceboat, it will get cold and some will inevitably be wasted. These little pans are the answer.

Pan (a) is made of stainless steel with a copper base and has sloping sides for easy pouring and a heat-resistant teak handle. It would also do for melting jam or jelly, or for warming liqueur before flambéing something. Pan (b) is made of porcelain and shaped like a miniature saucepan with a lip.

**Size.** D. 5 in. (127 mm).
**Material.** Aluminium pan, cast iron handle.

This French bain-marie saucepan is for making sauces. It is tall and narrow with a very short handle so that it can be crowded with others like it in a bain marie, or water bath, and is used to the same effect as a double boiler. Domestic

# Bain-marie saucepan

kitchens do not really need a special bain-marie bath; a wide, shallow roasting tin does just as well if you are making several sauces at once. Otherwise you can use any pan that is wider than the pan containing the sauce, and deep enough to allow water to come more than half-way up.

**Size.** D. $6\frac{3}{4}$ in. (172 mm).
**Material.** Aluminium.

The problem with asparagus is that the base of the stem needs much more cooking than the tender tips. To cook it properly, it should stand upright with the tips at the top, rather than lying down. This tall lidded pan overcomes the problem. It has a perforated sleeve inside with a handle at the top and three feet at the

## Asparagus pan

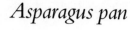
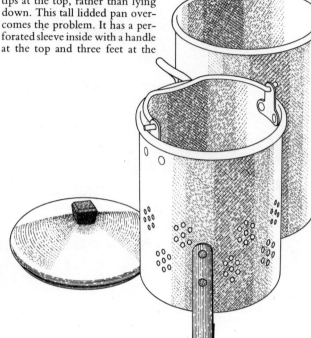

bottom. The asparagus stands in a bundle inside this basket, with salted water boiling up to about half-way up. By the time the tips are tender from steaming, the bottoms should have boiled sufficiently to be cooked. This is a very useful pan if you eat a lot of asparagus.

## Rice boiler

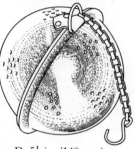

**Size.** D. $5\frac{1}{2}$ in. (140 mm).
**Material.** Aluminium.

To keep the pan clean while it cooks the rice and to simplify draining it, put the rice in this perforated aluminium ball and suspend it in boiling salted water until it is cooked. It has a chain with a hook at the end to hang it by and is hinged on one side with a clip on the other.

## Preserving or maslin pan

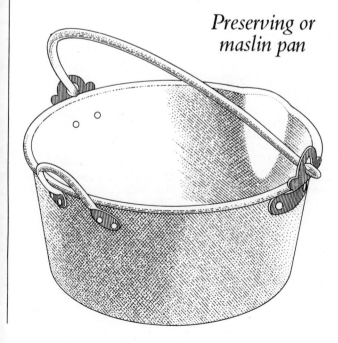

**Size.** D. $12\frac{3}{4}$ in. (324 mm).
**Material.** Aluminium.

This pan has a hinged semi-circular handle across the top which can be locked in an upright position to keep it off the rim and so cool. It also has an ear-shaped handle opposite the pouring lip. Preserving pans need to be large as the boiling jam bubbles up a lot. It is in any case not worth making jam in small quantities. These pans are wide and not too deep to help with evaporation.

Preserving pans are often made of copper because heat needs to be transmitted fast and furiously. The copper also gives fruit a very bright colour, particularly gooseberries, which stay green in a copper pan but go a dull pink in an aluminium one. (Tin linings would melt at the temperature of boiling jam.) The handles of copper pans are usually brass.

(a) **Size.** D. 6¼ in. (160 mm).
**Material.** Aluminium pan, plastic handles and knob.
(b) **Size.** D. 7¼ in. (185 mm).
**Material.** Tin-lined copper pans, ceramic bowl, brass handles.

Double boilers consist of two saucepans, a lower one which holds simmering water and an upper lidded one which fits inside it, and which holds the food – usually a sauce – to be cooked. Egg-based sauces which need gentle cooking, such as béarnaise, hollandaise and custard, are best cooked in a double boiler so that the indirect heat of the simmering water can be kept low enough to cook the sauce without curdling it.

Pan (a) has a top pan made of a thinner gauge aluminium than the lower pan: it should not be used as a pan in its own right as it is not heavy enough and might burn or warp over a high heat. The lid fits both pans. The advantage of this pan over pan (b) is its cheapness and the fact that the sauce in the top pan can be stopped from cooking and instantly cooled by removing it from the water. This is not so with the ceramic bowl of boiler (b); this retains heat and can only be cooled quickly by plunging the base into a bowl of cold water. There is no advantage in

# Double boilers

having the lower pan and lid made of tinned copper if it is only to hold boiling water, but it does look very pretty. It would look handsome at the breakfast table, full of porridge or kedgeree.

(a)

(b)

# Zabaglione pan

**Size.** D. 6 in. (152 mm).
**Material.** Tin-lined copper pan, gunmetal handle.

Zabaglione is a delicious froth made from egg yolks, sugar, Marsala and cream. Use a pan that is large enough to allow the raw egg yolks to triple in bulk as they are whisked while they cook. This pan can be held directly over the heat with one hand while you whisk with the other.

Zabaglione can also be made in a double saucepan, or in a ceramic basin or copper egg bowl standing over a pan of gently simmering water. As soon as the froth is made serve it still warm, in large goblet-shaped wine glasses.

This pan may seem rather too costly if you intend to use it only for making zabaglione, but you could justify the expense by using it as well for making egg-based sauces and custards.

# Steamers

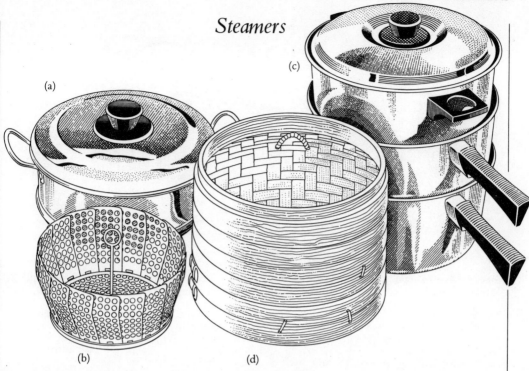

(a)

(b)

(c)

(d)

(a) **Size.** D. 8¼ in. (210 mm).
   **Material.** Aluminium.

(b) **Size.** D. 9½ in. maximum (242 mm).
   **Material.** Chromed steel.

(c) **Size.** D. 8¾ in. (223 mm).
   **Material.** Stainless steel pans, aluminium base, plastic handles.

(d) **Size.** D. 10 in. (255 mm).
   **Material.** Bamboo.

Steamer (a) is made of polished aluminium, perforated in the base; it has a tight-fitting lid and two ear-shaped handles. The base has six concentric ridges so that it can be placed over pans of six different diameters. It is large enough to take a fairly large cauliflower or a small chicken.

Steamer (b) is an expanding basket, made of interleaved panels, all perforated, so that it can be used inside pans of any size from 5½ in. to 9½ in. (140 to 242 mm) in diameter. It has a central stem to lift it by; you can remove this if you want to steam large objects. It stands out of the water on three little legs.

Steamer (c) is a three-tiered contraption. The bottom section can be used as an ordinary saucepan and has an aluminium base to aid heat conduction. The middle part is a steamer, and the top section is another pan which can be used on its own or as a double boiler over the bottom pan. The lid fits all three sections.

Steamer (d) is a Chinese bamboo lidded steamer for making the many and various delicacies – mostly dumplings – that go to make up the Chinese "dim sum". They come in many sizes and can be fitted in as many tiers as you want over a pan of boiling water. To stop the dumplings from going soggy, line each basket with a square of muslin.

Make sure when steaming food that the lid fits tightly. If it does not, improve the seal by lining it with folded cloth or foil.

# Set of lids

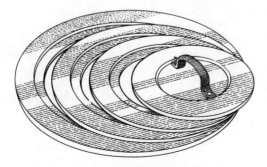

**Size.** 5¼ to 10¼ in. (133 to 260 mm).
**Material.** Aluminium.

This is an ingenious continental idea for a versatile lid that can be used on pans of different sizes. It can be used as it is – 10¼ in. (260 mm) wide – or broken down into three smaller lids.

# Fish kettle

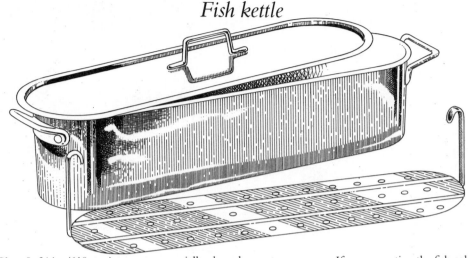

**Size.** L. 24 in. (610 mm).
**Material.** Aluminium.

The best way to poach a salmon, or indeed any fish, is whole rather than cut up. This is no problem if the fish is small, in which case any pan will do, but large fish need specially shaped pans to accommodate them without curling them up.

Cold salted water or a court bouillon should be brought slowly to the boil with the fish in it. The heat should then be turned off and the fish left to cook until it is done.

If you are eating the fish cold, let it cool in the liquid; if hot, lift it out on the rack to drain.

This fish kettle would need two burners on a domestic stove. Squarer fish kettles are also available for fish such as halibut and turbot.

# Idli steamer

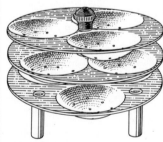

**Size.** D. 6½ in. (165 mm).
**Material.** Aluminium.

An idli steamer consists of three tiers, with three little round hollows on each tray, so that nine idli—steamed dumplings made of ground rice and lentils—may be steamed at one go. The steamer has three short legs so that it can stand in a shallow bath of boiling water inside a lidded saucepan. Idli are a speciality of Southern India.

# Egg poachers

(a) **Size.** D. 7¼ in. (185 mm).
    **Material.** Aluminium, plastic handles.
(b) **Size.** W. 2½ in. (65 mm).
    **Material.** Aluminium.
(c) **Size.** H. 3¼ in. (84 mm).
    **Material.** Ceramic.

Poacher (a) steams rather than poaches eggs: it is not a poacher in the strict sense of the word because the egg is not immersed in boiling water. It has three round, non-stick cups which hold the eggs. These are fitted into a lidded tray which stands over boiling water.

Poacher (b) is an egg-shaped poacher. Break an egg into it—it won't disappear through the holes—and stand it in boiling water. (The water should cover the egg.) Both poachers (a) and (b) should be buttered before use.

Pot (c) is a ceramic egg coddler. Eggs cooked in this screw-top mould emerge like shell-less boiled eggs. It stands in a pan of boiling water. Double-sized coddlers take two eggs. Coddlers are said to have been invented by Kipling which is why coddled eggs are sometimes known as Kipling eggs.

(a)

(b)    (c)

# PRESSURE COOKERS

Pressure cookers can be used to cook any food that is otherwise steamed, stewed or boiled. Because of the high temperature inside them, they cut cooking time by up to 50 or 70 per cent and save fuel. However, these high temperatures are better suited to things like steamed puddings, stocks, soups and the preliminary cooking of oranges for marmalade than they are to meat, which tends to be reduced by such treatment to flabby, tasteless shreds. Pressure cookers may also be used for bottling fruit and blanching vegetables for the freezer.

They work on the principle of increasing the boiling temperature of water and trapping the steam produced. At sea level water boils at 212°F (100°C) and however fast and furiously it does so, the temperature will go no higher and the water just evaporates as steam. By putting a container (the pan) under pressure the boiling temperatures are increased. Most cookers operate on three pressures: low, with 5 lb. (2·26 kg) pressure creating a temperature of 228°F (109°C); medium, with 10 lb. (4·53 kg) pressure creating a temperature of 240°F (115°C); and high, with 15 lb. (6·79 kg) creating a temperature of 250°F (121°C).

Some cookers have just one pressure, usually high or medium, and this slightly restricts their usefulness. High pressure is generally used for cooking meat, vegetables, fish and Christmas pudding; medium for softening fruit when jam making and for bottling vegetables; low for steaming puddings with a raising agent and for bottling fruit.

When cooking in a pressure cooker, the food is put in the cooker with the necessary liquid and the lid is tightly closed. The cooker is put over a high heat until the liquid boils and steam comes out of the vent. At this point a pressure weight must be put on. When the cooker starts to hiss, indicating that the necessary pressure has been reached, the heat is turned very low for the remainder of the cooking time. Should any part of the cooker not function properly, there is a safety valve which lets out the steam so that the cooker does not explode. Cooking completed, you can either turn off the heat and wait for the pressure to come down in its own time (which means that the food continues to cook) – usually 15 to 30 minutes – or you can stand it in cold water or run cold water over the lid. This brings the temperature down in a minute or so and stops cooking straightaway.

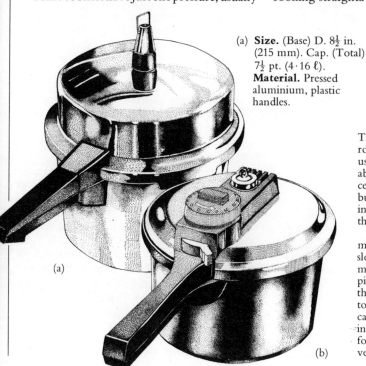

(a)

(b)

(a) **Size.** (Base) D. 8½ in. (215 mm). Cap. (Total) 7½ pt. (4·16 ℓ). **Material.** Pressed aluminium, plastic handles.

(b) **Size.** (Base) D. 7½ in. (190 mm). Cap. (Total) 9½ pt. (5·5 ℓ). **Material.** Drawn aluminium, plastic handles, timer and housing.

The domed lid of cooker (a) allows room for the tall preserving jars used for bottling fruit or vegetables. The weight has a graduated central core which rises as pressure builds up inside the cooker and indicates at which point to turn the heat down.

Cooker (b) depressurizes automatically, either quickly or slowly, at a pre-set time by moving a lever on the lid. A pinger timer rings at the end of the cooking period to remind you to turn off the heat. A central panel can be slotted into the perforated inner basket to divide it neatly – for cooking two different kinds of vegetable, for example.

# FRYING PANS, SAUTEUSES AND DEEP FRYERS

Fried food is cooked in fat or oil rather than water, steam, stock or sauce. The cooking process is usually brief and rapid, and the results are characteristically crisp and crunchy. There are three distinctly different methods of frying and three distinctly different types of pan – shallow frying pans, sauteuses and deep fryers.

## Frying pans

These use just enough fat or oil to cover the base of the pan and are used for cooking thin, flat pieces of food, such as escalopes, fillets of fish, slices of liver, hamburgers, slices of bread, fish cakes, rissoles and, of course, sausages, bacon and eggs.

Heat needs to be transmitted rapidly and evenly to this type of food, so these pans should be made of heavy gauge, heat conducting metals. They have wide, flat bases and shallow sides, sloping outwards to give space for lifting and turning the food. Handles are usually long and straight to make lifting and manoeuvring the pan easy. Frying pans have no lids, as the retention of moisture would only make fried food soggy, but mesh lids with long handles can be used to reduce splattering.

Ordinary frying pans are suitable for most simple frying, including sealing pieces of meat before they go in a stew, but their sides are too angular and steep for special things like omelettes and pancakes. These are cooked in shallow pans with curving sides. Very wide pans with two small handles are made for cooking paella, and large oval pans with long handles are made for frying fish.

## Sauteuses

Sauteuses, sauté pans or plats à sauter are frying pans with deep sides. They are used to cook larger pieces of food in deeper fat or oil. They are not used nearly as much in English and American kitchens as they are in France. This is our loss, for these pans are extremely useful.

As their name suggests, these pans are used to toss the food as it fries ("sauter" means to leap or jump) so that it gets crisp and brown on all sides, without laborious lifting and turning. To cook croûtons, sauté potatoes or little glazed onions, put at least $\frac{1}{4}$ in. (6 mm) of oil into the pan and add the food only when the oil is really hot. Then, as it cooks, hold the handle with both hands and sharply toss the pan away from you so that the little frying pieces rise up in the air and return to the pan. Drain them in a chinois sieve when they are done. (It is easier to toss food in pans with sloping sides.) Use the sauteuse to seal largish pieces of chicken before cooking them further in the same pan. Remove the pieces once they have become golden and drain off excess fat or oil before deglazing the pan with wine or stock. Return the chicken pieces to the pan, add more stock to simmer them until tender, and finally thicken the sauce. These pans are not usually provided with lids in France, but in America they are known as "chicken fryers" and have lids.

## Deep fryers

These are for frying food that needs total immersion in boiling oil or fat – this includes chips, fritters, doughnuts, beignets, pieces of chicken or fish in batter, and such delicacies as Chinese fried noodles or Spanish churros.

There is always a danger that a large quantity of boiling oil might get spilt or, still worse, catch fire, so the best pans are absolutely stable, with a mark showing the maximum safety level for oil. Boiling fat has a nasty tendency to foam up and spill over as cold or wet food goes into it. Many pans are therefore supplied with lids for use in an emergency and to enable you to use them as stockpots or stewpans as well as fryers. They usually have wire baskets so that all the food can be lifted in and out at once. These baskets may also be used for blanching vegetables.

Deep-fried food should be as dry as possible before it goes into the fat, otherwise the fat will splatter dangerously. Batter-coated food, although wet, crisps and dries the instant it is immersed so long as the fat is hot enough. It has the added advantage of being cooked in an insulating coat so that the contents do not cook too fast or transmit their flavour to the fat. Oil that is used to fry battered fish should not absorb a trace of fishy flavour. Egg and bread-crumbing has the same insulating and crisping effect as batter but take care to filter the fat or oil after cooking as small particles left in it will burn and transmit a bitter taste.

## Frying pans

(a) **Size.** D. 10 in. (255 mm).
**Material.** Mild steel.

(b) **Size.** D. 8½ in. (215 mm).
**Material.** Mild steel.

(c) **Size.** D. 9 in. (230 mm).
**Material.** Enamelled cast iron.

(d) **Size.** D. 6½ in. (165 mm).
**Material.** Enamelled cast iron.

Pan (a) is the classic shape for a frying pan, with low, straight, sloping sides. It is made of heavy-gauge untreated mild steel with a pressed steel handle riveted to the pan. In time this metal goes completely black, giving the pan a non-stick surface. Be careful not to let it rust before it has built up this patina.

Pan (b) has curved rather than straight sides. This makes it look rather like an omelette pan, but the sides are in fact too high in proportion to the width of the base to make really successful omelettes.

Pan (c) has a lip on each side. This is for pouring off the sauce you have made by deglazing the caramelized juices left after frying little tournedos, or escalopes. Food tends not to stick too much on a smooth enamelled surface like this. The handle gets very hot as it is cast with the rest of the pan.

Pan (d) is also of cast iron. vitreous enamelled in black.

## Paella pan

**Size.** D. 14 in. (355 mm).
**Material.** Mild steel.

This pan is shaped like an ordinary shallow frying pan but, because it is so large (paella pans usually are) and heavy when full, it has two handles to carry it by instead of one long one. It is made of heavy-gauge untreated mild steel with steel handles.

Paella is a Spanish rice dish in which all the ingredients are cooked in this one pan, usually over an open fire or charcoal. Begin with pieces of chicken and continue with pork, chorizo sausages, and squid. Then add rice, saffron-flavoured stock and tomatoes. Towards the end, add mussels, clams and prawns in their shells, and bits of green pepper or peas for colour. Paella is always served straight from the pan.

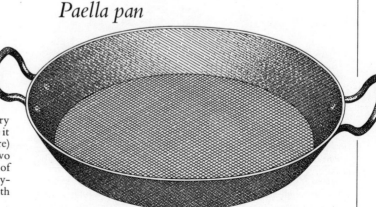

(a) **Size.** D. 9 in. (230 mm).
**Material.** Steel, wooden handle.
(b) **Size.** D. $10\frac{1}{4}$ in. (260 mm).
**Material.** Aluminium, plastic handle.
(c) **Size.** L. $6\frac{1}{2}$ in. (165 mm).
**Material.** Aluminium.
(d) **Size.** D. $10\frac{1}{2}$ in. (267 mm).
**Material.** Steel.
(e) **Size.** L. 16 in. (405 mm).
**Material.** Aluminium, iron handle.

## Special pans

The crêpe or pancake pan (a) is extremely shallow with very sloping sides. The pan is light so that it is easy to turn the crêpe over by tossing it in the air; the low sides are all that is necessary to contain a paper-thin crêpe and are a help when it comes to sliding it on to a serving dish. Once seasoned, the pan should never be washed.

Wide though pan (b) may seem, it is in fact just the right size for a two- or three-egg omelette. To make a successful omelette, the raw mixture should spread thinly over the base of the pan, it should cook very quickly, and it should be stirred constantly until it sets. Then tilt the pan so that the omelette can be rolled into a sausage shape and fall out of the pan and on to a plate from the side opposite the handle. This is why the sides are curved and not too high.

Pan (c) is rectangular and is for making special layered Japanese omelettes (tomago dashimaki). These are folded up towards the end of the pan as they are made, with two or three successive ladlefuls of the raw mixture cooked in the same pan and rolled round the preceding one. The finished roll is then wrapped in a cloth or mat (sudare) to set. The handle is slightly angled to help with the rolling up, and the cooking is done with chopsticks.

Pan (d) looks exactly like a frying pan but is made of a lighter-gauge steel and has large round holes in the base. It is used to roast chestnuts over an open fire or charcoal brazier.

Pan (e) can accommodate one or two large sole, several herrings, or a fair-sized plaice. Remember to fry the white side of flat fish first so that when you serve the fish the dark side is underneath.

# Sauteuses

(a) **Size.** D. 12 in. (305 mm).
**Material.** Tin-lined copper, brass handle.

(b) **Size.** D. 11¼ in. (285 mm).
**Material.** Tin-lined copper, stainless steel handle.

(c) **Size.** D. 7 in. (178 mm).
**Material.** Tin-lined copper, copper handle.

(d) **Size.** D. 9 in. (230 mm).
**Material.** Enamelled cast iron.

The first three pans are made of very heavy-gauge copper, lined with tin; they are extremely expensive but so good to cook with that they are worth the cost.

Pan (a) has a brass handle and straight sides, and is large enough to cook sautéed chicken, blanquette of veal or beef olives for about ten people.

Pan (b) has curved sides and a stainless steel handle and is ideal for sautéing potatoes as well as being a useful, general-purpose cooking pot. You need some strength to lift it as it weighs 4½ lb. (2 kg) when empty – but that is only half as heavy as pan (a).

Pan (c) is too small for large quantities of meat or sauce, but good for making a little treat for yourself and a pampered friend. It has a copper handle and is very heavy – about 3 lb. (1·4 kg) – for its size.

Be careful not to heat these pans when empty as the tin lining will blister. In any case, they conduct heat so well that a medium heat should be enough to brown most food. Like the other sauteuses, pan (d) has deeper sides than an ordinary frying pan. It is made of black matt enamelled cast iron and its handle is cast with the pan. It has two lips on the rim for pouring and a lug on the side opposite the handle to help when lifting. This pan is made with a lid to it so that you can braise and stew in it as well as fry.

# Anti-splash lid

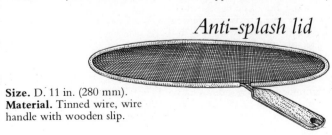

**Size.** D. 11 in. (280 mm).
**Material.** Tinned wire, wire handle with wooden slip.

This wire mesh lid is put over a frying pan when cooking very splattery foods. It will control splashes of fat and help to keep the cooker clean.

# Deep fryers

# Potato nest baskets

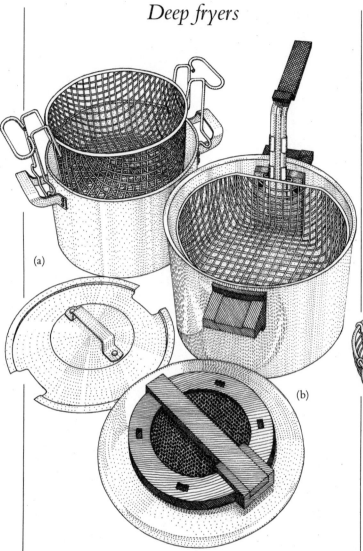

(a)

(b)

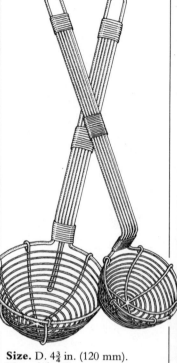

**Size.** D. $4\frac{3}{4}$ in. (120 mm).
**Material.** Wire.

The smaller of these wire ladles fits inside the larger one and the two are clipped together. Fine chips or potato slices are fried in the larger basket, with the smaller basket holding them in a nest-like shape. The starch in the potatoes helps to hold the nests together. The nests can be filled with savoury titbits.

(a) **Size.** D. $9\frac{1}{4}$ in. (235 mm).
   **Material.** Aluminium pan and lid, wire basket.
(b) **Size.** D. $9\frac{1}{2}$ in. (242 mm).
   **Material.** Enamelled aluminium pan and stainless steel lid, plastic wire basket.

Deep fryer (a) has a lid with slots which accommodate the handles of the basket when it is submerged in water or fat inside the pan. The handles of the basket have extensions which allow them to rest on the handles of the pan; this allows the basket to sit above the level of fat, so that chips, fritters and so on can drain. The pan has two small

handles rather than one long one which could catch on your arm and tip the whole thing over.

Deep fryer (b) has a deodorizing filter fitted into its lid; this filter is made of charcoal and should be removed after 20 to 30 fry-ups. It works very well, allowing steam to escape but keeping the disagreeable smell of cooking fat to itself. The basket holds up to $2\frac{3}{4}$ lb. ($1\frac{1}{4}$ kg) of chips. The pan is marked with lines for the minimum and maximum safe levels of oil—up to about 4 pt. ($2\cdot5$ ℓ)—and has a thermometer which indicates, by colour, the heat of the fat in the frying pan.

*Before frying, coat the potato slices in cornflour so that they stick together and not to the wires.*

# Electric deep fryers

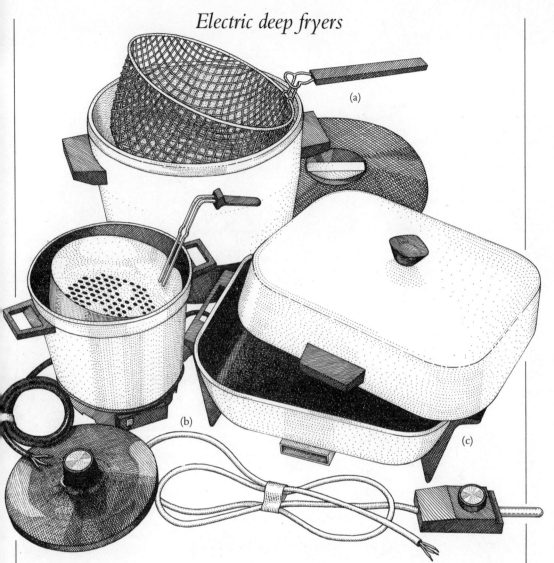

(a)

(b)

(c)

(a) **Size.** D. 9 in. (230 mm).
**Material.** Enamelled
aluminium pan and lid,
wire basket, plastic handles.

(b) **Size.** D. 7 in. (178 mm).
**Material.** Enamelled
aluminium pan, aluminium
basket, plastic lids, base and
handles.

(c) **Size.** W. 12 in. (305 mm).
**Material.** Enamelled
aluminium pan and lid,
plastic handles and feet.

Electric deep fryers are thermo-statically controlled so that the fat can be kept at the temperature you require. Pan (a) can be used to simmer stews or soups at a temp-erature just below boiling point, or to cook jam at a temperature just above it. It is capacious enough for soup for eight or ten people. It is equipped with a galvanized wire basket for deep frying.

Pan (b) is a small version of pan (a) and is ideal for one or two people. It has a non-stick lining, a thermostat to control tempera-ture, and a light to show that it is switched on. It does not indicate when the desired temperature has been reached, however, so you have to test the oil with a fat thermometer or by browning a cube of bread in it (SEE MEASURING EQUIPMENT). Its small size also makes this fryer good for table-top dishes like fondue bourguig-nonne. The pan has two lids – one for covering cooled oil in the pan, and the other, looser-fitting, for keeping it all clean when not in use.

Pan (c) can be used to braise, stew, roast, steam and boil, as well as fry foods. The lid is high enough to cover a small chicken or two ducklings. It has a non-stick lining. The temperature is thermostatically controlled and ranges from simmering to 424°F (200°C). This pan is totally wash-able, unlike pans (a) and (b), as the electric heating element is detach-able. It is ideal for cooking in cramped conditions – in a bed-sitter for example.

211

(a) **Size.** D. $6\frac{1}{2}$ in. (165 mm).
(b) **Size.** D. 6 in. (152 mm).
(c) **Size.** D. $7\frac{1}{2}$ in. (190 mm).
(d) **Size.** D. 9 in. (230 mm).
**Material.** All wire.

This is a selection of baskets in various shapes to fit deep frying pans of different diameters. They can also be used to blanch vegetables in boiling water, a necessary process if you are freezing them.

Basket (a) is fairly deep and made with very fine wire mesh so food cannot escape. Basket (b) is similar, but has extra reinforcement in the form of a metal frame outside the basket. Basket (c) is shallower than the others, and has larger holes. Basket (d) is collapsible and folds down flat which means it can be kept in a drawer.

## Frying baskets

## Chinese wok

**Size.** D. 14 in. (355 mm).
**Material.** Mild steel.

A wok is used over gas or a live fire; a metal ring or collar is set round the burner for the pan to stand firmly and the flames rise up to the base.

Rapid shallow "stir frying" is done with the simultaneous use of a spatula and a ladle (see SPOONS). Once food is cooked, it can be pushed to one side, leaving the centre of the pan free for new ingredients. Large pieces of food need deeper fat or oil and can be drained in the semi-circular rack which clips round the rim. A small rack in the centre of the wok is all that you need to support a dish or bowl of food for steaming; the water boils beneath it and a domed lid covers the whole thing. The same equipment can be used for smoking food, with a mixture of burning tea leaves, rice and brown sugar in place of the water.

# GRILLS AND GRIDDLES

Grills and griddles are designed to cook food very fast, with a minimum of fat. They are heated from beneath and transmit heat more directly than grills on domestic ovens where the heat comes from above.

The best of these pans are made of cast iron or cast aluminium—both metals that conduct heat well. They are thick and heavy so that they will not buckle over intense heat, and flat and low-sided because little or no fat is used. They are similar in appearance to frying pans; some have long handles, others have nothing more than a hand-hold at the side. This is in fact all that is needed, as a grill or griddle—once in place over the heat—does not need to be moved about or tipped up like a frying pan or sauteuse.

## Grills

Grills are used for cooking steaks, chops, gammon rashers, fish and so on. The cooking surface is sometimes flat and smooth, but more usually it is corrugated. The corrugations channel away the fat that runs out of the food, allowing the outside of the food to char and crisp up nicely. They also brand it with stripes which can be made into criss-cross or diamond-shaped patterns. Another advantage of a corrugated pan is that food sticks to it less readily than it does to a flat pan.

A grill should always be heated beforehand, to provide a searing temperature. Test it for temperature by flicking a drop of water on it—it sizzles if the metal is hot enough. It should then be smeared lightly with melted fat or oil.

## Griddles

These are closely related to grills and are also known as girdles and bakestones. The name "bakestone" gives a clue to this tool's origins. It may be completely flat and smooth with no sides at all, or it may have circular hollows for cooking special things such as flat, round drop-scones or spherical aebleskiver (Danish apple dumplings). Large smooth stones heated on an open fire are the precursors of the bakestone or griddle and are still used by nomadic tribes to bake flat chapatti-like breads.

A heavy iron or aluminium griddle is in fact the best tool to use in a modern kitchen for baking chapattis, as well as oatcakes, galettes (buckwheat pancakes) or any of the many other kinds of unleavened breads or pancakes.

Griddles need only a little oil or fat to prevent the food from sticking.

## Waffle irons

Waffle irons and sandwich toasters are like double-sided grill pans, hinged together at one end, with long handles projecting from the other. The plates of a waffle iron are deeply indented with a grid-like pattern. The grooves contain the waffle batter, which is poured into the lower, greased plate as soon as the iron has heated up sufficiently over a burner. The top plate is lowered on to it and the handles are clipped together. As soon as the underside of the waffle is browned, the iron is turned over to cook the other side.

Waffles can be eaten with maple syrup, sugar, lemon juice, jam, ice cream or fruit. Irons can also be used to make toasted sandwiches. Special sandwich toasters are available, but these will not make waffles.

Waffle irons are of Scandinavian origin. Having made your own waffles, you can see where and how ice cream cones and wafers originated.

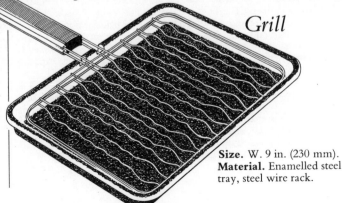

### Grill

This is one of the cheapest and most useful utensils in the book. It consists of a double-sided wire rack held by flanges over a thin enamelled tray. It grills food very efficiently; heat penetrates the tray rapidly because it is so thin and because it has open slots across its base. Food is held between the bars of the rack. As soon as one side is done, you detach the rack from the tray, turn the rack over, and cook the other side.

**Size.** W. 9 in. (230 mm).
**Material.** Enamelled steel tray, steel wire rack.

# Griddles

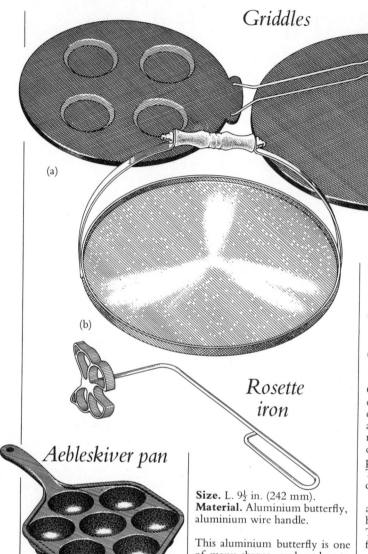

(a)

(b)

(c)

## Rosette iron

## Aebleskiver pan

**Size.** D. 8 in. (204 mm).
**Material.** Cast iron.

Aebleskiver pans are used in Denmark to make round, puffed-up dumplings, each stuffed with a slice of apple. They are served, dusted with caster sugar, with afternoon coffee. The pans have semi-spherical indentations. These are buttered, and when the butter is foaming, the batter is poured in and an apple slice put in each. As soon as the underside is done, the dumpling is turned over to cook the other side.

**Size.** L. 9½ in. (242 mm).
**Material.** Aluminium butterfly, aluminium wire handle.

This aluminium butterfly is one of many shapes—such as hearts, pine trees, stars and wheels—that can be attached to the aluminium handle. These irons are Swedish and are used to make crisp little fried batter cookies. The iron is dipped into hot frying oil and then into batter, taking care that it doesn't come over the top of the iron. The batter-coated iron is then dipped into the fat again and held there until the mixture is crisp and golden. It should come off the iron quite easily. Drain it on paper, then coat it in sugar. More elaborate cookies can be made by topping them with crème pâtissière and fresh fruit.

(a) **Size.** D. 9½ in. (242 mm).
**Material.** Enamelled cast iron, stainless steel wire handle.

(b) **Size.** D. 12 in. (305 mm).
**Material.** Cast aluminium, wooden handle.

(c) **Size.** D. 11 in. (280 mm).
**Material.** Cast iron.

Griddle (a) is made of enamelled cast iron and has four circular depressions in it and a small rim all round the edge. It is used for making perfectly round little pancakes and drop-scones or, if you prefer, perfectly round fried eggs. The handle, of stainless steel wire, can be folded flat.

Griddle (b) has a small low rim all round its edge and a hooped handle with a wooden holder. The handle is hinged so that it lies flat for storage.

Griddle (c) is thinner than griddle (b) but, being made of cast iron, it is also heavier. It is flat with a small hand-hold at one side. Similar but larger griddles are used in France to make Breton galettes (buckwheat pancakes), which are served with eggs, sausages or cheese. The batter is spread evenly with a special wooden "ratteur".

This griddle is English and is used for drop-scones or oatcakes. It could also be heated in the oven and used as a bakestone for bread or pitta. This griddle is used in the same way as (b).

# Grill pans

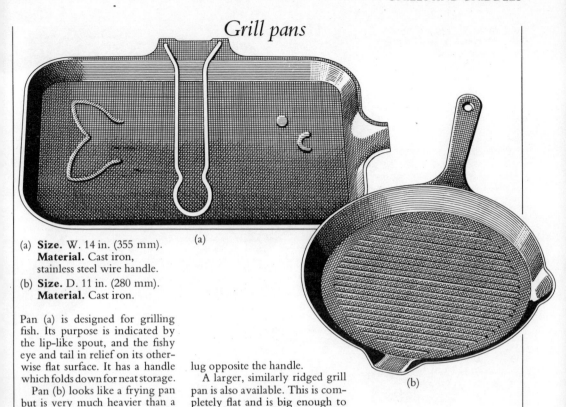

(a)

(b)

(a) **Size.** W. 14 in. (355 mm).
**Material.** Cast iron,
stainless steel wire handle.
(b) **Size.** D. 11 in. (280 mm).
**Material.** Cast iron.

Pan (a) is designed for grilling
fish. Its purpose is indicated by
the lip-like spout, and the fishy
eye and tail in relief on its otherwise flat surface. It has a handle
which folds down for neat storage.

Pan (b) looks like a frying pan
but is very much heavier than a
normal pan and it is ridged
across the cooking surface. It also
has a spout on one side for pouring
off any accumulated juices, and a
lug opposite the handle.

A larger, similarly ridged grill
pan is also available. This is completely flat and is big enough to
go across two burners. It will
easily accommodate four chops,
as well as a few halved tomatoes
and some mushrooms.

# Salamander

**Size.** L. 18 in. (458 mm).
**Material.** Cast iron, wooden
handle.

If you heat this iron until it is red-
hot, whether in gas flames or over
a live fire, it can be used to brown
the surface of gratins or sugar-
coated desserts, making a delicious
crisp brown crust or caramel coating without disturbing or heating
the rest of the food beneath it. The
same effect can be achieved under
a hot grill, but there is a greater
likelihood of spoiling the rest of
the dish by over-cooking or curdling. This iron is most useful for
crème brûlée, a rich cold custard
made of cream and egg yolks
which should be covered in a
sheet of hard, smooth, thick caramel (see SOUFFLÉ DISHES). If you
dampen the sugar after sprinkling
it thickly on the custard, the salamander works better. If you don't
have one of these special tools, you
could use a small, old-fashioned
cast iron collar iron.

This salamander is made of cast
iron, with a wooden handle. It is
small enough – 2 in. (50 mm) in
diameter – to be held over individual custard cups.

A red-hot poker is sometimes
used to brand decorative criss-
cross patterns on meat – branded
in this way it looks as if it's been
grilled even if it's been roasted.

(a) **Size.** W. 7½ in. (190 mm).
   **Material.** Cast aluminium, plastic-coated handles.
(b) **Size.** D. 7 in. (178 mm).
   **Material.** Cast aluminium, plastic-coated handles.

# Waffle irons

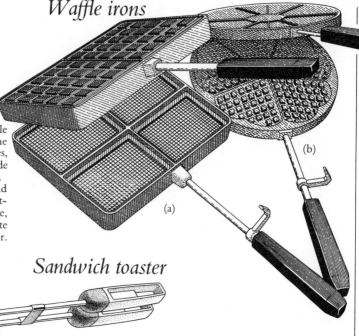

(a)

(b)

Waffle iron (a) has reversible plates; waffles are made on the side which has deep grooves, toasted sandwiches can be made on the other, less indented, side.

Waffle iron (b) makes round waffles. Circular, fan or heart-shaped irons are also available, as well as irons with intricate patterns for Swedish krumkaker.

# Sandwich toaster

**Size.** W. 4½ in. (115 mm).
**Material.** Stainless steel, plastic handles.

Sandwich toasters consist of two hollow plates hinged together. Bread, buttered on the outside, is placed on one plate, the filling goes on top and another piece of bread (again with the butter facing out) goes on that. The toaster is put over the heat, which fries the bread and bakes the filling. Fillings may be anything you like—thinly sliced meat, tinned fish, cheese, fruit, or even chocolate.

# Infra-red electric grill

**Size.** L. 12¼ in. (310 mm).
**Material.** Enamelled steel, turned steel baking dish.

Infra-red grills are heated by electric coils and supplied with infra-red radiation, which penetrates food more rapidly and efficiently than the heat from electrically heated elements alone. They consist of two detachable non-stick plates. The electric coils and infra-red equipment lie behind, in two brightly coloured trays which are hinged together in such a way that any thickness of meat up to 1½ in. (38 mm) can be put between them. They will also bake food in the baking dishes provided with the machines. The grills take between seven and ten minutes to heat up; an indicator light goes off when the grill is hot enough to cook on. This grill works on only one temperature; others can be set to high,

medium and low heats.

Recipe books supplied with the grills recommend using them with the baking tin for the astonishingly rapid cooking of pizzas, quiches, simple puddings and even sponge cakes, as well as for grilling meat or fish in the usual way, and for toasting sandwiches. Some people, however, prefer meat cooked on a conventional grill as they like the contrast

of very burnt outsides and less well cooked middles.

Because of the infra-red rays, these grills can also be used to cook unthawed frozen foods. Excess fat or oil should be poured off through the small holes at the corner of the grilling plates. Food can be cooked in foil if you want to avoid smoke and spattering fat, but this slows down the cooking time considerably.

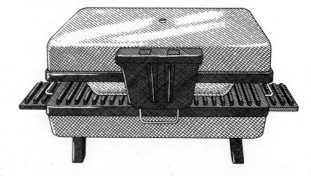

# BARBECUES

All barbecues consist of a metal box or tray for fuel and, balanced over this, a metal grid or grids on which food is grilled by the charcoal fire below. Some barbecues are set on a stand or on legs, which may have wheels or be fitted into a trolley. All except for the very simplest have a windshield, or a half or full hood – sometimes called a cover or kettle top. Most models have slots or hooks at various heights above the charcoal so that the grilling racks can be placed higher or lower above the fire, depending on the heat. Most larger models also have a rôtisserie spit, powered by a battery motor, on which a whole chicken or small joint of meat can be barbecued, basting any other smaller items below as it cooks. A whole turkey or large joint can be cooked in some of the big kettle models without the aid of a rôtisserie.

There are dozens of shapes and sizes of barbecues but, despite their diversity, they are all used in much the same way. Essentially, they grill or spit-roast food over burning charcoal, which should be lit well ahead of time so that it becomes a glowing mass by the time the food is placed over it.

Charcoal gives off carbon monoxide when burned, so barbecue cooking must be done out of doors, in an open space well clear of over-hanging trees or nearby bushes or dry grass. Paved ground or a patch of hard earth is best. If possible choose a site sheltered from pre-vailing winds or draughts to minimize the risk of flying sparks. These are essential safety factors, and also make barbecue cooking a more pleasant activity.

Foods can be marinated or seasoned before being grilled or spit-roasted. Steaks and chops should be snipped round the edges to prevent curling, and the skin of small whole fish should be slashed on each side. Poultry drumsticks should have their ends wrapped in foil, so that they can be held in your hand while being eaten. Small food portions should be turned at least once while grilling, using tongs or a spatula rather than a fork: piercing them releases their juices, thus drying them out and making the fire spit. Fatty foods may also make it flare up, in which case it should be doused with water from a sprinkler bottle.

For spit-roasting on large models, the fire can be laid towards the back of the barbecue so that drippings fall into a driptray placed under the meat or bird and in front of the fire. In this way flare-ups are avoided and the drippings are saved for making well flavoured gravy.

## Cleaning
The barbecue should be cleaned as soon as it has cooled. Soak racks in hot water containing strong detergent, and scour or scrub racks and the bottom of the grill – particularly if it was not lined with aluminium foil. Cleaning it thoroughly is worth while for sweet-smelling, pleasant barbecuing next time round.

## Fuels to use
Charcoal is by far the form of fuel most often used for barbecuing because it is easy to use and store; it is also cheap to buy and there is little waste. It burns evenly, packs down into a glowing mass and gives off few flames.

Softwood burns fast and gives off a good deal of resinous smoke, so it tends to char the food and give it an acrid flavour. Hardwoods with a low resin content are added to charcoal in some large kettle barbecues in the form of chips or chunks for their aroma and because they give larger cuts of meat and poultry long slow cooking without charring; but charcoal alone is used in most smaller models.

Charcoal comes in two forms, lumps and briquettes. Lumps are usually made from both softwood and hardwood, so one of their dis-advantages is that they may burn at different rates, and the softwood lumps may flare and flavour the food. Another disadvantage of lumps is their varying size. Larger pieces may have to be broken up, and since they burn faster than briquettes, they need topping up more often.

Briquettes are usually made from hardwood compressed into block form. They give off more intense heat than lumps, burn more evenly and need less attention. Being uniform in size, they are easier to store and arrange. Their one disadvantage is that if untreated, they take longer than lumps to ignite. How-ever, it is possible to buy treated briquettes which light easily.

# Barbecues

(a) **Size.** L. 17 in. (430 mm). **Material.** Cast iron body, wooden handles.

(b) **Size.** L. 16 in. (405 mm). **Material.** Alloy steel body and pans, wooden handles.

(c) **Size.** H. 28 in. (710 mm). **Material.** Alloy steel body, grid and spit, wooden spit handle.

(d) **Size.** H. 29 in. (737 mm). **Material.** Alloy steel body, aluminium ash pan and legs.

Barbecue (a) is a hibachi and is the simplest type of barbecue. The Japanese word "hibachi" means a fire bowl–and a hibachi consists of just that: a fuel container with a grilling rack or racks on top. This model is rectangular; round and square models are also available. This one stands low on the ground–or you can put it on a garden wall or steps. Some hibachis have a detachable stand or legs. Draught vents in the sides of the fuel holder help in lighting and maintaining the fire.

This model will cook enough food for four people. More elaborate models have dividers in the fuel containers, or even two separate "fire-bowls", so that you can cook for four people using one fuel compartment, or for eight people using both. There is also a version with three fuel compartments. Even these hibachis are usually quite small, so you can transport them easily. This makes them very useful for cooking hot food on a picnic or for supplying hot snacks to supplement cold buffet food at an outdoor party.

Barbecue (b) is larger than most hibachis and has a windshield and optional spit. It is lightweight yet unusually stable, so is suitable for use on rough ground–for example when camping.

This barbecue is large enough to cook a full meal for six people and would be a useful thing to have when your normal fuel supply fails. There is a larger size which cooks a generous meal for eight to ten. Both sizes have adjustable grilling heights, and two racks with wooden handles for lifting off the fire easily. This type of barbecue is compact and probably

one of the safest–so highly suitable for a family with children.

Barbecue (c) is often called a brazier or party barbecue. It is rather like a hibachi on stilts but it has a flatter tray to hold the charcoal. This model has a windshield, others have half hoods and some also have an undershelf for holding food and cooking equipment. This barbecue has slotted sides giving adjustable spit-roasting and grilling heights. It has a spit rod and an optional motor. A brazier of this size should cook ample food for 12 to 18 people.

Most brazier barbecues have tubular legs or a pedestal stand and are therefore less stable than this type which has sturdy A-shaped legs.

Barbecue (d) is a large example of the most elaborate type of barbecue–these are known as kettles or kettle-topped barbecues because of their rounded or domed hoods. Vents control the heat.

The complete hood means that joints or birds can be, in effect, oven-roasted with a char-broiled flavour in the closed kettle–this means you don't need a spit. In large models, a complete hood and cover makes it possible to cook small joints or birds by indirect heat. The joint is positioned on the food grill directly over a pan placed centrally on the charcoal grill below. The charcoal is piled each side of the pan producing heat which is reflected off the inside of the cover and lower bowl. This

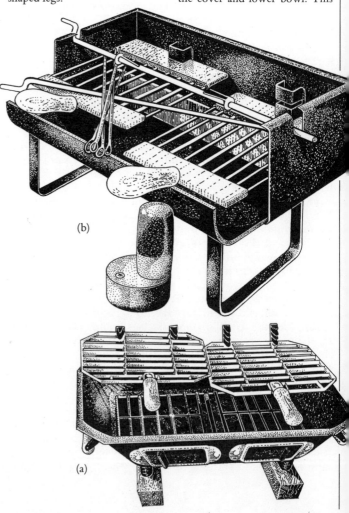

(b)

(a)

cooking method keeps food more moist than other forms of barbecuing and also decreases the cooking time.

A disadvantage of most kettles is that the grill rack is inset, without handles, and may therefore be hazardous to lift off while hot; food has to be removed with a spatula or tongs, and refuelling and removing dead ash may present problems. A great advantage of the model shown here is that dead ash drops into an ash pan under the kettle. Fresh charcoal can be added without removing the grill rack.

This kettle has tubular legs and wheels so that it is lightweight and easy to move. It has a shelf for food and cooking gear.

(d)

(c)

# SMOKERS

There are two ways of processing foods in wood smoke: hot smoking and cold smoking. In hot smoking, the food is heated as well as being bathed in smoke, and comes out of the smoker cooked, with a smoky flavour. In cold smoking – or, more correctly, almost-cold smoking – the food is salted, usually in spiced brine, before being smoked. This process preserves the food without cooking it. Cold-smoked foods can be kept for longer than hot-smoked foods which should not be kept for any longer than ordinary cooked foods of the same sort.

## Hot smokers

There are two kinds of hot smokers: small box smokers and large kettle smokers, known as "smoke 'n' pit" smokers. The small smokers have the advantage of being portable and easily transported by car or bicycle, ready-filled with picnic food. They also stand more steadily on uneven ground. The large smokers, on the other hand, enable you to smoke large quantities of food at a time – for a party, for example. They are also more versatile; by omitting liquid or increasing the heat, you can turn them into barbecues, roasting ovens or steamers.

All hot smokers consist of the same basic parts, and are set up and used in much the same way. The main structure is a casing or smoke-box which holds the food. The smoke-box contains either a baffle plate or damper which controls and directs the flow of smoke. Every smoker uses fuel to supply smoke and fuel for heating. In small smokers, the smoke comes from wood dust and the heat from methylated spirit – either in liquid form or in solid tablets – placed under the casing. In the large kettle types, a hardwood chunk is added to charcoal in the bottom bowl of the smoker; the wood chunk supplies the smoke and the charcoal the heat.

Hot smoking small portions of food does not take long. Small fish, chicken joints, chops and steaks will cook in about 20 minutes. A whole chicken will cook in a large box-smoker in 45 to 50 minutes. In a large kettle smoker, most foods will cook in about the same time as when cooked by conventional methods, but a large turkey, ham or spare ribs may take six hours or more.

## Cold smoking

Cold-smoked foods – preserved but not cooked – are processed for storage rather than for eating at once. Most foods can be eaten just as they come from the smoker but a few – such as well brined bacon joints – may need soaking and cooking before they can be eaten.

A cold smoker is set up and used in much the same way as a small box smoker, but smoking takes longer – up to eight or ten hours for large items such as sides of smoked salmon – and the smoker must be refuelled at regular intervals during that time. Hardwood chips provide the smoke.

Food must be marinated in a suitable brine and then dried off before cold smoking. The smoker can be set up while they are drying. Smoking times are, within limits, a matter of personal choice. As a general guide, salmon sides and large white poultry are smoked to most people's taste in about eight hours; smaller dark-fleshed birds in four to six hours. Safe storage times depend on how long they have been salted and smoked.

## Cleaning

Covering the baffle plate of a smoke-box or lining the fuel bowl of a kettle smoker with aluminium foil will help when cleaning up used fuel later.

A smoker holds burning heat for some time after use, so the temperature must be checked before cleaning. Any unused charcoal or hardwood chips should be removed and saved for another smoking session. Burned wood dust should be scraped or washed out and disposed of. Then the metal parts of the smoker should be washed with hot water and detergent and allowed to dry off. Do not use abrasives or wire wool. Any congealed fat or clotted fuel must be brushed or rubbed off; it would otherwise give a bitter taste to food.

(a) **Size.** L. 13 in. (330 mm).
**Material.** Enamelled steel box, aluminium wire rack.

(b) **Size.** H. 19¼ in. (490 mm).
**Material.** Enamelled steel body, chromed nickel racks, wooden handles.

# Hot smokers

Smoke box (a) uses wood dust to provide smoke and methylated spirit to supply heat. The wood dust is scattered on the floor of the smoker's casing and covered with the baffle plate. The fuel pans are filled with methylated spirit and placed inside the frame under the smoker. Place the smoke-box squarely on the stand, on a level, flame-proof surface, well clear of anything flammable. Stand the rack on the baffle plate, which should be covered with aluminium foil to keep it clean. Put the food on the rack, put on the cover, and finally light the spirit. Don't open the smoke-box while smoking is in progress. Smallish portions of food will be cooked when the spirit has burned out. Smaller and larger smokers are also available.

In the larger kettle smoker (b), a chunk of hardwood and charcoal are put in the lower bowl of the smoker; the wood chunk supplies smoke and the charcoal heat. The fuel bowl should be lined with aluminium foil to keep it clean. There is also a second bowl, sited above the fuel bowl, in which you can put water, beer, cider or wine which will keep large cuts of meat or birds moist. This bowl also acts as a baffle plate; it directs the flow of smoke towards and all around the inner surface of the casing so that it reaches and smokes the top and sides of the food as well as the underneath. The charcoal fire is lit, the rack positioned inside the casing, the prepared food placed on the rack, and the cover put on the smoker. Again, the smoker should not be opened while smoking is in progress. By the time the food is ready, the charcoal will have burned low enough just to keep the food warm.

You can get an extra section to fit between the bottom part and the cover; this will extend this smoker dramatically and enable it to smoke up to 45 lb. (20 kg) of food at a time.

# Cold smoker

**Size.** H. 32 in. (812 mm).
**Material.** Enamelled steel box, aluminium racks, steel hooks.

The main casing of this cold smoker is similar to that of the hot smoke-box, but the smoking and heating fuels, instead of being directly under the food, are in a compartment outside the smoke-box so that they can be replenished without opening it. This outer compartment is known as the smoke-generator housing. A hole in the side of the smoke-box admits the smoke from the outer housing.

Inside the main casing are two racks. Small items can be laid on these racks, but large ones – sides of smoked salmon or turkeys, for example – are best hung from the steel hooks supplied so that smoke can circulate all around them.

Wood dust is scattered in the smoke generator housing with small hardwood chips on top, and methylated spirit is put in the fuel pans underneath. This is lit when the food is in the smoker and the lid is securely in position. The hardwood chips should begin to smoulder within 20 minutes; thereafter they should be topped up with larger chips at two 45-minute intervals, and then at 90-minute intervals until smoking is complete.

# FONDUES

One of the most popular forms of table cooking is a fondue. The names come from the French "fondre" meaning "to melt". Classically it consists of cheese and wine melted together in a pot over a flame. Cheese fondues were invented by the Swiss to use up dry, hard, stored cheese. Everyone helps himself from the same pot by dipping in chunks of bread with a figure-of-eight movement: this keeps the fondue creamy to the end. Finally, the crust that has formed at the bottom of the pot is scraped off and divided among the diners. Cheese fondues are made in earthenware pots.

For a meat fondue, oil is heated in a metal pot, and cubes of meat are dipped into it. They are served with a selection of sauces—béarnaise, tomato and chilli, for example—and with tomato quarters, cucumber slices, onion rings, and so on.

Provided you are sure of your culinary skills, and are not afraid of cooking in public, flambéing—or cooking food over a spirit heater with a high flame—is another excellent way of providing a number of people with things such as crêpes or omelettes which need to be eaten the instant they are ready.

(a) **Size.** H. 8½ in. (215 mm), assembled. Cap. 3 pt. (1·7 ℓ). **Material.** Copper pan lined with stainless steel; copper spirit heater and tray; wrought iron stand.

(b) **Size.** D. 8 in. (204 mm). Cap. 2½ pt. (1·4 ℓ). **Material.** Earthenware.

(c) **Size.** H. 5 in. (127 mm). **Material.** Stainless steel and cast iron structure, butane gas burner.

For a meat fondue cubes of meat skewered on fondue forks are rested in hot oil and cooked at table. The copper pan (a), or any other metal pan which conducts heat very efficiently, is best for this. A caquelon can be used in place of the copper pan on this stand which has a small spirit burner as a heat source.

The heatproof earthenware caquelon (b) is glazed within and is the ·best pot for preparing a cheese fondue. The initial preparation can be done on a conventional hob to speed things up and the caquelon can be placed over a butane gas burner, heating candle or methylated spirit burner to maintain the heat at table.

The butane gas heater (c) is designed for cooking food, or flambéing it, at table. It is easily regulated with a dial for a number of heat settings.

(a)

(b)

(c)

# TOASTERS

As long as you have a cooker with a grill, a toaster is a convenience rather than a necessity in the kitchen. That said, toasters are quicker than cooker grills and considerably cheaper to use. The best toasters are pop-up ones and have slots large enough to take slices of all sorts of bread as well as thicker things like crumpets. They also have heat settings which control the degree of brownness.

Never poke into a toaster with a knife or other metal implement unless you have first switched it off and unplugged it.

(a) **Size.** L. $9\frac{1}{2}$ in. (242 mm).
   **Material.** Chromed steel.
(b) **Size.** L. $7\frac{1}{4}$ in. (185 mm).
   **Material.** Chromed steel.
(c) **Size.** L. 16 in. (405 mm).
   **Material.** Chromed steel.

Toaster (a) is a typical pop-up toaster which raises the toast above the heating elements when it is done. This four-slice toaster speeds up breakfast toast production and has a dual heat control so you can toast to two different degrees of brownness at the same time. The two-slice toaster (b) works similarly.

The pop-up toaster (c) incorporates a small grill and oven with a special setting so you can use it as a slow cooker — useful in a kitchen where space is limited.

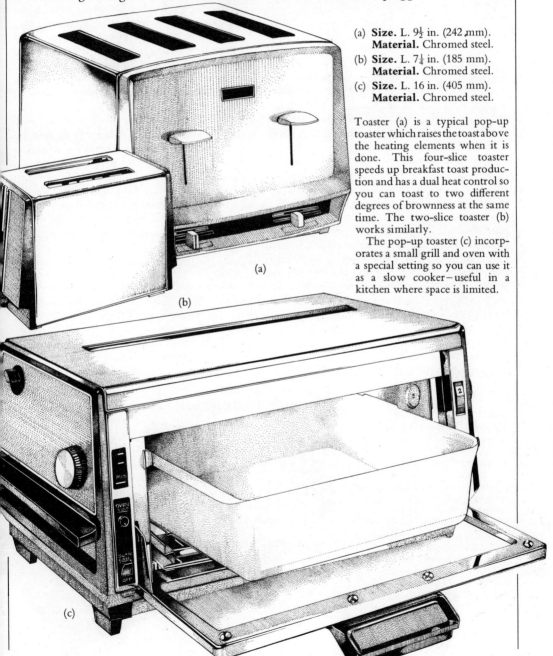

(a)

(b)

(c)

# WARMERS AND COOLERS

Keeping food and drink at the right temperature is very important, whether they are hot or cold. A lukewarm second helping, especially of fried food, is most unappetizing, and there is a great difference between a bottle of warm white wine and a bottle served nicely chilled.

## Warmers

Food warmers are designed not for cooking food, but for keeping it warm once it is ready for the table. They also enable you to serve hot second – or even third – helpings at the table. A great advantage of keeping food warm with one of these devices is that it does not dry out in the same way as it does in an oven. A food warmer is also cheap to run.

There are a great many different kinds of food warmers available. The simplest kind of all is heated by little candles which are similar to night-lights. Candle warmers have one great advantage over electric ones in that they are not affected by power cuts or electricity failures. They are also more reliable since there is nothing than can go wrong, as long as you do not run out of candles. They are cheaper than electric warmers, they do not need to be positioned near a power point, and there is, of course, no danger of tripping over an electric lead.

Conversely, the advantage of electric food warmers over candle warmers is that they tend to be more versatile: they often have temperature controls and some have an extra hot corner to keep coffee warm while you eat. Some can be switched off and the lead removed once they have reached their maximum temperature; they will then hold this temperature up to an hour.

The simplest kind of electric warmer is the heated tray, with two insulated handles for easy carrying. For those who like to eat in an armchair while watching television, there is a coffee table available with a built-in hotplate. Some electric food warmers incorporate ceramic serving dishes which double as casseroles and can be put in the oven. Some also have a special place for warming plates. Trolley versions are available, which have a heated tray set into the top of a trolley. These are useful for wheeling hot food from one room to another, and can be pushed round the dining table for serving like a dessert trolley in a restaurant. Really sophisticated versions have heated shelves and serving compartments inside a wood-finish cabinet on castors, and will keep an entire meal hot for hours.

## Coolers

Coolers for chilled drinks are kept cold either by insulation or with ice cubes. There should be a constant supply of ice cubes in your refrigerator or freezer.

Insulated bags and boxes and thermos flasks are very useful for keeping food and drink hot or cold on camping expeditions or picnics.

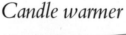

## Candle warmer

**Size.** L. 13½ in. (343 mm).
**Material.** Enamelled steel base, stainless steel grid.

This warmer is kept hot with two squat candles which sit underneath the stainless steel grid. The candles are held in little metal pots, and are extinguished by small metal plates which slide over the top of them. Round warmers are available as well as rectangular ones.

Candle warmers will keep a meal hot for an hour or so, without renewing the candles, and are therefore extremely cheap to run.

**Size.** L. 24¼ in. (615 mm).
**Material.** Aluminium frame, wooden handles, glass heating surface.

This electric tray has an extra warm part at one corner to keep coffee hot while you eat your meal. The tray can be heated to a temperature of 200°F (93°C) and the hot spot to a temperature of 248°F (120°C). The glass heating surface is resistant to stains.

## Electric warming tray

## Ice trays

(a)

(b)

(c)

(d)

(a) **Size.** L. 10½ in. (267 mm).
**Material.** Plastic.
(b) **Size.** L. 10½ in. (267 mm).
**Material.** Rubber.
(c) **Size.** L. 9½ in. (242 mm).
**Material.** Plastic.
(d) **Size.** L. 8½ in. (215 mm).
**Material.** Aluminium tray, plastic divider.

The simplest form of cooler is an ice cube, whether for reviving a drink or for soothing a burnt hand. Make ice either in the frozen food compartment of the refrigerator or in the freezer. If you need a lot and don't have enough trays, ice cubes can be stored in plastic bags in the freezer – squirt them with soda water first to prevent them sticking together.

Ice tray (a) is made of plastic and makes triangular ice cubes. If you are likely to want just the odd cube at a time, an ice tray made of flexible rubber (b) is best, as it's particularly easy with this type of tray to take out one or two ice cubes at a time. An ice tray with individual compartments which lift out (c) is also good if you don't want many cubes at a time. A metal tray with a plastic divider (d) needs more effort to extract the cubes, but has the advantage of doubling – with the divider removed – as a tray for making ice cream.

## Ice buckets

(a)

(b)

(a) **Size.** D. 6½ in. (165 mm).
**Material.** Plastic.

(b) **Size.** D. 4¾ in. (120 mm).
**Material.** Glass bucket, chromed steel handle.

An ice bucket is necessary when you are serving a lot of drinks, and need more than just the odd ice cube or two.

Ice bucket (a) has thick, ridged glass sides. Plastic ice bucket (b) has thick plastic sides and a close-fitting lid, and will keep ice cubes for at least four to six hours. Other well insulated buckets are also available in cork and leather with removable plastic or glass containers inside for easy cleaning.

Ice tongs (see TONGS) to transfer ice from buckets to glass are more hygienic and less chilly than using your fingers.

225

## Cooling jug

**Size.** 10 in. (255 mm).
**Material.** Glass jug, chromed steel lid.

This jug will keep drinks cool out of the refrigerator and will not dilute them; it is, at the same time, a pretty serving jug but is rather heavy to hold. It has an inner tube which screws into the lid and which holds crushed ice. It has a very close-fitting lid.

Glass bowls which have a little compartment underneath for crushed ice are also available. These are ideal for serving caviar.

## Drink coolers

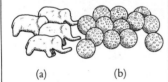

(a)                              (b)

(a) **Size.** L. 2 in. (50 mm).
    **Material.** Plastic.
(b) **Size.** D. 1 in. (25 mm).
    **Material.** Plastic.

These plastic drink coolers are filled with water and, when frozen, will cool a drink without diluting it. They are also useful for cooling salads.

Coolers (a) are shaped like elephants and are alas, coloured pink. Coolers (b) represent golf balls.

## Wine cooler

**Size.** D. 8½ in. (215 mm).
**Material.** Aluminium.

A wine cooler is indispensable if you want to keep a bottle of wine chilled once out of the refrigerator – for example, at a dinner party or in the garden. It will also lower the temperature of a bottle of wine much more quickly than is possible in a refrigerator; whereas it will take a good two hours in a refrigerator (not the freezing compartment – this is too violent) to chill a bottle of wine on a warm day, a quarter of an hour or so in a bucket of ice and water will be sufficient. It is important to put water in the cooler as well as ice; ice alone will merely chill the wine in patches. The level of water should be up to the same level as the wine.

White, rosé and sparkling wines are best served chilled. So are fortified wines served as aperitifs and a few red wines such as Beaujolais Nouveau and those of the Loire valley in France. Other red wines should be served "chambré" – at room temperature. Wines that are to be chilled must never be allowed to get too cold. A wine that is icy cold will lose its taste – and, just as important, its bouquet. Never keep wine in the refrigerator for too long as after a few hours it will take on a flat and unpleasant taste and smell. Most people do not recommend putting ice in wine – unless, of course, you particularly like it diluted or if you drink it with soda water.

There are many "rules" about the temperatures at which different wines should be served. But you should follow your own tastes and experiment to find out what you like best.

There is nothing, as far as the wine is concerned, to stop you using an ordinary bucket filled with ice and water, but a proper wine cooler is obviously more elegant. Wine coolers are made of many different materials – copper, stainless steel, even silver.

This wine cooler, made of aluminium, is big enough to hold a bottle of wine plus plenty of ice and water without spilling it or damaging the bucket. It has two sturdy handles which are easy to hold – an important consideration as, once full, it will be fairly heavy.

Silver ice coolers are also available and are perhaps more suitable as champagne buckets. These are expensive, but may well be within your budget if you are a regular champagne drinker.

# RACKS, TRIVETS AND HEAT-DIFFUSERS

Racks are used primarily to keep roasting meat or poultry clear of the fat and juices dripping from them. They can also be used as trivets, in a pan of the right size, to keep a container of steaming food clear of the heat from the burner below the saucepan.

Racks are also needed when cakes are turned out from their tins. Any open wire grid will do as long as it allows air to circulate below the cake as well as all around it so that the cake can cool without going soggy. The same sort of rack can be used when icing cakes with soft icing or when glazing cold food with aspic; the surplus drains off without collecting in a pool as it would on a plate. To ensure that your vol au vents all rise to the same height, you can fix a rack at the appropriate distance above the baking sheet. Special racks are made for this purpose, which are worth having if you often make vol au vents.

Trivets are smaller than racks as a rule, but stronger because they have to support the weight of heavy pots. Metal ones stand in the bottoms of pans of steaming water to hold containers – pudding basins, terrines, custard dishes and so on – away from direct heat. Small saucers will serve this purpose almost as well. Wooden trivets act as stands for hot pots or pans, protecting the surface beneath from scorching and helping to avoid the sudden change in temperature which could crack a hot porcelain dish if you were to put it straight down on a cold tiled surface.

### Heat-diffusers

These help to prevent direct heat from coming into contact with the base of a pan by standing between it and the burner. They are made of asbestos or perforated metal mesh. Asbestos mats should not be used with natural gas.

(a) **Size.** L. 11¾ in. (298 mm).
(b) **Size.** L. 9 in. (230 mm).
**Material.** Both tinned steel wire.

Rack (a) is a straightforward rectangular rack; rack (b) is also rectangular but is supplied with two detachable sides which slot into it to form a cradle. The width varies according to which bars the sides are slotted into. It is particularly useful with poultry, which needs to be turned on all sides to get thoroughly browned.

## Roasting racks

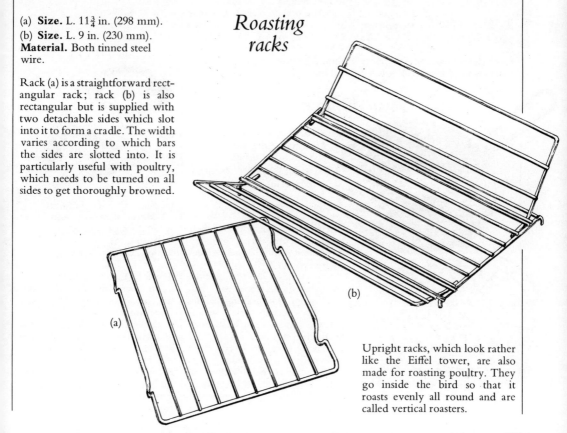

(a)

(b)

Upright racks, which look rather like the Eiffel tower, are also made for roasting poultry. They go inside the bird so that it roasts evenly all round and are called vertical roasters.

## Cake racks

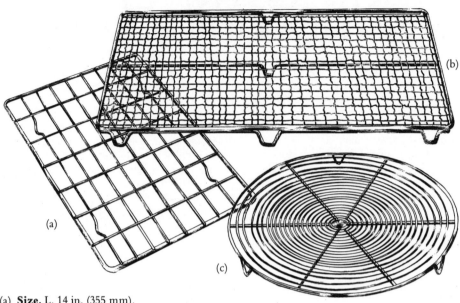

(a)

(b)

(c)

(a) **Size.** L. 14 in. (355 mm).
(b) **Size.** L. 18 in. (458 mm).
(c) **Size.** D. 11 in. (280 mm).
**Material.** All tinned steel wire.

Rack (a) has a fairly open grid and is rectangular. Rack (b) is also rectangular but it is made of a much closer mesh and is therefore more suitable for light cakes. Rack (c) is circular, with reinforced spokes, making it strong enough to take quite a hefty cake.

All these racks have feet so that air can circulate beneath them. Cake racks are sometimes made without feet, in which case they should be stood over the top of a baking tin.

## Heat diffusers

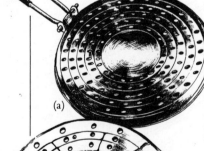

(a)

(b)

(a) **Size.** D. 8 in. (204 mm).
    **Material.** Alloy steel, plastic-coated handle.
(b) **Size.** D. 7$\frac{1}{2}$ in. (190 mm).
    **Material.** Alloy steel.

These mats shield pots and their contents from direct heat by diffusing it through sheets of perforated metal.

Mat (a) has a sheet of asbestos sandwiched between the two metal sides. The folding handle is plastic-coated, which means that you can move the mat about even when it is hot.

Mat (b) is similar in construction, with two grooved and perforated discs of metal with an air space between them. It diffuses heat efficiently and is very strongly made.

## Trivets

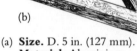

(a)

(b)

(a) **Size.** D. 5 in. (127 mm).
    **Material.** Aluminium.
(b) **Size.** Each side. 6 in. (152 mm).
    **Material.** Beechwood.

Trivet (a) is circular and will hold a container 1$\frac{1}{4}$ in. (32 mm) above the bottom of a pan full of water for steaming.

Trivet (b) is wooden, triangular and flat. It goes beneath the pot as a protective mat. It prevents polished tables from being ruined by contact with hot pans and protects heated ceramic dishes from the sudden shock of very cold surfaces.

# CAKE DECORATING EQUIPMENT

Ordinary, everyday food is best left looking plain and simple, neatly presented but with a minimum of fancy work. But for festive occasions and celebrations, when the company is wearing its best and the house is wreathed in garlands, the feast on the table had better be decorated as well.

The food upon which the most time and effort are likely to be lavished is cakes. Wedding cakes tend to be the most elaborate of all, though Christmas, christenings, birthdays and other anniversaries also call for suitably decorated cakes. The success of cake decorating depends as much on a steady hand and an artistic eye as on anything else, but even the most experienced cake decorator will agree that the battle is more than half won by having the right equipment. A cake may look as elaborate as a baroque cathedral, but the tools of the trade are in fact quite simple. However, as with many kitchen tools, the best are often those made for the professionals and, although these may cost more than their domestic equivalents, they are usually worth having, especially if you do a lot of baking.

There are many ways of decorating cakes and many types of icing. Whipped cream can be used to decorate sponge cakes, and meringue can be piped to make elaborate creations such as vacherins. Most icings, such as butter cream, fudge and glacé, are soft. Royal icing, on the other hand, is hard and this is the type of icing with which most of the tools in this section are used.

## What you need

The most important piece of equipment for royal icing and anything other than the simplest decorations, is a turntable on which to stand the cake so that it—rather than you—can turn as you work. A turntable should be strong enough to bear the weight of the largest cake you are likely to want to decorate—a professional turntable will support a cake of 60 lb. (27 kg). It should spin smoothly, without wobbling.

Royal icing is smoothed over a layer of marzipan and for this it is best to use a 6 in. (152 mm) palette knife (see KNIVES). A smaller,

4½ in. (115 mm) palette knife can be used for mixing colours into the icing. A really smooth surface can be achieved with a stainless steel ruler, while the sides can be smoothed with a scraper or given a ridged pattern with a serrated scraper.

Once the royal icing has dried and hardened, the decorating can begin. Cake patterns are available for those who lack the confidence to design their own cakes. With these you transfer the design on to the cake by pricking it through the pattern with a pin or a fine skewer. If you prefer to design your own patterns, you will find that however good your eye it is easier to make symmetrical patterns with some kind of marker which divides the surface into circles or wedge-shaped sections.

Having marked out the design, you can turn your hand to detail. Flowers and latticed baskets, cradles or pyramids are usually piped separately, using plastic flower and net "nails" as a base on which to work. However, the true professional can just as easily use a little knob of marzipan as a base for a flower or a leaf and create beautiful webs of icing directly on the cake. Lastly comes the thrilling and nerve-racking application of the finishing touches—lines, scrolls, stars, rosettes and letters, which are piped directly on to the cake.

For all these jobs you need a piping tool. Icing kits for domestic use invariably contain a syringe to which a variety of nozzles can be fixed, but once again the professional often makes do with something far simpler—a little cone of paper, with a nozzle dropped into the open point at the bottom or, for meringues and whipped cream, a large forcing bag made of nylon or plastic. The flow of icing, meringue or cream is much more easily controlled by the gentle pressure of your hand on top of the bag than it is with a syringe, where you use your thumb to press a plunger down into the tube.

Icing syringes and forcing bags can equally well be used for choux pastry, decorative petits fours, stiff mayonnaise and creamed vegetables, so if you don't make many cakes, there are plenty of other occasions in the kitchen when they will come in handy.

# Turntables

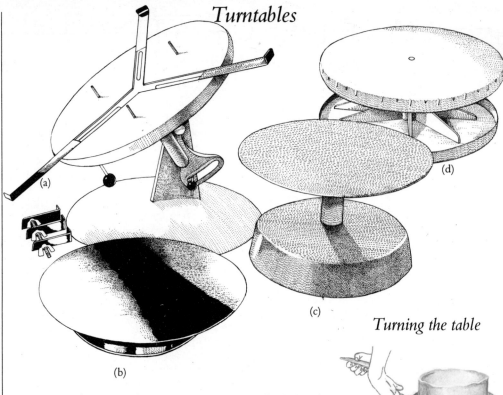

(a)

(b)

(c)

(d)

## Turning the table

(a) **Size.** D. $10\frac{1}{2}$ in. (250 mm).
**Material.** Enamelled cast iron with chromed steel attachments.

(b) **Size.** D. 9 in. (230 mm).
**Material.** Aluminium.

(c) **Size.** D. 9 in. (230 mm).
**Material.** Enamelled cast iron.

(d) **Size.** D. 9 in. (230 mm).
**Material.** Plastic.

Turntable (a) is very sophisticated with a number of aids for the professional cake decorator. The top is ridged with concentric circles to help you place the cake dead centre on the stand. Three sharp little pins help to anchor the cake. There are two sets of adjustable arms which have lipped edges to hold cakes measuring from 6 in. (152 mm) diameter up to $16\frac{1}{2}$ in. (420 mm) diameter. There is a little handle underneath the revolving top to turn it. The top can be tilted at four different angles to help with particularly delicate work. It can be prevented from revolving by tightening a screw on the spindle – this also helps to keep the top firmly attached to the base. The spindle should be kept well oiled so that the top rotates easily.

Turntable (b) is very flimsy by comparison with the others, and will not withstand any great weight. Although the revolving stand rotates smoothly enough for the amateur cake decorator, it lacks the silky smooth action that a keen craftsman would appreciate. It is also likely to wear out long before any great number of anniversaries have been celebrated.

Turntable (c) is very heavy and will hold cakes of a massive weight – up to 60 lb. (27 kg). Its spindle should be kept well greased so that the stand revolves smoothly.

Turntable (d) is pleasingly simple, cheap and sturdy – ideal for the keen amateur. It consists of three pieces – base, top and spindle. The top and base are exactly the same, so you can use it either way up. The rotation is perhaps not quite as smooth as that of a professional turntable, but it will support a cake weighing up to 60 lb. (27 kg). It is light, easy to clean and calibrated round the edges of both top and base to help you mark out the pattern.

*Turn the table with your left hand while you work on the cake with your right (or vice versa if you are left-handed). Turn it smoothly in one movement in a clockwise direction (anti-clockwise if you are left-handed). This enables you to give the royal icing on the side of a round cake a smooth finish with a plain plastic scraper, or to give it a ridged effect with a serrated scraper.*

# Rulers

(a) **Size.** L. 15 in. (380 mm).
   **Material.** Stainless steel.
(b) **Size.** L. 14 in. (355 mm).
   **Material.** Plastic.

Ruler (a) can be used to give a mirror-smooth surface to the icing on top of your cake. It is completely rigid which helps when levelling the icing. This particular ruler has no calibrations but a ruler with markings in inches and centimetres can be useful, for example when cutting croissant dough into equal pieces or for measuring cake tins.

The plastic ruler (b) is known as a decorator's level and has one serrated edge for making ridges in the icing and one straight edge. It doesn't have the same rigidity as a stainless steel ruler. It is marked in inches outwards from the centre – this is a great help when marking out a symmetrical pattern on a cake.

## Levelling the cake

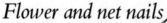

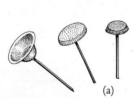

*Spread the icing over the cake top with a palette knife. Holding the ruler at each end, place the edge on the far side of the cake. Draw it steadily towards you with a paddling action.*

   *For a really professional finish,* *it is necessary to apply three or four coats of royal icing to the cake. It is therefore not important if you don't achieve a perfectly smooth surface with the first coat. Allow each coat to dry thoroughly before applying the next.*

# Flower and net nails

(a) **Size.** H. 3 to 4 in.
   (75 to 100 mm).
   **Material.** Plastic head, wire stem.
(b) **Size.** H. $3\frac{1}{2}$ to $4\frac{1}{2}$ in.
   (90 to 115 mm).
   **Material.** Plastic head, wire stem.

The flower nails (a) are useful for making miniature piped flowers. Petals are piped individually. Each layer of petals must be dry before the next is applied.

   The net nails (b) are for making three-dimensional woven or latticed basket, cradle and pyramid shapes of Royal icing.

# Serrated scraper

**Size.** L. 3 in. (75 mm).
**Material.** Plastic.

This scraper has a serrated edge which will make a ridged pattern in the icing on the side of the cake. There are also plain scrapers which give a smooth finish (see SCRAPERS).

# Cake markers

(a) **Size.** D. $1\frac{1}{2}$ to $6\frac{1}{2}$ in.
   (38 to 165 mm).
   **Material.** Aluminium.
(b) **Size.** L. $4\frac{1}{4}$ in. (107 mm).
   **Material.** Plastic.

Marking rings help you to divide the surface of the cake so that your design will be symmetrical. The marking rings (a) come as part of a domestic icing set. There are five rings, each marked off into eighths.

   The more versatile of the two, cake marker (b) consists of two wedges which pivot on a pin. You can use it to find the centre of a cake, to draw circles and to divide the cake into equal portions. One wedge has a cut-out in it shaped like an S scroll and the other has a C scroll. You can transfer these shapes to the cake by pricking out the shape with a pin or a fine skewer.

# Applying almond paste

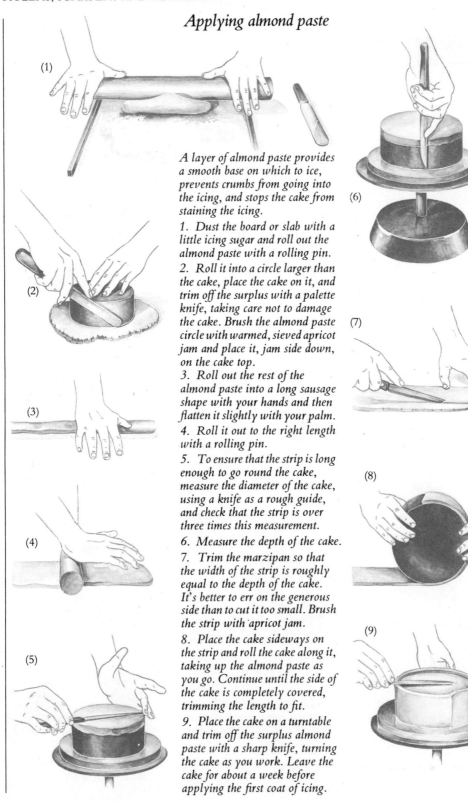

(1)

(2)

(3)

(4)

(5)

(6)

(7)

(8)

(9)

A layer of almond paste provides a smooth base on which to ice, prevents crumbs from going into the icing, and stops the cake from staining the icing.

1. Dust the board or slab with a little icing sugar and roll out the almond paste with a rolling pin.

2. Roll it into a circle larger than the cake, place the cake on it, and trim off the surplus with a palette knife, taking care not to damage the cake. Brush the almond paste circle with warmed, sieved apricot jam and place it, jam side down, on the cake top.

3. Roll out the rest of the almond paste into a long sausage shape with your hands and then flatten it slightly with your palm.

4. Roll it out to the right length with a rolling pin.

5. To ensure that the strip is long enough to go round the cake, measure the diameter of the cake, using a knife as a rough guide, and check that the strip is over three times this measurement.

6. Measure the depth of the cake.

7. Trim the marzipan so that the width of the strip is roughly equal to the depth of the cake. It's better to err on the generous side than to cut it too small. Brush the strip with apricot jam.

8. Place the cake sideways on the strip and roll the cake along it, taking up the almond paste as you go. Continue until the side of the cake is completely covered, trimming the length to fit.

9. Place the cake on a turntable and trim off the surplus almond paste with a sharp knife, turning the cake as you work. Leave the cake for about a week before applying the first coat of icing.

# Royal icing

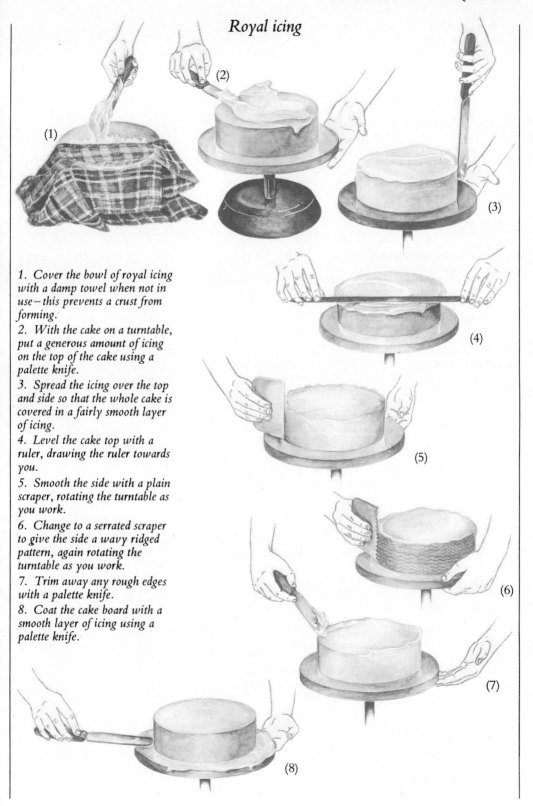

1. Cover the bowl of royal icing with a damp towel when not in use – this prevents a crust from forming.

2. With the cake on a turntable, put a generous amount of icing on the top of the cake using a palette knife.

3. Spread the icing over the top and side so that the whole cake is covered in a fairly smooth layer of icing.

4. Level the cake top with a ruler, drawing the ruler towards you.

5. Smooth the side with a plain scraper, rotating the turntable as you work.

6. Change to a serrated scraper to give the side a wavy ridged pattern, again rotating the turntable as you work.

7. Trim away any rough edges with a palette knife.

8. Coat the cake board with a smooth layer of icing using a palette knife.

(a) **Size.** L. 13½ in. (343 mm).
   **Material.** Nylon.
(b) **Size.** L. 16 in. (405 mm).
   **Material.** Plastic.

Before the manufacture of nylon these bags were made of canvas, which worked perfectly well but was difficult to wash and dry. Nylon, on the other hand, is easy to wash and dry, and has now almost completely replaced canvas. If the nylon is of good quality, it has the added advantage of not "weeping", which canvas bags tend to do unless they are very closely woven.

The best nylon bags are double stitched along the seams as well as glued. The top should be hemmed and the nozzle end reinforced with an extra layer of nylon. You can also get plastic forcing bags. These are relatively cheap but will not last as long as nylon ones. Besides this, plastic is less flexible than nylon and so less sensitive to slight changes in hand pressure. A loop or hole at the top is useful to hang the bag up to dry.

# Forcing bags

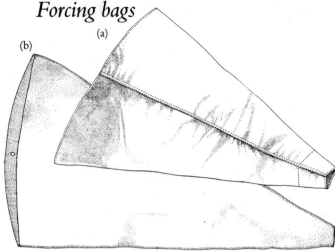

(a)

(b)

Forcing bags are available in large, medium and small sizes. The largest ones are for piping meringue or choux paste. Medium-sized bags are used for piping whipped cream. The smallest are for icing, though professionals use disposable paper cones and dispense with the bother of washing. The nylon bag (a) is medium-sized and made to professional standards with good seams, hems and reinforcements. It has a loop to hang it by, which is useful when drying.

The plastic bag (b) is a little larger and has bonded seams. It is relatively cheap and works well but is unlikely to last as long as bag (a).

## Filling the forcing bag

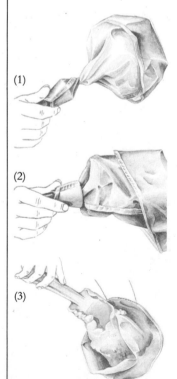

(1)

(2)

(3)

*1. Insert a nozzle into the forcing bag and, with the top of the bag turned over and one hand inside the bag, twist the nozzle end round so that there is a twist in the bag just above the nozzle.*

*2. Then push the twisted section of the bag firmly inside the nozzle. This closes off the nozzle while you fill the bag.*

*3. Fill the bag, using a spatula.*

*4. Gather up the top of the bag.*

*5. Push down with your fingers so that the bag untwists, allowing the filling to pass into the nozzle.*

*6. Force out the filling by exerting pressure on the bag with the fingers and palm of one hand. Guide the nozzle with the other hand.*

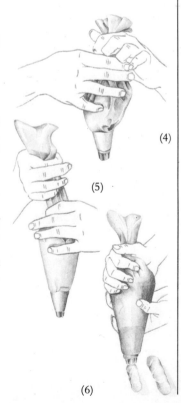

(4)

(5)

(6)

## Piping meringue

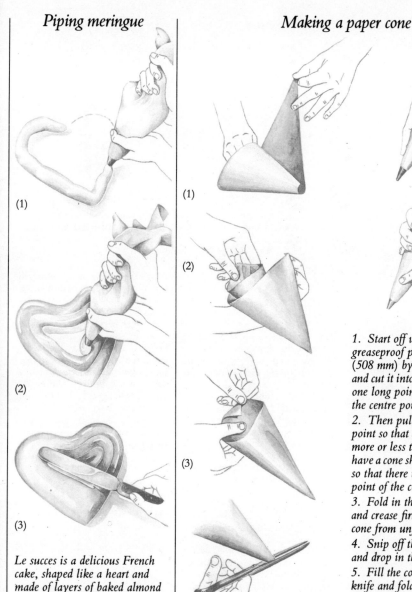

(1)

(2)

(3)

(1)

(2)

(3)

(4)

(5)

(6)

(7)

## Making a paper cone

1. Start off with a sheet of greaseproof paper about 20 in. (508 mm) by 30 in. (762 mm) and cut it into two triangles. Fold one long point inwards towards the centre point.

2. Then pull up the other long point so that all three points are more or less together and you have a cone shape. Pull up tightly so that there is no hole at the point of the cone.

3. Fold in the top flap twice and crease firmly to prevent the cone from unfolding.

4. Snip off the point of the cone and drop in the piping nozzle.

5. Fill the cone using a palette knife and fold over the top of the cone to give it a flat top for the thumb to press down on.

6. Hold the bag with the forefingers of each hand on either side and press downwards with the thumb only.
Steady the nozzle with the other hand.

7. To use a big cone for large quantities of meringue or cream, exert pressure on the cone with the fingers and palm of one hand, keeping it closed with the thumb. Again, guide the nozzle with the other hand.

Le succes is a delicious French cake, shaped like a heart and made of layers of baked almond meringue filled with almond butter cream and iced with chocolate butter cream.

To make a meringue heart, first draw the heart shape with the point of a rubber spatula on the greased baking sheet. Then, using a forcing bag with a ½ in. (12 mm) nozzle, pipe out the heart-shaped outline of meringue (1). Continue working around and inwards (2) until you have filled in the outline completely. Smooth the top of the meringue lightly with a palette knife (3).

# Forcing and icing nozzles

# Icing syringe

**Size.** H. 6½ in. (165 mm).
**Material.** Chromed steel tube, aluminium lid and handle, nylon plunger.

Icing syringes are generally thought to be more difficult to operate than forcing bags, but some people do find them easy enough to handle.

An icing syringe consists of a hollow tube which holds the icing, with a nozzle of the appropriate size and shape which is fitted to the bottom end of the tube. The icing is forced through the nozzle by a nylon plunger fixed to a handle. The tube is closed at the top by a lid with two finger grips at the sides.

(a) **Size.** H. 2 in. (50 mm).
 **Material.** Tinned steel.
(b) **Size.** H. 2 in. (50 mm).
 **Material.** Tinned steel.
(c) **Size.** H. 2 in. (50 mm).
 **Material.** Plastic.
(d) **Size.** H. 1¾ in. (45 mm).
 **Material.** Plastic.
(e) **Size.** H. 1¼ in. (32 mm).
 **Material.** Stainless steel.
(f) **Size.** H. 1¼ in. to 1½ in.
 (32 to 38 mm).
 **Material.** Nylon.

These hard little cones are the crucial part of an icing or forcing bag. The pattern you pipe depends on the size and shape of the hole at the tip of the nozzle.

There are four basic shapes: round, star, scroll and petal. A plain round tube draws lines and words and in the hands of a skilled operator it will create ropes, trellises, lacy patterns and dots. Star and scroll tubes produce stars, scallops, twisted ropes, fluted scrolls and wavy borders. Petal tubes, as their name suggests, are for making flowers, petal by petal and, because they're flat, they can also be used to make ribbons and basket weaves.

Forcing nozzles are larger than icing nozzles and usually have plain or starred holes. Icing nozzles are available in a great many sizes and shapes. Some

icing sets contain as many as 20 different nozzles. Since they are not very expensive, you might like to build up a large collection of them.

The round tubes (a) and (b) are for use with forcing bags. They are strongly made with tidy unobtrusive seams. Tube (a) has a rim round the base which helps to make a closer join between bag and nozzle, particularly important when piping slithery mixtures like mayonnaise or cream. The ½ in. (12 mm) diameter of the hole is right for all profiteroles and langues de chats. Use a larger tube for éclairs.

The star tubes (c) and (d) are also for use with forcing bags. They both make much the same pattern but (c) will produce more deeply indented ridges. Use these tubes for piping scrolls of mashed potato. Both these tubes have ridged bases.

The set of six metal icing nozzles (e) includes a medium-sized round tube, a six-pointed star tube, an eight-pointed star tube, two scroll tubes and a petal tube. They are neatly seamed but their delicate tips can get damaged.

The set of 15 nylon nozzles (f) contains an excellent selection of the four main shapes of icing tube. These nozzles are seamless and are not easily damaged.

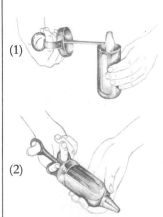

*Fill the syringe with icing and insert the plunger (1). To force out the icing through the nozzle, push the plunger handle down with your thumb and hook a finger on to each of the two finger grips. Guide the nozzle with your other hand (2).*

## Making a feather design

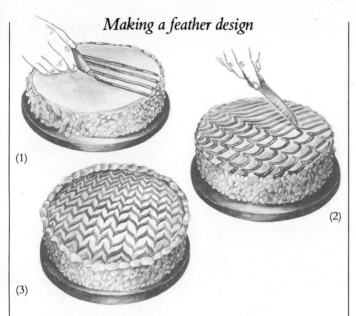

(1)

(2)

(3)

This is an extremely simple technique which produces a surprisingly effective pattern. It is traditionally used on glacé-iced sponge cakes. First ice the cake with white glacé icing. Then pipe fine chocolate lines on to the cake with a plain round tube (1). Draw the point of a knife across the lines while they're still wet (2). Then draw the knife point across the chocolate lines again, working in the opposite direction and in between the rows you've already done to give a feathered effect (3).

## Simple lattice work

(1)

(2)

(3)

Working on a turntable and using a medium fine writing nozzle in a paper cone, pipe diagonal lines round the top edge of the cake at $\frac{1}{4}$ in. (6 mm) intervals (1). Wait for these lines to dry and pipe a second layer of diagonal lines, working in the opposite direction to the first. Work third and fourth layers of diagonal lines over the first two, but make them slightly longer than the original ones to give a neat finish (2). Remember to allow each layer to dry before applying the next. Using a medium shell nozzle, pipe small shell shapes round both edges of the lattice pattern to cover up the ends of the piped line (3). This lattice pattern can then be repeated round the base of the cake.

## Running out

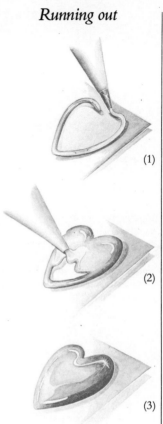

(1)

(2)

(3)

Cut a small square of waxed paper on which to work. If you don't have the confidence to pipe the outline of your shape – in this case a heart – directly on to the paper, you can either place the waxed paper over a template or, better still, draw the outline on the wrong side of the waxed paper. Using a fine round nozzle, pipe out the outline of the heart (1). Then, using a paper cone without a nozzle, fill in the piped outline to the required depth (2). Try not to damage the outline with the tip of the cone, though if you do knock it by accident, it is less likely to be damaged by the paper than by a nozzle. The end result should be a perfectly shaped, glossy, slightly domed heart (3). When the heart is dry, it can be removed from the paper and stuck to the cake with a little icing.

## Making a wishbone

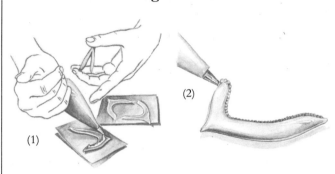

(1)

(2)

Pipe wishbone run outs in the usual way and, when dry, remove them from their waxed paper. Pipe a line of icing on to the flat side of a wishbone run out (1) and press another wishbone on to it so that the two flat sides stick together. Clean off any surplus icing that squeezes out with a knife. Conceal the joins by piping small shell shapes along them (2), and allow to dry. Stick the wishbone into position on the cake with a little icing.

## Using net and flower nails

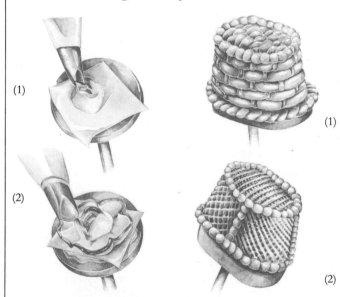

(1)

(2)

(1)

(2)

To make a flower, attach a square of waxed paper to a flat flower nail with icing. Using a petal nozzle, start at the centre of the flower (1) and gradually build up the flower, working outwards and adding more layers of petals (2). Wait for each layer to dry before piping the next.

Cup-shaped flower nails are used in a similar way, but are greased rather than covered in waxed paper.

To use a net nail, grease it with colourless cooking oil and then pipe the pattern – basket-weave (1) or lattice work (2) – on to the nail, waiting for each layer to dry before applying the next. If the icing does not come off the nail easily, hold it over a current of warm air.

## Dropped lattice work

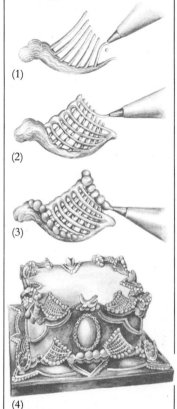

(1)

(2)

(3)

(4)

The lattice is suspended from raised scrolls piped on the cake. Using a fairly fine scroll nozzle, pipe a base scroll on the top and base of the cake. Each scroll has three progressively smaller scrolls piped on top, working towards the outer edge of the cake. The scrolls should be piped with a finer nozzle each time, and each one should be dry before you pipe the next.

1. Start the lattice by piping a guideline.
2. Then, starting at the outer end of the guideline, pipe lines from the guideline to the top outer edge of the bottom scroll. Working towards the centre of the cake, pipe lines in the opposite direction.
3. The ends of the lines can be hidden with small shell shapes.
4. Repeat the process on all the scrolls for a really impressive effect.

# PAPERS, PLASTICS, FOIL, STRING AND CLOTH

In a well organized kitchen, one drawer should be set aside and kept full of these commonplace articles. Take precautions against last-minute panics by stocking it with plenty of clean plastic bags, rolls of foil, various sorts of paper, string and cloth. This will avoid frantic searches in the writing desk or mending basket for the paper to make papillotes or a nice piece of cloth to wrap the pudding in – all you need will be there in the kitchen, ready for use.

## Decorative papers

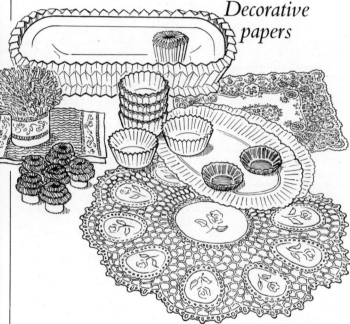

Special decorative paper frills can be bought from stationery shops as well as kitchen supply shops.

There are small frills for dressing up cutlets or the bones which stick up on guards of honour and crowns of lamb; and larger frills are for the knuckle end of cooked ham. Other decorative papers include pleated ruffs for pie dishes and little fluted cups for fairy cakes or home-made chocolates. Doilies to line and decorate serving dishes, are made in a great variety of patterns, colours, shapes and sizes.

## Plastic film and bags

Plastic film and bags are comparatively recent additions to the cook's batterie de cuisine but it is difficult to imagine being without them.

Plastic makes a good air-tight container, as long as it is tightly sealed and not punctured or torn anywhere. This makes it useful for cooking "en vessie" – this is a French method of steaming meat or poultry in a pig's bladder, submerged in boiling water. Use special plastic roasting bags for this. These also help with straight-forward roasting, conserving the juices and keeping the oven clean, yet allowing the outside of the meat or poultry to go crisp and brown. Ordinary plastic bags melt in contact with high heat or naked flames, so don't attempt to use them for roasting or steaming.

Plastic film and bags are essential for storing food in the refrigerator or freezer (see STORAGE). Light plastic film is sold in rolls and is ideal for sealing pâtés, wrapping round cakes, and for covering bowls of food in the larder or refrigerator. It is transparent and has a useful way of clinging as if glued to any smooth surface and also to itself, thus making tight seals without the bother of tying or taping.

Bags for frozen food are usually made in a stronger gauge plastic than the ordinary ones you might use for wrapping sandwiches or keeping food in the refrigerator. Freezer bags are sometimes coloured to help with easy identification of meat, fish, vegetables, and so on. Special tape and labels are needed to seal and label food packages in the freezer – they stick even in freezing temperatures. Plastic bags are usually sold with wire ties to close them.

Large plastic bags make excellent containers in which to rest dough while it proves – make sure they are big enough for the dough to expand. Plastic bags also make good containers for resting pastry – it won't dry out or develop a skin while it firms up in the refrigerator. They are ideal too for marinating meat or game; the marinade can be "stirred" without opening the bag – simply pick it up and put it down again a couple of times.

# Papers

Paper is sold for kitchen use in rolls or sheets. It never makes a completely air-tight container or cover, like plastic or foil, but it can be used as a barrier against grease, to envelop food in steam, to blot and mop up moisture, and to make purely decorative frills.

The three most useful types of paper in the kitchen are: grease-proof (or, in America, parchment) paper, which is similar to tracing paper; waxed paper; and absorbent paper, also known as kitchen paper. You may also sometimes find brown paper, rice paper and cellophane useful.

The uses of greaseproof paper are many. Buy it in large sheets if possible; rolls are also available, but once this paper has been rolled it is difficult to make it lie flat. Use it to make paper cones for piping icing (see CAKE DECORATING EQUIPMENT); butter it and use it to line cake tins or pastry flan cases before weighting them down with beans; cut a circle of it to put over simmering green vegetables – its light weight keeps them under the water and they won't discolour as much as they would under a metal lid; dampen it and place two or three layers of it over a pie once the pastry lid has cooked to prevent the lid from burning while the pie continues to cook; butter it and cover a roasting turkey to prevent it from browning too soon; and use it to make papillotes (envelopes) for meat or fish. Non-stick greaseproof paper is also available – this needs no greasing.

Waxed paper is similar to grease-proof paper but it has a film of wax on one or both sides. This makes it less likely to stick to moist foods like raw meat or fish and, if you use it to wrap food, you can seal it by pressing two waxed sides together with a hot iron. Use it as a wrapper round a roll of maître d'hôtel butter (butter mixed with chopped green herbs); this can be sliced into rounds after chilling and the paper peels off easily. Put sheets of waxed paper between cooked pancakes, raw hamburgers and flattened fillets of meat or fish so that they can be easily separated after freezing. Cover jams and chutneys with little waxed paper discs before sealing them to prevent the growth of mould. Heavy-gauge waxed paper bags and cartons make good containers for frozen foods.

Absorbent kitchen paper, often sold with dispensers that can be fixed to the wall, is invaluable for mopping up spills and quickly cleaning out pans. It also makes a useful blotter for fritters, chips and poached eggs. It can be gently laid over the surface of hot stock or consommé to absorb any stray globules of fat.

Rice paper, made of a thin sheet of rice starch, is used when making macaroons and meringues. It lines the tin and sticks to the bottoms of the cakes, thus forming an integral – and edible – part of them.

Ordinary white typing paper is also useful in the kitchen. It is stronger and better looking than greaseproof paper and stays put once creased or folded. Use it to make dinner-party papillotes, soufflé dish collars, decorative paper frills and patterns for cake decorating. A smooth sheet of paper also makes the best vehicle for funnelling breadcrumbs, flour, beans or grain into a jar.

Paper napkins are stronger than kitchen paper and can be used as filter papers for consommé, coffee or hot fat.

Brown paper makes a good insulator for wrapping round lightweight cake tins if you don't want the contents to cook too fast.

Paper bags – like the ones used in shops – can be used for flouring pieces of meat before frying them: put the seasoned flour into the bag, add the meat, hold the bag firmly shut and shake it about. Another use for a paper bag is to help remove the skin from green or red peppers. Char the skin over a flame or under a hot grill and then put the pepper into a paper bag and close it tightly; this creates steam and the skin is then much easier to peel.

Cellophane paper makes jam-pot lids and cake wrappers. Although it looks fragile, it is quite heatproof, and is popular in Oriental cookery for papillotes. The contents show through so they should be as pretty as possible.

Lastly, don't forget to keep a good supply of sticky paper labels for the freezer and for jars and bottles of preserves.

## Making papillotes

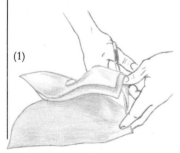

(1)

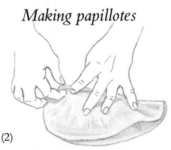

(2)

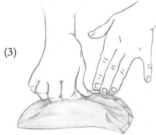

(3)

Fold the paper or foil in half; make sure that it is large enough to contain the food that is to be cooked inside it. Cut a semi-circle for chops and a heart-shape for fish, which is fatter at one end than the other (1). Grease the paper and put the meat or fish (along with any seasoning or chopped vegetables) in the envelope (2). Seal the edges by crimping them into small pleats (3), finishing with a little twist at the end. Serve the papillote unopened.

# Aluminium foil

This is another modern material. It can be used for many of the same things as greaseproof paper or plastic, sealing in air or moisture, but also conducting heat to the food inside. Use it lightly oiled or greased for papillotes and as a cover for roasting meat or poultry. It is also excellent as a wrapper for baking fish. Foil is easy to seal—simply pinch the edges together and they will stay put—but it tears easily on sharp edges. There is a view that the shinier side reflects

more heat than the less shiny side; if you believe this to be true, wrap food for baking with the shiny side inwards.

Foil can also be cut into strips, folded once or twice for reinforcement, and used as a makeshift flan ring or cake hoop. You can make any shape you like—round, square, oval or heart-shaped—and save yourself the expense of buying a special tin. Save buying a steamer too; simply put the food you wish to steam in a bowl, place it in a

roasting pan full of water, and cover the whole thing with foil before putting it in the oven.

Foil makes an excellent, long-lasting wrapper for storing cakes or pâtés but it should first be lined with waxed paper as the acid in some foods can destroy it.

Special heavy-gauge aluminium dishes and pie plates which can go from freezer to oven to freezer (wait for the food to cool first) are also available. These usually have cardboard lids.

## Making a flan ring

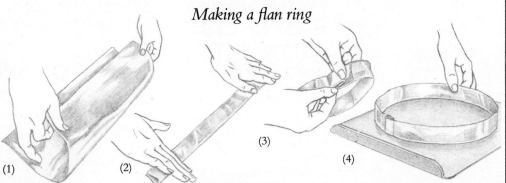

(3)

(1)                    (2)                    (4)

1. Fold a sheet of foil three or four times, lengthways.

2. Pinch the ends together, with the fold outside.

3. Form the ring into the shape you need.
4. Stand it on a baking sheet.

# Cloths

You will need three sorts of cloths in the kitchen—for general purposes, for straining, and for wrapping. Keep cloths clean—especially tea towels.

Buy plenty of butter muslin if you intend to make curd or cream cheese; put the dampened cloth over a colander, tip in the curds, tie the cloth into a bag and let the whey drip into a bowl underneath. Use butter muslin to line cheese moulds (see MOULDS). Wrap a ballottine of duck or chicken in muslin before cooking it. It will brown through the cloth in the frying pan. Then it goes into the stock to be poached and the cloth will help it to keep its shape while it cooks. It is not removed until the ballottine has cooled. Thickly buttered muslin may also be used to protect the breast of a turkey while it roasts.

Line metal steamers with muslin before steaming dumplings.

Strain vegetables through muslin before making them into a purée. Cloth absorbs moisture best and keeps floury things from going soggy.

Use muslin or torn-up pieces of sheet or tea towels to wrap puddings in for boiling. Always scald the cloth with boiling water first, and then flour it. This makes a skin inside which prevents the pudding from sticking to the cloth. If you want to make doubly sure that the pudding does not stick, line the cloth with greased greaseproof paper.

Special cloths are used to strain jellies (see STRAINERS) but if you want to economize, use old tea towels, sheets or table-cloths instead.

You will need a large old table-cloth to cover the table for making strudel pastry. A folded tea towel underneath a mixing bowl will stop it from skidding or spinning

while you mix or beat. There are also many occasions when a tea towel comes in useful for things other than drying the dishes: to cover bowls against flies or dust, to pat things dry before frying them, to dry salads, to make a seal round the rim of a steamer and, folded in four, to absorb steam from cooking rice.

If you are preparing cuts of meat for the freezer, use a roll of cotton stockinette. This prevents hard edges of bone from cutting through an outer wrapper of plastic.

Not to be forgotten, is the chef's torchon or dishcloth, worn almost like a badge of office, tucked into his apron belt or back pocket and always ready to wipe a dish clean before arranging food on it and to protect his hands from the heat of a cooking pan handle. Oven mitts are useful too, but much less professional looking.

# String

A ball of fine white string will come in handy in the kitchen. The best way to keep it in the kitchen is to put it in a special box with a hole in the lid so that the end hangs out, ready to be snipped off at whatever length you like; this means that you keep the string clean and don't have to hold the ball with sticky, bloody or greasy hands.

String is probably most often used for trussing. It is also necessary for tying bouquets garnis together and for fastening paupiettes, beef olives and boeuf à la ficelle. A bag of spices will not get lost while you boil pickles if you tie it to the handle of the saucepan. You will also need string to secure pudding cloths round basins, to keep the flaps in place on a saddle of lamb, and to wind round ballottines and stuffed meat.

Use white cotton tape to tie bundles of asparagus, rather than string which might cut the stems. Keep a darning needle and a reel of black button thread handy – this is useful for mending tears in a boned duck or chicken and, being black, can easily be found when your want to remove it.

## Trussing a chicken

*1. and 2. With the bird on its back and its wing tips tucked behind the shoulders, draw the string under the tail, crossing it over, and take it round the end of each drumstick.*

*3. Draw it tightly up between the drumsticks and the thighs.*

*4. Turn the bird over. Take each end of string under the folded wings and over the shoulders.*

*5. Pull the string tightly and tie a knot between the shoulders.*

## Tying a butcher's knot

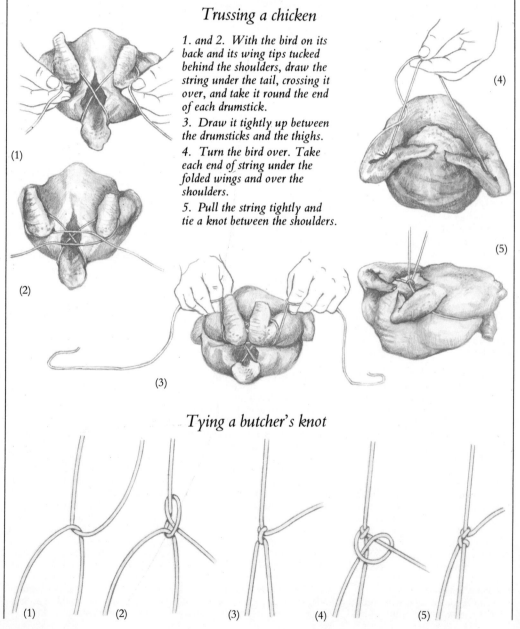

(1)

(2)

(3)

(4)

(5)

(1)    (2)    (3)    (4)    (5)

# OPENERS AND CORKSCREWS

Even if you strongly disapprove of convenience foods, it is unlikely that you can manage without a can opener. Can openers come in all shapes and sizes, from little ones you can slip in your pocket to fairly large wall-mounted ones. Multi-purpose electric kitchen tools often have a can opening attachment, useful if you have arthritic hands or very weak wrists. These disabilities can also make opening tightly sealed jars and bottles a problem. Gadgets to give you extra grip or provide better leverage on a stubborn lid or stopper may not be essential to the kitchen but they can save time and temper.

Another sort of opener – the corkscrew – also has a place in the kitchen; a glass of wine not only refreshes the cook, but brings richness and flavour to many dishes. Corkscrews were first made in the eighteenth century, when they were called bottle screws; before that corks and stoppers on bottles were loosely fitted and projected from the top of the bottle so that they could be pulled by hand – or even with the teeth. The best corkscrews have spirals with rounded edges; sharp edges tend to break the cork. Openers for crown corks are also needed when fruit juices or beer are required for a recipe.

(a) **Size.** D. 4 in. (102 mm).
 **Material.** Rubber.
(b) **Size.** L. 9 in. (230 mm).
 **Material.** Nickel plated steel.
(c) **Size.** L. 5 in. (127 mm).
 **Material.** Chromed steel.
(d) **Size.** L. 9 in. (230 mm).
 **Material.** Plastic and stainless steel.

These gadgets deal with the most firmly stuck or screwed-on lids and stoppers. Those with metal jaws will scratch or dent lids – which may not matter for run-of-the-mill pickle jars, but can be disastrous if the lid in question belongs to something precious.

The rubber opener (a) will damage nothing it opens. It has a textured surface to improve your grip and works best on bottle caps and small lids. It is easiest to use if held in your weaker hand with the jar grasped by the stronger.

The long handles on opener (b) give good leverage but the ends

## Jar and bottle openers

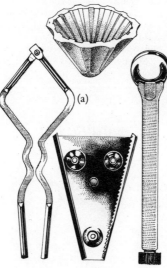

(a)

(b)   (c)   (d)

tend to dig into your palm when opening large lids. They are more comfortable, and equally efficient, when the smaller, central section is being used to open bottle caps.

The wedge-shaped opener (c) screws under a shelf or work surface. You slide the lid between the flanged edges and then twist the jar or bottle. It can unscrew lids from $\frac{3}{4}$ in. (20 mm) to 3 in. (75 mm) in diameter.

Most fiddly of the four to operate, opener (d) has a flexible steel hoop that is released by a screw at the end of the handle. It can be adjusted to deal with lids up to 4 in. (102 mm) in diameter. The hoop can be retracted, squeezing small rubber jaws to undo lids as tiny as $\frac{1}{2}$ in. (12 mm) diameter. The rubber jaws can be lifted aside completely to allow the steel hoop to encircle very large lids, but without the grip that the rubber jaws provide the band can slip.

(a) **Size.** $3\frac{1}{2}$ in. (90 mm).
 **Material.** Nickel plated steel.
(b) **Size.** H. $3\frac{1}{2}$ in. (90 mm).
 **Material.** Chromed steel.
(c) **Size.** L. $4\frac{1}{2}$ in. (115 mm).
 **Material.** Nickel plated steel.

Openers like these are occasionally needed in the kitchen; some are incorporated on the handles of kitchen scissors and can openers for this reason.

## Crown cork openers

(a)   (b)   (c)

Opener (a) is the basic type, while the dual-purpose opener (b) will prise off a bottle cap and then can be snapped back in place on to the rim of the bottle to reseal it. Opener (c) is multi-purpose. At one end is a crown cap opener and at the other is a can piercer, useful for cans of liquids where there is no need to remove the entire lid. The opener also has a good corkscrew.

# Can openers

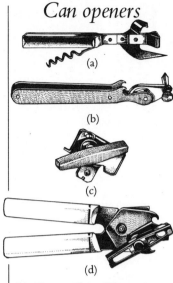

(a)

(b)

(c)

(d)

(a) **Size.** L. 5½ in. (140 mm).
**Material.** Blued steel blade, nickel plated steel handle.

(b) **Size.** L. 6 in. (152 mm).
**Material.** Nickel plated steel, lacquered handle.

(c) **Size.** L. 3 in. (75 mm).
**Material.** Chromed steel and plastic.

(d) **Size.** L. 7½ in. (190 mm).
**Material.** Chromed steel and plastic.

The best can openers work smoothly and effortlessly, leaving no jagged edges.

It is not possible to remove the top cleanly with either opener (a) or (b) and they both need some effort to operate. Opener (b) is worked by a ratchet and is an efficient opener of all cans including those that are square or rectangular.

Butterfly-handled openers cut clean edges with no sharp projections. Left-handed versions are also available. With opener (c), you simply hook the blade over the rim of the can and turn the butterfly. It is extremely efficient, producing a clean, safe edge. Give the butterfly a reverse turn at the end to free the can.

Unlike most other butterfly can openers, opener (d) works not with a blade and cog wheel, but with a gear-driven cutting wheel like those found on many wall-mounted can openers. It is extremely smooth in operation.

# Wall-mounted can openers

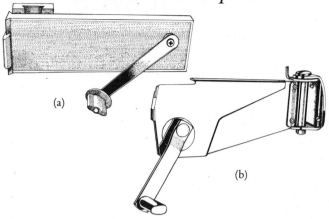

(a)

(b)

(a) **Size.** L. 8½ in. (215 mm).
**Material.** Chromed steel and plastic.

(b) **Size.** L. 7½ in. (190 mm).
**Material.** Chromed steel.

In a small kitchen, a wall-mounted can opener is never too far from your work surface and can be most convenient. These types of opener hold the can by the rim, even when the top is completely removed.

Opener (a), unlike many wall-mounted openers, has a cutting blade and cog wheel, which makes it particularly easy to clean. You fit the can to the blade by first raising the handle. It works efficiently and smoothly. The bracket is designed to hold the opener in one position for working and another for storing. This makes it less convenient than opener (b) which can be folded back against the wall.

Opener (b) has a magnet to hold the top suspended until you are ready to throw it away and it can be set for use at three different angles. All wall-mounted can openers should be cleaned occasionally with a brush.

# Sardine key

**Size.** L. 6½ in. (165 mm).
**Material.** Chromed steel.

The essential key is not always provided with a sardine can – and, even if it is, it often needs brute strength or the end of a spoon put through the handle as a lever to operate it. This patent, everlasting key makes the job simple. You slip the metal flap on the can into a slot at the end of the key and twist. The extra length in the key means less effort in rolling back the lid. Clear the lid from the key by screwing the wing-nut down.

# Cork retriever

**Size.** L. 6½ in. (165 mm).
**Material.** Chromed steel.

If a cork breaks while you are trying to draw it, you can gently reinsert the corkscrew at an angle or push the remainder of the cork down into the wine. You can then retrieve the cork with this ingenious tool. Slide it into the bottle, hook the projecting lug under the cork and pull it back up the neck. A piece of string with a knot on the end can be used in the same way.

(a) **Size.** H. 5 in. (127 mm).
**Material.** Chromed steel.

(b) **Size.** L. 4¾ in. (120 mm).
**Material.** Chromed steel.

(c) **Size.** H. 4½ in. (115 mm).
**Material.** Chromed steel.

(d) **Size.** H. 7 in. (178 mm).
**Material.** Boxwood.

(e) **Size.** H. 6¾ in. (178 mm).
**Material.** Chromed steel.

(f) **Size.** H. 4½ in. (115 mm).
**Material.** Plastic.

(g) **Size.** L. 6½ in. (165 mm).
**Material.** Plastic.

(h) **Size.** H. 19½ in. (495 mm).
**Material.** Brass.

The more rounded the edges and open the spiral of a corkscrew the better its grip on the cork and the easier it will be to operate. The size and strength of your hands also have some bearing on the type of corkscrew you should use.

The most basic types of corkscrew require brute strength and, if used inexpertly, can jolt and disturb the wine.

The simple corkscrew (a) does not have a good spiral and is therefore more likely to break a cork than the multi-purpose corkscrew (b) which has a well formed spiral, round in section. It is used by professional wine waiters and is called the "waiter's friend". The hinged lever rests on the edge of the rim as the cork is pulled. With practice this is an easy corkscrew to operate. The little knife blade cuts the lead seal over the cork.

The flat, flexible prongs on the cork puller (c) are eased down beside the cork with a rocking action. The cork is then pulled out with a twist of the wrist. It can also be used to replace corks and is particularly good for drawing fragile ones.

Corkscrews like (d) and (e) that pull against the rim of the bottle require less effort to use and make for much smoother opening. The top handle on corkscrew (d) is twisted down to screw the spiral into the cork. The lower one is then twisted in the same direction to raise it again with the cork. The lever corkscrew (e) has two side arms which rise as the spiral is inserted. You close them to withdraw the cork. It has a solid cored spiral, so is not so good as corkscrew (d) which has an open spiral.

## Corkscrews

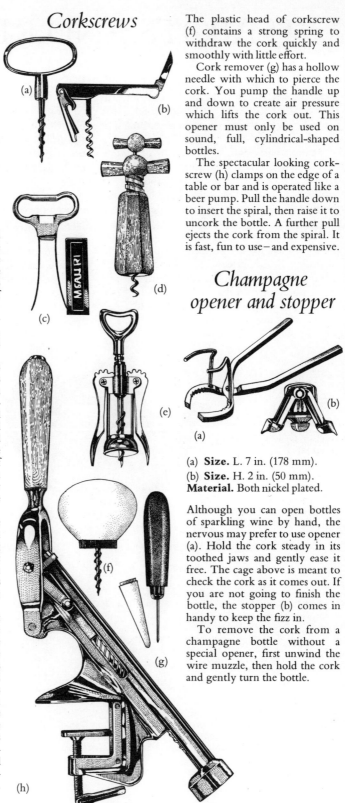

The plastic head of corkscrew (f) contains a strong spring to withdraw the cork quickly and smoothly with little effort.

Cork remover (g) has a hollow needle with which to pierce the cork. You pump the handle up and down to create air pressure which lifts the cork out. This opener must only be used on sound, full, cylindrical-shaped bottles.

The spectacular looking corkscrew (h) clamps on the edge of a table or bar and is operated like a beer pump. Pull the handle down to insert the spiral, then raise it to uncork the bottle. A further pull ejects the cork from the spiral. It is fast, fun to use – and expensive.

## Champagne opener and stopper

(a) **Size.** L. 7 in. (178 mm).

(b) **Size.** H. 2 in. (50 mm).
**Material.** Both nickel plated.

Although you can open bottles of sparkling wine by hand, the nervous may prefer to use opener (a). Hold the cork steady in its toothed jaws and gently ease it free. The cage above is meant to check the cork as it comes out. If you are not going to finish the bottle, the stopper (b) comes in handy to keep the fizz in.

To remove the cork from a champagne bottle without a special opener, first unwind the wire muzzle, then hold the cork and gently turn the bottle.

# TEAPOTS AND KETTLES

A good cup of tea – be it Indian, China or herbal – is best made by infusing the leaves in a teapot; the water must be boiling and, in Britain at least (where tea is more or less the national beverage), that water is best boiled in a kettle.

Teapots come in a huge variety of shapes, sizes and materials. Obviously, if you are determined to have a pot that matches your tea service or to use one that has been in the family for generations, you must be prepared to put up with any of its disadvantages. But if you are choosing a new teapot, the three main points to look for are a spout that pours well, a handle that is comfortable to hold and large enough to keep your hand away from the heat of the pot, and a lid that stays put even when you are pouring out the last drop of tea.

A kettle, which is a peculiarly British utensil, has many uses in the kitchen other than boiling water for tea. It is much quicker, for example, to heat water for vegetables or pasta in an electric kettle than it is to heat it in a pan on the hob. Whether you buy an electric or a non-electric kettle, always choose one with a comfortable handle. Check that when it boils the steam vents will not direct scalding steam on to your hand, and if you like to save time choose one with a spout that is big enough to take water straight from the tap – this saves the trouble of taking the lid off every time you fill it. If you have an electric cooker and you're buying a non-electric kettle, check that it can be placed on an electric hot plate – some kettles are not suitable. With an electric kettle, look for well fixed, stable feet.

## Teapot

**Size.** H. 6¾ in. (172 mm).
**Material.** Porcelain.

Traditionalists swear by the brown glazed teapot with its comfortable, old-fashioned shape. This teapot, known as "Brown Betty", has a hole in the top of the lid for steam to escape. It will hold a good number of cups of tea and the lid fits quite securely.

Keep your teapot for tea only. Tea contains tannin which coats the inside of the pot and can eventually spoil the taste of the tea. To prevent this clean the pot from time to time with a solution of bicarbonate of soda. Unless you can be quite sure that your pot is free of any deposits of tannin, it is a good idea to keep a special teapot for herb teas.

## Tea infusers

(a) **Size.** H. 1 in. (25 mm).
    **Material.** Stainless steel.
(b) **Size.** H. 2 in. (50 mm).
    **Material.** Chromed steel.
(c) **Size.** L. 5¾ in. (146 mm).
    **Material.** Nickel plated steel.

(a)

(b)

(c)

These small tea infusers are designed to make single cups of tea. They work like teabags but you can fill them with any kind of tea you like – Indian, China or herbal. They are used directly in the cup.

Infuser (a) is shaped like a teapot. You fill it with tea, place it in the cup with its chain hanging over the edge of the cup and pour on boiling water. When the tea is sufficiently infused remove it. There is a little tray on which to stand the infuser after use. Infuser (b) is shaped like a little acorn, with perforations on the sides and top. It comes apart in the middle and has a chain with a hook on the end, so you can hook it over the rim of a tea cup.

Infuser (c), shaped like two spoons joined together, is less decorative than the other two, but equally efficient.

## Making a cup of tea

*To make a perfect cup of tea, first warm the pot before adding the tea. The amount of tea usually recommended is one teaspoon per person plus one for the pot, but some people may find this too strong. In any case, it rather depends on the size of the teapot and on the amount of water. Pour freshly boiling water on to the tea and let it "draw" for a few minutes. Stir before serving.*

## Fur collector

**Size.** D. 1 in. (25 mm).
**Material.** Stainless steel.

In hard water areas, the inside of a kettle is likely to become furred up—coated with a chalky deposit. This can be prevented by putting a fur collector inside the kettle. This looks like a little roll of crumpled-up wire mesh. As soon as the mesh becomes coated with fur, it should be held under running water and squeezed between the fingers until the fur has been removed. It can then be reused. A couple of marbles inside the kettle will serve the same purpose, but tend to make boiling a kettle a rather noisy business.

A kettle can be defurred with a proprietary fur remover or with an infusion of citric acid crystals.

## Kettles

(a)

(b)

(a) **Size.** H. 7 in. (178 mm).
**Material.** Stainless steel body, copper base, plastic handle.
(b) **Size.** 6 in. (152 mm).
**Material.** Plastic.

Although non-electric kettles take longer to boil than electric ones, some people prefer them. They are obviously more reliable as there is nothing mechanical to go wrong but there is always the chance of them boiling dry. They are certainly cheaper to run if you have a range cooker that is providing heat all the time. Kettle (a) is made of stainless steel with a flat copper base. This is suitable for electric plates as well as for gas and range cookers. It has a capacity of 4½ pt. (2·5 ℓ) and a whistle which sounds when the water boils.

Aluminium and brightly coloured enamelled kettles are also available, which are cheap and pretty but not very long-lasting.

Electric kettle (b) is a sophisticated device. It is made of moulded plastic, and has a water gauge showing the maximum—3½ pt. (2 ℓ)—and minimum amounts of water the kettle will hold. It has one great advantage:

it will not work unless the minimum amount of water is in it, so there is no chance of burning out the element by accidentally switching it on when it's empty. It is filled through the spout and operated by a push button. It switches itself off automatically when the water boils, thus saving fuel and eliminating the risk of water boiling away and the kettle becoming damaged.

An automatic kettle with a buzzer which sounds when the water boils is also available. This is handy if you tend to put the kettle on and then forget it—thus needing to bring the water back to the boil later when you finally get round to making that cup of tea. The best tea is made with fresh cold water that has just come to the boil. The longer water boils, the "flatter" and less oxygenated it becomes.

Non-automatic kettles are cheaper than automatic ones and are often more reliable as there is less to go wrong.

Never immerse an electric kettle in water, and make sure that the electric socket is kept dry. Elements can be easily replaced when they become burnt out.

# COFFEE MAKERS AND JUGS

The simplest and quickest way of making coffee–and some claim the best–is to pour boiling water on to freshly ground coffee in a jug or coffee pot. This method is much the same as that of making tea. First warm the jug, then put in a measure of medium-ground coffee–a level dessertspoon per cup is about right; pour on freshly boiling water, stir, put on the lid and allow to stand for three or four minutes; drag a spoon across the surface to settle the grounds before serving. The only

disadvantage of this method is that it requires practice and careful measuring of the coffee to control the strength. Correctly made, it should not need straining into the cups. To keep it hot, use a heated tray (see WARMERS).

If this method does not suit you, there is a huge variety of special coffee makers available, some much more sophisticated (and expensive) than others, with measures, gauges, strainers, filters and heaters all built in to enable you to make the perfect cup of coffee.

## Filter coffee makers

(a) **Size.** H. 5 in. (127 mm).
   **Material.** Plastic.
(b) **Size.** H. 9¼ in. (235 mm).
   **Material.** Earthenware.
(c) **Size.** H. 9½ in. (242 mm).
   **Material.** Glass body, wooden collar, leather thong.
(d) **Size.** H. 2½ in. (65 mm).
   **Material.** Chromed steel body, plastic handles.
(e) **Size.** H. 11½ in. (292 mm).
   **Material.** Aluminium body, plastic knob and handles.
(f) **Size.** H. 10½ in. (267 mm).
   **Material.** Porcelain.
(g) **Size.** H. 10 in. (255 mm).
   **Material.** Plastic.
(h) **Size.** H. 11¾ in. (298 mm).
   **Material.** Chromed and plastic body, teak handle, glass knob.

Plastic filter (a) adds a touch of refinement to the simple jug method of making coffee. The plastic filter, with a disposable paper filter inside, fits on top of the jug, and the coffee goes inside the paper filter. You wet the grounds with a little boiling water and then pour on more boiling water, topping up the filter until you have the desired amount of coffee.

This method does away with the need to strain the coffee but, because of the time it takes for the water to filter through the grounds, coffee made in this way is likely to be even colder than that made by the jug method unless a heated tray is used. The

filter method however does make good coffee, which is without bitterness or sediment.

The filter coffee pot (b) works in exactly the same way but looks much nicer, as jug and filter are made of matching glazed earthenware.

Jug (c) is also used with filter papers. It is a one-piece vessel shaped like an hour glass and made of heat-resistant glass. It has a wooden collar in the middle, tied to the coffee maker with a leather thong. The collar serves as an insulated handle.

An individual coffee filter (d), similar to the type used in continental cafés, is useful when you want to make a single cup of coffee. It sits on top of a coffee cup and holds coffee grounds between two perforated grids; you simply pour on boiling water and put the lid on top to keep it hot. When the coffee has filtered into the cup, you place the filter on the inverted lid so that it doesn't drip on the table.

The Neapolitan pot (e) consists of two aluminium containers of equal size. One container has a spout, the other has a screw-topped filter basket. Cold water goes into the container without a spout and the basket, filled with coffee, is dropped into place. The spouted container goes upside down on top. As soon as steam starts to appear from a little hole in the lower container, the whole thing is turned over, allowing the hot water to filter through the coffee into the spouted container.

The elegant porcelain filter pot (f) consists–starting at the bottom –of a pot with spout and handle, a cylinder with handles and a perforated base in which to put the coffee, and a perforated saucer-like section into which you pour boiling water. A lid sits on top of the whole thing, and also fits the pot itself.

If you drink a lot of coffee and like it made by the filter method, an electric machine with a built-in hotplate (g) may be a worthwhile buy. This works by heating water in a container and passing it through a filter full of coffee into a jug. This jug stands on a hotplate where it is kept at a thermostatically controlled temperature well below boiling point. (Coffee should never be allowed to boil.)

There is a more sophisticated version available which has two filter speeds, giving coffee of different strengths, and another model which can be programmed to switch on automatically for an early-morning cup of coffee.

A coffee percolator (h) works in much the same way in that boiling water passes through the coffee grounds, and then drips through a strainer, leaving the grounds behind. But, with this method, boiling water circulates through the coffee continually which is why coffee percolators are often criticized for "stewing" the coffee. They are also a very uneconomical way of making coffee, using about twice as much coffee as other filter methods.

(a) **Size.** 12 in. (305 mm).
**Material.** Plastic.
(b) **Size.** H. 9 in. (230 mm).
**Material.** Aluminium body,
plastic knob and handle.
(c) **Size.** H. 9½ in. (242 mm).
**Material.** Aluminium
body, plastic knobs.

For those who like strong Italian
coffee, an espresso coffee maker
is the answer. The espresso method
uses about the same amount of
coffee as filter methods. Espresso
machine (a) makes the espresso
coffee served in many coffee bars
and Italian restaurants.

Pot (b) is a smaller non-electric
version. Water is heated up in the
base until it boils and is forced, by
pressure, through a metal basket
filled with ground coffee. The
coffee is then ready to be poured
from the top section. The one
disadvantage of this type of pot is
that you need to watch it and
remove it from the source of heat
as soon as the water starts to rise.
This coffee maker is made of
aluminium and tends to discolour
with use. Stainless steel versions
are also available.

The espresso maker (c) is a
complicated-looking device but
works on the same principle as
(b). The coffee is put into a small
container which fits under the top
of the main body of the machine.
Cold water is poured into a hole
in the tube section of the main
body. The machine is put on the
heat and the coffee drips into the
jug below the coffee container.
There is also an attachment for
making capuccino – steam comes
out of a thin spout to froth up and
heat the milk.

*Espresso coffee
makers*

(a)

(b)

(c)

**Size.** H. 3 in. (75 mm).
**Material.** Tin-lined brass.

Although, strictly speaking,
Turkish coffee can be made in any
jug or pot that can be put on the
hob this small long-handled pot is
the sort of vessel that is traditionally used for doing so. To
make Turkish coffee, bring water
to the boil in the pot, remove
from the heat, and stir in very

*Turkish coffee
maker*

finely ground Turkish coffee and
sugar to taste. Replace the pot
on the heat and bring it to the
boil. Remove from the heat
immediately then bring back to
the boil twice more.

The coffee should be allowed
to stand for two or three minutes
to allow the grounds to settle. The
sediment will remain at the bottom of the pot if the coffee has
been made correctly.

# Vacuum coffee maker

# Plunge-filter coffee maker

# Coffee essence maker

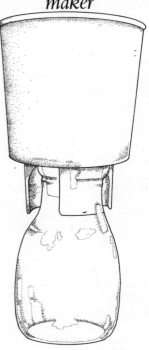

**Size.** H. 15 in. (380 mm).
**Material.** Glass containers, plastic stand and handle.

This works in a similar way to an espresso machine but makes coffee that tastes more like the filtered version. Water is heated in the lower glass container and is forced up, by vacuum, into the upper container which contains the ground coffee. The coffee then drains down into the lower container. It can be used either on the hob or on a spirit heater.

**Size.** H. 9¼ in. (235 mm).
**Material.** Glass jug, chromed steel frame and lid, plastic handle.

This attractive glass coffee maker makes coffee by the infusion method – as in the simple jug method. The difference is that once the boiling water has been poured on to the ground coffee you plunge the filter unit down into the container, thus trapping the grounds in the base and enabling you to pour the strained coffee directly from the jug.

**Size.** H. 14½ in. (368 mm).
**Material.** Glass lower container, plastic upper container.

This is the device for those who wish to make their own coffee essence. It consists of a lower glass container and a plastic container, fitted with a filter and a little plug, which sits on top. Place ground coffee and cold water in the top container and leave for about 12 hours. Then remove the plug and allow the essence to drip into the lower container. The coffee essence should be bottled and stored in the refrigerator and can then be used as required. It should be made up in the same way as any instant coffee – with boiling water in a cup. It can also be used to flavour cakes and puddings.

## —— Choosing coffee for different methods ——

| Method | Roast | Degree of grinding |
|---|---|---|
| Espresso | High | Fine |
| Filter | Low | Fine |
| Jug | Medium | Medium |
| Neapolitan | Low | Medium-fine |
| Percolator | Low or medium | Medium-coarse |
| Plunge-filter | Medium | Medium-fine |
| Vacuum | High | Medium-fine |

# WINE MAKING AND BREWING EQUIPMENT

With a little space and equipment, including some everyday household utensils, you can produce good wines and excellent beers very cheaply at home. Today, not only specialist shops but also some chemists and supermarkets, sell wine and beermaking equipment and standardized, packaged ingredients. Cans of grape concentrate and concentrated beer wort are very reliable; they are made to certain formulae and are less unpredictable in fermentation than ingredients gathered by someone starting from scratch.

*Basic principles*
The more refined the ingredients and the simpler the recipe, the less equipment and the more basic the whole process is. For basic winemaking you only need to put grape concentrate into a narrow-necked jar of adequate size; add the correct amounts of water and sugar, then put in the yeast. You then fit the jar with an airlock, stand it in a warm place and allow the mixture to ferment. The final steps are to drop in some campden tablets to kill off any stray bacteria and to siphon the wine off its sediment into another container. Finings can be added to clear it and the finished product is siphoned into bottles. Beer is even less complicated to make with a concentrated beer wort. With some concentrates the whole process can take as little as three weeks.

Enthusiasts who prefer to blend their own ingredients rather than buy ready prepared cans of concentrate will need additional equipment – particularly if they intend to make wine or beer in fairly large quantities. The essential thing, whatever the process followed, is to sterilize all the equipment and to keep air from getting into the must (wine during fermentation) or the wort. Otherwise airborne yeasts and bacteria can make the wine or beer sour, vinegary and generally undrinkable.

*Equipment*
Always choose sound, good quality equipment in the correct size and material for the job. Food-grade polythene, plastic and nylon utensils and containers are light, tough and easy to clean. They should be clear or white in colour as the dyes in black or strongly coloured plastic containers can affect the contents. (You can get round this by putting transparent or white bin liners in them.) Glass vessels are excellent, but are heavy and of course breakable. The one gallon (4·5 ℓ) demijohn is a very popular and conveniently sized jar for winemaking. Never use metal containers for fermentation.

Polythene fermentation bins graduated to $5\frac{1}{2}$ gal. (25·1 ℓ) are available, but you can also improvise them. An ordinary polythene dustbin of 6 to 11 gal. (28 to 50 ℓ) capacity is useful for large amounts. Mark it off yourself on the outside with a pen or nail varnish. For small quantities a lidded household bucket can be used. Never use secondhand plastic containers which have been used for other purposes as these can hold tainting smells and flavours.

Narrow-necked containers are needed for dandelion, elderberry and other country wines, which are started in bins and then are strained into containers which can be fitted with airlocks. Apart from the demijohn which is used for fermenting small quantities of wine, you can also use carboys holding up to 5 gal. (22·7 ℓ). Plastic jerrycans can also be fitted with airlocks.

*Storage*
Wine should never be stored in plastic containers. Glass containers are best for long-term wine storage, but shield red wine from the light if it is kept in clear glass since the colour may be affected. Traditional salt-glazed earthenware crocks and oak casks can be used but are more difficult to clean than glass. Beer can be stored in bulk in plastic containers and special pressure barrels and domes are available in various sizes to store beer on draught and save the work of bottling. Always use proper wine or beer bottles as they are designed to withstand a certain amount of pressure. Make sure that they and their corks are sterilized and use green bottles for red wines.

# Beginner's kits

(a)

(b)

(a) **Size.** Cap. 1 gal. (4·5 ℓ).
**Contents.** One glass demi-john, H. 12¾ in. (324 mm), sterilizing solution, plastic funnel, 2·2 lb. (1 kg) grape concentrate, sugar, yeast compound, airlock, cork bungs, campden tablets, PVC tubing, siphon tap, six wine bottles, corks.

(b) **Size.** Cap. 1 gal. (4·5 ℓ).
**Contents.** Polythene fermentation bin, H. 12½ in. (317 mm), sterilizing solution, 12 oz. (340 g) concentrated brewing wort, dried yeast, sugar, plastic spoon, PVC tubing, eight beer bottles and caps.

Kits like these are probably the best way to begin wine or beer-making. These kits contain the the basic utensils and ingredients (apart from water) to produce 1 gal. (4·5 ℓ) of wine or beer in about three weeks.

Kits take up little space and, be-cause you can produce in small quantities, allow you to make a variety of wines and beers with-out filling your home with bottles and bins.

253

## Press

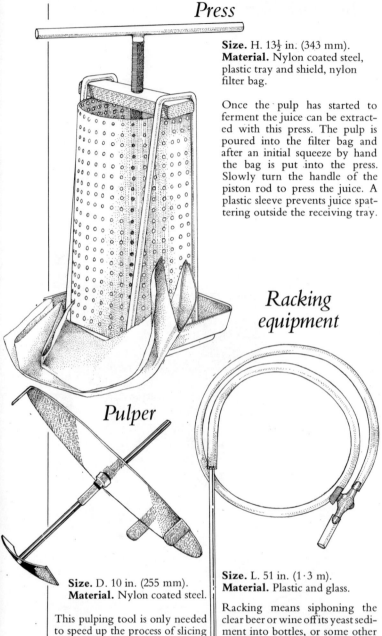

**Size.** H. 13½ in. (343 mm).
**Material.** Nylon coated steel, plastic tray and shield, nylon filter bag.

Once the pulp has started to ferment the juice can be extracted with this press. The pulp is poured into the filter bag and after an initial squeeze by hand the bag is put into the press. Slowly turn the handle of the piston rod to press the juice. A plastic sleeve prevents juice spattering outside the receiving tray.

## Racking equipment

## Pulper

**Size.** D. 10 in. (255 mm).
**Material.** Nylon coated steel.

This pulping tool is only needed to speed up the process of slicing and crushing fruit or vegetables, if you are making large quantities of country wine. Attach a power drill to the spindle that protrudes through its cover and place the cover over a standard household bucket filled one-third full with ingredients. Slowly raise and lower the drill to work the cutter through them. The manufacturer claims that it will pulp a load of apples in ten seconds.

**Size.** L. 51 in. (1·3 m).
**Material.** Plastic and glass.

Racking means siphoning the clear beer or wine off its yeast sediment into bottles, or some other container, placed at a lower level. Basically a piece of tubing approximately 48 in. (1·2 m) long is all that is needed, but a siphon tap fitted on one end can make the job easier by controlling the rate of flow. Otherwise it is necessary to stop the flow by pinching the end of the tube. A siphon rod with a specially shaped end can be attached also to prevent any sediment being siphoned up.

## Airlocks

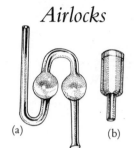

(a)                                    (b)

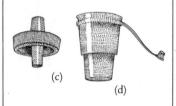

(c)

(d)

(a) **Size.** H. 5¼ in. (133 mm).
    **Material.** Glass.
(b) **Size.** H. 3 in. (75 mm).
    **Material.** Plastic.
(c) **Size.** H. 1¾ in. (45 mm).
    **Material.** Polythene.
(d) **Size.** H. 2½ in. (65 mm).
    **Material.** Polythene.

Airlocks, or fermentation locks, are fitted into narrow-necked containers to let carbon dioxide produced by the fermentation bubble out, and to prevent oxygen or unwanted airborne yeasts, which might spoil the wine, from getting in. Some have sterile water as a seal and this gives an indication of the stage fermentation has reached by the amount of bubbles passing through. Others operate with valves.

Most airlocks are fitted through cork or rubber bungs. Rubber bungs are less likely to be displaced by gas pressure and can be reused, but they can give a rubbery tang to wine if the fermentation period is long. Cork bungs cannot be used again.

Airlocks (a) and (b) are filled halfway up with water. Airlock (c) needs no water. It has a valve containing a ball-bearing in the cap on the top and can be fitted into a bored bung or be screwed directly into a standard, threaded jar. The most versatile of the four, airlock (d), can also be used as a bung, plugging the inner air tube with the little plastic stopper provided.

## Filter

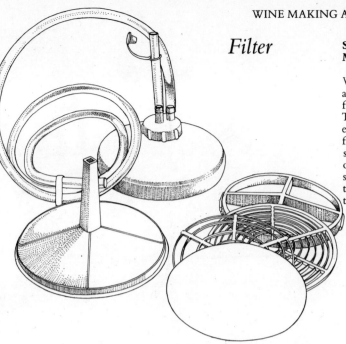

**Size.** H. 7 in. (178 mm).
**Material.** Plastic.

Wine will normally clear naturally over a period of time, but filtering speeds up the process. This equipment is not really necessary with quick wine kits and finings are often used instead by some wine makers. This filter fits over a receiving jar. The wine is siphoned directly into it, passing through a filter pad and then into the jar.

## Thermostatic heaters

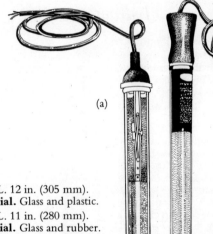

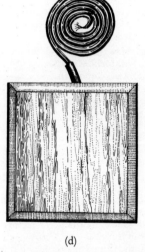

(d)

(a) **Size.** L. 12 in. (305 mm).
**Material.** Glass and plastic.
(b) **Size.** L. 11 in. (280 mm).
**Material.** Glass and rubber.
(c) **Size.** L. 20 in. (508 mm).
**Material.** Plastic.
(d) **Size.** 6½ in. (165 mm) square.
**Material.** Plastic.

These electric heaters keep wine and beer at a temperature of approximately 75°F (24°C) during fermentation. They are not essential equipment, but are a boon in cold weather, or if you keep your bins and jars in unheated places. They are efficient and cheap to run.

Heater (a) is for beer making, and can be submerged in the brew; it consists of a glass tube with a

pre-set heating element inside. A neon light glows when it is working. It can heat containers of up to 10 gal. (45 ℓ) capacity and can also be used for heating up to 5 gal. (22·7 ℓ) of wine. The wine heater (b) is similar to heater (a) but is intended for use in narrow necked containers. It has a rubber bung, bored to take an air lock.

The pre-set heated belt (c) wraps round the outside of a jar or bin. Belts come in various lengths to fit most containers. Alternatively you can stand a fermentation jar on the pre-set heated tray (d). Larger trays accommodate up to four jars at a time.

Some thermostatic heaters can be adjusted to vary temperatures slightly for different types of wine.

255

## Corking tools

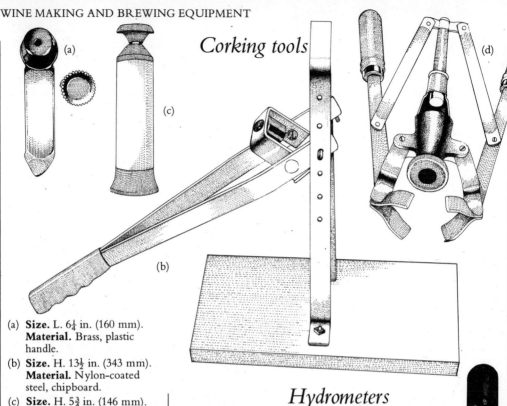

(a) **Size.** L. $6\frac{1}{4}$ in. (160 mm).
   **Material.** Brass, plastic handle.
(b) **Size.** H. $13\frac{1}{2}$ in. (343 mm).
   **Material.** Nylon-coated steel, chipboard.
(c) **Size.** H. $5\frac{3}{4}$ in. (146 mm).
   **Material.** Plastic.
(d) **Size.** L. $13\frac{1}{2}$ in. (343 mm).
   folded.
   **Material.** Alloy steel, wooden handles.

Crown corks have to be pressed and crimped over the rims of bottles with special tools. The small hand corker (a) is adequate for most bottling. The brass head is placed over a crown cork on the rim of the bottle and then hammered to fit the cork in place. The corking machine (b) is a table model, suitable for all sizes of bottle and is worth the investment if you are bottling in quantity. Polythene caps are re-usable and can be fitted easily by hand, but do not give such a good seal.

Wine bottle corks can be put in by hand using corker (c). It consists of a tube and plunger. The cork is dropped into the tube and the plunger is pushed down to ram it home. Two-handed corking machines such as (d) make the job easier, but are more expensive.

Polythene caps can also be used to seal wine bottles, though they are less efficient than corks and should not be used if the wine is to stand for a long time.

## Hydrometers

(a) **Size.** L. $8\frac{3}{4}$ in. (223 mm).
   **Material.** Glass.
(b) **Size.** L. $9\frac{1}{2}$ in. (242 mm).
   **Material.** Polystyrene.
(c) **Size.** L. $16\frac{3}{4}$ in. (425 mm).
   **Material.** Glass, plastic suction bulb.

Hydrometers tell you how much sugar there is in wine or beer by measuring the density of the liquid. This is important as it indicates when fermentation has ceased and the liquor can be bottled. It also gives you some idea of its eventual alcoholic strength. Many wine and beer makers rely on taste and eye when making these judgements – but it is reassuring to have an assessment confirmed, however expert you are.

To test the density of liquid in a wide-necked container, all you have to do is place the sterile hydrometer directly into it. With narrow-necked containers, you have to siphon a little off into a trial jar to test it. The wine maker's hydrometer (a) can also be used for beer. It is not so robust as the polystyrene hydrometer (b) which can be used for beer or, by adding a weight to the base, for wine.

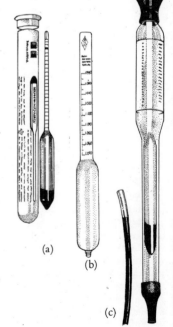

Hydrometer (c) can also be used for beer or wine. It lies inside a graduated glass tube with a squeeze bulb at one end and a nozzle at the other. You suck the sample directly into the tube for measuring.

# GLASSES

Most kitchen cupboards contain a collection of odd glasses–plain, robust and, frankly, cheap–which get pressed into use when recipes call for a measure of wine or brandy. They save better quality glassware from coming to grief among the chopping boards and mixing bowls and can be very useful in the kitchen.

When a glass is used as a measure, the quantity intended is usually the amount served as a drink (about $\frac{1}{2}$ to $\frac{2}{3}$ full), not a glass filled to the brim, but it does not really matter if you over or under fill it as the amount needed for any dish is rarely critical. Ordinary wine glasses vary considerably in size anyway, so use your discretion when measuring.

The floured rim of a wine glass makes a good cutter for dough (see DOUGHNUT CUTTER) and can also be used to cut pastry circles for tartlets and pies.

Wine glasses are sometimes used for hors d'oeuvres and desserts such as shrimp cocktails, custards or ice creams but this is not a good idea; there is always a risk of a glass breaking when you are eating anything more solid than a frothy zabaglione–which is the one dish that is appropriate in a wine glass.

The Paris goblet (a) and the tulip wine glass (b) are good shapes, as any type of wine can be served in them. The slight inward curve of the rim allows the bouquet of the wine to be savoured at its best. A 10 fl. oz. (28 cℓ) capacity glass is the most useful size. The flutes (c) and (d) are nowadays more generally used for champagne and sparkling wines than the once popular saucer-shaped glasses. With a flute less wine is exposed to the air, so the wine remains sparkling longer. The copita (e) is the traditional Spanish sherry glass and has a capacity of approximately 3·5 fl. oz. (10 cℓ). The elongated bowl funnels the concentrated bouquet of the wine upwards, allowing the drinker to savour it. A copita should be filled only half full.

Most liqueurs are spirit-based and strong in alcohol. The glasses (f) are therefore tiny and should be filled almost to the brim. They can also be used to serve neat spirits such as schnapps or vodka. An average glass holds 0·82 fl. oz. (2·3 cℓ). At the other extreme are the balloon-shaped goblets, (g), for brandy; some of which are made in very large sizes. Connoisseurs prefer slightly waisted glasses (h), which are easily warmed in the hand and hold the vapour from the spirit more effectively. A more elongated version of this shape, glass (i), is used for port.

Particular wine growing regions often have special glasses for the wines they produce. A typical regional glass is the shallow-bowled Anjou, (j), with its slightly sloping sides, in which Loire wines are served. Another is the Alsace glass, (k), reminiscent of a shallow Paris goblet in shape. This is common in Germany also, where the stems are tinted brown or green according to region. The stems are tall to keep white wine from being warmed by the hand.

The slightly flared, flat-based tumbler is traditional for whisky, (l), for it is large enough to accommodate ice, water or any mixer preferred.

# YOGHURT, ICE CREAM AND DRINK MAKERS

If too much of your shopping time and house-keeping money is spent on buying commercially made yoghurts, ice creams and soft drinks, it may be worth investing in special equipment for making such things at home. Apart from saving time and money you will be able to please yourself with the contents and flavourings, using natural ingredients instead of the synthetic ones so often found in bought products. The equipment is very simple to use.

(a) **Size.** D. 11½ in. (292 mm).
**Material.** Plastic and aluminium.
(b) **Size.** D. 8½ in. (215 mm).
**Material.** Plastic and aluminium.

## Ice cream makers

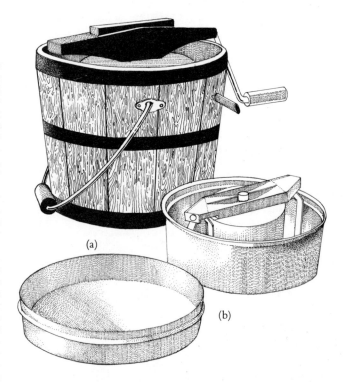

(a)

(b)

Perfect ice creams and sorbets consist largely of air; without it they resemble blocks of ice and are not nice to eat, no matter how luxurious the recipe. You can put the mixture to freeze and interrupt the process two, three or four times while you beat the ingredients in a bowl with a strong whisk, but this is not nearly as satisfactory as using an ice cream maker.

The manual ice cream maker (a) is more fun to operate than electric ones. The mixture is poured into a lidded container with a stationary paddle inside it. The container sits in the bucket, packed round with crushed ice and salt. (The salt lowers the temperature of the ice.) You turn the handle to spin the container round, pushing the mixture past the paddle as it freezes. The whole operation, which is usually willingly undertaken by greedy children, takes only twenty minutes and in that time makes at least 1 gallon (4·55 ℓ) of ice cream. The container is removed from the bucket, sealed with a cork and the ice cream left to ripen. This type of ice cream maker can be bought with an electric motor. Both models need about 6 lbs. (2·7 kg) of crushed ice and 1 lb. (450 g) of salt.

Electric ice cream makers small enough to fit in the freezing compartment of a refrigerator are usually called "sorbetières". They do not make a great deal of ice cream at a time. The one shown here, ice cream maker (b), takes just over 1½ pt. (900 mℓ) of mixture, which expands slightly when frozen. The ring-shaped, lidded container (useful for making ring-shaped ices) has the motor in the centre. The flat flex passes through the seal on the door of the refrigerator to the power point. Paddles set on the motor stir the mixture. They lift out automatically when the ice cream is stiff, but the motor goes on until it is turned off, getting slightly warm if you leave it too long. You lift it out, replace the lid on the container and leave the ice to firm up and "ripen" until it is needed. This model can also go in a freezer, but bear in mind that it works much faster in direct contact with the floor of the freezer than it does balanced on a pile of frozen food. The time taken to produce ice cream varies according to recipe, temperature, and position in the freezer. You can buy sorbetières with two compartments, so that different flavours can be made at once. These are slightly larger, as the motor is mounted outside.

**Size.** L. 10 in. (255 mm).
**Material.** Plastic case,
glass jars, electric heater.

Making yoghurt at home is very
easy using a plain commercial
yoghurt as a starter. You also
have the advantage of being able
to use creamy milk, or even cream
itself, if you like. It is perfectly
possible to make good yoghurt in
a vacuum jar, or a container inside
a well insulated storage tin, but
some special yoghurt makers will

## Yoghurt maker

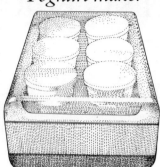

bring milk to the correct temperature and maintain it so that
the yoghurt is made quickly and
reliably.

This yoghurt maker produces
yoghurt in four hours. Some
models switch off automatically
when the yoghurt is ready, but
this has a disc to remind you when
you should switch off. Remember
to keep the contents of one jar to
start the next batch. You can get
extra jars so that more can be made
before the first batch is eaten.

(a) **Size.** H. $16\frac{1}{4}$ in. (412 mm).
    **Material.** Plastic.
(b) **Size.** H. $19\frac{1}{2}$ in. (490 mm).
    **Material.** Stainless steel cup,
    enamelled and stainless steel
    base.
(c) **Size.** H. $9\frac{3}{4}$ in. (248 mm).
    **Material.** Polished
    aluminium and plastic.

Given a fair amount of use drink
making machines will pay for
themselves in a relatively short
period of time. Drink maker (a)
makes all kinds of carbonated soft
drinks and mixers for alcoholic
drinks. It is powered by a carbon
dioxide cylinder and comes with a
supply of 8 fl. oz. (227 mℓ) bottles.
You fill these with water to the
marked line and insert each into
the machine in turn, pushing the
button to carbonate the water.
You then pour a measured amount
of flavouring into the bottles,
which can be capped and stored
until needed.

For children and sweet-toothed
adults the milk shake machine (b)
saves expensive trips to milk bars.
It is electric and consists of a mixing
spindle on to which you attach a
stainless steel mixing beaker of
$1\frac{1}{2}$ pt. (900 mℓ) capacity containing the required ingredients.
Once switched on it takes only a
few seconds to blend them into a
frothy mixture. The machine can
also be used for mixing cocktails.

The soda water syphon (c)
works on a slightly different
principle from drink maker (a).
The main flask is filled with water
and then the contents of a small
carbon dioxide cartridge fitted in
the cap are slowly pumped into it.
Flavouring concentrates can be
bought to make soft drinks with a

## Drink makers

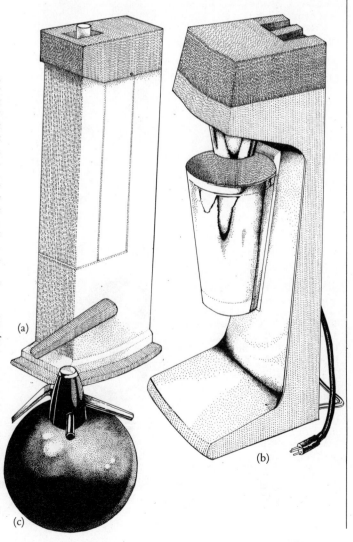

soda syphon but in this case the
flavour is poured into a glass, or
added to an alcoholic drink, and
then topped up with soda water.

(a)

(b)

(c)

# MEASURING EQUIPMENT

Measuring equipment is essential in any kitchen, since guesswork can cause culinary disasters. Volume measures are available both for dry ingredients and for liquids; some are dual-purpose. It is important to understand which measuring system your equipment and your recipe books relate to: British imperial, American, or metric. Many recipe books give conversion tables so that you can convert from one system to another. But measuring equipment is not expensive and it is worth buying enough tools to follow any of your recipe books without doing awkward conversions. Likewise, it's worth buying scales marked in both imperial and metric.

Audible timers are useful for those with unreliable memories. And, while many cooks get by without thermometers, they are useful for checking oven and freezer temperatures, and essential for jam and sweet making.

(a) **Size.** L. $5\frac{1}{2}$ to $6\frac{1}{2}$ in. (140 to 165 mm). **Material.** Plastic.

(b) **Size.** L. $3\frac{1}{2}$ to $4\frac{1}{4}$ in. (90 to 107 mm). **Material.** Stainless steel.

(c) **Size.** D. $2\frac{1}{4}$ to $3\frac{1}{4}$ in. (57 to 84 mm). **Material.** Stainless steel.

(d) **Size.** D. $2\frac{3}{4}$ to $3\frac{1}{4}$ in. (70 to 84 mm). **Material.** Aluminium.

(e) **Size.** L. $9\frac{1}{4}$ in. (235 mm). **Material.** Plastic.

## Spoons and cups

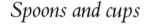
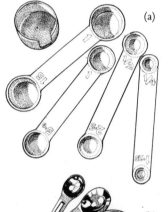
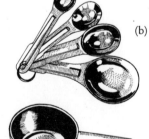

It is important with cup and spoon measures to know whether they relate to British or American sizes and which you need for any particular recipe. Check whether the recipe you are following specifies heaped or level spoons. If the latter, level off the ingredients with the back of a knife blade.

Spoons (a) are standard British spoons. This is a set of four double-ended plastic spoons measuring from $\frac{1}{4}$ teaspoon to 1 tablespoon (3 teaspoons) at one end and from $1 \cdot 25$ ml to 15 ml at the other. There is a holder for all the spoons which you fix to the wall—the spoons fit inside one another in order of size like Russian dolls and the largest spoon fits neatly inside the holder.

Spoons (b) are standard American spoons. There are four spoons measuring from $\frac{1}{4}$ teaspoon to 1 tablespoon. They have holes in their handles and are all attached to a ring by which to hang them. These are stainless steel but you can also get plastic ones as well as beautiful China spoons.

The four stainless steel cups (c) are standard American sizes, holding $\frac{1}{4}, \frac{1}{3}, \frac{1}{2}$ and 1 cup.

The four aluminium cups (d) are standard British sizes and hold $\frac{1}{4}, \frac{1}{3}, \frac{1}{2}$ and 1 cup. Each one fits neatly inside the next in size. They have holes in their handles so that you can tie them together and hang them up.

The American slide measure (e) is a handy tool with both spoon and cup measures for dry ingredients. The large scoop section measures from $\frac{1}{4}$ teaspoon to $\frac{1}{2}$ cup, and the handle section measures from $\frac{1}{4}$ teaspoon to 1 tablespoon. The measures are marked along the edge like a ruler. There is a sliding barrier—rather like a dam—which you set in the scoop or handle section for the required quantity. You then fill the appropriate section with the ingredient to be measured and level it off with the back of a knife. The only problem with this all-in-one measure is that you have to wash up between measuring sticky ingredients. Also, its capacity is rather small. This tool is fun to use but rather gimmicky. Where (rough) measures in spoonfuls are required, it is much easier to use the measuring tools found in your cutlery drawer.

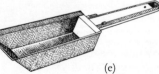

(a) **Size.** H. 5¾ in. (146 mm).
   **Material.** Glass.

(b) **Size.** H. 5¼ in. (133 mm).
   **Material.** Polypropylene.

(c) **Size.** H. 6 in. (152 mm).
   **Material.** Aluminium
   container, plastic base.

These measures are versatile and easy to use. Where the order of ingredients in a recipe is of no importance, you can dispense with scales and use the same container for measuring all your ingredients, provided you deal with the dry ones before the liquids. Measuring dry goods by volume is not as accurate as measuring them by weight, but it is a quick and easy method, accurate enough for most recipes. To obtain a correct reading you have to shake the container slightly to level the contents.

Measure (a) is a toughened glass beaker which will withstand boiling water and washing in a dishwasher. It has clear markings in grammes for flour, potato flour, cocoa, rice, tapioca, sugar and

## Liquid and dry measures

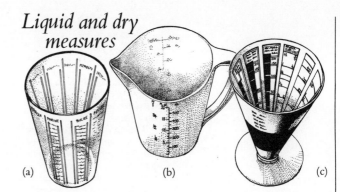

(a)    (b)    (c)

semolina, as well as for liquids.

Measure (b) is made of polypropylene – resistant to boiling water, light and unbreakable. It is slightly less easy to read than other similar beakers because the measures are marked in relief rather than in ink. It is marked in ounces for sugar and flour, and for liquids up to 1 pt., 20 fl. oz. and 500 ml.

Although it is small, the aluminium beaker (c) is one of the best measures available. It has calibra-

tions for an enormous variety of dry ingredients, including pulses, dried fruit, tapioca, rice, semolina, rolled oats, breadcrumbs, desiccated coconut, cornflour, cocoa, ground almonds, shredded suet, sugar and rice. It has liquid measures in British cups, pints and gills in millilitres, and in American cups and pints. There are a few metric and imperial equivalents on the outside of the measure which might serve as a useful reference.

(a) **Size.** H. 4¾ in. (120 mm).
   **Material.** Pyrex.

(b) **Size.** H. 5¾ in. (146 mm).
   **Material.** Polypropylene.

(c) **Size.** H. 6 in. (152 mm).
   **Material.** Plastic.

These three jugs are for measuring liquids. They are all marked in imperial and metric.

Jug (a) is made of Pyrex and will withstand boiling water and washing in a dishwasher. You can also put it in a bain marie or in a pre-heating oven. It has clear markings up to 1 pt., 18 fl. oz. and 500 ml.

Similar measuring jugs are available in plastic which is not so strong, and in stainless steel with markings inside the jug which are not so easy to read.

Jug (b) is made of polypropylene which is designed to withstand boiling water. It will bounce when dropped and is much lighter than Pyrex which is a particularly important consideration with such a large jug as this one. It is slightly opaque, which means it is not quite so easy to see the level of liquid inside the jug. It is marked up to 3½ pt., 70 fl. oz. and 2 ℓ.

## Liquid measuring jugs

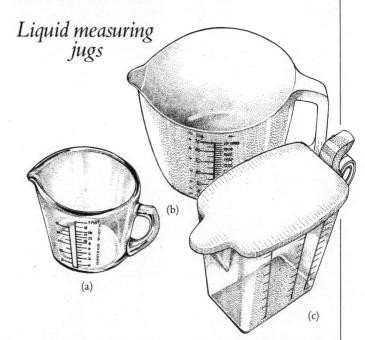

(b)

(a)

(c)

Jug (c) is made of clear blue plastic with blue markings which are perhaps less clear to read than those on the other two. It is also less resilient than jugs (a) and (b). It has a well-fitting lid, which opens and closes easily by a lever

at the handle. The lid is particularly useful if you want to store a measured quantity of liquid in the refrigerator for any length of time. It is marked up to 2 pt., 40 fl. oz., 1 ℓ, 10 dℓ, and 1000 ml.

# Scales

(a) **Size.** L. 12¾ in. (324 mm). **Material.** Enamelled cast iron base, aluminium pan, cast iron and brass weights.

(b) **Size.** H. 7 in. (178 mm). **Material.** Enamelled cast iron base, brass pan.

(c) **Size.** H. 8 in. (204 mm). **Material.** Steel base, aluminium face, plastic bowls and support.

(d) **Size.** H. 8¼ in. (210 mm). **Material.** Plastic.

(e) **Size.** H. 7½ in. (190 mm). **Material.** Plastic.

(f) **Size.** L. 12 in. (305 mm). **Material.** Enamelled steel base, plastic tray.

Measuring by weight is much more accurate than measuring by volume. The scales you choose will depend on how accurate you need them to be and what capacity you require.

Scales divide into two types: balance scales and spring balance scales. The dial of a spring scale is marked in both imperial and metric, but in order for a balance scale to be used for both systems you will need to have two sets of weights.

The balance scales (a) have a pan on the one side for the ingredients to be weighed and a platform for weights on the other. The ingredients weigh the same as the weights when the two sides balance—hence the name of this type of scale. They are accurate and easy to use and have a stream-lined base which is easy to wipe clean. If you are weighing a quantity of something which threatens to overflow the pan, put it into a plastic bag and put this on the pan.

Weights, either imperial or metric, are bought separately. The larger weights are made of cast iron, and the smaller ones of brass. The imperial weights weigh from ¼ oz. to 2 lb. and the metric ones from 5 g to 1 kg. A set of each will enable you to follow recipes in either measuring system without any problems of conversion.

The main problem with this type of scale is that it takes up a fair amount of room. It is also quite heavy and unwieldy, so it is best kept on a work surface rather than hauled in and out of a cupboard each time you use it. As long as you have room for it, this shouldn't be any great disadvantage since a balance scale is as attractive as it is efficient.

Spring balance scales (b), (c), (d) and (e) are all very easy to use. You simply place the item to be weighed in the pan and read the weight on the calibrated face. Most are dual marked in imperial and metric. The dial registers according to the degree to which the spring is depressed. The problem with this type of scale is that it tends not to be very accurate. The needle frequently needs re-setting to zero and may eventually cease to give correct readings. So although these scales are relatively inexpensive to buy, their life expectancy is considerably less than that of the balance scale (a).

Spring balance scale (b) has a pleasingly old-fashioned appearance. It weighs only in kilos and has a capacity of 10 kg.

Scale (c) is a pretty and unusual little version of the spring balance scale, but it has a small capacity—2 lb. or 1 kg. A plastic clip holds the indicator needle in place when not in use to prevent damage. It has two bowls which also act as volume measures—they measure up to 300 g of flour, 350 g of sugar, semolina and potato flour, and 0·5 ℓ of liquid.

Scale (d) has a neat and compact design. It has a choice of two trays, or you can use a plate or bowl if you prefer, remembering to adjust the dial to zero before you start. You can weigh successive ingredients without emptying the tray by bringing the dial back to zero or to the nearest even division. The magnified dial on the front shows measurements in imperial and metric. The measurements go up to 9 lb. or 4 kg. The smaller plastic tray fits inside the bigger one, and they invert over the machine when not in use to act as a tidy dust cover. In this position, the machine measures only 5 in. (127 mm) high, so it can easily be kept out of the way in a cupboard.

The jug scale (e) combines a kitchen scale with a liquid measuring jug. The scale is marked in imperial and metric up to 5 lb. and 2·2 kg. The smoked plastic jug is calibrated up to 2 pt. and 1 ℓ and inverts over the scale as a dust cover when not in use.

The beam scale (f) is as accurate and as reliable as the balance scale (a) but not nearly so easy to use. Along the front of the base there is a double row of calibrations—the top one in pounds and the bottom one in ounces. Each row has a slide. You move the upper slide to the correct number of pounds, and the lower slide to the ounce indicator which causes the scale to balance. There is a knob on the right-hand side to lock the scale when not in use, and another knob on the left-hand side to adjust it. It weighs up to 22 lb. 4 oz. A beam scale can be rather fiddly for small quantities but is excellent for weighing large joints of meat or large quantities of garden produce to the exact ounce. You can also get metric versions, and there are baby weighing attachments available. If you do buy a beam scale, it would be a good idea to have another, smaller scale for when you want to weigh small quantities.

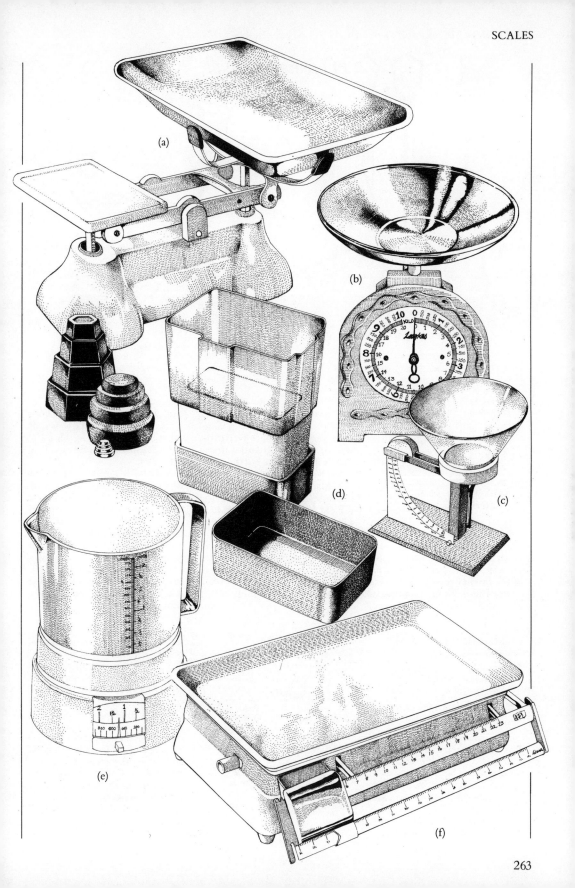

(a)

(b)

(c)

(d)

(e)

(f)

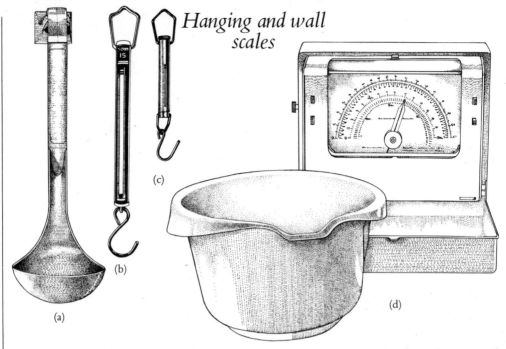

## Hanging and wall scales

(c)

(b)

(a)

(d)

(a) **Size.** H. 12 in. (305 mm).
**Material.** Plastic.

(b) **Size.** H. 10½ in. (267 mm).
**Material.** Aluminium.

(c) **Size.** H. 6¼ in. (160 mm).
**Material.** Brass.

(d) **Size.** H. 10½ in. (267 mm)
with weighing pan.
**Material.** Plastic.

Where countertop space is limited, it is useful to have a scale which hangs on the wall within easy reach of your work surface. All the scales shown here are versions of the spring balance.

The ladle scale (a) has imperial and metric calibrations up to 7 oz.

and 200 g. It is really useful only for measuring small quantities. The ladle can be hand held or hung from a holder which is fixed to the wall. It is heat-resistant, so it can also be used to serve hot food, and it can be washed in a dishwasher.

For large items which won't fit into a scale pan, pocket balances (b) and (c) are useful. These have a hook at the top to hang them up and a hook at the bottom on which to hang the item to be weighed. If you are weighing a chicken this is quite straightforward; other things may need to be put in a bag before weighing.

Pocket balance (b) is marked in

imperial and metric up to 4 lb. and 2 kg. The brass pocket balance (c) is tiny but will take a weight of up to 20 lb. (9·06 kg). It is the sort of scale that is often used by fishermen.

Scale (d) is a sophisticated wall version of the spring balance scale and folds up when not in use. It weighs in imperial and metric, up to 6 lb. 12 oz. and 3 kg. It has a taring (zeroing) device for weighing successive ingredients and can be used either with the weighing pan or with a special mixing bowl, both of which are suspended underneath the scale and are easily fitted and removed.

(a) **Size.** D. 2½ in. (65 mm).
**Material.** Plastic.

(b) **Size.** D. 3 in. (75 mm).
**Material.** Metal body,
plastic casing.

(c) **Size.** H. 3¼ in. (84 mm).
**Material.** Plastic.

If you have an unreliable memory, you could use a kitchen timer with an alarm bell; it can be set to go off when it is time to take something off the cooker or out of the oven.

Timer (a) is a compact little device which sits flat and can be

## Timers

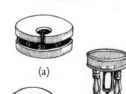

(a)

(b)

(c)

set to register up to one hour in one-minute intervals.

Timer (b) looks like a conventional alarm clock and can be set to ring after any time from one minute to five hours. You can also get a one-hour version.

The egg timer (c) will ensure that you have perfect three-minute eggs. It is made of plastic and works like a miniature hourglass. However, if you like eggs boiled for a little longer, cook them while listening to the overture to the *Marriage of Figaro*; it lasts exactly four and a half minutes.

## Roasting temperatures and times

| Meat | | °F | °C | Gas | Time |
|---|---|---|---|---|---|
| **Beef** | top quality | 425 | 218 | 7 | 15–20 min. per lb. (450 g) plus 15–20 min. |
| | medium quality | 375 | 191 | 3 | 25 min. per lb. (450 g) or 30 min. if boned. |
| | cheap quality | 325–350 | 163–177 | 3–4 | 40 min. per lb. (450 g). |
| **Bacon** | | 350 | 177 | 4 | 20 min. per lb. (450 g) plus 20 min. 15 min. before completion of cooking time, raise temperature to 425°F (218°C, gas 7). |
| **Chicken** | | 375 | 191 | 5 | 20 min. per lb. (450 g) plus 20 min. |
| **Duck** | | 325 | 163 | 3 | 30 min. per lb. (450 g). Start cooking at 375°F (191°C, gas 5) for first 30 min. |
| **Game** | | 400 | 204 | 6 | Young birds take 30–40 min., older birds 40–60 min. Start cooking at 450°F (232°C, gas 8) for first 10 min. Very old birds are better casseroled. |
| **Goose** | | 400 | 204 | 6 | 15 min. per lb. (450 g) plus 15 min. |
| **Lamb** | | 350 | 177 | 4 | 25 min. per lb. (450 g) plus 30 min. |
| **Pork** | | 375 | 191 | 5 | 30 min. per lb. (450 g) plus 30 min. |
| **Turkey** 12 to 14 lb. (5·4 to 6·4 kg) | quick method | 450 | 232 | 8 | 3 hr. Cover completely with kitchen foil. |
| | slow method | 325 | 163 | 3 | 4 hr. 15 min. Protect legs with kitchen foil and cover breast with bacon. |
| **Veal** | | 425 | 218 | 7 | 25 min. per lb. (450 g) plus 25 min. |
| **Venison** | | 375 | 191 | 5 | 30 min. per lb. (450 g) plus 30 min. Start cooking at 450°F (232°C, gas 8) for first 10 min. |

## How much meat to buy per person

**BEEF**
Brisket, chuck or blade steak, flank, leg and shin, rib, silverside, sirloin and topside (boneless):
6 to 8 oz. (170 to 225 g).
Brisket, rib and sirloin (on bone):
8 to 12 oz. (225 to 340 g).
Aitch-bone: 12 oz. (350 g).

**VEAL**
Best end of neck, breast, fillet, knuckle and shoulder (boneless):
4 to 6 oz. (115 to 170 g).
Leg and loin (on bone):
8 to 12 oz. (225 to 340 g).
Best end of neck, breast, knuckle and shoulder (on bone):
1 lb. (450 g).
Chops: 1. Cutlets: 1 or 2.

**LAMB**
Loin (boneless):
4 to 6 oz. (115 to 170 g).
Best end of neck, leg, loin and shoulder (on bone):
12 oz. (340 g).
Breast, middle and scrag end (on bone):
8 to 12 oz. (225 to 340 g).
Chops and cutlets: 1 or 2.

**PORK**
Belly, fillet, leg and loin (boneless):
4 to 6 oz. (115 to 170 g).
Blade, fillet, leg, loin and spare rib (on bone):
8 to 12 oz. (225 to 340 g).
Hand and spring: 12 oz. (340 g).
Chops: 1. Cutlets: 1 or 2.

**OFFAL**
**Liver**
ox, calf's, lamb's, pig's:
4 oz. (115 g).
**Kidney**
ox: 4 oz. (115 g).
calf's: $\frac{1}{2}$ to 1, lamb's: 2.
pig's and sheep's: 1 or 2.
**Heart**
ox: $\frac{1}{4}$, calf's: $\frac{1}{2}$, lamb's: 1.
**Sweetbreads**
ox, calf's, lamb's: 4 oz. (115 g).
**Oxtail:** $\frac{1}{4}$.
**Tripe:**
4 to 6 oz. (115 to 170 g).
**Tongue:** 4 oz. (115 g).
**Brains:** 1 "set".

## Oven thermometer

**Size.** L. 5¼ in. (133 mm).
**Material.** Glass mercury thermometer, stainless steel surround.

Even the most expensive oven may have a slightly inaccurate thermostat. If, in spite of the readings on the dial, your cakes or roasts are always either raw in the middle or burnt to a frazzle, your thermostat needs attention. If it cannot be improved, you should buy an oven thermometer which enables you to check the temperature in different parts of your oven and to correlate it with that set by the oven thermostat. Make sure you buy a thermometer with markings which correspond to the temperatures on your cooker.

This is the most accurate type of oven thermometer. It has divisions which relate to slow, moderate, hot and very hot oven temperatures. The thermometer can be stood on or hung from an oven rack.

## Meat thermometer

**Size.** L. 4½ in. (115 mm).
**Material.** Stainless steel body, glass dial.

If you lack the confidence or experience to know when a roast is done by a combination of timing, temperature and pressing it with your fingers, you may want to use a roasting thermometer. By piercing the meat with a roasting thermometer towards the end of the cooking time, you can check the temperature of the inside of the joint. Choose a thermometer with a thin probe so that it doesn't make large holes in the meat and let out juices and heat. Don't poke it in too often or leave it in the meat throughout the cooking time. Insert the spike so that its tip is as near the centre of the meat as possible. The roast is ready when the pointer on the dial reaches the appropriate wording. After use, the thermometer should be wiped clean, and not immersed in water. It has markings for well done, medium and rare meat.

## Freezer thermometer

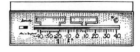

**Size.** L. 5¼ in. (133 mm).
**Material.** Glass spirit thermometer, plastic surround.

A freezer thermometer indicates whether your refrigerator or freezer is operating at the correct temperature. This is important for the prevention of bacteria growth and for the efficient processing of fresh food when it is first frozen.

This thermometer can be hung or stood in the freezer or refrigerator. It should be moved around from time to time to show up any dangerous hot spots. The blue plastic surround is marked from −40 to + 40°C and indicates safe freezer and refrigerator temperatures, and British Standard star ratings for storing frozen products.

## Multi-purpose thermometer

**Size.** L. 6¾ in. (172 mm) with case.
**Material.** Glass spirit thermometer, plastic top and case, steel clip.

This thermometer is marked from 0 to 100°C and from 40 to 220°F. It can be used for any job in the home – not necessarily the kitchen – that does not necessitate checking temperatures below freezing or above boiling point. You can also use it for checking the temperature in your kitchen or airing cupboard, when making yoghurt or raising dough, for example. Special yoghurt thermometers are also available.

## Deep-frying thermometer

**Size.** L. 12 in. (305 mm).
**Material.** Glass mercury thermometer, stainless steel surround, plastic handle.

This thermometer is marked from 100 to 500°F. It has an adjustable hook at the back to hold it to the side of the pan, and the plastic handle at the top enables you to touch the thermometer without burning yourself. Clip the thermometer into place in the cool oil and watch the indicator climb to the desired temperature as the fat heats up. Avoid overshooting the mark, as this could spoil the oil. The temperature will drop when you put the food in and then rise slowly again.

## Dairy thermometer

**Size.** L. 11½ in. (280 mm).
**Material.** Glass alcohol thermometer, plastic case.

This thermometer is used for checking the temperature of milk when making yoghurt or cheese. It is marked from 10 to 230°F.

# Candy thermometer

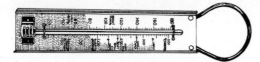

**Size.** L. 10½ in. (267 mm).
**Material.** Glass spirit thermometer, brass surround, copper hook.

This thermometer is designed for sweet or candy making and is marked from 20 to 180°C and from 100 to 350°F. It also has markings which indicate the various stages of boiling up water and sugar, and the right temperatures for jam and yoghurt. Try to get a reading from the hottest area of the pan – that is the centre.

Never plunge a thermometer directly into a pan of hot liquid. Always stand it in a jug of warm water first or put it in the pan before the heating process begins. After use, allow it to cool on a dry surface before washing it.

## Temperature guide

| Oven temperatures | °F | °C | Gas |
|---|---|---|---|
| very cool | 250–275 | 121–135 | ¼–½ |
| cool | 300 | 149 | 1–2 |
| warm | 325 | 163 | 3 |
| moderate | 350 | 177 | 4 |
| fairly hot | 375–400 | 191–204 | 5–6 |
| hot | 425 | 218 | 7 |
| very hot | 450–475 | 232–246 | 8–9 |

| Oil and fat temperatures for deep frying | °F | °C | Time taken to brown a small cube of bread |
|---|---|---|---|
| Fritters, doughnuts, onion rings, fresh fish .... | 350–360 | 177–182 | 60 seconds |
| Croquettes, rissoles pre-cooked meatballs, other cooked food ....... | 360–380 | 182–193 | 40 seconds |
| French fries, cheese straws, home-made crisps ................ | 370–390 | 188–199 | 20 seconds |

| Water temperatures | °F | °C |
|---|---|---|
| Freezing point | 32 | 0 |
| Blood heat (lukewarm) | 98 | 37 |
| Simmering | 205 | 96 |
| Boiling | 212 | 100 |

| Sugar boiling for sweet (candy) making | °F | °C |
|---|---|---|
| Smooth | 215–220 | 102–104 |
| Soft ball | 235–245 | 113–118 |
| Firm or hard ball | 245–265 | 118–130 |
| Soft crack | 270–290 | 132–143 |
| Hard crack | 300–310 | 149–154 |
| Caramel | 310 | 154 |

# Salometer and hydrometer

(a)                    (b)

(a) **Size.** L. 11½ in. (292 mm).
  **Material.** Glass.

(b) **Size.** L. 6¾ in. (172 mm).
  **Material.** Glass hydrometer, tinned steel testing jar.

Relying on your taste buds to gauge the density of salt brine would be both unpleasant and inaccurate. Salometer (a) consists of a weighted glass tube with markings from 0 to 100. You read the density according to how far the tube sinks into the brine. The more salt there is, the higher the salometer will float. The 100 mark represents a saturated solution – one holding all the dissolved salt it can take.

A quick guide used by some cooks is to put an egg or raw potato into salt brine: if it floats, the solution is sufficiently salty.

The hydrometer (b), or pèse syrop, measures the density of sugar syrup. This is important when making jelly, jam or ice cream, or when bottling fruit.

It works like a salometer, by registering the point to which the weighted tube sinks. The more sugar, the higher the hydrometer will float. The tube is marked from 0 to 40, according to the Baumé scale.

There are also special hydrometers for making wine and beer (see WINE MAKING AND BREWING EQUIPMENT).

# STORAGE

Kitchen storage should be accessible. There's no point in possessing a magnificent batterie de cuisine if you have to climb up steps or rummage at ankle-height in cupboards every time you want a sieve or wire whisk.

For efficiency the first rule of kitchen storage is to keep things near where you need them – but not cluttering the work surfaces.

Rule two is to plan the best place for everything. You should keep heavy items, for example, where you can lift or reach them without injuring yourself. Avoid balancing big things precariously on top of smaller ones.

Rule three is to estimate how often you use things and store them accordingly. No one minds climbing up a step-stool to reach the carving dish for the Christmas or Thanksgiving turkey, but it's silly to keep often-used saucepans on top of cupboards.

*Hard cash – or ingenuity*
If you're planning a kitchen from scratch it's sensible to spend money on good storage, and budget for it as a major item. If you are improving a kitchen you might find that ingenuity is more valuable than cash.

Modern kitchen units, even the cheaper ones, come fitted with useful storage aids. So with a whole kitchen layout to plan it's certainly worth looking around to find the range whose extras most suit your needs. You can get cupboards with pull-out, cantilevered racks for storing large electric mixers and supporting them in use and others that have pull-out wire baskets for storing vegetables. There are units to fill wasted corner space. They come fitted with large circular racks which swing right round and are used for storing cans, packets, or cleaning materials. Several manufacturers make tables that fold away into kitchen units; these not only increase the work surface available, but also provide a place where two people can eat quite comfortably.

Consider storage when choosing kitchen equipment too. Sets of saucepans, bakeware or crockery that stack or nest together save space – as do pans or implements with handles that allow them to be hung up.

Drawers can be used for more than clean tea towels, small implements and cutlery – you can put such things as saucepans lids and spice jars in them too. Some manufacturers make specially wide, deep drawers under hob units to store saucepans and frying pans. Ceiling or wall storage on wrought-iron racks hung with butcher's hooks is another way to keep pots and pans and small tools.

Faced with improving an existing kitchen, there are many inexpensive modifications you can make. You can increase shelf space in wall units by adding another shelf above the central one to allow you to store two rows of small things. You can fit a set of pull-out wire baskets stacked one above the other between shelves or fix a basket on the back of a cupboard door. Load it with fairly light articles – such as saucepan lids – so that the hinges are not strained.

Shelves are perhaps the simplest storage system of all but have the disadvantage that they get dirty more quickly than cupboards or drawers and are harder to keep looking neat. While a stack of cake tins is perfectly acceptable on a cupboard shelf, it doesn't look quite the same in open view. One way to get the advantages of shelf storage – easy access and the ability to see everything at a glance – is to fit roller blinds to the top shelf and pull them down when you've finished work for the day and want the kitchen to look tidy.

You can partition drawers with strips of plywood dropped between pieces of quadrant beading, to make it easier to separate wooden spoons from whisks, from skewers . . . and the same partitioning, done vertically, in a cupboard, will neatly pigeon-hole baking sheets, cooking racks, cake tins and trays. Non-stick bakeware should be stored in separate polythene bags to protect the surface.

Make the most of a small space by buying matching hooks and fitting them neatly in groups to hang such things as measuring spoons, mugs and kitchen scissors. Adhesive hooks are only satisfactory for light things of about 2 oz. (50 g) weight and should be stuck on surfaces of a recommended type. Otherwise you must use hooks that screw into the wall, with plugs, or hooks mounted on peg board.

*Chests and uprights*
Chest freezers open at the top and are slightly cheaper to run than uprights as less heat is lost from an open lid than through an open door. They are good for holding large, awkwardly shaped joints of meat or fancy cakes, but are

difficult to stack efficiently and it can be hard to get small packets out from the bottom. It is also difficult to keep things in any sort of order in chest freezers, unless each type of food is stored in a separate basket.

Upright freezers usually come fitted with shelves and pull-out baskets and are much easier to reach into, stack and sort through. They also save floor space, as do combined refrigerator-freezers, but cannot hold as much as the largest chest freezers. Whatever type you choose they are only economical and efficient if they are kept full.

The type of freezer you need depends on such factors as the size of your family; how much you entertain; whether you freeze home-grown produce or live a long way from good food shops; whether you intend buying carcass meat in bulk and feezing your own cooked meals, or prefer filling up with packaged convenience foods—and, more mundanely—on how much space you have.

*Defrosting*
Freezers require very little maintenance apart from regular defrosting. This usually needs to be done about once or twice a year—perhaps more often if you open and close your freezer frequently. It is a fairly simple operation and manufacturers usually provide comprehensive instructions. Pick a time when stocks are low and can be put temporarily in a refrigerator or be wrapped in newspaper or old towels.

*Larders and food cupboards*
A larder is unfortunately no longer a standard requirement in new houses and most people today do not have one and so have to store food either in a refrigerator or in kitchen cupboards. This is a pity since a larder is a convenient halfway stage between the two.

If you have space for a larder make sure that it is dry and well ventilated at a temperature of around 50°F (10°C). You should cover any windows that open with perforated zinc to keep flies out. Build as many shelves as possible, allowing sufficient space for storing large things on some of them. Old-fashioned larders usually have one slate or marble shelf on which perishable foods can be placed to keep cool and this idea is worth incorporating in a modern larder. Other shelves may be tiled to help keep food cool and to make cleaning easy. It is also a good place to bring refrigerated foods up to room temperature.

Ideally a kitchen cupboard where cans and packets are stored should be just as cool, dry and well ventilated as a larder.

Keeping times vary for different foods and you should make sure that things get used up in rotation and those which were bought first don't get pushed to the back of the cupboard.

Goods sold in packets can safely be kept in them until opened and should then be transferred to an airtight container. It is best not to buy cans with dents or rust marks, as the contents could be damaged.

*Vegetable storage*
Vegetables are best kept in a cool, dark, fairly dry place if they are to remain as fresh as possible. The floor of the larder (if you have one) can be stacked with baskets for the storage of root vegetables; leave the lower shelves free for greens or salads. Onions keep well in nets, or plaited into ropes which can hang on the walls of a cool shed or outhouse. If you have no larder, keep vegetables in the coolest, darkest part of the kitchen or, as long as they are protected from frost and mice, out of doors on a shady porch or balcony. Salads keep excellently in a refrigerator as long as they are wrapped in plastic to prevent them from drying out, but no green or salad vegetable improves with keeping, so try to buy them (or fetch them from the garden) as near to the time when you want them as possible.

The same observations apply to fruit. Apples and pears are the easiest to store for any length of time. All others should be eaten as near to the time they were picked as possible; soft fruits deteriorate particularly fast.

*Refrigerators*
Refrigerators vary in size and differ in design, from table-top, wall-mounted and free-standing models to those that can be built into kitchen units. Some have frozen food compartments in which commercially frozen food can be stored. Larder refrigerators have none and provide more space within the refrigerator body. They are designed for people who already own a freezer and do not need a refrigerator with storage space for frozen food.

Always make sure when buying a refrigerator that it suits your purposes. If you want to chill wine, see that the bottle rack will hold tall bottles; decide if you really want to keep eggs in your refrigerator, an egg rack in the door could be wasted space if not; if the shelves are close together, see if there is a "gate" shelf which lifts up to allow you to place large joints of meat on the shelf below; check whether the dairy compartment in the door is sufficiently large; see also that the space set aside for milk will easily hold your daily supply.

*Efficient running*

A refrigerator must be sited in a cool, dry place where air can circulate around it. Never place one near a cooker or other heat source as this makes it less economical of fuel. Any build-up of frost and ice makes it work less efficiently.

Always cool cooked food before placing it in a refrigerator and make sure that everything is wrapped or covered so that it does not dry out and there is no chance of smells or flavours cross-transferring. The temperature inside a refrigerator varies. The coldest part is at the top near the frozen food compartment, while the crisper at the bottom and the compartments in the door are the least cool spots. Keep raw meat, poultry and fish in the coldest place; cooked dishes and cheese on the middle shelves; salads and vegetables in the crisper in the bottom; milk in the door—if a shelf is provided—and butter and other fats in the dairy compartment.

## Frozen foods storage times

**Meat**
Beef.....................1y.
Lamb, pork, mince, offal....6m.
Sausages, bacon
  (smoked,unsmoked)......3m.
Poultry ..................1y.
Game....................6m.

**Fish**
White fish...............6m.
Oily and smoked fish ......2m.
Shellfish................1m.

**Vegetables**
Onions and peppers........6m.
All other types............1y.

**Fruit**
In sugar syrup............1y.
In dry sugar .............6m.

**Dairy Produce**
Butter ...................6m.
Cheese...................6m.
Cream...................3m.
Eggs (separated or beaten)...6m.

**Baked goods**
Bread...................1m.
Cakes (uncooked) ........2m.
Cakes (cooked)...........4m.

## Refrigerator storage times

| Stars | Temperature | Storage time |
|---|---|---|
| * | 21°F (− 6°C) | 1 week (ice cream for 1 day) |
| ** | 10°F (−12°C) | 1 month (ice cream for up to 1 week) |
| *** | 0°F  (−18°C) | 3 months (ice cream for up to 1 month) |

Fresh fruit and poultry.....2–3d.
Fresh fish ...............1d.
Fresh milk ..............2–4d.
Butter...................2–4w.
Cheese .................1–2w.
Salad vegetables..........3d.
Other fresh vegetables .....3–7d.

## Storage times for cans and packets

Canned fish in oil; canned meat
  (not ham)................5y.
Canned fish in tomato sauce .....1y.
Canned ham; if over 2lb. (1kg.)
  store in refrigerator........6m.
Canned vegetables.............2y.
Canned fruit .................1y.
Fruit juice (canned)...........1y.
Fruit juice (bottled) ..........3m.
Baby foods (canned and bottled).1½y.
Milk (evaporated)..........6–8m.
Milk (condensed) ..........4–6m.
Milk (powder)..............2–3m.
Dehydrated foods..........1y.
Dried fruit ...............2–3m.
Shelled nuts (including coconut).1m.
Gelatine...................1y.

Suet (unopened)...............1½y.
Suet (opened)..................2m.
Cornflour ...................1y.
Flour (plain).................6m.
Flour (self raising)..........2–3m.
Flour (wholemeal)............2m.
Baking powder .............2–3m.
Bicarbonate of soda .........2–3m.
Dried yeast .................6m.
Breakfast cereals (unopened) ....3m.
Breakfast cereals (opened).......3w.
Whole grains ...............2–3m.
Rolled oats, oatmeal ........2–3m.
Pulses .....................1y.
Pasta ......................1y.
Rice ......................1y.
Sugar (icing, brown) ..........1m.

Sugar (all other types)..........1y.
Syrup .....................1y.
Treacle ....................1y.
Jam .......................1y.
Jellies .....................1y.
Oils .......................1y.
Vinegar....................2y.
Ketchups ..................1y.
Herbs and spices ...........6m.
Tea........................1m.
Coffee (instant and ground,
  sealed).................1y.
Coffee beans (in airtight
  container)................6m.
Coffee beans, ground (in
  airtight container).........2w.
Cocoa .....................4m.

(a) **Size.** H. 6 in. (152 mm).
**Material.** Glass.

(b) **Size.** H. 9 in. (230 mm).
**Material.** Glass.

(c) **Size.** H. $14\frac{1}{2}$ in. (368 mm).
**Material.** Glass, cork stopper.

(d) **Size.** H. $4\frac{3}{4}$ in. (120 mm).
**Material.** Stoneware, cork stopper.

(e) **Size.** H. $7\frac{1}{2}$ in. (190 mm).
**Material.** Salt-glazed earthenware.

(f) **Size.** H. $3\frac{3}{4}$ in. (95 mm).
**Material.** Glass.

(g) **Size.** H. $4\frac{1}{4}$ in. (107 mm).
**Material.** Glass, wire clip, rubber seal.

(h) **Size.** H. $2\frac{1}{2}$ in. (65 mm).
**Material.** Glass, alloy steel lid and seal, rubber washer.

(i) **Size.** H. $12\frac{3}{4}$ in. (324 mm).
**Material.** Glass, wire clip, rubber seal, porcelain stopper.

Containers for such things as pulses, pasta, grains and herbs should be useful in the following ways: they should be easy to get hold of with one hand; their size and shape should be appropriate to their contents; they should be easy to keep clean; and they should be airtight. Some plastic and wooden containers retain smells and should not be used for pungent foods or spices. The glass storage jars (a) and (b) have ground-glass stoppers. They look pretty, but are not airtight, although some types are provided with plastic seals to make them so. They can be used for storing tea, coffee, herbs and spices, but remember that these commodities deteriorate in strong light. The cork-stoppered pasta jar (c) is not

## Storage containers

tall enough to hold the longest spaghetti, but looks pretty filled with other types of pasta.

Many people re-cycle such things as instant coffee jars or honey jars as containers for their kitchen shelves; the stoneware mustard jar (d) with its cork bung is a particularly pleasant shape. The $3\frac{1}{2}$ pt. (2 ℓ) capacity jar (e) with its straight sides and wide neck is easy to reach into and fill, but is not airtight. Herbs and spices are best bought in small quantities as they quickly lose

their taste and aroma. They should be kept in small airtight jars, like (f), which do not let in the light. Whole spices (nutmegs, peppercorns, cloves) can be kept loose in little drawers or boxes.

The preserving jar (g) has a wire clip and rubber seal which make it completely airtight. The smaller jar (h) has an inner sealing disc over which the metal lid is screwed during the bottling process. The freezer has superseded traditional bottling and preserving in many households but these jars – even if they are no longer used for preserving – make ideal airtight storage containers. The smaller jar is a handy size for small items (glacé cherries, angelica) using the screw-top lid without the inner seal. The cruchon (i) is similar to a preserving jar with a wire clip. It has a rubber seal on its porcelain stopper to make it completely airtight. It is used for storing home-made squashes.

## Salt crock

**Size.** H. 8 in. (204 mm).
**Material.** Glazed earthenware.

Salt needs to be always to hand but has to be kept dry. The traditional salt crock, although open to the air, keeps salt in good condition and is easy to reach into to take a handful or a pinch as required. Alternatively, a wooden salt box can be hung on a wall to save space on the worktop.

## Bread crock

**Size.** H. 13½ in. (343 mm).
**Material.** Terracotta.

Containers for storing bread must not be airtight as this would quickly make the bread go mouldy. They should be well ventilated and dry to keep the bread soft, but with a crisp crust.

Many types of metal container are used, of which the sturdiest are enamelled steel bins, but earthenware bread crocks, both glazed and unglazed are equally satisfactory. This terracotta crock is tall enough to hold most standard-sized loaves. If you are short of space choose tall rather than wide or long bins or crocks.

## Egg rack

**Size.** H. 12¾ in. (324 mm).
**Material.** Beechwood.

Eggs are less likely to crack while being boiled and are easier to use if stored at room temperature.

Wire or wicker baskets hold a large quantity, but eggs are best kept wedged separately – pointed end downwards – in racks. This wall-mounted rack should be fixed somewhere cool.

## Food covers

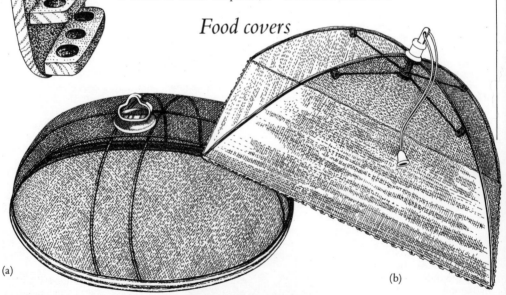

(a)

(b)

(a) **Size.** L. 16 in. (405 mm).
**Material.** Tinned steel wire mesh.

(b) **Size.** L. 14¼ in. (362 mm).
**Material.** Cotton net, tinned steel wire, plastic.

Covers that will keep flies, wasps and other insects off food are invaluable during the summer. The dome-shaped cover (a) can be hung on the wall when not in use and will protect a large joint of meat. The cotton cover (b) folds up like an umbrella and can be stowed conveniently in a kitchen drawer.

(a) **Size.** 12 × 7 in.
(305 × 178 mm).
**Material.** Beechwood,
alloy steel.

(b) **Size.** 15 × 10½ in.
(380 × 267 mm).
**Material.** Wood.

(c) **Size.** H. 12 in. (305 mm),
plus handle.
**Material.** Wicker.

The kitchen is not the ideal place
to store wine since the fluctuations
in temperature can cause it to
deteriorate. Wine should be
stored at an even temperature –
somewhere between 45° and 60°F
(7° and 15°C). A cellar is the
ideal place to keep it, provided
it is cool. If it is festooned
with central heating pipes you
should insulate them. This will
not only cut your fuel bills but
will prevent your choicest wines
maturing too quickly. Light also
affects the colouring of wine.

The bottles should be stored on
their sides so that the corks are
kept moist by the wine and so
that they do not dry out, shrink
and let air into the bottle to spoil
the wine. Keep the labels uppermost so that you can read them
without turning the bottles.

You can stack bottles of the
same wine one upon the other,
but if you buy various sorts of
wine you do need some sort of
rack that allows you to select a
bottle without disturbing others.
You can use the cardboard box
in which the wine is delivered as
a makeshift rack, but it will
collapse eventually – and will soften fairly quickly if kept in a
damp cellar.

Racks designed especially for
storing wine keep each bottle
correctly positioned without any
danger of breakage. They can be
made of various materials, including steel wire, plastic coated
steel wire, and even cubes of
perspex. The ones shown here
are both practical and decorative.

Racks like (a) are the most solid
and durable and stack one above
another. The folding rack (b) is
cheaper, but takes up more room
and holds fewer bottles. The
wicker basket (c) is very decorative. It can hold six wine bottles
– and can be transported conveniently.

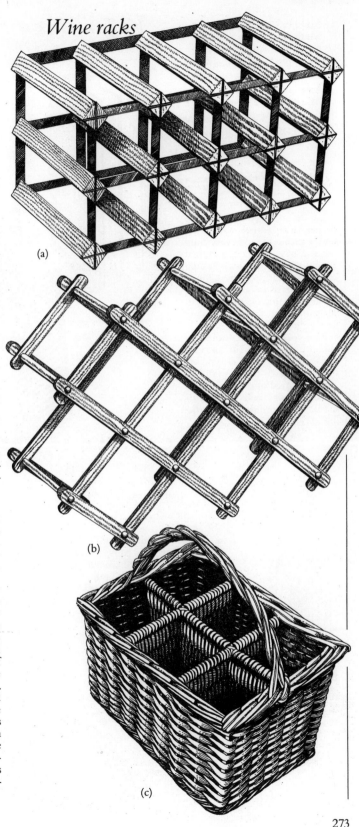

*Wine racks*

(a)

(b)

(c)

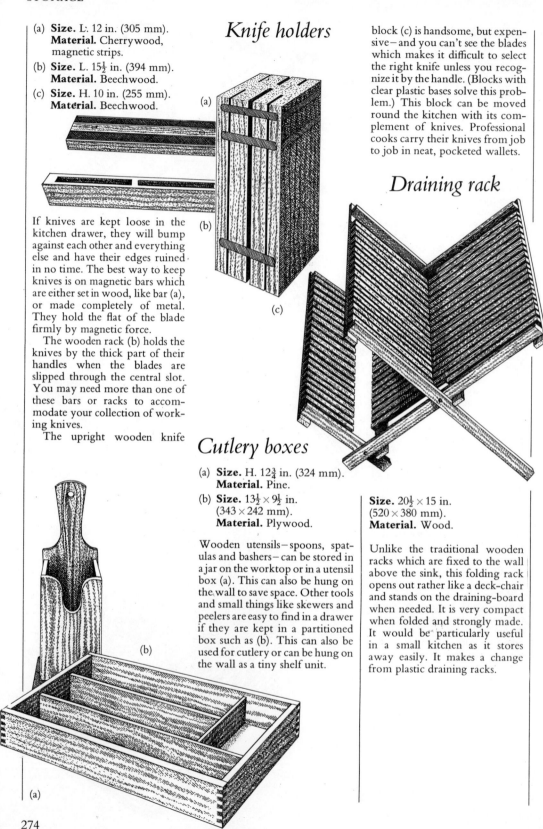

(a) **Size.** L. 12 in. (305 mm).
**Material.** Cherrywood, magnetic strips.
(b) **Size.** L. 15½ in. (394 mm).
**Material.** Beechwood.
(c) **Size.** H. 10 in. (255 mm).
**Material.** Beechwood.

## Knife holders

If knives are kept loose in the kitchen drawer, they will bump against each other and everything else and have their edges ruined in no time. The best way to keep knives is on magnetic bars which are either set in wood, like bar (a), or made completely of metal. They hold the flat of the blade firmly by magnetic force.

The wooden rack (b) holds the knives by the thick part of their handles when the blades are slipped through the central slot. You may need more than one of these bars or racks to accommodate your collection of working knives.

The upright wooden knife

block (c) is handsome, but expensive—and you can't see the blades which makes it difficult to select the right knife unless you recognize it by the handle. (Blocks with clear plastic bases solve this problem.) This block can be moved round the kitchen with its complement of knives. Professional cooks carry their knives from job to job in neat, pocketed wallets.

## Draining rack

## Cutlery boxes

(a) **Size.** H. 12¾ in. (324 mm).
**Material.** Pine.
(b) **Size.** 13½ × 9½ in.
(343 × 242 mm).
**Material.** Plywood.

Wooden utensils—spoons, spatulas and bashers—can be stored in a jar on the worktop or in a utensil box (a). This can also be hung on the wall to save space. Other tools and small things like skewers and peelers are easy to find in a drawer if they are kept in a partitioned box such as (b). This can also be used for cutlery or can be hung on the wall as a tiny shelf unit.

**Size.** 20½ × 15 in.
(520 × 380 mm).
**Material.** Wood.

Unlike the traditional wooden racks which are fixed to the wall above the sink, this folding rack opens out rather like a deck-chair and stands on the draining-board when needed. It is very compact when folded and strongly made. It would be particularly useful in a small kitchen as it stores away easily. It makes a change from plastic draining racks.

# Cup stacker

**Size.** H. 6¾ in. (172 mm).
**Material.** Plastic-coated steel wire.

This cup stacker is one of a range designed for storing tableware in cupboards. The upturned cups lie one upon another with their handles pointing out through the central gap for easy lifting.

# Saucepan frame

**Size.** D. 20 in. (508 mm).
**Material.** Alloy steel.

Tiered, free-standing saucepan racks are fine if you have a large kitchen, and look very pretty, but they have to be moved when the floor is cleaned and need to be put where they cannot be knocked over. This semi-circular frame is much more useful. It has hooks for four saucepans and is fixed to the wall. Straight bars lying flat on the wall and circular frames which hang on chains from the ceiling are also made. Other kitchen tools can also be hung from these frames.

# Tea-towel holder

**Size.** L. 7¾ in. (197 mm).
**Material.** Plastic, alloy steel, synthetic bristle.

Tea towels need to be kept off the floor and dry. A hinged rack with arms which can be fixed near a heat source is the best alternative to the back of a kitchen chair, which is the usual place for a tea towel.

This unobtrusive holder is screwed or fixed with adhesive strip to walls or woodwork. Two rows of bristles, mounted in metal, grip tea-towels pushed between them. The strips are made in three different sizes.

# Bookstand

**Size.** 16 × 11 in. (405 × 280 mm).
**Material.** Perspex.

Most kitchens have a shelf for cookery books. This sturdy, transparent stand keeps the one you are using open at the right page and guards it from splashes or grease marks.

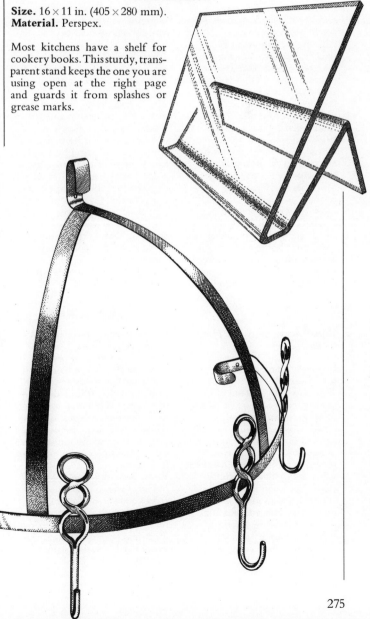

# GLOSSARY
# OF MATERIALS

Today there is a bewildering array of tools and utensils in a wide variety of materials. Some need particular care if they are to last and perform well. It helps to know something about these materials, but labelling is often confusing with names which are not always immediately identifiable to anyone but a metallurgist, timber merchant or expert in plastics. The list below is designed to clarify things a little by giving a simple definition of each material, listing the types of kitchen tool made of it, and adding some notes on care and cleaning.

## Ceramics

**Earthenware.** (*Casseroles, gratin pans, moulds, jugs, mixing bowls, basins and dishes.*)
Although it appears to be thicker, heavier and stronger than bone china, earthenware is rather fragile; it chips and breaks very easily. It is unvitrified (i.e. not fused like glass) and is therefore porous if left unglazed. Before glazing it is a warm, brick-red colour or a pale, creamy yellow. Glazes can be coloured or transparent. Earthenware is a good material for dishes that need long, slow cooking as it retains heat and moisture well. It is also cheap.
CARE. Glazed earthenware should be washed immediately after use in hot detergent suds. Stuck-on food can be removed by soaking. Do not use detergents or soap on unglazed earthenware. Scrub it in hot water to which a little salt or vinegar has been added.

**Porcelain.** (*Gratin dishes and fondue pots, tableware, tea and dinner services.* **Unglazed:** *pestles and mortars.*)
This is completely vitrified (i.e. glasslike) non-porous and acid resistant whether glazed or unglazed. It is harder than bone china, can withstand heat and can be used for oven-to-table ware. However, it will crack if exposed to sudden changes of temperature. Ovenproof porcelain conducts heat well but should be used with a heat-diffusing mat on top of the stove and a heat conducting tray in the oven.
CARE. Wash in hot suds using a soft brush or cloth.

**Stoneware.** (*Casseroles, storage jars, bowls and tableware.*)
This is semi-vitrified and impervious to liquids, so does not need glazing – although decorative glazes are usually added. It is fired at a higher temperature than earthenware and is ideal for dishes that need long, slow cooking. It is a little more expensive than earthenware.
CARE. As for glazed earthenware.

**Terracotta.** (*Chicken bricks, diables, milk coolers, pots for baking bread.*)
Reddish clay usually left unglazed. It is very porous. Fairly inexpensive.
CARE. Wash in hand-hot water without soap or detergents; add a little salt or vinegar instead.

## Glassware

**Borosilicate glass.** (*see Heat-resistant glass.*)

**Crystal.** (*Glasses, decanters, bowls, dishes.*)
This glassware contains a percentage of lead oxide which varies according to quality.
CARE. Wash pieces individually in hand-hot detergent suds in a plastic bowl, or a sink with a plastic or rubber mat. Dry while still warm with a non-fluffy cloth. Use a soft brush to clean cut glass. Don't put crystal in a dishwasher as it will become permanently dulled in time. Remove stains by soaking overnight in suds containing a few drops of ammonia. Rinse glasses thoroughly.

**Flameproof glass.** (*Casseroles, pie dishes, saucepans.*)
This type of glass, known as "Pyroflam", can be used on the hob as well as in the oven. It is brilliant white. It is made from pyroceram, a material used on the nose cones of space rockets. It is stronger than heat-resistant glass and can withstand sudden, extreme changes in temperature. It is expensive.
CARE. Soak dishes in hot water before washing in hot suds to remove burnt-on food. Use a nylon brush or scourer to remove food particles. You can use liquid abrasive cleaners, but avoid harsh abrasives which will spoil the smooth finish of the surface.

**Heat-resistant glass.**
(*Casseroles, bowls, pie dishes.*)
This contains boric oxide which toughens it and makes it able to withstand temperature changes, but sudden extremes should be avoided. Known as "Pyrex".
CARE. As flameproof glass.

**Pyroceram.** (*see Flameproof glass.*)

**Soda lime glass.** (*Bottles, jars, carafes, flasks, everyday glassware.*)
It can be hand-blown, but is usually press-moulded or blown.
CARE. Wash in hand-hot suds, rinse in warm water and dry immediately while still warm. This glass will eventually dull if put in dishwasher.

# Metals

**Aluminium.** (*Kitchen gadgets, juicers, ricers, waffle irons, percolators, pots, pans, bakeware, kettles, colanders.*)
A cheap, lightweight, rust-resistant metal which conducts heat well if it is of a sufficiently heavy gauge. It can be pitted by certain substances found in food. Heavily pitted pots should be replaced, as they are not easy to clean and can be a health hazard.
CARE. Wash aluminium in hot water with detergent, rinse and dry. Use a brush, or nylon or wire wool scourer to deal with obstinate food particles. Remove stains by boiling a weak solution of vinegar and water, or by stewing rhubarb trimmings in the pan. This also removes discoloration caused by cooking eggs or any other alkaline foodstuff. Never use washing soda.
NB. Never leave foodstuffs in aluminium pans. Turn food out into ceramic or plastic containers for storing.

ANODIZED ALUMINIUM
Aluminium with a protective coating which improves resistance to discoloration. Do not put coloured anodized aluminium in a dishwasher as the colour can fade.

CAST ALUMINIUM. (*Presses, tools, griddles, waffle irons.*)
Aluminium shaped by being poured in a molten state into a mould.

DEEP DRAWN ALUMINIUM. (*Pressure cookers, heavy-gauge and high-sided pans.*)
Sheet aluminium of thicker gauge (over $\frac{1}{8}$ in. – about 4 mm – thick), pressed to shape while being spun on a lathe. The extra thickness provides more metal for forming deep-sided utensils.

PRESSED ALUMINIUM. (*Pots and pans.*)
Sections of sheet aluminium – usually under $\frac{1}{8}$ in. (3 mm) thick – shaped in a press or by spinning on a lathe with sideways pressure. This technique is used in hollow-ware manufacture.

**Brass.** (*Pestles and mortars, toasting forks, oriental tools and cooking pots, handles on copper pans, decorative rivets and collars on knives, bottle openers.*)
An alloy of copper and zinc.
CARE. Wash in hot detergent suds, rinse and dry thoroughly. If brassware used for cooking is cleaned with metal polish, it must be thoroughly washed afterwards.

**Cast iron.** (*Pots, pans, grill pans, casseroles, griddles, baking sheets.*)
Iron run in a molten state into moulds where it is cooled and hardened. This is an excellent conductor of heat. It is hard, but brittle and very heavy. It is smoother than matt black vitreous enamelled cast iron.
CARE. Avoid washing cast iron pans. Clean them by wiping them with absorbent paper after use. If food is stuck on, rinse in detergent and warm water and scour very lightly with a brush or nylon pad. Dry well and oil lightly before putting away. In time a non-stick patina builds up, which is especially valuable on griddles and frying pans.

**Copper.** (*Pots, pans, egg bowls, moulds, fondue pots, skillets, kettles, coffee pots, zabaglione pans, preserving pans.*)
One of the earliest metals used by man. It can react toxically with the acids in some foods, especially if they are kept in prolonged contact with it. Modern copper cooking utensils are therefore usually lined with tin, and sometimes with stainless steel or silver. Unlined copper pans can be used for boiling sugar which has no chemical reaction with copper and would, in any case, melt a tin lining. Some pans which look like copper are, in fact, aluminium coated with copper. These are cheaper than solid copper pans. Copper, if thick and heavy, is an excellent conductor of heat.
CARE. Be careful not to overheat tinned copper pans, especially when empty, as the tin could begin to melt. Use wooden spoons and spatulas when

possible and if you have to use a metal lifter make sure not to score the surface. Wash in hot water or detergent after use, using a cloth, soft pad, or brush. Soak before washing to remove any stuck-on food. Rub with a soft cloth after washing and drying to keep the shine. Use a good proprietary cleaner on the outside when necessary – or a combination of salt and lemon juice or salt and vinegar. Never use scouring powders or wire wool pads.

**E.P.N.S.** (*see Silver plate.*)

**Inox.** (*inoxydable*) French for stainless steel.

**Molybdenum.** An alloy added to steel to improve corrosion resistance, or so some manufacturers claim. About 1% molybdenum is added to martensitic stainless steel for kitchen knives.

**Rockwell.** This scale measures the degree of hardness of steel. Most knives have a Rockwell number approaching the ideal range of between 55 and 58. Some cheaper knives have a hardness of 45. Above 58 a knife becomes progressively harder to sharpen.

**Rostfrei.** German for stainless steel.

**Silver.** (*Tea pots, jugs, coffee pots, cutlery, tableware, linings to copper pans.*)
Because it is such a soft metal silver is usually combined with copper to give it hardness. It is the best of all metals for the conduction of heat, but its cost precludes its use for pots and pans.
CARE. Rinse immediately after use (especially if the meal has included eggs, pineapple, green vegetables, fish, mustard, sauces, chutneys or pickles). Wash in hot detergent rinse in clear, hot water and dry on a soft cloth, buffing to a shine on another dry cloth. Occasionally polish with proprietary cleaner, rinse and dry. Never use abrasives or rub harshly. Don't put in dishwasher.

**Silver plate.** (*Grape scissors, nutcrackers, flambé stoves.*)
Also called E.P.N.S. or electro-plated silver. Produced by depositing a thin layer of silver on nickel by electrolysis. Very thin layers of poorer quality E.P.N.S. soon wear from use and polishing and the nickel shows through.
CARE. As silver.

**Steel.** A fairly light, very strong, malleable alloy consisting mainly of iron and carbon. Other metals are added in varying amounts, depending on the qualities required.

ALLOY STEEL. (*see Mild steel.*)

BLUED STEEL. (*Blades of cutters, baking tins.*)
Mild steel heat-treated to give it a very dark blue, almost black finish. It has some resistance to rust.
CARE. As tinned steel.

CARBON STEEL. (*Kitchen knife blades, cutters, grinding plates and cleavers.*)
An alloy of iron and carbon. When used for knife blades it may contain anything from about $0.6\%$ to $1.30\%$ of carbon, so that it can be heated to a high hardness level. The higher the carbon content of the steel from which a knife is made, the longer the sharp edge will last. Carbon steel will rust and stain.
CARE. Wash immediately after use, rinse and dry thoroughly. Remove stains with a little scouring powder or a mildly abrasive scouring pad. Sharpen carbon steel knives before use and store carefully to avoid damaging their edges.
**NB.** Don't soak in water or leave in contact with foodstuffs.

CHROMED STEEL. (*Scissors, kitchen tools and gadgets, corkscrews.*)
Also called chromium plate. This is deposited electrolytically and is usually the final layer, after the steel has been coated first with copper and then with nickel.
CARE. Wash in hot detergent, rinse and dry. Avoid harsh abrasives.

HIGH CARBON STEEL. (*see Carbon steel.*)

MILD STEEL. (*Baking tins and sheets, tartlet rings, frying pans, enamelled pots, pans, plates, mugs and kettles.*)
Also called alloy steel. Lighter than cast iron, but just as vulnerable to rust, which is why it is often plated with tin, nickel or chrome, or is enamelled.
CARE. Unplated mild steel baking tins and pans build up a non-stick patina as long as they are not washed in very strong detergents and are well dried before being put away. Wash as cast iron.

NICKEL PLATED STEEL. (*Kitchen tools, gadgets, lifters, spoons.*)
Mild steel with a thin layer of nickel applied by electro-plating. Sometimes a coating of chrome is added for brightness.
CARE. Wash in hot detergent, using a brush if necessary. Rinse and dry thoroughly in a warm place. Avoid prolonged soaking.

PRESSED STEEL. (*see Mild steel.*)

STAINLESS STEEL. (*Knife blades, cutlery, tableware, pots, pans, lifters, strainers, graters, sieves, juicers, pestles and mortars, bowls, kettles.*)
There are many different sorts of stainless steel. Most kitchen knives are made from martensitic stainless steel, which contains at least $12\%$ chrome and it is this that renders the steel stainless and rust resistant. It also contains between $0.15\%$ to $0.80\%$ carbon. The higher the carbon content, the higher the hardness and the longer the edge will last.
Stainless steel used for pots and pans contains a proportion of nickel and chrome. Pans are sometimes marked 18/8 or 18/10 – this indicates that the steel contains $18\%$ chrome to 8 (or 10)$\%$ nickel. Stainless steel does not conduct heat well, so the bases of pans usually consist of some other metal sandwiched between stainless steel layers.
CARE. Wash in hot detergent suds, using a soft brush or nylon scourer. Special stainless steel polishes should remove marks. Soak off burnt-on foods. Avoid bleach, harsh abrasives, silver-cleaning liquids. Rinse after contact with lemon, vinegar, any chemicals.

SURGICAL STEEL. A term applied to stainless steel containing at least $0.50\%$ carbon.

TINNED STEEL. (*Kitchen gadgets, graters, bakeware, cutters, sieves, strainers, food mills.*)
Sheet steel coated thinly with tin, either by electro-plating or by dipping in molten tin. This gives a corrosion resistant and non-poisonous finish.
CARE. As nickel plated steel.

**Stove enamel.** (*Pie dishes, teapots, casings on kitchen equipment.*)
Paint baked on to steel.

**Vanadium.** A very hard, white metal which occurs in a few rare minerals. It is used in alloys and a little can be added to non-stainless or to stainless steel to prevent it becoming brittle.

**Vitreous enamel.** (*Pots, pans, pie dishes, gratin dishes, casseroles, skillets.*)
A layer of powdered glass (frit) fused to cast iron and steel at very high temperatures, or at a lower temperature to aluminium, which has a lower melting point. (Enamelled aluminium is therefore not so heat resistant as enamelled cast iron or steel.) Vitreous enamelled cast iron pans are thicker and heavier than enamelled steel pans and conduct heat more efficiently.
CARE. Wash in hot detergent suds using a soft nylon brush or nylon scourer when necessary. Soak pans to soften burnt-on food. Remove stains with a weak bleach solution. Do not use abrasives.
**NB.** Never place an empty pan on a high heat. This can damage the enamel.

**Wire.** (*Sieves, cutters, whisks, salad shakers, handles.*)
This is made of stainless or mild steel; the latter is usually dipped in tin, chrome or nickel to protect it from corrosion.
CARE. As nickel-plating, if coated. Otherwise as stainless steel.

# *Plastics*

These vary widely in their types, composition and properties, but they all have one thing in common – during their manufacture they were at some stage either liquid or semi-liquid and at that point were shaped by heat or pressure or a combination of both.

Some are intended to resemble and take the place of natural materials such as wood, stone, fabrics or metals, while others are simply made to be cheaper, easier to care for, or lighter to handle. They differ greatly in their properties. Some are rigid, some flexible; some transparent, others opaque; some will soften under gentle heat, others can withstand boiling; some are tough and virtually unbreakable, others may be brittle and easily cracked. All are light to handle, pleasant to the touch and easy to clean and care for.

THERMOPLASTICS. These soften and melt when heated sufficiently.

GENERAL CARE. Wash in hot detergent suds using a soft cloth or soft washing-up brush. Use a mild bleach solution if necessary to remove stains. Avoid contact with most solvents, especially paint strippers, dry cleaning fluid (carbon tetrachloride), undiluted bleach, petrol, nail varnish or nail varnish remover, white spirit, methylated spirit.

**ABS** (*see Acrylonitrile butadiene styrene.*)

**Acrylic.** (*Cutlery handles, food covers, tableware, beakers which look like glass.*)
Rigid, shiny, brittle sounding when tapped. Scratches easily.
CARE. Remove superficial scratches with a little metal polish, rubbed lightly over.

**Acrylonitrile butadiene styrene.** (*Domestic appliance housings; e.g. mixers, blenders.*)
Lightweight, very tough, high resistance to heat, acid and general wear.

CARE. Wipe with a damp cloth wrung out in warm detergent suds. Remove stains with a damp cloth dipped in liquid abrasive.

**Cellulose acetate.** (*Tool handles.*)
Tough, resilient, similar to cellulose nitrate, but less flammable, though it burns easily. Wide colour range. Resistant to oil and petrol.
CARE. Avoid acids and alkalis, soaking in water, direct heat.

**Cellulose nitrate.** (*Handles of inexpensive knives, brushes and tools.*)
Once called celluloid. Very tough, but very flammable. Resistant to most chemicals.
CARE. Avoid naked flame or intense heat; strong acids or alkalis, very hot water.

**Nylon.** (*Sieves, containers, bottles, pot scourers, beakers, brush and broom tufts, parts and fittings on mixers.*)
Very tough, almost unbreakable, smooth, waxy surface when moulded. Resistant to most chemicals and solvents, wear and abrasion. Can be boiled.
CARE. Store empty containers with lids off as odour can develop. Avoid strong acids, direct heat and sunlight.

**Polycarbonate.** (*Beakers, food covers, containers and dishes.*)
Tough, clear (looks like glass), almost unbreakable.
CARE. Some types are dishwasher-safe, but follow manufacturer's instructions.

**Polyethylene.** (*Washing-up bowls, buckets, waste bins, storage boxes, waste disposal bags, squeeze bottles, bottle caps, chopping boards.*)
Also called Polythene, Alkathene.

LOW DENSITY: smooth, waxy feel, very flexible.

HIGH DENSITY: coarser texture, stiff and hard.
Both types can absorb odours, so not suitable for long-term storage of foodstuffs, especially fats and oils.

CARE. Avoid abrasives and scourers. High density type can be cleaned in boiling water, following the manufacturer's instructions.

**Polypropylene.** (*Tableware, food mills, pudding basins, mixing spoons, bowls.*)
One of the lightest plastics. More rigid than polyethylene and able to withstand higher temperatures. Resistant to most acids, alkalis, solvents and staining.

**Polytetrafluoroethylene.** (*Non-stick coatings.*)
Also called PTFE, Teflon, Release Coatings, Fluon. Resistant to most common chemicals; some types scratch easily.
CARE. Wipe with soft kitchen paper before washing according to maker's instructions. Avoid scourers and scouring powders, metal implements. Do not use at high temperatures and do not leave empty pans, or pans containing hot fat only, on a heated hotplate. Store pans in plastic bags to avoid scratching the non-stick coatings.
NB. Once the coating begins to flake away, it is best to scour the rest off, if possible. The pan will still clean easily.

**Polystyrene.** *Also called Styron.*

STANDARD: (*Bowls, tableware, gadgets and tools.*)
Rigid, slightly brittle, highly polished, has a ringing sound when tapped lightly. Can be easily broken if dropped or banged hard. Burns easily when exposed to heat.

TOUGHENED: high impact, or high density. (*Bread bins, storage boxes.*)
Strong, rigid, not so shiny as standard type. Softens at a higher temperature. Wide colour range.
Both types can become electrostatically charged and many articles are lacquered to prevent this.
CARE. Remove electrostatics by wiping with a cloth wrung out in detergent solution.

**Polyvinyl chloride.** *Also called PVC.*

RIGID OR UNPLASTICIZED. (*Soft drink bottles, food containers.*) Glossy, almost transparent, unless pigmented. Resists abrasion, water, most liquids, many solvents.

FLEXIBLE, PLASTICIZED: (*Tablecloths, aprons.*) Resembles polythene sheeting, but softer and more rubbery. Easy to cut. Resists water, most liquids, many solvents. CARE. (Both types.) Avoid contact with spirit-based wax polishes.

THERMOSET PLASTICS. These are chemically altered during manufacture and become completely non-softening, though they can burn or char.

**Laminated plastic.** *Also called Warerite, Formica, Sephanite.* (*Counter tops, tables.*) Resistant to most chemicals and heat from coffee or teapots. Made by bonding several resin-impregnated paper sheets together under pressure and at high temperature. The top, decorative sheet is protected with melamine film. CARE. Clean with a cloth wrung out in hot detergent suds. Remove food stains with a liquid abrasive cleaner. Clear tea or coffee stains with a mild bleach solution. Avoid contact with hot baking tins, heavy, hot casseroles and heated pans, especially those with heavy, flat bases. Don't chop on it with sharp knives or clamp mincers to it.

**Melamine formaldehyde.** (*Storage jars, storage boxes, tableware, surfaces.*) Rigid, almost unbreakable but can crack and stain. CARE. Wash plates and kitchen surfaces soon after cutting fruit, or after contact with bottled sauces, pickles etc. Avoid contact with hot saucepans and baking tins. Long contact with alkalis.

**Urea formaldehyde.** (*Trays, tableware, measuring spoons.*) Hard, brittle with a smooth glossy surface. Resists boiling water for a short time. CARE. Remove stains with detergent powder on damp cloth. Avoid contact with bleach, soap solutions, acids and abrasive; soaking in hot water.

# Wood

Wood is a relatively cheap natural material, easily worked, pleasant to look at and to touch and easy to clean. However it can be split, warped, burnt and scarred if not used with care.

GENERAL CARE
If made of well-seasoned wood, kitchen tools should withstand washing, but don't leave them soaking in water as they may soften or split. Wipe them with a damp cloth if this is sufficient to clean them. Otherwise scrape off any food scraps and wash them in hot suds; rinse, give a final rinse in cold water and dry in a cool, airy place.

If tableware is sealed or has a special finish to make it water or dirt resistant, follow the maker's instructions for cleaning. Alternatively, wipe tableware with a damp cloth and dry it in an airy place away from direct heat. Remove stains by rubbing lightly along the grain with a fine steel wool pad dipped in olive oil. Articles which are seldom used, or are washed frequently, can be rubbed over with a soft cloth moistened with oil.

**NB.** Wood retains odours; utensils used for spicy or very aromatic foods should be kept exclusively for this use.

**Ash.** (*Tool handles, carving, chopping and pastry boards.*) A tough, brownish-white hardwood with a prominent, ripple-like grain.

**Beech.** (*Scoops, spoons, spatulas, tool handles, chopping and pastry boards, rolling pins, shortbread moulds, potato mashers.*) A pale, cream coloured hardwood with a straight grain; fine textured with small spindle-shaped markings.

**Birch.** (*Some kitchen tools, whisks.*) A white to reddish-brown, close-grained hardwood.

**Box.** (*Pepper and salt mills, spoons, ladles, pastry trimmers, butter curlers, corkscrew handles.*) A hard-textured, close-grained, yellowish hardwood. Small tools are easily chipped.

**Deal.** (*see Pine.*)

**Iroko.** (*Bowls and boards.*) A very strong, golden brown, coarsely but evenly textured hardwood. Often used instead of teak.

**Maple.** (*Tool handles, bases.*) Also called Field maple, Rock maple, Hard maple. Hard-wearing, yellowish-brown hardwood, that takes a very high polish.

**Oak.** (*Carving boards, salad bowls.*) Very hard yellowish-brown to deep, warm brown hardwood.

**Pine.** (*Spice racks, wine racks, egg racks, knife racks, storage boxes, varnished and painted handles.*) Includes: whitewood and spruce. Straight-grained softwood, white to yellow with small, tight knots, or brownish with reddish streaks. It takes paint and varnish well, but is soft, easily scarred and chipped. Not suitable for chopping boards.

**Reconstituted wood.** (*Handles.*) These, as the name implies, are wood chips impregnated and bonded with polyester resins or other plastic resins to produce a wood-like material with the washable qualities of plastic.

**Sycamore.** (*Kitchen utensils, spoons.*) Creamy to yellowish-white hardwood with a fine, wavy grain.

**Teak.** (*Salad bowls, fruit bowls, chopping boards.*) Straight-grained golden brown hardwood, now in very short supply. Iroko is often used in place of it.

# Other materials

**Basketwork.** (*Strainers, baskets.*)
CARE. Scrub regularly in warm water. Burn baskets infested with woodworm.

**Bamboo and cane.** (*Strainers, steamers, baskets, handles, tongs.*)
CARE. As wood.

**Bone.** (*Knife handles, toothpicks.*)
CARE. Avoid immersing bone handles of knives when washing up, as water will loosen the fixing material of the handles and can split and discolour them. Wash bone tools in warm suds, rinse and dry immediately. Remove stains with a weak solution of bleach or by rubbing gently with a scouring powder. Avoid soaking. Do not put in dishwasher.

**Composition stone.**
(*Millstones, sharpening stones.*)
Man-made artificial stone.

CARE. Carborundum: Wipe sharpening stones clean of oil after use. If water was the lubricant, rinse and dry carefully.
Millstones: These should not be washed. Regularly dismantle the mill and brush free any accumulated flour to prevent contamination from stale flour.

**Horn.** (*Knife handles, spoons, salad servers.*)
CARE. Wash in hand-hot detergent suds, rinse and dry. Prevent horn from drying out and cracking by rubbing in pure beeswax or light cooking oil and polishing with a soft cloth. Avoid bleaches, abrasives and very hot water. Do not put in dishwasher.

**Marble.** (*Pastry slabs, pestles and mortars.*)
A crystalline form of limestone; hard, heavy, close-grained, cool and beautiful. It is also expensive and fragile.

CARE. Clean by wiping with a damp, soapy cloth. Care should be taken to see that it is dried thoroughly as marble is easily pitted by prolonged contact with water. Remove slight stains with lemon juice or vinegar. Use a mild, liquid abrasive on more persistent ones. Acid foodstuffs also pit marble so wipe up spills immediately.

**Reed.** (*Bannetons, mats, baskets.*)
CARE. Wash only if really necessary. Swish in warm suds, rinse in cool water. Shake off moisture and dry thoroughly. Avoid soaking.

**Stone.** (*Pestles and mortars.*)
CARE. These heavy implements are washed when necessary in hot water without soap or detergent. Once the roughened surfaces have become worn they must be re-knapped to restore the necessary grip.

# Cleaning materials

Good old-fashioned brushes are still the best implements for cleaning most things. A selection of brushes and scourers which can be kept in a pot or placed on a rack near the sink should help you remove bits of burnt-on food, tannin stains, or earth from vegetables in a matter of minutes. Don't forget that brushes themselves need cleaning from time to time. A weekly soak in a mild solution of domestic bleach, or baby's bottle sterilizing liquid, will keep them free of germs and remove stains from bristles. Replace brushes fairly regularly if they get a lot of use. The old ones can always be re-cycled as heavy-duty scourers for gardening tools.

**Washing-up brushes** can be used on non-stick surfaces if the bristles are fairly soft. Some brushes have a flattened end on the handle to enable you to scrape off particularly stubborn bits of dirt. Do not use it on non-stick surfaces.

**Bottle brushes** come in many sizes. The largest are long enough to clean demijohns and bottles for wine making. The smallest are useful for cleaning teapot spouts. Medium-sized ones are excellent for dealing with vacuum flasks and decanters.

**Potato brushes** have strong short nylon bristles which cope effortlessly with encrusted mud on root vegetables.

**Scourers** are useful for giving more immediate contact with what is being cleaned and are particularly good for keeping the outsides of pans clean and shining.

**Washing-up scouring pads** are available in a wide range of materials. Some are made of nylon, others are a wire tangle or a combination of materials. Some pads also include an abrasive scouring agent which is good for cleaning burnt pans. Avoid using wire scourers on non-stick surfaces.

# INDEX

## A

Aebleskiver pan 214
Airlocks 254
Almond paste, *applying* 232
Almonds, *skinning* 8
Aluminium foil 241
  *making a flan ring* 241
Apple, *arranging slices* 8
  corer 63, 69
  patent peeler 62
Artichoke fonds
    *preparing* 21
Asbestos mats 227
Aspic cutters 75
Asparagus
  pan 201
  peelers, *preparing with* 61

## B

Baguette tin 160
Bain marie saucepan 200
Baking
  beans, *blind baking* 166
  pots 182–187
  sheets, *preparing* 165
  tins for cake, bread,
    pastry 152–171
Balance scales 262, 263
Ball sieve, rotating 91
Ballers 64
Balmoral loaf tin 157
Banneton 150
Barbecues 217–219
  brazier 218
  fuels to use 217
  hibachi 218
  kettles 218, 219
Barquette moulds 168
  *lining* 111
  *making strawberry boats*
    168
Baskets
  deep fryers 210–211
  frying 212
  potato nest baskets 210
  salad shakers 142
  wine bottle 273
Basters, bulb 137
Bat, meat 87
Bateau moulds 168
  *lining* 111
  *making strawberry boats*
    168
Baumé scale 267
Basins and bowls 148–151
  banneton 150
  pudding 150
    *preparing basin for suet*
      *pudding* 150
Bean
  pots 186
  slicers 68
Beam scale 262, 263

Beaters and whisks 132–135
  blenders and
    liquidizers 144
  coiled whips 134
  electric hand-held
    mixers 145
  electric table mixers 146
  *spoons for beating* 123
Beef
  *carving* 48
  *quantities to buy per person*
    265
  *roasting temperatures and*
    *times* 265
  slicer 46
Beer making 252–256
  airlocks 254
  beginner's kits 253
  corking tools 256
  hydrometers 256
  racking equipment 254
  thermostatic heaters 255
Birch whisk 134
Biscuit
  baking sheets 165
  *crumb base* 125
  cutters, assorted 72, 73
  "langue du chat" tin 162,
    163
  *making Swedish Christmas*
    *biscuits* 72
  multi-sided cutter 73
Blender, pastry 84
Blenders and
    liquidizers 144
  electric hand-held
    mixers 145
  electric table mixers 146
  food processors 147
  homogenizers 137
Blocks, chopping 106
Boards 105–8
  carving 108
  chopping (and
    blocks) 106
  pastry 107
  slicing 108
Boat moulds 168
  *lining* 111
  *making strawberry boats*
    168
Boilers
  asparagus pan 201
  bain marie saucepan 200
  double 202
  rice 201
  sugar 200
Bombe, ice cream
    mould 178
  *making a bombe* 178
Boning knives 38–42
  *boning breast lamb, pork*
    *or veal* 41
  *boning chicken, chicken leg*
    39
  *boning leg lamb, pork or*
    *veal* 42
  *boning loin lamb, pork or*
    *veal* 36

Boning knives cont.
  *boning shoulder lamb, veal*
    43
  *butterflying a leg of lamb*
    41
  *cooked sole* 114
  *guard of honour* 41
  *preparing crown roast* 40
  *quartering a duck* 38
Bookstand 275
Bottle openers 85, 243, 245
Bottle, cruchon 271
Bottling jars for storage 271
  thermometers 266–267
Bowls 148–151
  banneton 150
  copper egg bowl 148
  gazpacho 151
  mixing 149
  pudding basins 150
    *preparing for suet*
      *pudding* 150
  salad 151
    *chapon au salade* 151
  serving 151
Box graters 80
Brandy glasses 257
Brandy snaps, *wrapping with*
    *spoon* 123
Bread
  crock 272
  *croissant cutter* 77
  *herb bread* 111
  *kneading dough* 7
  knives 52
  *shaping a cottage loaf*
    123
  *simple plait* 161
  *six-strand plait* 161
  storage times 270
Bread tins 152, 159, 160,
    161, 162
  baguette 160
  Balmoral loaf 157
  brioche, *making* 159
  earthenware pot 162
  English loaf 160
  *filling bread tins* 161
  flowerpot 162
  pain de mie 160
Breadcrumbs
  *crushing with rolling pin*
    109
Brewing and wine
    making 252–256
  airlocks, fermentation
    locks 254
  beginner's kits 253
  corking tools 256
  filter 255
  hydrometers 256
  press 254
  pulper 254
  racking equipment 254
  thermostatic heaters 255
Brioche tins 159
Brushes, pastry 121
Bulb basters 137
Burger presses 179

Butcher's
  chopping blocks 105,
    106
  knives and saws 34
    *cutting up half a pig* 35
    *making a rack of lamb* 37
  knot 242
Butter
  curlers 85
  moulds 172
  *storage times* 270
  warmer 200
  *Butterflying leg of lamb*
    41

## C

Cake
  *assembly of Black Forest*
    *cherry cake* 51
  *dusting with dredger* 141
  *keeping fruit cakes*
    *flat* 157
  *making Swiss roll* 157
  *smoothing off* 157
  testers 117
Cake decorating 229–238
  *applying almond*
    *paste* 232
  *applying royal*
    *icing* 233
  flower and net nails,
    *using* 231, 238
  forcing and icing nozzles,
    syringe 236
    *running out* 237
  forcing bags, *filling* 234
  lattice work 231, 238
  *making feather*
    *design* 237
  *making paper cone* 235
  *making a wishbone* 238
  markers 231
  *piping meringue* 235
  rulers 231
    *levelling a cake* 231
  serrated scraper 231
  turntables 230
Cake racks 228
Cake tins 152–159, 162, 163
  Balmoral loaf 157
  brioche, *making* 153
  croquembouche 153
  dariole mould 157
  deep, round, square and
    heart-shaped,
    *lining* 154, 155
  *insulating a large*
    *cake* 155
  kugelhopf, *making* 158
  popover pans 163
  savarin 158
  shallow, round,
    square 156
    *turning out a sponge* 157
  small tins 162, 163
  tube tins 158

282

# ▬ AUTHOR'S ACKNOWLEDGMENTS ▬

*It would not have been possible to compile this book without the generous help and advice of many people. I am particularly grateful to Linda Dwyer at Divertimenti in Marylebone Lane, London, for allowing me to borrow tools from the shop, and also to the staff of Pages in Shaftesbury Avenue, of the Elizabeth David shop in Bourne Street and of the kitchen tool department at Harrods for giving me the same facilities.*

*Demonstrations and practical help with techniques were generously given at the cookery school "La Varenne", run in Paris by Anne Willan, who also introduced me to one of her ex-pupils, Liz Wolf, without whom many of the techniques shown here would have remained secrets known only to the trade.*

*Above all I am particularly grateful to the team who edited and designed the book. It was headed by Bridget Morley, who art directed, co-ordinated and daily provided support and sustenance for editors Jenny Barling, Jeanne Ruzicka, Anne Johnson and Louis Jordaan, as well as for designers Dave Whelan and Julia Goodman. I am also extremely grateful for all the fetching and carrying done by Gill Saunders and to many of my friends for all their encouragement; for the kind loans of precious objects from their own kitchens.*

*Many thanks to the following people who obtained or lent special tools and showed me how to use them:*
Elizabeth Lambert Ortiz (Latin American and Japanese tools)
Susumu Okada of the Ajimura restaurant, Covent Garden, London (Japanese tools)
Christl Roehl (German tools)
Caro Hobhouse, Tony Fry and Anna Whaley (Italian tools)
Janetta Parladé (Spanish tools)
Stanley Olson, Susan Cox and Frank Biancalana (American tools)
Viola and Ivan Martins and Lira Mendef (Indian tools)
Pauline Viola at the Danish Food Centre, London (Danish tools)
Sergio Costa and T. R. Moldrich at Costa's Coffee Boutique, London (coffee machines and grinders)
Michael and Mary Ford of the Mary Ford Cake Artistry Centre, Southbourne, Bournemouth (cake decoration)
Salvatore Conte of Bifulco's Stores Ltd., Soho, London (butchery techniques)
Steve Hatt, fishmonger, of Islington, London (fishmongery techniques)
Mme. V. Vignaud and Michael Young, Maison Bertaux, Soho, London (pâtisserie)

*Many thanks to the following people for technical advice:*
Peter Trier, of Clarbat (London), on cast iron ware
Mrs. C. J. Freeman of T. G. Green Ltd., on pottery and ceramics
Russell Jay at the British Steel Corporation, on steel
E. A. Oldfield at the Cutlery and Allied Trades Research Association, on metal and knives
Dennis Slater, Master Cutler, of H. M. Slater Ltd., on knives
N. J. Hawkins of Rudson, Wood & Co. Ltd., on wooden tools
R. J. Jefferies of I. C. I., on hollow-ware

*Dorling Kindersley would like to extend special thanks to the following people:*
Ann Savage, who set the standard for the illustrations and produced many of them, Tricia Calderhead, Tony Lodge, Shirley Willis, Valerie Kirkpatrick, the staff of Negs, Denis Walker and all the staff of Vantage, and Patrick of Evans Nugent Transport.

*Artists*
Bil Brooks
Tricia Calderhead
Anne Howard
Hayward and Martin
Carole Johnson
Tony Lodge
Andrew Macdonald
Gary Marsh
Andrew Popkiewicz
Ann Savage
Susan Smith
Shirley Willis

*Special thanks also to the following writers:*
Laura Taylor (*pressure cookers, fondues, toasters, warmers and coolers, teapots and kettles, coffee makers and jugs, yoghurt, ice cream and drink makers, openers and corkscrews, measuring equipment, storage*)
Sue Biro (*wine making and brewing equipment, glasses*)
Maggie Black (*barbecues and smokers*)
Dorothy Davis Farmer (*glossary of materials*)

*Many thanks to the following manufacturers and suppliers:*
Addis Ltd.; George Baker Ltd. (Bakaware wire tools); The Boots Co. Ltd.; S. Brannan & Sons Ltd.; Brooks Productions Ltd. (Barbecues and smokers); B.S.R. Housewares Ltd. (Swan and Judge pans); Clarbat Ltd. (Le Creuset and Cousances ware); College Housewares; M. Gilbert Ltd. (cutlery and gadgets); Graham & Green, London; The Grape and Grain, London; T. G. Green Ltd. (ceramics); Hamilton-Dale (Bel tools); Home Brewin', Purley, Surrey; I.C.T.C. (Electrical) Ltd.; Leon Jaeggi & Sons Ltd.; Kitchen Devils Ltd.; Krups (UK) Ltd.; Metal Box Ltd. (Tala ware); Moulinex Ltd.; Frank Odell Ltd. (Barbecues and smokers); Prestige Group Ltd.; Proctor Silex Division SCM (UK) Ltd.; Rima Electric Ltd.; Robot Coupe, France (Magimix); Rumbelows Ltd.; H. M. Slater Ltd.; Spong & Co. Ltd.; Sunbeam Electric Ltd.; Tefal Housewares Ltd.; Thorn Domestic Appliances (Electrical) Ltd. (Kenwood); Timothy Whites, Br. 3051; Tower Housewares Ltd.; Weber Stevens Products Co. Inc. (Barbecues); Wilkinson Sword Ltd. (Nutbrown); Wirax Wirewares Ltd.

*Typesetting*
Vantage Photosetting Limited, Southampton

*Reproduction, printing and binding*
W S Cowell Limited, Ipswich